Proclaiming the Gospel
to the Indians and the Métis

PROCLAIMING the Gospel to the INDIANS and the MÉTIS

RAYMOND J.A. HUEL

The University of Alberta Press

Western Canadian Publishers

First published by
The University of Alberta Press
and Western Canadian Publishers

The University of Alberta Press
Athabasca Hall
Edmonton, Alberta, Canada T6G 2E8

Copyright © The University of Alberta Press 1996
ISBN 0–88864–279–2

CANADIAN CATALOGUING IN PUBLICATION DATA
Huel, Raymond Joseph Armand.
    Proclaiming the Gospel to the Indian and Metis

    (The Missionary Oblates of Mary Immaculate in the Canadian North
    West)
    Co-published by: Western Canadian Publishers.
    Includes bibliographical references and index.
    ISBN 0–88864–279–2

    1. Oblates of Mary Immaculate—Missions—Northwest, Canadian—
History. 2. Indians of North America—Missions—Northwest, Canadian—
History. 3. Missions—Northwest, Canadian—History. I. Title. II. Series.
BV2300.O2H83 1996   266'.271'089972   C96–910094–9

Printed on acid-free paper.
Printed and bound in Canada by Best Book Manufacturers, Louiseville, Quebec.

The University of Alberta Press acknowledges the Alberta Foundation for the
Arts, a beneficiary of the Lottery Fund of the Government of Alberta, for their
financial support in the publication of this book.

COMMITTED TO THE DEVELOPMENT OF CULTURE AND THE ARTS

△ △ △ △ △ △ △ △ △ △ △ △ △ △ △ △ △ △ △ △

CONTENTS

△ △ △ △ △ △ △ △ △ △ △ △ △ △ △ △ △ △ △ △

ABBREVIATIONS

AOM   Archives oblates de Montréal
AD   Archives Deschâtelets
ADPA   Archives of the Diocese of Prince Albert
HBC   Hudson's Bay Company
NAC   National Archives of Canada
NWC   North West Company
OMI   Oblates of Mary Immaculate, Fonds Alberta-Saskatchewan
Adm.   Administration
DP   Dossiers du Personnel
Écrits   Écrits de Mgr Grandin
PP   Papiers Personnels
PAA   Provincial Archives of Alberta

△ △

FOREWORD

With the publication of Raymond Huel's *Proclaiming the Gospel to the Indians and the Métis: The Missionary Oblates of Mary Immaculate in Western Canada, 1845–1945*, the third volume in the Western Oblate History Project, the critical study of the Missionary Oblates of Mary Immaculate in Western and Northern Canada is continued in a positive and scholarly beneficial manner. The first volume, *Les Oblats des Marie Immaculée dans l'Ouest et le Nord du Canada, 1845–1967*, by Donat Levasseur, OMI, admirably set the stage with a narrative overview by an Oblate intimately familiar with the Order's history and workings. Unabashedly an Oblate, Levasseur's work reflected both the strengths and the deficiencies of a history from the pen of a participant. In terms of later volumes, Levasseur provides a knowledge of the working of the order that enhances the reader's appreciation of the succeeding volumes.

Martha McCarthy's *From the Great River to the Ends of the Earth: Oblate Missions to the Dene, 1847–1921* is the second volume in the series. Derived from McCarthy's doctoral studies in the later part of the 1970s, the work profitably reflects the strengths of scholarship from a scholar outside of the order but empathetic to its goals as well as the trials and tribulations it experienced. Reflecting the scholarly climate of the 1980s, McCarthy, using the limited sources available, sensitized herself to the socio-cultural context in which the Oblates worked in the north. The results constitute a major contribution not only in the study of the Oblates but in the writing of religious history in this country.

Raymond Huel's *Proclaiming the Gospel to the Indians and the Métis: The Missionary Oblates of Mary Immaculate in Western Canada, 1845–1945* is a milestone not only in terms of the Missionary Oblate series but in terms of the writing of religious history in Canada. The work ably reflects Huel's experience in scholarly writing on various aspects of the francophone experience in Western Canada. His volume in the five-volume series, *The Collected Writings of Louis Riel / Les Ecrits Complets de Louis Riel* (Edmonton: The University of Alberta Press, 1985), is but a particular example. Equally important is Huel's experience as the general editor of the Western Oblate History project. More than familiar with the limitations of hagiographic religious histories as well as the shortcomings of "politically correct" secularists writing on religious historians, Huel positions his study not only in terms of the existing historiography but in terms of the history itself. Forthrightly yet empathetically he confronts the issues arising out of the history of the Oblates. The result is an admirable history of a community of men whose motives and abilities run the gamut of human experience. In the process Huel has created a study that will become the hallmark against which other studies of this nature will be judged.

John E. Foster

△ △ △ △ △ △ △ △ △ △ △ △ △ △ △ △ △ △ △ △

PREFACE

The Missionary Oblates of Mary Immaculate were the dominant Catholic clergy in western Canada. In focusing on the missionary work of the Oblates among the peoples of the First Nations, the Indian and Métis populations who inhabited that region, this study examines but one aspect of the many activities undertaken by that congregation. The Oblates were first and foremost a French-speaking order and, as such, were an élite in the French Catholic community be it in Quebec or in western Canada. The Oblates were also educators and directed secondary and post-secondary institutions such as *Collège Mathieu* in Gravelbourg, Saskatchewan. In Winnipeg, the Oblates published newspapers in four languages to serve the needs of the multi-lingual Catholic population that had settled in the prairies. In Alberta and Saskatchewan the Oblates were very much involved in the establishment of a French language press and promoting the union of the dispersed French Catholic population. The Oblates also acted as colonizers and hoped to settle large numbers of French-speaking settlers in the West. Equally important was the role the Oblates played in establishment and consolidation of the Catholic Church in the western Canada. Until 1911, all of the bishops in western Canada were Oblates and all were suffragans of the Ecclesiastical Province of Saint-Boniface.

The Oblates played a complex and important role in the history of the western and northern regions of Canada and were associated with most of the momentous events in the development of those areas. Nevertheless, the history of the western Oblates was not well known and, furthermore, what was known was fragmented. The Oblates were the first to recognize this deficiency and, after prolonged discussion and planning, they established the Western Oblate History Project in 1986. Administered by Western Canadian Publishers, this project was to provide funds to researchers interested in preparing critical monographs of the Oblate experience in the Canadian North West. The research undertaken to prepare this volume was subventioned by Western Canadian Publishers.

The subject of Oblate missions is so intricate that this study should be regarded as an introduction to the missions of the prairie provinces. Similar studies will have to be undertaken for British Columbia, the Yukon, the Northwest Territories and the Arctic regions to provide a complete overview of the Oblate missionary experience in the western and northern regions of Canada. In addition to these topics, there is ample material for in-depth case studies of missions such as Île-à-la-Crosse and St. Albert that played a pivotal role in the expansion of the missionary frontier. It is also time to go beyond the "great man" approach and prepare biographical studies of Oblates other than the more prominent ones or those who attained ecclesiastical office. Furthermore, the biographies of Albert Lacombe, Vital-Justin Grandin, Joseph Hugonnard and Alexandre Taché that have been written some time ago are in need of revision to reflect newer intellectual traditions, the availability of more comprehensive and complimentary archives as well as a more secular outlook.

A history of Oblate missionary efforts would be incomplete without an examination of the response of the First Nations people to the apostolic process and the establishment of a missionary edifice. This study, however, does not pretend to be a comprehensive analysis of that interaction. At the time of initial contact the First Nations were preliterate and left no written records but they possessed an oral tradition that provides an accurate account of its past. The Oblates provided an extensive chronicle of their encounter with Indians and by utilizing the canons of ethnohistory as elaborated by specialists such as James Axtell[1] and Bruce Trigger,[2] it is possible to use these sources to gain valuable insights on the interaction of those who were being evangelized. Axtell has suggested "a good working principle" for studying missions and missionaries: "each side of the Christian curtain has to be studied from its own perspective."[3] From the perspective of a missionary, conversion was motivated by Christianity's superior spirituality and the desire to be redeemed. For Indians, the motives for conversion were far more complex and rooted in the "elemental fact of ethnic survival" in the face of social, cultural and economic challenges.[4] If these two fundamental viewpoints are ignored the end result will not be a "more objective understanding" of the missionary process but the substitution of a contemporary politically correct terminology for "old prejudices."[5]

Given the time span of one century, the immense area and the large number of tribes that inhabited the North West, it was necessary to establish parameters that would contribute to producing a study that was both meaningful and comprehensive. Fortunately, the chronological limits did not entail serious problems. The first date, 1845, is obvious because it represents the arrival of the Oblates in Red River to assist Bishop Norbert Provencher and begin their initiation to missionary work among the Saulteaux and Métis of southern Manitoba. The terminal date, 1945, is more arbitrary. It coincides with the hundredth anniversary of the Oblate Apostolate in the Canadian North West and represents a turning point in the history of Canada's First Nations. They had not disappeared as a result of assimilation, the ravages of disease, alcohol and other debilitating factors. Not only were the First Nations peoples more numerous, they were becoming more articulate and increasingly militant in an attempt to protect their identity and heritage as well as promote their socio-economic interests.

While chronology did not present an insurmountable problem, the size of the North West and the different tribes that inhabited the region had the potential to seriously undermine the one-volume study that initially had been envisaged. In considering these dilemmas, it became apparent that a judicious reduction of the area to be examined would also reduce the number of tribes that were involved. Consequently, it was decided to limit the study to the three prairie provinces of Manitoba, Saskatchewan and Alberta thereby excluding British Columbia, the Mackenzie basin and the Arctic. However, since ecclesiastical and religious jurisdictions do not always follow civil boundaries, reference will sometimes be made to Kenora and Fort Francis that, while in Ontario, were nevertheless included in the Diocese of St. Boniface and the Oblate

Province of Manitoba. Pembina and St. Joseph in North Dakota presented an identical situation until they were detached from St. Boniface. The Vicariate Apostolic of Athabasca-Mackenzie once included territory that is in the Province of Alberta.

In the period under consideration, civil and religious boundaries in the Canadian North West underwent significant change at numerous intervals. In order not to confuse the reader, Oblate missions and schools are identified by referencing them in parentheses to contemporary provincial boundaries because the latter are more obvious and better known. The maps on pages 26 and 98 also will assist the reader in locating the places discussed.

By introducing the reader to the Oblate Apostolate in western Canada, it is hoped that this study will be a point of departure for a series of scholarly studies dealing with the multi-faceted activities of the Oblates of that region. In addition to this introductory function, this study attempts to place the Oblate experience within its proper context. The Oblates were the product of a specific age and culture and their outlook, values and aspirations were conditioned by that experience. Furthermore, their missionary activities were carried out within the framework of a Roman Catholic Church that sought to create a perfect replica of itself in every country where it had been established. These clones became, and remained, foreign institutions rather than indigenous churches that reflected the needs and aspirations of the people they served. A study of Oblate missionary activity that does not consider these factors cannot be regarded as valid and authoritative.

△ △

ACKNOWLEDGEMENTS

Many individuals contributed to making this study possible and deserve my gratitude and appreciation. The late Gaston Carrière, OMI, invited me to join the Western Oblate History Project and Félix Vallée, OMI, was instrumental in launching the project and creating Western Canadian Publishers to administer its operations. I am indebted to Western Canadian Publishers for underwriting my research and travel expenses and to its director, the late Guy Lacombe, who provided me and other researchers with invaluable assistance and encouragement. My work was facilitated by the expert knowledge of Oblate archivists: the late Donat Levasseur, OMI, of the Archives Oblates de Montreal, Romuald Boucher, OMI, director of the Archives Deschâtelets in Ottawa, Gaston Montmigny, OMI, of the Grandin Province Archives. Claude Roberto of the Provincial Archives of Alberta facilitated access to the Alberta-Saskatchewan Oblate collection housed in the Provincial Archives in Edmonton. I am indebted to Olive Hébert of the Archives Deschâtelets for her assistance in locating material and verifying footnotes. I am also grateful to a large number of Oblates whom I met during a year's study leave while living in Oblate residences in Ottawa and Edmonton. This was indeed a rewarding experience because it allowed me to transcend the written word and come to know the Oblates first hand as well as share in their life and witness their spirituality.

I am also grateful to the University of Lethbridge that provided me with study leaves to undertake the research and complete the preparation of this manuscript. I am indebted to my colleagues, Malcolm Greenshields, Tom Robinson and Brian Titley, for their encouragement and advice. A special thanks should also go to John Foster at the University of Alberta for writing the Foreword and his continued support of the Western Oblate History Project. My wife, Laureen, and family deserve special mention for the divided attention they experienced during the time this study was being researched and written.

This book has been published with a grant from the Humanities and Social Sciences Federation of Canada, using funds provided by the Social Sciences and Humanities Research Council of Canada.

△ △ △ △ △ △ △ △ △ △ △ △ △ △ △ △ △ △ △ △

INTRODUCTION

From Marseille to the Canadian North West

At a time when the missionary has been removed from his lofty pedestral, a study of the apostolic and pastoral activities of the Missionary Oblates of Mary Immaculate among the Native and Métis populations of the prairie provinces in the period 1845–1945 is indeed a challenging task. Since their arrival in Red River in 1845, the Oblates have been, and remain, the dominant Catholic missionary order in the western and northern regions of Canada. Their experience is a fascinating chapter in the history of the introduction of Catholicism in the Canadian North West and a reflection of complex relationships between individuals, institutions, cultures, religions and the frontier. It is also the study of an attempt to make the indigenous inhabitants of the North West conform to a preconceived image of the ideal Christian society and culture.

While the main thrust of this study is on the Oblates, their activities did not take place in a vacuum. In their interaction with the First Nations, the Oblates came into contact with the Hudson's Bay Company, which controlled transportation and supplies in the interior. Without access to these facilities, early Oblate missions could not have been established or sustained. The Oblates also had to relate to the federal government that had jurisdiction over the Indians who had signed treaties in the North West and responsibility for providing education and health care to those populations. Christ's injunction to baptize all nations was also heard by Protestant denominations who became keen competitors on the missionary frontier. Oblate missions and activities were funded by Catholics in Europe and, in the missions, female religious communities provided an important support role. It is not possible to provide equal emphasis to these other integral components of the apostolic process but an effort has been made to identify them and to outline their relationship to and interaction with the Oblates.

The post WWII era witnessed the breakup of colonial empires, the emergence of a more liberal spirit, a condemnation of the repression of indigenous cultures and traditions that imperialism had fostered in the name of progress and development. With respect to religion, Vatican II (1962–65) fostered a more ecumenical attitude among denominations and contributed to fostering a keener appreciation of spiritual traditions that were outside traditional Christian forms. Long before Vatican II, however, the Oblates had recognized that their apostolate, with its emphasis on conformity to Roman Catholic norms and values, was being rejected by a large number of Natives who abandoned Christianity in favour of traditional forms of spirituality and worship. Confronted with this alienation and indifference and at times open hostility to Christianity, the Oblates began to critically examine their objectives and missiology and postulate new relationships that reflected the needs and aspirations of the second half of the twentieth century. In addition to their awareness of the disenchantment of the First Nations, the Oblates also recognized that these communities had come of age and could no longer be kept in tutelage and the old missionary apparatus had to be dismantled.

The focus on the prairie provinces made it possible to concentrate on the Oblate evangelization of tribes that spoke an Algonkian language and lived from the hunt. The southern part of the prairies was inhabited by the Plains Cree and Blackfoot as well as the Dakota and Saulteaux. The Ojibwa were to be found in northwestern Ontario and the Oji-Cree in southeastern Manitoba. The Assiniboines, or Stonies, spoke a Siouan language. Further north, the Oblates encountered the Woodland Cree and the Chipewyan (Dene), the largest Athapascan tribe. The Beaver were to be found in the Peace River region. The Métis or mixed-blood population was to be found in all parts of the prairies and often played a broker role between the Oblates and other Indians.

The Coastal Indians of British Columbia and the Inuit of the Arctic possessed a culture and lifestyle that differed significantly from that of the

Plains tribes and the Métis. The tribes along the Pacific coast were characterized by a civilization based on cedar and salmon while the Inuit, with their unique language, culture and lifestyle, contrast sharply with all other Aboriginal populations. Furthermore, the Oblates in British Columbia closely regimented and controlled the activities of Natives and their communities through the "Durieu system," a refinement of the *reducciones,* the older Jesuit enclaves of Paraguay. This attempt at total social control was absent in the prairie provinces. The evangelization of the Inuit of the western Arctic did not begin until the second decade of the twentieth century and presented its own unique challenges.

The prairie provinces and their First Nations populations were under the jurisdiction of the Dominion of Canada and there were no competing provincial governments as in British Columbia. Furthermore, the treaties signed between the Indians and Canada between 1871 and 1899 encompassed all of the Indians of the present western provinces whereas only Treaty 8 included the Indians living in the northeastern part of British Columbia.

Another important and unique characteristic of the Oblate apostolate in the prairie provinces is that it was the work of French-speaking clergymen. Consequently, the Oblates reinforced the ultramontane Catholicism of Quebec that zealously guarded and defended the prerogatives of the Catholic Church and the rights of the French language. In establishing the Catholic Church in the West the Oblates were promoting a cultural and religious extension of Quebec. This amalgam of race and religion produced a missiology that placed great value in the preservation of indigenous languages as a bulwark against Protestantization and subsequent Anglicization. To French-speaking Oblates, Henri Bourassa's eloquent defense of the French language, *La langue gardienne de la foi,*[1] was as valid a directive for their missions and schools in the North West as it had been for French-speaking minorities in Canada.

In British Columbia, the ecclesiastical hierarchy, Oblate administration and missionaries became increasingly English-speaking in the twentieth century and their missiology and schools reflected an assimilationist philosophy reminiscent of the "Irish" Catholic bishops of Canada who sought to make Catholicism more respectable and, hence, acceptable to the larger Protestant community by eliminating all "foreign" vestiges. High on the list of "foreign" impediments to be discarded was the historic association of Catholicism with the French population of Quebec. While not initially apparent and, to a large degree not anticipated, the different attitudes and responses of French- and English-speaking missionaries are another indication of the incredible complexity of the Oblate missionary phenomenon.

In ideological terms, the Oblate experience involved the export to the Canadian North West of a west European model of Christianity. It is a story of a deep cultural and spiritual conflict between individuals reared in a western European cultural and religious tradition that was deemed to be the finest manifestation of human endeavour and migratory hunters who, according to the missionaries, lacked the fundamental elements of civilization religion and perhaps even humanity. The Oblates also believed that the benefits that had accrued from their cultural traditions and spirituality were to be bestowed on less fortunate groups through the process of evangelization. Thus, it was through the process of proclaiming the Gospel that the contrast between missionary and those being evangelized becomes most evident. As James Axtell has argued: "Christianity is exclusive and intolerant . . . In the shadow of the Cross, all other beliefs pale into insignificance."[2]

The Oblate apostolate is also a frontier experience in which a French institution domiciled and adapted itself to the conditions in and the demands of the interior of the Canadian North West. During this process, the Oblate missionary effort underwent significant change as the Oblates examined and analysed the results of their apostolate. It began with a naive and optimistic attempt to assimilate Native people while Christianizing them. A century later, however, the Oblates became aware that their efforts were not succeeding and were being rejected or subverted by the Native community. In the meantime, the Oblates, as delegates of the Catholic Church, had to function within the limits of a predetermined ecclesiology that they were not at liberty to alter. Prior to Vatican II, the universality of the Catholic Church was identified and proclaimed by its conformity to the parent Roman institution.

As an institutional history the Oblate missionary effort encompasses the development of an adequate missionary strategy, the establishment, consolidation and expansion of missions and ancillary institutions such as orphanages, schools and hospitals. The missionary frontier is also the story of competing denominations, each striving to convert the largest number of individuals and denouncing the other in terms that lacked any semblance of Christian charity and meekness. The Oblates were able to establish strong bonds of personal friendship with the largely Anglo-Protestant officers of the Hudson's Bay Company as a result of a mutuality of interests in the isolated interior. The Oblate apostolate also involved the creation of an unholy alliance with the bureaucracy of a nominally Protestant government to provide education and health care services for the Native populations. In the process, normal problems associated with the provision of education and health care were exacerbated by rivalries between Catholic and Protestant.

In addition, the Oblate experience is an analysis of motivation as individuals willingly endured incredible physical distress, starvation and long periods of isolation to be able to partake in Christ's great commission to instruct and baptize all nations. This study does not begin with the premise that the work of the Oblates was providentially ordained but it does recognize that the individuals involved sincerely believed it was. While the Oblates were a unified and disciplined religious congregation, the work in the field was carried out by individuals each of whom possessed different skills and talents. Thus, Oblate missionary history is the story of human agents with personal aspirations and characteristics that sometimes were difficult to reconcile with holy orders and religious vows.

There is no doubt that the Oblates played a complex and important role in the history of the western and northern regions of Canada. Unfortunately, despite a long and fascinating experience transcending many disciplines, the western Oblates have not attracted the attention of scholars until recently. This was not an oversight by scholars but a reflection of prevailing circumstances and intellectual traditions. For many years the study of religion and, by implication, the study of religious activity such as missionary work, was deemed to be the prerogative of the participants themselves or of other clergymen or members of religious communities. Accounts were written by lay persons from time to time but these were the exception rather than the rule and, while they may not have reflected as obvious a denominational bias as did clerical accounts, their basic interpretation did not differ significantly.

It should be noted that the archives of religious congregations such as the Oblates are, in fact, private archives. Permission had to be obtained to examine these collections and their facilities were limited. The private nature of these archives made it difficult for lay persons and especially scholars in nondenominational universities to undertake serious research on the missionary activities of the Oblates. With respect to the Oblates, the utilization of their archives is complicated by the fact that the majority of their documents is in French.

In addition to these handicaps, the intellectual tradition within religious circles identified theology as the central element upon which to focus. Thus, the study of religion became an account of the "the saving events in which God entered into human history" and of the propagation of the message of redemption.[3] The study of the role and function of religion in society was not recognized as a valid field of inquiry by the earlier generation of clerical authors. Within the Catholic tradition, works on religious subjects were subjected to an elaborate process of scrutiny prior to being published. The *nihil obstat*, for example, accorded by a clergyman designated as censor, certified that nothing within nothing found within the pages in question was contrary to Catholic faith and morals. In addition, works had to secure the *imprimatur*, the authorisation of an ecclesiastical authority. With respect to the Oblates, a third permission, *imprimi potest*, was accorded by the author's religious superior.

Equally restrictive in view of objectivity, was the fact that the early literature dealing with the western Oblates was written to publicize their work and to stimulate interest in and financial contributions for their missions and institutions. It goes without saying that the challenge facing the Oblates in the missions of the North West was described in the most superlative of terms, the hardships they encountered, the incredible distances that had to be travelled were a response to a divine imperative and, hence, inconsequential. Protestant opponents were not only pictured as diabolical and very cunning but also possessing limitless resources with which to undermine the impoverished Oblates. These accounts had a profound impact on devout lay Catholics and provided them with an opportunity to participate in the extension of Christ's Kingdom in the Canadian North West through their financial contributions. The writings French Oblates serving in the North West served an additional purpose of reminding their countrymen under the anti-clerical Third Republic that the glorious pre-revolutionary tradition of Catholicism *Gesta Dei per Francos,* the actions of God through the deeds of the French, was being continued in the interior of Canada.

This literary genre was begun in 1866 by Alexandre-Antonin Taché, OMI, Bishop of St. Boniface who, in 1865, wrote *Vingt années de missions dans le Nord-Ouest de l'Amérique*. Taché's "notes" had been prepared at the request of the Superior General of the Congregation to publicize the work of the Oblates in the Canadian North West and subsequently were published serially in *Missions de la Congrégation des Missionnaires Oblats de Marie Immaculée*.[4] At the request of the Bishop of Montreal, Taché agreed to allow his account to be published in book format under the same title: *Vingt années de missions dans le Nord-Ouest de l'Amérique*.[5] Since Taché was a pioneer missionary and the first Oblate bishop in western Canada, *Vingt années de missions* enjoyed a wide circulation especially in his native Quebec.

Accounts compiled by Oblates from France targeted, as a secondary objective, a European market that was fascinated by the North American wilderness and its Native populations. In this latter category are to be found accounts written by two Oblate bishops who served in the Athabasca-Mackenzie districts: Émile Grouard, *Souvenirs de mes soixante ans d'apostolat dans l'Athabasca-Mackenzie*,[6] and Gabriel Breynat, *Cinquante ans au pays des neiges*.[7] An English version of another of book by Breynat appeared posthumously in 1955 as *Bishop of the Winds: Fifty Years in the Arctic Region*.[8] Only a small number of Oblate books appeared in English and this contributed to the Oblates and their work being less well-known among English-speaking Canadians.[9] One notable exception, Frank Dolphin's *Indian Bishop of the West,* a recent biography of Bishop Vital-Justin, is based on older hagiographic sources and is uncritical.[10] A far more valuable source for researchers is the translation of the diaries of Bishop Vital-Justin Grandin.[11]

Oblate missionaries also published their memoirs or accounts of their activities from time to time.[12] These personal accounts have been supplemented by the works of historians within the Oblate order. Foremost among these writers was the prolific historian-archivist Gaston Carrière who, while interested primarily in the Oblates of eastern Canada, nevertheless wrote biographies of prominent western Oblates such as Joseph Hugonnard and Ovide Charlebois.[13] In Alberta, Paul-Émile Breton published biographies of other prominent missionaries who had served in the region.[14] While the writings of Carrière and Breton were more sophisticated than the older personal narratives and involved considerable archival research, the biographies they produced were essentially the religious equivalent of the "great man" school of interpretation in secular historiography.

Carrière, who had produced a ten-volume documentary history of the Oblates in eastern Canada, had been expected to undertake a similar venture for the western Oblates but his numerous obligations prevented him from turning his attention to this task. His contribution to a more general history of the western Oblates consisted of comprehensive articles discussing the establishment of early Oblate missions in the North West, the relations between the Oblates and the personnel of the Hudson's Bay Company, and events in the careers of prominent Oblates such as Albert Lacombe and Alexis André.[15] Carrière's most significant contribution is his three-volume biographical dictionary of Oblates who served in Canada, and it is an indispensable tool for anyone studying the Oblates.[16]

Carrière's efforts were seconded by another Oblate, Joseph-Étienne Champagne, who published a short history of the Oblate missions in western Canada, *Les missions catholiques dans l'Ouest canadien (1818–1875)*,[17] which remains the only survey on the subject. While useful as historical sources, the personal accounts written by missionaries in the field and those prepared by other Oblates are limited by factors that are immediately apparent to the contemporary reader. There is an obvious denominational bias in the older personal accounts that extols the virtues of Catholicism and simultaneously casts serious doubts on the credibility of Protestant rivals. Protestants were not even accorded the status of competitors; they are dismissed as false prophets or minions of Satan. The writings of Carrière, Breton and Champagne do not reflect such a blatant confessional bias but, nevertheless, they are predicated on the premise that Catholicism is the one true religion and, *ipso facto*, the work of the Oblates was a continuation of Christ's commission to the Apostles to instruct and baptize all nations The most recent account written by an Oblate, Claude Champagne's *Les débuts de la mission dans le Nord-Ouest canadien: Mission et Église chez Mgr Vital Grandin, o.m.i., (1829–1902)*,[18] reflects the more recent trends in historical scholarship but is not completely detached from the tradition established by Carrière, Breton and Joseph-Étienne Champagne.

Oblate writings also reflect an ethnocentric perspective that is perhaps less readily identified than their religious partisanship. The Christian model exported by the Oblates to the North West was based on the norms, values and cultural traditions of western Europe. It was deemed to be the most perfect form of spirituality and a manifestation of the highest form of civilization ever attained by humanity. Consequently, this Christian model was to be imitated by all so that everyone might share equally in its benefits especially the Native populations of the North West whom the Oblates were evangelizing. To the Oblates, Christianity and the civilization of western Europe went hand in hand and each served to promote and enhance the interests and welfare of the other.

The severe criticism of the Oblates in contemporary society is due largely to their former ethnocentric perspective. Today the missionary in general, and the Oblate in particular, generally is not held in very high esteem by society at large. The missionary is no longer the benevolent patriarch, imbued with altruistic motives and prepared to suffer great hardship in order to minister to the needs of his flock. To a large degree, this classic imagery has been replaced by the dismal tableau of the missionary as an outsider, an unwanted and troublesome intruder attempting to subvert the society, culture and religion of those whom they were evangelizing.

Although products of a previous age and mentality, the comments of the western Oblates on the culture and religion of Native populations offend the sensitivities of contemporary society. Oblate descriptions of Native society and customs were influenced by a feeling of social, economic and cultural superiority. In their missionary work in the North West, the Oblates provided a concrete expression of the concept of "the white man's burden" long before it was popularized by Kipling. Within this context, the comments the Oblates made on the society of the First Nations reveal more about the culture and mentality of the Oblates and the society they represented than they do about the individuals they are supposed to describe. Terms like "savage," "pagan," "barbarian," "superstitious," "resistant to grace and redemption," "irresistible nomads," and others are not objective assessments of the life, culture and religion of the First Nations who inhabited the North West. What these comments really indicate is the gap that had to be bridged before the indigenous populations achieved the ideal socio-economic and religious order envisaged by the Oblates. In addition, accusations that the Oblates deliberately used residential schools under their jurisdiction to acculturate

Indians together with more recent allegations of sexual and physical abuse in those institutions have produced an unbalanced interpretation of their apostolate in western Canada.

At this point, the reader must be cautioned that this study will not examine or speculate on allegations of physical and sexual abuse in Indian residential schools administered by the Oblates. To begin with, this study focuses on the overall Oblate apostolate and, while residential schools became important adjuncts of mission, they are secondary to the main theme. More important, however, is the fact that a peripheral study would not do justice to the sensational and controversial subject of abuse. Only a detailed and thorough study conducted by someone well versed in pedagogy and social psychology could make a meaningful contribution to the debate. Furthermore, abuse in residential schools must not be studied in isolation but within the context of the educational system in general and the family and society at large. Without this larger picture, conjecture will prevail and conclusions at best will be tenuous and tendentious.

With the passage of time, the archives of the Oblates became less private and were opened to researchers, the clergy lost their monopoly on religious subjects and the nontheological dimension of religion and religious activity emerged as a valid field of inquiry. In the meantime, Oblates and other members of the clergy prepared theses using the congregation's voluminous archives.[19] Lay persons also began to use these archives to prepare theses that would be of great value to researchers and which illustrated the complexity of the Oblate apostolate in the North West. In this latter category are Jacqueline Kennedy's [Gresko] "Qu'Appelle Industrial School: White Rites for the Indians of the Old Northwest,"[20] and Martha McCarthy's "The Missions of the Oblates of Mary Immaculate to the Athapascans 1846–1870: Theory, Structure and Method."[21] In addition to the preparation of theses, the Oblate archives have been recognized as an important source of information by scholars interested in the encounter between missionaries and aboriginal populations, for example, Antonio Gualtieri's *Christianity and Native Traditions: Indigenization and Syncretism among the Inuit and Dene of the Western Arctic*[22] and John Webster Grant's *Moon of Wintertime: Missionaries and the Indians of Canada in Encounter Since 1534*.[23] In *Will to Power*, David

Mulhall examined the career of the controversial Adrien Gabriel Morice, pioneer missionary in the interior of British Columbia, from a very secular perspective.[24]

Other graduate students and researchers examined the Oblates but did so in a context secondary to their principal role as missionaries. Thus, the Oblates figured prominently in a thesis on the organization of French Catholics in Saskatchewan,[25] in an article on the French language press in western Canada,[26] in works on Louis Riel,[27] on the controversial Manitoba school question,[28] in urban histories[29] and in a diocesan history.[30] From time to time, the memoirs and journals of individual Oblates have been published.[31]

After one hundred and fifty years, it is indeed time to rewrite the history of the western Oblates. To begin with, time and changing circumstances have challenged traditional interpretations and found them wanting. The archives of the Oblates have been organized and are more accessible to researchers. Complimentary sources are to be found in the records of the Department of Indian Affairs, the papers of prominent Canadian statesmen and civil servants. The records of female religious communities such as the Grey Nuns who assisted the Oblates and those of competing Protestant religious denominations such as the Church Missionary Society will present equally intriguing perspectives. New intellectual trends, such as ethnohistory, have contributed to a more meaningful and realistic assessment of the missionary and the process of cultural interaction that evangelization entailed in western and northern Canada.

△ △ △ △ △ △ △ △ △ △ △ △ △ △

1

THE FRENCH ANTECEDENTS

If the missions of New France provided the Society of Jesus with a glorious chapter in its annals, the Canadian North West enabled a French order, the Missionary Oblates of Mary Immaculate to earn the accolade, "specialists in difficult missions," as a result of an impressive record of dedication and service in the midst of highly adverse conditions.[1] Originally created in 1815 by *abbé* Charles-Joseph-Eugène de Mazenod and named *La Société des Missionnaires de Provence,* the congregation's initial goal was to evangelize the poor and lower classes and reanimate a moribund Catholicism in southern France through religious exercises and the preaching of popular missions in the parishes and countryside.[2] Mazenod believed that the lower classes and the poor constituted a "precious" but unfortunately abandoned portion of the Christian community that had to be redeemed.[3] Ten years later, in 1825, as Mazenod was seeking pontifical approval for the order and its rules, he decided to change the name to *Oblats de Marie Immaculée* to avoid confusion with other religious communities that also incorporated the term *oblat* in their title.[4]

Given the original purpose of their order it is not surprising that the Oblates who came to the Canadian North West were not trained to carry out their work among Indian and Métis populations. In post-revolutionary France the intellectual quality of theological studies in the *grands séminaires* left much to be desired. To begin with, there were few priests for the pastoral work that had to be done and, hence, the length of theological studies was reduced to an absolute minimum. In addition, those who in charge of the preparation of the clergy were themselves poorly trained and lacked specialization because the Revolution had closed the faculties of theology.[5]

At the time he established the congregation, Mazenod was well aware of the lamentable state of affairs in French seminaries and he attempted to remedy the situation when the first Oblate scholasticate opened in Marseille in 1827. Mazenod deplored the hasty and incomplete formation of candidates for the priesthood and insisted that those entering the Oblate order receive a solid education in both ecclesiastical and religious subjects regardless of where they were sent to serve. However, secular subjects such as anthropology, sociology or linguistics were not to be found in the scholasticate's curriculum and a century would pass before their importance was recognized and missiology, the science of missions, became a discipline in its own right in Oblate institutions.[6] Mazenod was not averse to adding instruction in the English language to the curriculum after the Oblates had established themselves in England and in other parts of the British Empire such as Canada.[7]

While the post-revolutionary era had contributed to a less than ideal preparation of the Oblates as clergymen, it also accentuated their ultramontane beliefs as did the section of their constitution and rules that stressed obedience to the Pope. It was not surprising that the theological texts in use in the seminary at Marseille reflected a staunch ultramontane perspective.[8] Equally uncompromising was the conviction that the Roman Catholic Church was the only source of grace and salvation while the pretensions of all other denominations were deemed false and their adherents *ipso facto* were heretics.[9]

Consequently, it was argued that there could be no salvation outside the Roman Catholic Church and, furthermore, baptism, as an initiation into the Church and a revelation of its divine truths, was a necessary prerequisite to that salvation. This unequivocal premise influenced every facet of Oblate missionary activity and it contributed to the development of a missionary strategy whose primary objective was to carry the message of redemption as quickly and as efficiently as possible to non-Christian populations. Regardless of the cost and sacrifice, it was deemed necessary to continue the mandate that Jesus Christ, on the eve of His ascension into heaven, conferred upon his apostles through the injunction to teach and baptize all nations.[10]

This mandate would be continued until the end of time by the Church Christ established through the intermediary of its representatives. The Church's mission, like Christ's, was to extend and consolidate the Kingdom of God by bringing the message of redemption to humanity and by actively involving individuals in their own salvation.[11] Within this historical context the Oblate, as a member of the Roman Catholic Church, was the legitimate and official representative of that institution among non-Christians and, hence, responsible for the establishment of the Church in their midst. As a missionary, the Oblate was God's envoy, a pioneer, whose work would lay the foundation for the extension and consolidation of the Kingdom among non-Christians.[12] An 1881 Oblate directive on missions clearly identified the objective of missionary activity as the conversion of souls, the re-animation of faith and the strengthening of the Kingdom of God to ensure earthly happiness and the acquisition of eternal salvation.[13]

The directive went on to suggest the special characteristics the Oblate required in order to successfully discharge his mandate. Following the example of the saints, the Oblate must acquire and strengthen within himself the following traits: gentleness, chastity, humility, mortification, the love of souls, and a true piety.[14] As the earthly representative and delegate of God the missionary was to reflect the glory, honour and virtues of Christ. The missionary was to possess the zeal of the apostle Paul and Saint Francis Xavier and to imitate the former who was himself a follower of Christ.[15]

Announcing the message of the Gospel to peoples who had never heard of Jesus Christ and leading them to redemption was the most sublime and invigorating endeavour for the Oblates who were already convinced that they represented the true Christian Church. The co-operation and association with Christ in bringing about the salvation of mankind was deemed to be *l'oeuvre des oeuvres*[16] and it produced a spiritual ecstasy that enabled the Oblates to accept overwhelming challenges and, in the process, to endure incredible sacrifice and hardships. The challenges, the hardships, the suffering were not only accepted but openly sought because they were viewed as a means whereby God was testing the Oblates to ensure that they were worthy of following in the footsteps of the Apostles.

Mazenod was convinced that the vocation of the Oblates was part of this authentic apostolate that, through the message of the Gospel, brought about a knowledge and love of God and Christ in the hearts and minds of the people to whom it was addressed. After the initial announcement of the Good News, the Christian message was to be reinforced by teaching catechism to children and preaching popular missions among the poor. The "popular" or "parish" missions were a medium by which the Oblates preached and instructed the local population in their own language and in terms that were comprehensible to the people. Religious services accompanied the sermons and instructions. The preaching of popular missions was deemed to be the most efficient means of transmitting the message of redemption. Mazenod was opposed to the preaching of flowery and moving sermons that would have no lasting impact on the masses whom he was trying to reach. He preferred that the faith be implanted in them in a more lasting manner and that the knowledge of Jesus Christ crucified be indelible.[17]

Given their French background and ultramontane perspective, it was not necessary for the Oblates to be theoreticians and elaborate a complex conceptual model of their role as missionaries or present a systematic account of their conception of the Church. Using Vital-Justin Grandin, one of the early French Oblates who came to the Canadian North West as a case study, Claude Champagne demonstrated that the Oblate missionaries were primarily pastors and men of action.[18] As the legitimate and official delegates of the Roman Catholic Church, the Oblates were responsible for continuing Christ's commission to teach and baptize all nations by means of religious instruction, preaching and missions.

Mazenod regarded his Oblate associates as "true apostles" selected by Christ because, in the manner of the apostles of the biblical era, they were the first to carry the redemptive message of the Gospel to individuals who previously had been under the influence of Satan. So convinced was Mazenod that his Oblates were continuing the work of the Apostles that he exhorted them never to lose the least rosette from their crown. Furthermore, they were to find encouragement and consolation in their communal life and in the rules that governed their activities and never allow themselves to be overcome by the trials and tribulations of their earthly existence.[19] While all of the "foreign missions" that is, missions among non-Christian populations, came to be held in high regard by Mazenod because he perceived in them a reflection of the work of the first Apostles, the missions of the Canadian North West were even more highly esteemed because of their primitive state, their isolation and hardships. Furthermore, the true apostolic tradition was to be found in the missions of the Canadian North West where missionary and bishop performed manual labour as had Saint Paul.[20]

Initially the Oblates limited their work to Provence but, by 1831, members of the congregation had expressed the desire to carry their missionary work beyond that region. The arrival of the Oblates in eastern Canada in 1841, the Oregon Territory in 1847, Ceylon in 1847, Texas in 1849, South Africa in 1852, and British Columbia in 1858 was not only a concrete manifestation of this desire, it also provided a new orientation for the congregation. Henceforth, the Oblates would become increasingly committed to these *missions étrangères* especially those that contained non-Christian aboriginal populations. In 1850, Mazenod had already discussed the necessity of amending the congregation's constitution to reflect this new dimension in apostolic activity and, in 1853, a special appendix was added to the second edition of the *Constitutions et Règles*.[21]

This was Bishop Mazenod's *Instruction* relative to foreign missions that reiterated Oblate philosophy and procedure in the light of the experience and insights acquired in missionary activity overseas. As such, the *Instruction* was not a radical departure from traditional practice but a refinement of the congregation's primary objective of reviving the faith among the poor and providing for their religious needs through the intermediary of missions and religious exercises. The foreign missions were in fact a natural extension of religious instruction and exercises at the parochial level.[22] The *Instruction* accorded a high status to foreign missions that were regarded as "eminently suitable" to securing the glory of God and enhancing the status of the congregation.[23] It was recognized that not every Oblate was competent for this type of ministry and only those who demonstrated special characteristics would be selected. The desired qualifications included a strong sense of vocation, a desire to serve in the foreign missions, as well an appropriate character and behaviour. In addition, the candidate had to be in good health and possess the necessary strength to carry out his duties and face the hardships that might be encountered in the process.[24]

In the field, the Oblates were not only responsible for evangelizing non-Christian populations but also for inculcating among them a behaviour and lifestyle that reflected Christian virtues. For example, they were to regularize marriages in conformity with the precepts of Canon Law, to instil in children the fear of God and the necessity of avoiding temptation and sin, to inspire a sense of piety in women, and temperance and honesty among men. It was deemed important to train aboriginal populations in the necessities of communal life because, while this was a desirable goal in itself, it also would enhance apostolic work and contribute to the welfare of the mission. Consequently, the Oblates were to convince hunting populations to abandon their traditional lifestyle, learn to build homes for themselves, cultivate the land and, in the process, become "civilized" in accordance with accepted Euro-Christian values and traditions. Since prosperity was equated with the level of education a society received, the Oblates were to establish a school in each mission in which the young would be instructed in the rudiments of Christianity and at the same time receive a practical education to prepare them to live in a sedentary civilized society. While the Oblates were to concern themselves with promoting the material welfare of their charges, they were not to assume a leadership function in temporal matters because such matters were to be left to the people themselves.[25]

To facilitate the process of evangelization and the acquisition of fundamental Christian truths, the *Instruction* urged Oblates to follow the apostolic tradition and evangelize the people in their indigenous language. After having mastered the language, the missionary was to prepare a résumé of Christian doctrine in the form of a series of questions and answers. Neophytes were to memorize this summary and it would be explained gradually to them in terms and at a level of comprehension that were appropriate. Missionaries were also to incorporate these fundamental Christian truths into hymns and have them sung by their charges. The Oblates were to compile illustrated catechisms and to use any other means to more efficiently transmit the Christian message and to render it more forceful.[26]

With respect to the format of the regular mission the *Instruction* stated that it begin in the morning with the celebration of Holy Mass attended by persons of both sexes followed by the singing of hymns and a sermon. The purpose of this morning instruction was to present the neophytes with a simple but meaningful introduction to the precepts of the Christian faith by discussing the Apostle's Creed, the Ten Commandments and participation in the Sacraments. A second meeting would take place the same morning to instruct those who had not yet been baptized. Later in the day, adults would be confessed, children prepared for their First Communion, quarrels would be settled and domestic difficulties resolved. In the evening there would be another common religious exercise that everyone should attend. The subjects to be discussed included the individual's purpose on earth, the malice of sin, death, the Last Judgment, heaven, hell, and the life and passion of Christ. During this evening session the missionary was to use all his skills to instil among the neophytes a true fear of offending God. At the same time, he was to inculcate a loving devotion for the Blessed Virgin Mary.

The final day of the mission was to be a special event. There would be a general communion in the morning, followed by the baptism of adults and children around mid-day. After the evening sermon there would be the renewal of baptismal vows and promises. The mission would terminate with the solemn benediction of the Blessed Sacrament, a majestic ritual that produced a lasting impression in the minds and hearts of participants.[27]

The *Instruction* also contained very pragmatic procedural recommendations for the activities of Oblates serving in the foreign missions. In an area where the Oblate administration was not established in a regular manner all missions were placed under the immediate jurisdiction of a vicar of missions.[28] At the local level, the domicile of missionaries was called a residence and was placed under the authority of a director or superior. In those missions where the Oblate missionary was alone, the vicar of missions had to provide a lay brother or another missionary as a companion as soon as possible. Oblates who found themselves separated from other members of their community had to compensate by being more zealous and arduous, occupying themselves with their religious obligations and practicing Christian piety. Oblates were to devote one day a month to spiritual meditation and every year they were to come together for a retreat. Vicars of missions were responsible for maintaining a watchful eye on the health of those under their jurisdiction.[29]

Young Oblates who were beginning their missionary careers were to work under the supervision of a mature and experienced missionary. The establishment of a mission was to be confided to individuals with years of missionary experience. The *Instruction* also cautioned against the premature baptism of neophytes. It recommended that baptism be given only to those who had been sufficiently instructed and who offered positive indications that they would persevere in the Christian tradition. A similar caution was to be exercised vis-à-vis those who wished to present themselves for their first communion.[30]

Regardless of the distance separating the Oblates and members of their hierarchy, the *Instruction* insisted on regular communication between the constituent parts. Each missionary, for example, was to write to his director of residence once a month, to his vicar of missions once every three months, and to the superior general at least once a year.[31] This pattern of communication contributed to breaking down the barriers of solitude and isolation and it reinforced the spirit of communal religious life in those instances where circumstances rendered it impossible. Inadvertently, this directive created a voluminous correspondence that now rests in the various Oblate archives and has become an invaluable historical source for researchers. Many of these letters and reports on missions were reproduced in the order's quarterly publication, *Missions de la Congrégation des Missionnaires Oblats de Marie Immaculée,* and constitute a significant body of literature on the foreign missions in general and the Canadian missions in particular. This publication was inaugurated in 1862 by Joseph Fabre who succeeded Mazenod as superior general. Fabre continued Mazenod's practice of frequent communications with all members of the congregation and he established *Missions* to provide Oblates with a means to communicate with one another and to comment on their endeavours. A special invitation to collaborate was extended to Oblates engaged in missionary activities.[32] Like Mazenod, Fabre exhorted Oblates in the foreign missions to send him reports of their activities. Fabre stipulated two conditions: the reports had to be simple and *true*.[33]

The *Instruction* is not a theoretical, abstract document and it reflects the pragmatic character and nature of its author and the congregation he created. From its origins the Oblate order had two main goals: the personal sanctification of its members and missionary endeavours.[34] This apostolic effort was to be fulfilled through sacerdotal activities. Religious life, on the other hand, would not only enhance the priestly function; it would also contribute to personal salvation.[35] Regardless of where they served, the Oblates committed themselves to a programme of comprehensive apostolic activity based on the preaching of missions and conducting religious exercises among the local population.

Within this context, the *Instruction* was not a new orientation for missionary activity but a refinement of existing practices based on the experience acquired in evangelizing aboriginal peoples in Canada, Ceylon and South Africa. This internal flexibility and pragmatic philosophy, combined with Mazenod's innovative spirit, enabled the Oblates to improvise and adapt to the circumstances of the Canadian North West. This adaptation is even more remarkable in view of the fact that the missions of Red River and Quebec developed simultaneously and independently and so the experience and expertise acquired in one region could not assist missionaries in the other. Furthermore, missionaries tended to come directly to Quebec or to the North West and there was little exchange of personnel between the two regions. The Oregon missions and later those of British Columbia also developed independently of and in isolation from the missions of western and northern Canada.

While the evangelization of the Indian and Métis populations of the North West was the primary occupation of the Oblates, they had to assume auxiliary obligations such as the establishment of schools because the area initially lacked such institutions, be it at the parochial or regional level. As Catholics, the Oblates could not remain indifferent to the plight of orphans, the sick and the old, whose unattached or nonproductive status within the Native community destined them to a bleak future. The schools, orphanages and hospitals they established required financial support and at first the Oblates turned their requests to sources within the Catholic community such as *l'Oeuvre de la Propagation de la Foi* and *l'Oeuvre de la Sainte Enfance*.[36] When these sources became insufficient, the Oblates turned to the Canadian government that had jurisdiction over matters affecting Native populations in particular and the North West Territories in general. This alliance between church and state made it possible for religious groups such as the Oblates to provide and sustain much needed services at a time when few were interested in or concerned with the welfare of the First Nations people of Canada.

As a person constantly in contact with the Indian and Métis populations the Oblate missionary was an early witness to the destructive consequences of the presence of the white agricultural frontier on these two indigenous communities.[37] The disappearance of the buffalo and the erosion of the old ways and traditions were not only creating an upheaval within aboriginal societies, they were also threatening the less solidly entrenched Christian values among the neophytes. Through the extension of Christianity the Oblates hoped to ensure the salvation of the Native populations. By providing a practical education in their schools the Oblates hoped to prepare them for the socio-economic transformation that was taking place in their traditional hunting grounds. Individuals with less faith, dedication and determination would have refused the challenge contained in the congregation's motto, *Evangelizare pauperibus misit me*,[38] that found its concrete expression in the missions of the Canadian North West.

△ △ △ △ △ △ △ △ △ △ △ △ △ △   **2**

THE RED RIVER MISSIONS

It is ironic that the Oblates of Mary Immaculate, who became the dominant Catholic missionaries in the western and northern regions of Canada, were not the first Catholic clergymen to come to the North West. In terms of ecclesiastical administration that region came under the jurisdiction of the Diocese of Quebec, the only Catholic diocese in British North America after 1760 because British authorities initially were opposed to the establishment of a regular Catholic hierarchy.[1] Although the North West was a vast fur trade empire contested by both the Hudson's Bay Company (HBC) and the North West Company (NWC), individuals such as the Scottish philanthropist and colonizer, Lord Selkirk, were convinced that the area had potential for colonisation and agriculture as well. Consequently, in 1811, Selkirk sent out the first contingent of settlers to establish the Red River Colony at the junction of the Red and Assiniboine Rivers in what is today metropolitan Winnipeg.

The majority of Selkirk's settlers were Roman Catholic and, in Red River, this denominational affiliation was reinforced by the presence of French Canadian fur traders and the Métis, their mixed blood offspring. Since there was no Catholic priest in Red River, Selkirk invited Bishop Joseph-Octave Plessis of Quebec to establish a permanent mission in his colony. Officials of the NWC had also encouraged Plessis to send a priest to Rainy Lake where they hoped to establish a provisioning post for their brigades. For his part, Plessis desired to minister to the French Canadian and Métis populations of the North West who had been without spiritual guidance since the fall of New France in 1760 but initially his resources, both human and financial, would not permit this.[2]

While the NWC and the HBC were profit oriented and not overly concerned with issues associated with salvation they, nevertheless, realized that the presence of the clergy could have a positive and stabilizing influence on the country and its inhabitants, especially the Métis, who were essential to the fur trade as a proletariat. As the severe competition between the NWC and the HBC evolved into open confrontation and violence, both the NWC and Selkirk increased their efforts to gain Plessis's favour. Plessis was anxious to use every means at his disposal to promote the extension of the Church and, in the wake of the Seven Oaks massacre and a petition signed by 22 heads of families in Red River, he decided to establish a mission at Red River as Selkirk had recommended.[3]

In 1818, Plessis sent two priests, Joseph-Norbert Provencher and Sévère Dumoulin, to Red River to lay the groundwork for the establishment of the Church in the North West. Plessis provided the two clergymen with detailed instructions concerning their duties and responsibilities in the field. Their first objective was to rescue the Indian populations from the barbarism and subsequent disorder into which they allegedly had fallen. Their second objective was to minister to delinquent Christians in the area who were living licentiously and ignoring their duties and obligations as Christians.[4]

Basing himself on the experience of the Jesuits among the Hurons during the French regime, Plessis outlined the methods that should be utilized in this first attempt to evangelize the Native and Métis populations of Red River. Like the Jesuits, Provencher and Dumoulin were to Christianize these elements by preaching the Gospel in the local language or dialect. It was believed that the Gospel would be understood and could make its force felt if it were preached in the vernacular. The clergy were to regularize marriages between Catholics and members of indigenous populations and to insist on monogamous relationships. Plessis instructed the two priests to establish schools and to teach catechism to the young. They were to preach obedience to duly constituted authority and to remain neutral in the competition and conflict between the two rival fur trading companies.[5]

Upon their arrival in Red River, Provencher and Dumoulin began to minister to the Métis at St. Boniface (Manitoba) and Pembina (North Dakota) respectively because the barrier presented by language was reduced and the population possessed some connotations of the Catholic faith. Provencher believed that the Native elements would be difficult to convert because of their language, nomadic lifestyle, and licentious ways.[6] This focus on the Métis, however, forced the early missionaries to adjust the structure of the Church to accommodate the nomadic nature of a buffalo hunting society. Through the *mission ambulante,* which was a unique departure from the traditional parish or casual contact with itinerant tribes, the clergy were able to maintain contact with the Métis hunters in their wintering camps.[7]

The Pembina mission established by Dumoulin proved to be a source of contention between the Church and the HBC. As a result of the boundary settlement that followed the War of 1812, the mission was located in the United States. In addition, the HBC was encouraging the Métis to settle in Red River and Plessis was criticized for not having established schools and farms in that area. It was also thought that the existence of a mission at Pembina contributed to keeping the Métis dispersed and, hence, rather than risk alienating the HBC, Plessis instructed Provencher to concentrate on the St. Boniface mission. Many of the Pembina Métis continued to hunt while those who left the United States settled at White Horse Plains west of St. Boniface.[8]

In the period 1818–1833, no progress was made in evangelizing the Indian populations because of the language barrier and the very small number of priests at Provencher's disposal and some of them asked to return to Quebec after a short stay in the North West.[9] The arrival of *abbé* Georges Belcourt in 1831 seemed to presage a better future for the evangelization of the Indians.[10] He began by assisting Provencher in St. Boniface in addition to working with the Saulteaux near the Red River settlement and studying their language. Two years later, in 1833, Belcourt established a mission among the Saulteaux, which he named St. Paul des Saulteaux (Baie St. Paul).

Unfortunately, Provencher and Belcourt became involved in a controversy surrounding the most effective means of evangelizing the Indians. Based on his experience, Belcourt argued that the Saulteaux had to be gathered in settled agricultural villages if religious instruction were to succeed. Provencher was convinced that the missionary should follow the Indians and instruct them wherever they might be. Furthermore, the bishop believed that Belcourt's settlements would be both expensive and a waste of time.[11] In opting for an itinerant missionary approach Provencher believed that Native culture need not be altered before Christianity could take root. The missionary had only to preach and instruct his flock in the vernacular. Belcourt contended that Christianization could come about only when the Indians were settled in villages, took up farming and went to school.[12]

The conflict with Belcourt, while very serious in itself, was but one of the many problems that came to confront Provencher as he attempted to administer his vast diocese and minister to its diverse population. To begin with, although Provencher had the assistance of twelve secular priests from Quebec in the period 1818–1845, at no time did he have more than four at his disposal.[13] Ordained Bishop of Juliopolis *in partibus infidelium* and coadjutor Bishop of Quebec in 1822, Provencher was to find that this new episcopal dignity contributed little to his authority or his resources and he was still dependent upon Quebec and Montreal for both.[14] Provencher's position was inadvertently undermined in 1844 when the Holy See detached the North West from the Diocese of Quebec and erected it as the Vicariate Apostolic of Hudson's Bay and James Bay with Provencher as titular bishop. This ecclesiastical independence from the jurisdiction of the Diocese of Quebec would adversely affect Provencher's attempts to obtain sufficient resources and personnel from that quarter.[15]

In addition to these internal problems, Provencher had to maintain good relationships with the HBC especially after 1821 when it absorbed its competitor the NWC and had a monopoly on trade and was the *de facto* authority in the North West. Since it would be impossible to establish and sustain a mission without the support of the HBC and its facilities, the company's views and wishes would have to be considered seriously and the consequences of going against them carefully weighed. The abandonment of the Pembina mission was an example of the accommodation that had to be made to protect the interests of the Church. While Provencher succeeded in establishing and maintaining good relations with the HBC, this policy of accommodation was not looked upon too kindly by some of his clergy and the Métis who felt that company policy vis-à-vis trade was becoming unduly restrictive.[16]

The arrival in the colony of Protestant elements such as the Anglican Church Missionary Society, created another serious challenge for Provencher and his clergy. Protestant missionaries were deemed to have more resources at their disposal and, since the officers of the Bay were their co-religionists, Catholics felt doubly disadvantaged. When the HBC extended an invitation to the Wesleyans to establish themselves in the North West in 1839, Provencher and his clergy were convinced that the Company, like the government, was favouring the English Protestant element and attempting to confine the French Catholic missionary presence to Red River.[17]

Despite these problems and limitations Provencher persevered and the Catholic missionary frontier expanded. In 1842, a mission was established at Lac Ste. Anne, some 60 km west of Edmonton (Alberta) and it would become the stepping stone for expansion further north. Provencher also opened schools in St. Boniface and St. Francis-Xavier and hoped that this educational venture also would assist in the creation of an indigenous clergy.[18] In 1844, he secured the services of the Sisters of Charity of Montreal, the Grey Nuns, who adapted themselves to local needs especially in the fields of education, health care and social work.

Nevertheless, much remained to be done and Provencher was cognisant of the fact that there was little to show after a quarter of a century of missionary effort. The irregular visits or itinerant missions among the Native population were a "disheartening" experience. The *mission ambulante* among the Métis was more successful in maintaining a Catholic influence over this community but it represented an adaptation of ecclesiastical structures to local circumstances rather than an accommodation on the part of the hunters to the Church and its precepts.[19] There were strong differences of opinion between Provencher and his clergy and these simultaneously undermined his episcopal authority and hindered missionary efforts.

Additional personnel was required in Red River and, in 1843, Provencher hoped to obtain the services of the Society of Jesus, which had returned to Canada the previous year, but this never materialized. That same year, Provencher asked the HBC for permission to bring French clergymen into his diocese but the company's governor, Sir George Simpson, replied that he could not sanction a plan to bring "foreign priests" into the country.[20] Provencher then decided to call upon the Oblates to assist him and, in 1844, he informed Archbishop Joseph Signay of Quebec that his situation in Red River was intolerable because his clergy lacked unity of effort and a sense of direction.[21]

In this analysis of the problem Provencher overlooked the consequences of his own poor relationships and differences of opinion with his clergy. Be that as it may, Provencher hinted that only a religious congregation could provide a missionary thrust that was united and disciplined. In addition to accomplishing more, a religious order would entail less expense and this prospect was undoubtedly equally appealing to Provencher. Given the opposition of the HBC to the presence of "foreign" clergymen he suggested that the first Oblates be Canadian. Provencher also believed that Canadian clergy would be more acceptable to the Métis and French Canadian populations of Red River and he hoped that the Oblates would have numerous vocations in Canada thus lessening the need for French clergymen.[22]

Provencher's request for the services of the Oblates was enthusiastically supported by Bishop Ignace Bourget of Montreal who had become a "second father" to the Oblates stationed in Canada and who was urging Bishop Mazenod to accept more missions and parishes in North America.[23] On 10 October 1844, Bourget wrote a very convincing letter to Mazenod in support of Provencher's request for assistance contending that the missions of the North West presented a singular opportunity that should not be lost. The letter had the desired effect and Mazenod informed Joseph-Eugène Guigues, the superior of the Oblates in Canada, to reply positively to Provencher's request even if initially only two Oblates could be sent.[24] In the meantime, Guigues entertained reservations concerning the proposed establishment and hesitated but his equivocation ceased when, on 25 May 1845, Mazenod ordered him to write to Provencher indicating that two Oblates would be sent to assist to Red River.

As superior general, Mazenod designated Pierre Aubert, a French Oblate serving in Canada, as one of the clergymen to be sent to Red River and he instructed Guigues to select the most suitable Canadian Oblate to accompany him. This new Oblate establishment was irregular because its community numbered less than three but Mazenod affirmed that there were mitigating circumstances and he urged Guigues to cease his unrealistic objections.[25] Mazenod affirmed to Bishop Bourget that he had done more for the Canadian missions than he should have and yet he was being criticized for not doing more. Furthermore, Mazenod claimed that no one was bound to do the impossible and that some things had to be left to Providence.[26]

Even at this early stage in the development of the Oblate Apostolate in Canada Mazenod had very definite ideas on its structure. He advised Bishop Signay of Quebec that the Oblates were first and foremost the servants of bishops. They were to act upon their signal, obtain their directives from them and act only in conformity with their desires.[27] Mazenod was aware that the Jesuits had returned to Canada and he affirmed that the Oblates were "pygmies in the presence of such giants." The Oblates were to take the Jesuits as models but without comparing themselves to them or imitating them.[28] Mazenod was undoubtedly convinced that Providence had reserved a special destiny for the missions of the Canadian North West. Shortly after his arrival in Red River as superior, Aubert was informed by Mazenod that, as an apostle and a representative of the entire congregation, he was the vanguard of an army that would banish Satan and implant the cross of Christ in regions that hitherto had not known the true God.[29]

On 25 August 1845, Aubert and Alexandre Antonin Taché arrived in St. Boniface after a two-month voyage and presented themselves to Provencher. When Taché was introduced as a sub-deacon, Provencher glanced at his youthful figure and allegedly exclaimed that, instead of the men he required, boys had been sent.[30] Nevertheless, Provencher ordained Taché deacon on 31 August and priest on 12 October. The following day, Taché, made his profession of faith as an member of the Oblate order before Aubert, his religious superior. This had been authorized by Mazenod as superior general who was elated at receiving the news and declared that it was noble to make one's vows on the battlefield in front of the enemy that one had come so far to engage in battle.[31]

The two Oblates spent the first winter in St. Boniface being initiated to missionary life and studying the Saulteaux language under the direction of Belcourt. Taché ministered to the needs of the French Canadian and Métis populations of St. Francis Xavier. The following year, in 1846, Aubert was sent to Wabassimong, a mission on the banks of the Winnipeg River some 50 km. east of St. Boniface and he became the first Oblate to evangelize the Native populations in western Canada. Shortly after Aubert's departure, Taché was instructed to proceed north to Île-à-la-Crosse (Saskatchewan) in the company of *abbé* Louis Laflèche to continue the work begun earlier by *abbé* Jean-Baptiste Thibault among the Chipewyan (Dene) a tribe that became known as the *Montagnais* to the

Oblates.[32] Taché and Aubert were reinforced by the arrival, in late 1846, of Francis-Xavier Bermond and Brother Henri Faraud whose aptitude for languages was noted immediately when he began to study the Saulteaux language.[33]

In 1847, Aubert, accompanied by Faraud, returned to visit the Saulteaux at Wabassimong and continued on to Rainy Lake. At the same time, Bermond established himself among the same tribe at Duck Bay on the west shore of Lake Winnipegosis.[34] In an attempt to find a more accessible location and avert starvation, Bermond decided to seek a new location for the mission. In 1848, he established Notre-Dame du Lac Mission near the abandoned HBC post, Manitoba House, on the west shore of Lake Manitoba. The assistance of another French Oblate, Jean Tissot, who joined Bermond in 1849, made no appreciable difference to the success of the mission.

As a result of these encounters the Oblates, like the earlier secular clergy who had preceded them, came to the conclusion that the Saulteaux offered few consolations for the missionary. The Saulteaux were polygamous and, while many males agreed to have only one wife, they would invariably choose the youngest rather than the first as the Church insisted. Furthermore, the Saulteaux would convert or allow their families to be instructed only with the consent of the tribal elders.[35] The Saulteaux also had a strong indigenous spirituality that allowed them to radically interpret certain segments of the Christian message much to the dismay of the missionaries. The Saulteaux claimed, for example, that as the representative of God the missionary had to provide food and clothing to them because God would not allow his children to want. The Saulteaux also affirmed that the various nations each had their own prayers and that these could not be adapted and used by other groups.[36]

Thus, when Aubert and Faraud returned to St. Boniface from their visit to Wabassimong, the former was convinced that the mission was a failure and it was abandoned in 1847. The experience of Bermond at Notre-Dame du Lac was equally disappointing because the Saulteaux there also had turned a deaf ear to the message of salvation and, three years later in 1850, that mission also was closed. The decision to abandon the Saulteaux missions was taken reluctantly but, nevertheless, it was a rational one. In view of the circumstances, there was no alternative as a result of the lack of success in converting the Saulteaux.

Provencher justified the abandonment of the Wabassimong mission on the grounds that the Indians were not disposed to listen to the missionary or heed his message.[37] For his part, Taché attributed the failure of the Saulteaux missions to the fact that the tribe had frequent contact with less than desirable elements within the white population, was given to drink, was morally degraded and abused every favour.[38] The analysis provided by Provencher and Taché is only partially correct and reflects the limited perspective of the missionary. In this early stage of the Catholic missionary frontier, it was believed that all the Natives had to do was to accept the Christian message preached in their language and abide by its precepts. Furthermore, it was believed that this could be done without a major transformation or modification of Native society.

For their part, the Saulteaux resisted or refused to listen to the Christian message because they realized that the acceptance of Christianity would entail significant changes to their culture through the substitution of the values, traditions and morality of western European civilization.[39] At this point in time the Saulteaux were able to mount a successful "defence" against the Oblate "offensive" directed against their culture, institutions and spirituality. Consequently, a crisis situation did not develop to force the Saulteaux to turn to another culture and spirituality for assistance in meeting the challenge.[40]

The Saulteaux, like all indigenous populations, had evolved a strong religious spirituality that was intimately linked to their culture and the socio-economic basis of their society and Christian moral conventions such as monogamy and temperance were foreign to them. In such circumstances, the calibre of missionaries sent to evangelize them was critical. The failure of the Oblate effort among the Saulteaux is also attributable in part to Aubert who had great difficulty in speaking their language. Even Provencher admitted that Aubert had no natural competency or special talents for missionary work but he hoped that the Oblate's zeal would overcome that handicap. Provencher predicted that Aubert would succeed in a ministry where the language of communication was French and this evaluation proved to be correct.[41] The Oblates were not sociologists or anthropologists trained to impartially identify and assess the role and function of religion in a particular society. As missionaries, charged with preaching the message of salvation, their interpretation of what prevented the acceptance of the Christian message was articulated in terms of powerful countervailing evil forces rather than its unsuitability in a particular cultural milieu.

In the field, however, the Oblates were quick to realize that the Indian with which they came into contact was different than the character that appeared in contemporary literature. Tissot's European inspired image of an Indian who was docile and timid in the presence of a priest and who accepted Christianity as soon as the missionary spoke of God contrasted sharply with his experience among the obstinate Saulteaux.[42] For his part, Taché deplored the inaccurate descriptions of Indians composed by individuals who had insufficient knowledge and were ignorant of their language and customs. He was especially critical of "poetic descriptions" that depicted "the inhabitants of the woods as an ideal people." He admitted, furthermore, that initially he had believed in "the elegant descriptions and loving sympathies" of authors such as Chateaubriand and had been "truly astonished" when confronted with the reality of Indian life in the North West.[43] Unfortunately, not every missionary was able to abandon this imagery and come to grips with reality. For Honoré-Timothée Lempfrit, the first Oblate missionary in British Columbia, the romantic notions of Natives acquired in Europe caused him to entertain unrealistic aspirations and idealize the motives of the coastal tribes he evangelized.[44]

Some Oblates were able to make insightful observations on the non-religious aspects of Native life and culture. In some instances they were even able to transcend their own ethnocentric perspective. In a letter to his mother, Taché stated that Lac des Oeufs (Clear Lake, Saskatchewan) derived its name from the large quantity of bird eggs that were to be found on its islands. These eggs were an important dietary resource for the local Indians who were not always able to eat the eggs fresh. Taché described how they removed the embryo of a fertilized egg and then consumed the remainder as if it were fresh. He admitted that at first he had been unable to do the same but came to realize that, in this and in other matters, one's previous education and upbringing sometimes engendered prejudices and habits that should be cast aside. Taché also noted the custom in the North West of referring to animals by the female term for the species. Taché humorously suggested that this usage would please women who, if they were responsible for the preparation of dictionaries, would want to replace the term "man" by "woman."[45]

While their criticisms of the Saulteaux were severe, the missionaries in Red River demonstrated much more sympathy for the Chipewyan who appeared better disposed to accept them and heed their message. The receptiveness of the Chipewyan illustrates the complex response of the First Nations to the Christian message. John Webster Grant has argued that where Native societies were "relatively intact and the white man was a tolerated visitor, the initial reaction was usually to reject Christianity out of hand." But, when traditional spirits and rituals "had ceased to perform their expected functions satisfactorily" there was a tendency to adopt Christianity to fill the void.[46] According to Grant's paradigm, in this early phase of Oblate missionary activity, the Saulteaux, who had been exposed to a white presence and settlement, should have adopted Christianity whereas the Chipewyan, who were more isolated from such influences, should have rejected it. In practice, however, it was the Chipewyan who welcomed the Oblates and the dominant consideration for doing so was the presence of epidemic diseases carried by the boat brigades that resulted in many deaths.[47] In these circumstances, the Christian message was "powerful medicine" to counteract illness and, as a last resort, to ensure that those who died were prepared for and assured of life in the ancestral hereafter.

L'abbé J.-B. Thibault had encountered the Chipewyan at Île-à-la-Crosse in 1845 and had reported enthusiastically to Provencher that they spent their days and nights learning their prayers in order to be baptized as quickly as possible. This optimistic report, in conjunction with the lack of success of the Saulteaux missions, convinced Provencher to establish a permanent mission among the Chipewyan and Taché and Laflèche were instructed to proceed as far north as possible in the course of their apostolic duties.[48]

The two clergymen were well received by the Chipewyan at Île-à-la-Crosse and Taché noted that many of their beliefs were compatible with Christianity. They believed in only one God "the creator and guardian of all" and, like St. Paul, they believed in the presence of evil spirits that were the enemies of God and man. They prayed and made offerings to the divinity and sought its intercession in critical circumstances. Unlike Christians, however, they did not blaspheme the divinity.[49] Among the Chipewyan legends Taché noted that there were similarities with the Christian version of the creation and fall of humanity and the account of the flood and the ark. While the Chipewyan abhorred acts of violence and cruelty and had an aversion to stealing, they oppressed the weak such as women and orphans, Worse yet, immorality was a "great social plague" and polygamy the norm.[50] Taché was convinced that the "mitigating influence" of religion would erase oppression and engender a moral regeneration of this nation. Some of the poor conduct of the Chipewyan was due to the influence of French Canadian voyageurs who had engaged "in an orgy of corruption" among them and Taché felt "honour bound" to redeem their progeny as well as the nations they had degraded and debased.[51]

From Île-à-la-Crosse Taché visited Green Lake (Saskatchewan) and later Reindeer Lake further to the north-east by way of Lac la Ronge. In June 1847, he went on a mission to Portage la Loche (Saskatchewan) and then on to Fort Chipewyan on the shores of Lake Athabasca. The following year, 1848, Taché returned to Reindeer Lake and in the fall to Fort Chipewyan. He undertook another mission to the northern end of Reindeer Lake in Manitoba in 1849 but had to return when his guide did not arrive at the designated rendezvous. Taché was forced to undertake these lengthy and exhausting voyages because his companion, *abbé* Laflèche, was in poor health and remained behind to assume responsibility for the Île-à-la-Crosse mission. Until the arrival of Henri Faraud at Île-à-la-Crosse in July 1848, Taché had not seen another Oblate for more than two years. A lay brother, Louis Dubé, arrived at the mission in July 1849 to assist the missionaries, thus becoming the first Canadian Oblate lay brother to serve in the missions of the North West. In 1849, Faraud left Île-à-la-Crosse to establish Nativity Mission at Fort Chipewyan. With the abandonment of the Saulteaux missions two other Oblates, Tissot and Augustin Maisonneuve were sent to Île-à-la-Crosse in 1850.[52]

Thus, within five years of the arrival of the Oblates in Red River the missionary frontier had not only been displaced northward but it had expanded considerably and had undergone significant alterations as a result of local circumstances. The consequences of this expansion alarmed Mazenod and he voiced his concern upon being advised in 1846 that his priests would be alone for one year.[53] When, contrary to his instructions, missionaries continued to be sent out alone for long periods of time, Mazenod informed Taché that it would be preferable to have fewer missions.[54] After learning of the establishment of St. Joseph Mission at Fort

Resolution by Faraud in 1856, Mazenod admonished the latter for his zeal, suggesting that it would transport him far beyond the earth's limits to some bright star. Mazenod reflected that Faraud would experience no greater isolation in a stellar galaxy than that to which he was exposed on the shores of his glacial sea.[55]

As a means of overcoming the isolation of his missionaries Mazenod insisted that they communicate with him on a regular basis. Missionaries were to profit from the passage of the HBC brigade or northern packet to send him a lengthy and informative letter.[56] He was perturbed when the post contained no letters and admonished those who wrote only a few lines on heavy paper that was "pharisaically" weighed by the postal authorities.[57] In addition to breaking down the loneliness of Oblates, letters from the missionary frontier provided Mazenod with useful information with which to stimulate interest in the Congregation's activities, increase vocations, and solicit funds to maintain the missions and their personnel.

Provencher had received financial support from *l'Oeuvre de la Propagation de la Foi*, a French organization domiciled in Lyon and Paris, and, when the Oblates accepted responsibility for the Red River missions, Mazenod asked it to underwrite that establishment.[58] Mazenod also urged *l'Oeuvre* to continue paying the travel costs of Oblates en route to foreign missions and, in 1846, he asked for a special grant to cover the voyages of two Oblates from Marseille to Montreal and from there to St. Boniface.[59] Mazenod sent letters and reports from the missionaries of the North West to the directors of *l'Oeuvre* in order that they be published in its periodical, *Les Annales de la Propagation de la Foi*.[60] Thus, the Red River missions were made known not only to those associated with *l'Oeuvre* but to the general Catholic population of France that read the *Annales*. In terms of Oblate administration, the North American missions (Quebec, Red River, Oregon) were distinct entities and Mazenod insisted that *l'Oeuvre* respect this division and provide separate allocations rather than a lump sum to be divided among them. In addition to the administrative advantages this entailed, Mazenod believed that it would offer the readers of the *Annales* a "more striking justification" of the expenditure of their contributions in addition to providing more detailed information on the various Oblate missions in the world.[61]

In the meantime, Mazenod, who initially enthusiastically had supported the proposal to send the Oblates to Red River, came to have second thoughts concerning the results of this venture that the Oblates had contributed so much. Despite the zeal and sacrifice of missionaries like Taché, there were few conversions and the small tribes, separated by great distances, were, at best, visited sporadically. Mazenod was also concerned about the difficulties of communicating with Red River as well as the high cost of basic supplies and transportation. More ominous, however, was the fact that the Oblates serving there were often alone for more than a year and thus unable to confess themselves and satisfy the requirements of religious life. Mazenod claimed that of all the Oblate missions that of Red River mission was the most difficult and distressing and the results were insignificant. Cumulatively, these problems convinced Mazenod to abandon Red River and reassign the missionaries to duties that were less dangerous and produced more tangible results.[62]

Mazenod discussed the matter with his council of advisers and the order recalling the Oblates from Red River was being drafted when news arrived from Rome that Bishop Provencher had selected Taché as his coadjutor with right of succession.[63] Provencher's initial choice had been Louis Laflèche who had accompanied Taché to Île-à-la-Crosse in 1846 but Laflèche declined the nomination because his infirmities and poor state of health would prevent him from traveling.[64] In the meantime, Bishop Bourget had recommended that Provencher name an Oblate as his coadjutor because when a member of the congregation was also the ecclesiastical leader, bishop and missionaries shared the same work and there was more cohesion.[65]

For his part, Provencher felt that for political reasons, it was crucial that the Bishop of Red River be a British subject. In addition, since most of the clergy of the diocese would be foreigners it was imperative that their leader be a Canadian. Provencher listed other convincing arguments in favour of Taché's candidacy. It was imperative that the bishop know the country and the difficulties encountered by missionaries because an outsider might have unrealistic expectations and become discouraged when confronted with conditions in the North West. Furthermore, Taché knew the Indian languages and had the youth and strength to overcome the burdens associated with his ecclesiastical responsibilities. Reiterating Bourget's views, Provencher argued that, since the region could not provide its own clergy, the bishop had to be taken from the ranks of the order that furnished the missionaries.[66]

Although Mazenod shared the conviction that vicar apostolics should be chosen from the ranks of congregations that served in the region he believed that, in the case of Red River, the Oblates were unable to supply the necessary financial resources and, hence, firm guarantees of assistance would have to be forthcoming before he would allow a member of the congregation to accept ecclesiastical office.[67] In the end, Mazenod agreed to Taché's nomination because he regarded it as a providential intervention in favour of the continuation of the Red River missions that he was on the verge of abandoning. Taché's nomination would bind these missions more closely to the Oblates and Mazenod thought that apostolic efforts would be more fruitful now that bishop and missionary were not foreign to each other.[68] In the final analysis, Taché's nomination was not so much a consequence of his talents and experience but of a desire to endow the Oblate order with responsibility for and direction of the missions of the Canadian North West.[69]

As a result of Taché's nomination as coadjutor bishop, the Oblate missionary frontier in the North West underwent a period of consolidation and expansion. The congregation became more closely linked to these missions as Mazenod severed the link between the North West and the Oblate Province of Canada by creating Red River as an autonomous religious vicariate and designating Taché as Vicar of Missions, that is, as superior of all Oblates in the North West.[70] This process of consolidation was accelerated in 1853 when Provencher died and Taché assumed the direction of and responsibility for the diocese.

Beginning in the 1850s additional Oblate personnel came to Red River and the missionary frontier expanded far beyond the limits established by the early secular missionaries and Oblates. Experience and circumstances also dictated a change in missionary strategy. The itinerant missions, favoured by Plessis and Provencher, were abandoned and replaced by a series of permanent missions strategically located in the interior. Increasingly it was believed more had to be done than preach the Christian message in a language that could be understood by the faithful. The First Nations would have to give up their nomadic ways if they were to become and remain solid Christians and not be swept aside by the increasing white presence in the North West. In the final analysis, Christianity and civilization became indistinguishable objectives.

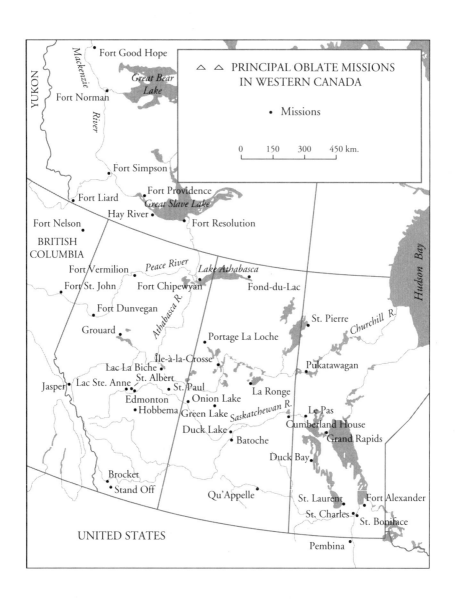

△ △ PRINCIPAL OBLATE MISSIONS
IN WESTERN CANADA

• Missions

0   150   300   450 km.

YUKON

Mackenzie

River

Fort Good Hope

Great Bear
Lake

Fort Norman

Fort Simpson

Fort Providence
Great Slave Lake

Fort Liard

Hay River

Fort Resolution

Fort Nelson

BRITISH
COLUMBIA

Fort Vermilion   Peace River   Lake Athabasca

Fort St. John   Fort Chipewyan   Fond-du-Lac

Fort Dunvegan

Athabasca R.

Grouard

Portage La Loche

St. Pierre

Churchill R.

Hudson Bay

Lac La Biche

Île-à-la-Crosse

Pukatawagan

Jasper   Lac Ste. Anne   St. Albert

Edmonton   St. Paul

Hobbema   Onion Lake   La Ronge

Green Lake   Saskatchewan R.

Le Pas

Duck Lake   Cumberland House

Batoche   Grand Rapids

Duck Bay

Brocket

Stand Off

Qu'Appelle

St. Laurent   Fort Alexander

St. Charles

St. Boniface

UNITED STATES

Pembina

△ △ △ △ △ △ △ △ △ △ △ △ △ △   **3**

THE MISSIONARY FRONTIER
AND THE OBLATES

Adaption and Innovation

Initially, the number of French Oblates who were interested in serving in the Canadian missions and possessed the skills and competence to do so was rather small. Mazenod insisted that his priests were to complete their theological studies prior to assuming ministerial duties because he was convinced that a missionary could not preach effectively without a comprehensive knowledge of doctrine complimented by an appropriate style and method.[1] In practice, however, the need to staff and later to reinforce the missionary contingent in Red River forced him to make exceptions. Ordinations were advanced and others were sent to the North West prior to being ordained. Mazenod, nevertheless, insisted that adequate theological studies be completed and superiors were to ensure that those who were sent in the field prior to completing their studies or being ordained received an adequate preparation and instruction including the study of Native languages.[2]

Despite an increase in vocations in France there were always shortages of personnel and, for a time, ordinations continued to be accelerated. Léon Doucet, the first priest to be ordained in Alberta, came to the North West as a *frère scolastique* and continued his theological studies at Lac Ste. Anne under the direction of Vital Fourmond. In 1870, Doucet was advised by Bishop Vital Grandin to make a retreat prior to his immediate ordination. Doucet objected on the grounds that he had not completed his theology, did not know all the ceremonies of the mass and had an

27   △ △ △

insufficient knowledge of Cree. Grandin replied that his ordination was necessary in order not to leave a large number of neophytes without the services of a clergyman.³ Another Frenchman, Joseph Le Treste, completed his noviciate at Lachine near Montreal and left for the North West after pronouncing his first vows. At Lac La Biche (Alberta), Bishop Henri Faraud made him advance rapidly through the ranks. Le Treste was made sub-deacon shortly after his arrival in July 1884, deacon in September and ordained in December.⁴

Shortages of personnel in France were complicated by the fact that not every Oblate was fit or willing to serve in difficult foreign missions such as those of the North West. Mazenod's most dreaded fear was having to recall an Oblate who had been unfaithful to this vocation and to forestall this eventuality he followed the policy of the Jesuits and sent only volunteers to the North West. Despite this precaution, Mazenod believed it necessary to carefully screen volunteers to distinguish between serious intentions and weak or impulsive ones.⁵ Mazenod's policy was to propose the foreign missions to the members of his congregation and wait for volunteers to respond positively. In 1854, for example, the only volunteer to come forward was Vital-Justin Grandin, who had been motivated by Taché's visit and talk to the novices at Notre-Dame de l'Osier in 1851. Mazenod desired to provide Grandin with a companion but the only other volunteer had a terrible fear of cold but did not object to going to Sri Lanka. Mazenod believed that it would not be wise to force this individual to serve in the difficult missions of the North West.⁶ Staffing problems were complicated by the fact that the noviciate at Lachine was unable to provide the personnel that was required for eastern Canada and the shortfall had to be made up from noviciates and seminaries in France, thus reducing the number available for the foreign missions.⁷

Isidore Clut was characteristic of the individuals selected by Mazenod for the North West missions. In 1857, Clut, a mature 25-year-old person, was a *frère scolastique*, who was not yet a sub-deacon and had a year of theological studies to complete. Mazenod informed Taché that if it were not necessary for Clut to leave immediately he would ordain him sub-deacon, deacon and priest within three weeks. Taché was authorized to ordain Clut when he deemed it appropriate but Mazenod advised him not to delay unnecessarily.⁸

In one of his reports to Mazenod, Taché complained about the short-comings of some of the missionaries that had been sent to Red River. The superior general replied that it was difficult to find individual who were willing to work in the midst of terrible conditions and hardships and that he considered himself fortunate when someone was not terrified by these difficulties and actually volunteered. Mazenod stated that he took these individuals as they were as long as he was convinced that they were virtu-ous and dedicated. He believed that imperfections would be overcome by experience, good will and the assistance of Providence and he advised Taché not to insist on the impossible.[9]

Despite the careful selection made by Mazenod some individuals found it difficult to adjust to conditions and life in the North West. One Oblate informed Mazenod that he did not want to learn the Indian lan-guages and wanted to return to France as a result of his poor state of health. Others had to be encouraged to persist in their endeavours.[10] While problems associated with finding sufficient vocations and the demoralisation of some of the missionaries in the field obviously disap-pointed Mazenod, such frustrations could not be voiced in public with-out jeopardizing the foreign missions.[11]

To be successful and effective as a missionary in the North West, how-ever, one needed more than the desire to serve in that region. If he were to be understood by those whom he was evangelizing, the missionary had to communicate in the language of his audience and be familiar with their customs and traditions. In addition, the process of evangelization could not be conducted in an artificial milieu nor could the missionary be isolated or set apart from his flock. In the tradition of the early Apostles, the Oblates would have to preach and instruct in the vernacular and live in the midst of their charges and adapt their activities to the lifestyle of the Métis and Native communities. This was the practice advocated by Mazenod who was very annoyed when he learned that an Oblate was reluctant to undertake a serious study of the languages necessary to per-form his ministry.[12]

The first Oblates to the North West faced the greatest difficulties in learning the necessary languages because they had few tools at their dis-posal. Ten months after arriving in St. Boniface, Taché admitted that he had experienced great difficulty in learning the Indian languages. He could speak a few words of Saulteaux but he would have to abandon this language to study Chipewyan since he was being sent to Île-à-la-Crosse. He believed, however that his study of the Saulteaux language would still be valuable because the grammar of Indian languages was similar.[13] In his new post Taché studied both Cree and Chipewyan but initially had to teach prayers in French because he lacked an interpreter. By the spring of 1848, however, Taché had acquired a fair knowledge of Chipewyan and had adopted a syllabic script for it.[14]

Like Taché, Henri Faraud had begun to study Saulteaux in Red River followed by Cree and Chipewyan at Île-à-la-Crosse. Faraud described Cree as a language that was very pleasant and "most ingenious" whereas Chipewyan presented difficulties that were "virtually insurmountable." He had to use his knowledge of Cree to learn Chipewyan because his assistant was the same blind Indian who had assisted Taché and who could not understand French. After a few weeks, Faraud could converse with the blind Indian and a short while later he could catechize in Cree. In 1849, Faraud was sent to Nativity Mission at Fort Chipewyan (Alberta) where he began to seriously learn Chipewyan and to compose a detailed study of that language. This study was sent to Taché who had it copied for use by other missionaries. Faraud was a talented linguist and by 1851 he was teaching his flock to read and sing in French, Cree and Chipewyan.[15] Some time later at the Lac La Biche mission, Faraud made good use of his expertise in languages by providing a daily period of instruction for the missionaries stationed there.[16]

The mastery of these new languages was facilitated by the previous classical education the Oblates had received especially the detailed and analytical study of the Greek and Latin languages. These linguistic studies provided them with the model from which to create a paradigm for the new languages they had to learn and to compile dictionaries and grammars. The Native languages fascinated the Oblates who studied them in depth. Albert Lacombe who mastered Cree and Blackfoot claimed that these languages were nearly perfect. Like Latin they were invariable and would remain so unless there were significant socio-economic changes. What most impressed Lacombe was the fact that, despite a complicated grammatical structure, an eight-year-old child spoke as correctly as the most talented orator.[17] Valentin Végréville was another talented linguist who came to Île-à-la-Crosse in 1852 and by 1858 could speak Cree as easily as his native language. As a matter of fact, by 1856, colleagues were complimenting him that he could speak Cree *"comme un vieux sauvage."*[18]

It was crucial for the Oblates to become as proficient as possible in the indigenous languages. To begin with, it facilitated the presentation and comprehension of their preaching and instruction. In addition, the Oblates realized that if they did not have a good command of the language and hesitated and fumbled in their presentation, they would not be taken seriously by their audience. In such instances the Indians claimed that the missionaries spoke like children and, hence, they would be treated accordingly.[19] Thus, it was not surprising that the early Oblates devoted much time and effort to mastering the aboriginal languages. At Nativity Mission, for example, Vital Grandin was able to utilize the preliminary notes left by Faraud and Henri Grollier but he had neither grammar nor dictionary. He began by copying the prayers, hymns and catechisms compiled by his predecessors and then obtaining as accurate a translation as possible. He later obtained the services of an elderly Indian woman who was unable to follow her tribe and she provided him with more specific instruction by replying to his queries concerning the names of objects, and singular and plural forms. Grandin even administered confession in Chipewyan but he freely admitted that he "heard" more confessions than he understood.[20] As a result of his experiences Grandin, when he became bishop, advised his missionaries to associate with children in order to learn the proper accent and intonation.[21]

The notes, dictionaries and grammars compiled by the early Oblates made it easier for those who came later to study the aboriginal languages. Isidore Clut acknowledged the assistance of Végréville's notes in his study of the Cree language. At Nativity Mission Clut occupied himself exclusively with the study of Chipewyan that he regarded as *"l'arme principale"* for the work he was undertaking. Prior to the arrival of the Chipewyan for the mission, Clut would memorize a few hymns and prayers in that language and, while this impressed the Indians, they were aware of the extent of his linguistic skills.[22] Clut's study of Chipewyan was facilitated by Faraud's expert knowledge of that language and the use of the book that the latter composed. According to Clut, this instrument dissipated the difficulties normally encountered in learning Chipewyan and when the substance of Faraud's book was explained in the "classical manner," rapid progress was assured.[23] When Faraud died in 1890, he was the undisputed linguist among the Oblates of the Mackenzie Basin as a result of his command of Chipewyan, Cree, Beaver, Slave, Dog Rib and some Inuit.[24]

Émile Grouard was the Oblate who demonstrated "extraordinary dispositions" for the study of aboriginal languages. Grouard arrived at Nativity Mission in 1862 and began to study Chipewyan under Clut's direction. In April 1863, Clut informed Bishop Taché that Grouard had preached without an interpreter and predicted that the pupil would soon surpass his mentor. Grouard had received two hours of instruction a day and with his incredible memory and skill at pronunciation, the young missionary was able to learn in one winter what had taken years for others.[25] In 1883, Grouard was at St. Charles Mission, Fort Dunvegan (Alberta), studying the Beaver language while teaching Cree to another missionary. With the assistance of a Beaver Indian who spoke Cree, Grouard was able to learn the Beaver language and translate hymns, prayers and catechisms previously composed in Cree by Lacombe. Grouard himself composed ten hymns in the Beaver language.[26] Seven years later, in 1890, Grouard was among the Inuit at Fort McPherson (Northwest Territories) and in the month that he spent among them he began to study their language and was to compose two hymns in their language. He reported that these were listened to with astonishment and attention.[27]

As the Oblates became more familiar with the Native languages they revised the notes and texts they had prepared earlier prior to having them published. As could be expected, there were errors because they were attempting to translate complex liturgical and theological concepts. In one instance, the Oblates were astounded to behold that, in one of their Chipewyan hymns, the term they had used initially was a more accurate reflection of the Lutheran conception of the Eucharist than it was of the Catholic doctrine of transubstantiation.[28]

Unfortunately, not every Oblate displayed the zeal and aptitude of a Grouard in mastering the indigenous idioms. As bishop, Grandin admonished young missionaries who believed that they could perform their duties without a knowledge of the Indian languages or who displayed a lack of enthusiasm to study them.[29] On the other hand, some found it impossible to learn despite determined efforts to do so and were consequently frustrated.[30] Of more significance perhaps was the fact that talented linguists such as Laurent Le Goff and Valentin Végréville were obstinate and demanding individuals who would not assist younger missionaries and under whom the latter refused to study.[31] In the end, the ministry of those who had not mastered the languages suffered. Valentin Fourmond learned Cree in his later years and was never able to pronounce it well. He was informed one day by a Métis that they could not understand his Cree and that he should preach in French because then they might be able to understand a few words.[32] At Lac Ste. Anne, Zéphirin Lizée, who had experienced great difficulty in learning Cree, was profoundly humiliated by a Protestant Indian who reminded him that after a year at the mission he could not speak the language properly.[33]

In the beginning, when the Oblates had little or no knowledge of the aboriginal languages, interpreters had to be used but their services were never used extensively or for lengthy periods of time. Instruction to small groups was usually provided by the missionary himself even if he experienced problems with the language. When it was necessary, the Oblates had recourse to interpreters for the more formal instruction and preaching before a larger audience on Sunday. The problems associated with interpreters went beyond their ability to correctly convey the substance of complex doctrinal concepts that were foreign to them. Some took advantage of their position to enhance their status in the Native community or to claim that they were more powerful than the clergy.[34]

In addition to being necessary for the successful transmission of the Christian message, a knowledge of the Indian language also provided the missionary with insights into the Indian character and culture. These insights permitted the Oblates to tailor their ministry to accommodate certain traits in the Indian character and temperament. The Oblates were quick to note that while the Indian was an expert in matters of living and surviving in the wilderness, the sign of the Cross would have to be explained to them one hundred times before they could cross themselves properly. Similar frustrations were encountered in teaching them to say the rosary. In contrast, Indians quickly grasped the melody of a hymn and sang with gusto and were very adept at learning to read with the assistance of syllabic script.[35] For his part, as a young missionary at Nativity Mission, Grouard found it advantageous to grow a beard. He claimed that this beard, although still short, created the impression among the

Indians that he was much older than his 22 years and hence they took him seriously.[36]

After having mastered the necessary Indian languages and learned to adapt to the country and its inhabitants, the Oblates had to develop a missionary strategy and missiology that was appropriate to the Canadian North West. Like the secular clergy who had preceded them the Oblates had no specialized training for the work they were to undertake and they had yet to acquire experience in the foreign missions. Nevertheless, the Oblates did not begin their apostolic venture haphazardly without a clear view of the objective and lacking a sense of direction. The experience acquired by Provencher's clergy and during the first years of the Oblate presence in the North West provided a point of departure. Given the immensity of the task that lay before them, the Oblates would have to work as a highly motivated team pursuing a goal known to and accepted by all. Individual, uncoordinated efforts, even if made by the most dedicated of individuals, would not ensure success and this had been clearly demonstrated by the problems that had negated the efforts of Provencher's secular clergy.

As a religious congregation whose purpose it was to work among the poor, the Oblates possessed an internal discipline as well as a sense of unity of action. They had received a solid preparation in scripture and theology and had perfected the concept of popular missions in France. The practice used by the Oblates in these popular missions, that is, living and working among the poor and instructing them in their own language, was not only pragmatic but readily modified to suit different conditions.

In view of the fact that there were no established parishes in the North West beyond settled areas such as St. Boniface and St. Albert (Alberta), the traditional three to six week mission given in French parishes was impractical if not impossible. It was replaced by shorter missions whose commencement, frequency and duration were dictated by local conditions and the lifestyle of the Native populations. Missions were held in areas where Indians gathered to hunt fish or trade and, hence, they had a predictable seasonal cycle. Missions tended to be held, and later permanent establishments built, near an existing HBC post. These posts were usually located in strategic locations and the Indians were accustomed to coming there at fixed times to trade their furs. In addition, these posts were situated in areas that had sufficient water, firewood and food to sustain the Indians who camped there. By making the mission coincide with the exchange of furs the missionary could capitalize on the presence of a captive audience. It is doubtful if Indians would have traveled any distance from their traditional hunting grounds or trading rendezvous for the sole purpose of obtaining religious instruction.

From a logistical point of view it made sense for the missionary to establish himself near a HBC post otherwise an independent source of transportation and supply would be required to support the mission. In the short term, the Oblates used the Bay posts as a source of supply and the company's brigades as a source of transportation because it was cost effective and it permitted the Oblates to concentrate their personnel and resources on their primary objective of evangelizing the Indians. This dependence on a commercial company for such essential services created problems for the Oblates and to protect their interests and reduce costs they later established Notre-Dame des Victoires Mission at Lac La Biche as a supply base and point of transshipment for the missions of the Mackenzie basin and organized their own transportation system.[37]

While company policy and the antipathy of a few of its officers at times created hardship for the Oblates and their missions, it was not unusual to find strong personal bonds of friendship developing between the officers of the HBC and the missionaries as a result of their common experiences in the field. Differences of class, race and religion were overcome by living together in the environment and interrelating with the same Native populations. In addition, the Oblates did not interfere in the affairs of the HBC nor did they take part in the fur trade.[38] The Bay's officers were quick to note that Oblate missions attempted to be self-sufficient and were not very demanding on the Bay's supplies and transportation system. Another officer remarked that the Oblates offered more support to the company than did Protestant missionaries.[39]

As Catholic missionaries, the Oblates impressed upon the Indians the moral necessity of honouring their contractual obligations and this benefited the HBC that had advanced goods to the Indians in return for their furs later in the season. The Oblates generally disliked free traders because their presence was disruptive and threatened long standing relationships. In 1859, shortly after the HBC's exclusive monopoly on trade beyond Rupert's Land was not renewed by the British Parliament, Taché made his views known on free trade to Simon James Dawson who had been sent by the Canadian government to explore the North West. Taché claimed that free trade would be the greatest misfortune to afflict the Indians and it would lead to their destruction because it would be impossible to control the introduction of alcohol. He argued that only one company should be allowed to trade, that alcohol should be prohibited as an article of trade and the price of trade goods and furs should be regulated by the government. Taché affirmed that he was not promoting the interests of the HBC but, he did not wish to see it replaced by another whose policies might result in a worse state of affairs. Taché's most serious complaint against the Bay was that it allowed the use of alcohol in all but three of its districts. The arrival of free traders had increased the use of spirits and Taché feared the situation would become "alarming" if the authorities permitted absolute free trade without adopting "energetic measures" to protect the Indians.[40]

Some 25 years later, Émile Grouard reiterated the same convictions after spending a month at Grande Prairie (Alberta) where the Bay had established a post to counter the influence of free traders. He found that the presence of the Bay post facilitated the instruction of Indians "because they are less troubled about their trade, and having no temptation of double dealing, they keep their conscience free from dishonesty." Grouard preferred to see the Indians trading with the HBC as they had done in the past and he was convinced that free traders would not benefit the Indians. Since the traders could not be stopped, Grouard predicted that the problems that accompanied their presence would spread across the country.[41]

In the field, the Oblates made certain that the activities of personnel attached to a mission did not compete with the commercial interests of the Bay. At Reindeer Lake (Manitoba), for example, a mission employee had obtained a large quantity of caribou hides despite the fact that he had been forbidden to do so. When this was brought to the attention of the superior of the mission the latter proposed to reprimand the individual so severely that he would either cease or leave the mission's employ. While the possibility of losing an employee at such a remote mission would be a calamity, the superior believed that he had no choice in the matter because he was not willing to compromise the future of the missions for the actions of one individual.[42] At Fort Dunvegan, it was not the actions of mission employees that the Bay complained about but those of the missionaries themselves. When complaints reached Bishop Faraud he immediately sent Grouard to investigate the matter. Faraud informed the chief factor of the district that he detested such unwarrantable ventures into commerce and that Grouard would terminate them.[43] For his part, Grouard informed Auguste Husson, the resident missionary, that he could not interfere or take part in the trade and that he had to limit himself to exchanging the products of his garden for some of the free trader's own provisions.[44]

Notwithstanding the friendship of officers and the services provided by the company itself, Oblate missions had to strive to become self-sufficient. Given the limited financial resources of the Oblates missions had to be located in areas where they could be supplied and maintained and where costs would not be prohibitive. When an establishment was contemplated the area was reconnoitered to ensure that it possessed adequate local resources. Missions had to be located where there was an abundant supply of wood for construction purposes as well as heating in the winter months. The presence of nearby lakes and rivers that contained fish facilitated the feeding of the mission's personnel during the winter as well as the dog teams, which consumed enormous quantities. Arable soil was very important because a garden and crops could be cultivated to reduce cost of purchasing and transporting foodstuffs and alleviate an otherwise bland diet. The gardens and cultivated fields added a touch of white civilization to a mission in the midst of the wilderness and this contributed to the morale of missionaries.[45]

In addition, the exploitation of arable soil by the missionaries provided Indians with tangible evidence of the virtues of agriculture. For their part, nomadic tribes would not remain long in an area that lacked game fish and firewood and they would be forced to camp elsewhere. Indians tended to stay longer in an area that provided more than the minimum of basic necessities. The lengthier stay was advantageous to the missionary because it enable him to provide more thorough and effective instruction to his charges.[46]

In the final analysis, the factors that determined when and where a mission was conducted or established were not related to a comprehensive Oblate plan or strategy but with pragmatic responses to particular situations and needs. There were only a small number of Oblates and they had very limited resources at their disposal and, consequently, missions could not be established in areas where it was convenient for the missionary but where there were strong indications that it would succeed. The Saulteaux, for example, had responded negatively to the secular clergy and later to the Oblates. Despite the fact that the Saulteaux were relatively easy to reach from St. Boniface, it made little sense to continue their evangelization in view of their recalcitrance. The evangelization of the Chipewyan, on the other hand, presented more difficulties in terms distance and language but their more positive disposition and the anticipation of a successful Apostolate compensated for the additional hardships that were incurred.

The presence of rival Protestant missionaries was a factor that endangered the success of an Oblate mission and it had a significant influence on when and where the Oblates established their missions. The objective of all missionaries, Catholic and Protestant, was to reach and convert the largest number of Indians in the shortest possible time. Thus, the presence or impending presence of a rival denomination or, far more serious, the establishment of a rival mission, prompted the Oblates to establish themselves first and claim a territorial imperative. If Protestants had already erected a mission, Catholics built one nearby and sometimes directly across from the competing establishment.

In the quest for souls, Catholic and Protestant competed against one another with a zeal that reinforced Christianity's exclusiveness and intolerance. While this rivalry was taken for granted by the missionaries, it was bewildering to the Indians whose spirituality lacked dogmatism as well as the derision and condemnation of the beliefs of others.[47] As the Assiniboine chief Dan Kennedy remarked, "the Indian had to learn the whiteman's language to break the first commandment" because there were no profane words in their vocabulary.[48] In Canada, rivalry between Christians was heightened by cultural and linguistic factors that had been transplanted from Europe during the French-English rivalry for colonial domination in North America. With respect to the North West, a Catholic mission effectively meant a French presence while a Protestant one indicated an English presence. This fact of life was not lost on the astute Indians who identified Catholicism as "*la religion des Français*" and Protestantism as "*la religion des Anglais.*" Indians also identified the

Catholic clergy as "*les priants français*" and Catholic ceremonies and rituals as "*la prière française.*"[49]

The rivalry between Catholic and Protestant clergymen in the North West antedated the arrival of the Oblates. Bishop Provencher's secular clergy were suspicious of their Anglican competitors but rarely referred to them whereas the latter mentioned the former regularly in their correspondence. The secular clergy ignored the presence of their Protestant counterparts and did not take them seriously. The Catholic clergy possessed a superior theological training and preparation and this contributed to their reluctance to engage in bitter diatribes with their rivals.[50] Despite a passionate opposition in their apostolic efforts, Oblate and Protestant missionaries displayed no outward physical hostility to each other. For the most part, the Oblates continued the tradition of their predecessors and ignored the existence of their rivals. Nevertheless, individual Oblates were convinced that their Protestant rivals not only possessed unlimited resources but also were unscrupulous competitors determined to undermine the efforts of the Oblates by any means.[51] In the post-treaty era, the competition between Oblate and Protestant missionaries became more acute as both groups approached the federal government for funds to provide education and health services to Indians. Confessional schools and hospitals were a means of establishing a strong territorial imperative in cultural and religious terms and these institutions allowed the rival elements to "work wonders."[52]

Proximity to a Bay post offered certain material benefits for early Oblate missions but that institution also attracted Protestant missionaries who preferred the comforts it had to offer rather than living among the Indians. Consequently some missions were located a short distance away to protect neophytes from being exposed to heretical doctrines. Some posts were also notorious for the liquor traffic and other vices associated with civilization and this was another inducement to locate a short distance from the post.[53]

While there were many physical discomforts associated with early mission life, isolation was an even greater hardship for the Oblates. Missionaries were often alone for lengthy periods of time but even more significant was the fact that solitude made it difficult if not impossible to fulfil the rules of the order with respect to confession, retreats and com-

△ △ *Bishop Ovide Charlebois on a portage.* (AD)

munity life. When Taché arrived at Île-à-la-Crosse in 1846 two years
would pass before he would see another Oblate. In 1851 Faraud complained that he had been alone for two years and that his isolation would
last for another year and perhaps two. While in principle this was unacceptable to the Oblates, Faraud rationalized it by suggesting that it was
dictated by circumstances.[54] The situation did not improve significantly
with the passage of time. In 1863, for example, Clut was left alone at
Nativity Mission because his two Oblate colleagues were required elsewhere. Clut did not cherish the thought of remaining alone for an entire
year and he informed Taché that he was experiencing temptations and
required the assistance of a spiritual director quite apart from the fact that
the mission could not be administered effectively by one person.[55]

The following year, in 1864, Clut expressed his frustration upon learning that the superior general's delegate and canonical visitor, Florent
Vandenberghe, would not proceed to Fort Chipewyan as expected. Clut
claimed that his long beard would turn white before the arrival of another
canonical visitor to Nativity Mission and he equated the Portage La
Loche (Methy Portage, Saskatchewan) to the Pillars of Hercules, which
neither Taché nor a visitor would ever overcome. In his earlier communication Clut had underlined the consequences of isolation on one's spiri-

△ △ *Joseph Egenolf preparing building lumber at St. Peter Mission,*
Reindeer Lake, Manitoba. (AD)

tual well being but now he chose to identify the demoralizing effects on
the individual. Isolated from the outside world and, in the absence of visits from remarkable individuals, missionaries in the interior were in the
process of becoming "*missionnaires sauvages.*"[56] In 1887, Ovide Charlebois
was sent to Fort Cumberland (Saskatchewan) and served there by himself until 1903 thus earning the well deserved accolade, "*Solitaire du
Cumberland.*" In his first four years at his post Charlebois had a companion for only one and one-half months.[57]

The establishment of a mission was a very trying period because, in
addition to his apostolic work, the missionary had to perform a multi-
tude of tasks that were indispensable to the success of his work. He had to
construct a chapel and residence, cultivate a garden, hunt and fish to
ensure an adequate food supply. He had to prepare his meals, mend his
clothes and travel great distances often in less than ideal circumstances
and in the worst of conditions. He also had to learn the Indian language
and fulfil the obligations incumbent on a Catholic priest and member of
a religious community. It must be remembered that these activities often
were carried out under conditions that were far from ideal. Moreover, the
missionary was often alone at his post or on mission because service personnel in the form of lay brothers or mission employees were not avail-

able in sufficient numbers. The supplies sent to the missions consisted of the minimum required to support the missionary and his enterprise. If they failed to arrive at the mission the Oblate's vows of poverty, humility and obedience took on a more meaningful dimension.[58]

Once the difficulties associated with the period of establishment had been surmounted, the consolidation phase brought forward challenges that were equally trying. Reflecting on his experiences as a missionary and a bishop, Henri Faraud claimed that it would be a simple matter to establish and develop missions if Satan and heresy were the only enemies. According to Faraud, what often paralysed and ruined missions was the inaptitude, the lack of foresight and zeal displayed by the personnel who were attached to them.[59] A successful missionary required more than a vocation and a willingness to serve in difficult and remote areas and the physical strength and stamina to do so; he also needed unwavering patience, the ability to relate to those whom he was evangelizing and to accept them as brothers. In a letter to a young missionary who was experiencing difficulties, Bishop Taché suggested that Indians admired those who loved them and would listen to those who were interested in instructing them but would shun missionaries who avoided them and scorn those who detested them.[60] Unfortunately, not every Oblate possessed these qualities. Valentin Végréville was not liked by the Chipewyan of Reindeer Lake as a result of his commercial activities and the lack of interest and affection that he displayed for his charges.[61] Albert Lacombe adapted readily to the Indian populations and was esteemed by them. But, his success as a missionary engendered envy among his fellow Oblates especially the ones who came from France and who alleged that Bishop Taché favoured him because he was a native Canadian.[62]

Even after a mission was established and placed under the direction of highly motivated individuals much remained to be done. The apostolic venture was far from finished when the Natives were converted, baptized and well disposed to Christianity. According to Faraud, this was only the beginning of the process because, when one built a large fire, what endured was not the initial flame of the kindling but the larger pieces of wood that were subsequently ignited. Comparing this fire to faith among the Indians, Faraud affirmed that the faith of neophytes had to be stimulated and this would require considerable care and patience.[63]

Faraud's assessment was supported by the experience of missionaries in the field. While on a mission to Green Lake in 1873, Léon Doucet reported that the Indians were indifferent if not hostile to religion. Had he not sought them in their lodges, none would have come forward to receive instruction. He made a special effort to ascertain their dispositions and the reasons for their indifference. He discovered that the Indians had been instructed previously but, because it had not been possible to follow up and sustain this initial overture, they had lapsed into indifference. Doucet believed that if the Natives received regular visits from a missionary many of their prejudices would disappear and a small but solid nucleus of Christians would be created.[64] The period of consolidation and stabilisation of Oblate missions in the North West substantiated Faraud's contention that much remained to be done and Doucet's observations that sporadic visits were inefficient and, in fact, probably counter productive. Indians who had been instructed by the Oblates and who had lapsed into indifference for whatever reason were very difficult to reach let alone return to the fold.

After active service in the field few of the missionaries retained romantic concepts of the Indian and their ardent desire to convert. In their letters published for public consumption in periodicals such as *Missions,* the Oblates alluded to the sterling character of Indians and their willingness to convert after having heard the missionary. In their private correspondence, however, the missionaries were more circumspect. Upon hearing from Augustin Maisonneuve that the Indians at Lac La Biche were poorly disposed, Grandin stated that those of Fort Chipewyan were no better and that the previous fall Faraud had chased more of them out of the Church than he had baptized. Grandin indicated that Henri Grollier was far from praising his flock at neighbouring Fond du Lac (Saskatchewan).[65]

In this early phase of the Oblate establishment the influence of the Native community and its environment was significant. To begin with, evangelization was carried out in the appropriate Indian language and it was incumbent on the Oblates to master it because there was no compelling reason for Indians to learn French. In addition, the whole missionary process was adapted to the lifestyle and seasonal activities of Indians. Missions, for example, were built in areas where Indians usually gathered and instruction and religious services were provided when

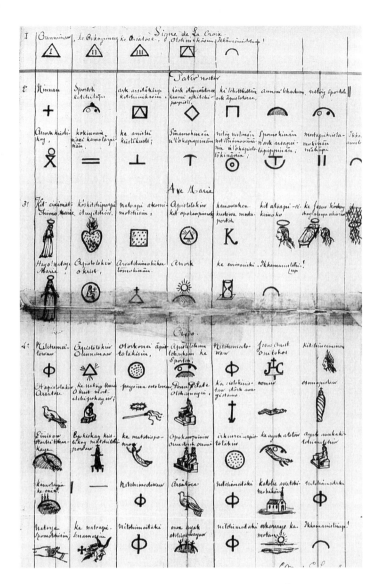

△ △　*Prayers in Blackfoot syllabics prepared by Émile Legal.*
(PAA, OB 10005)

Indians assembled for well defined seasonal activities such as trade and
hunting. The Oblates adopted pedagogical techniques that made their
ministry more appealing to the Native audience that respond positively to
the use of music, coloured illustrations and syllabic script. During this
period it was not the Oblates who determined what tribes would be evan-

gelized but the Indians themselves. When the Saulteaux refused to heed the Christian message the Oblates had little choice but to turn their personnel and resources to a more receptive audience. However, as the Oblates consolidated their efforts and white settlement advanced in the North West, the influence of Natives declined but they were never reduced to mere pawns to be manipulated at the whim of missionaries.

THE OBLATE MISSIONARY FRONTIER

Consolidation and Expansion

In September 1846, when a youthful Alexandre Taché and his colleague *abbé* Louis-François Laflèche arrived at Île-à-la-Crosse, Roderick McKenzie, the seasoned trader in charge of the HBC post, could not help being surprised. The two clergymen had been sent out to establish a mission despite the fact that they could not speak the language nor did they did have an interpreter or anyone to assist them in gathering food, cutting wood or hauling water.[1] Shortages of personnel dictated that missionaries be sent to a mission in the shortest possible time after their arrival in St. Boniface and, furthermore, the logistics of the fur trade imposed an immutable seasonal calendar to which missionaries had to accommodate themselves.

Thus, it was in the field and not in the classroom that the Oblates acquired the necessary experience and expertise to evangelize the Native and Métis populations of the North West. With respect to the establishment of their initial missions, the Oblates followed in the footsteps of the secular clergy that had preceded them and established themselves at Île-à-la-Crosse, first visited by *abbé* Thibault in 1845, and Lac Ste. Anne, first visited by that same individual in 1842.[2] From these central missions the Oblates moved out into new areas and established satellite missions thus expanding their apostolic frontier.

The establishment of a mission was followed by a period of consolidation and expansion that coincided with and paralleled the experience and skills acquired by the missionaries themselves in the performance of their apostolic duties and adaptation to a new environment. The facilities at strategic, central missions such as Île-à-la-Crosse were expanded and enhanced and these missions took on an added importance. In 1847, within a year of having arrived at the mission, Taché began to cultivate a garden and had purchased a cow to provide butter and milk.[3] By 1853, many significant improvements had been made to the material status of the mission and its personnel was no longer dependent on fish for sustenance. The gardens had produced 200 bushels of potatoes, in addition to oats, peas, beans, onion and cabbage. The fifteen cattle had produced three-hundred pounds of butter. While all of this resulted in a better diet for the missionaries, Taché also noted that it gave the mission a pleasant air of civilization.[4]

The Oblates quickly extended the missionary frontier far beyond the earlier limits established by their predecessors and the ability to promote expansion became an important consideration in selecting the site of new Oblate missions. Taché, who first visited Fort Chipewyan on Lake Athabasca in 1847, decided to establish Nativity Mission there because it was an ideal location for visits to the Peace River country, Great Slave Lake, Fort Simpson (Northwest Territories) and the north shore of Lake Athabasca. Providence Mission on Great Slave Lake was selected as the site of the administrative centre of the new Vicariate Apostolic of Athabasca-Mackenzie in 1861 because it could provide the vital services of supply and transportation for the northern missions. Vital Grandin who selected the location gave it the name *Providence* to reflect this critical function.[5]

However, not all the missions fulfilled the roles that had been anticipated for them. Fort Dunvegan was deemed to be the central point in the Peace River district as a result of its central location, fertile soil, temperate climate and the large number of Indians who gathered in that region. Accordingly, St. Charles Mission was established there in 1866 to exploit these natural advantages as well as service three other outlying stations: St. Henri (Fort Vermilion, Alberta), St. Jean Pierre (Fort St. John, British Columbia) and Notre-Dame des Neiges (Portage des Montagnes rocheuses on the Peace River near Hudson's Hope, British Columbia). Unfortunately, a host of problems associated with personnel and resources prevented St. Charles Mission from developing into the strategic centre of the Peace River region.[6] For its part, Providence Mission never became the administrative centre for the northern vicariate or the principal source of supply and transportation for the Mackenzie basin missions. Henri Faraud the first Vicar Apostolic of Athabasca-Mackenzie preferred to reside at Lac La Biche, the mission that had been placed under his temporary jurisdiction and that became the entrepôt for the northern missions. Isidore Clut, his coadjutor, did not reside permanently at Providence Mission.

In addition to planning for future establishments, the Oblates also re-evaluated the status and location of their existing missions in the light of the experience they had acquired and the objectives they hoped to accomplish. The mission at Lac Ste. Anne had provided Oblates like Albert Lacombe with a point of departure for their missions to other areas and the Grey Nuns had established themselves there and provided education and health care. In 1860, however, Bishop Taché decided to relocate the mission a short distance from Fort Edmonton where the Oblates had established St. Joachim. The new location, which Taché named St. Albert, in honour of Albert Lacombe's patron saint, had a greater agricultural potential and also facilitated the meeting of the Blackfoot in their travels.[7] As a result of its natural and geographical advantages, St. Albert quickly became the dominant mission in the region and its status was enhanced when Vital Grandin, Taché's coadjutor, established himself there in 1869. In 1871, St. Albert was the most important settlement in terms of population and agriculture in the North West Territories.[8]

In the case of other missions, such as Lac La Biche, relocation did not involve as great a distance or effort. The original site for the Lac La Biche mission had been chosen by Taché and René Rémas in 1854. The following year, Augustin Maisonneuve and Jean Tissot were sent out to establish the mission and they concluded that the original site left much to be desired. It was believed that the proposed site was too close to the HBC post, it might also attract a Protestant missionary and, furthermore, fishing was poor. Consequently it was decided to relocate the mission some ten kilometres to the west of the post.[9] The location of Notre-Dame des Victoires Mission was of crucial importance because Taché had envisaged Lac La Biche as the point of supply and transshipment for the more northern missions because it was located strategically near the Churchill and Mackenzie river watersheds.

△ △ *Albert Lacombe and Bishop Vital Grandin in traditional pose.* (PAA, OB 3164)

The expansion of missions also took place in the central and northern regions of western Canada where the Oblates had already established themselves in strategic locations. One of the driving forces behind this expansion was the intrepid Albert Lacombe who began his career in the west at Fort Edmonton in 1852. Lacombe had met the Blackfoot and the Plains Cree while serving at Lac Ste. Anne and in 1865 he asked to be relieved of his duties at St. Albert in order to follow these tribes in their travels across the prairie.[10] After spending some time with the Cree, Lacombe decided to establish a mission in their midst. In 1865, he selected the site for Saint-Paul des Cris (Brosseau, Alberta), which became the first Catholic Indian mission in Alberta as well as the first attempt at establishing an agricultural colony among the Indians. The mission was located on the banks of the North Saskatchewan river where the Cree felt protected because their traditional enemies the Blackfoot did not want to cross the river to attack them.[11]

Under Lacombe's supervision, a large parcel of land was cultivated, divided into family plots and sown with oats and potatoes. Afterwards, the Cree left for the summer buffalo hunt but returned later to quickly harvest their crops before leaving for the winter hunt.[12] After completing the necessary manual labours and ensuring that all was in order, Lacombe accompanied the Cree on their hunts and instructed them. With the termination of hostilities between the Cree and the Blackfoot, the former dispersed into small camps, while the Métis moved further south. This dispersal accentuated the mission's handicaps in the form of rodents, poor agricultural land and little firewood.[13] In 1870, the mission was decimated by an epidemic of smallpox and Lacombe was left alone to care for the sick, minister to the dying and bury the dead.[14] The following year, since resources did not permit moving the mission to a more suitable location, it was decided to temporarily abandon the mission and visit the Cree during the summer.

The Oblates derived important lessons from their experience at Saint-Paul des Cris. To begin with, the problems associated with poor soil and lack of firewood underscored the need for careful selection of mission sites. More important, however, was the innovation in missionary technique introduced by Lacombe's itinerant ministry. Previously it had been thought that the only way to instruct Indians was to rendezvous with them at a fur trading post. Lacombe demonstrated that it was possible to evangelize the Indians by accompanying them *à la prairie* and instructing them in their camps.[15]

With the closing of Saint-Paul des Cris the Cree were not abandoned because Lacombe's ambulant mission was continued by Constantine Scollen and Léon Doucet. In 1877, it was decided to establish a new mission among the Cree, Saint François-Régis, at Fort Pitt (Saskatchewan). This was a departure from Lacombe's practice of following the Indians and living in their camps but the location had distinct advantages. To begin with, there was always a significant number of Indians and Métis who resided permanently near the fort. Furthermore, the region was one that was visited by large numbers of Indians who were hunting, trading or receiving treaty payments and the mission would make it possible to minister to these Natives locally or permit missionaries to accompany them in their travels. The establishment of this mission effectively terminated the proposal to inaugurate a Protestant one.[16]

In the meantime, the attention of the Oblates turned to another plains tribe, the formidable Blackfoot. Lacombe had already established contacts with them while at Lac Ste. Anne but intertribal war, disease and limited resources on the part of the Oblates precluded any serious attempt at evangelization. These hostilities did not deter the Oblates but, in their travels across the prairie, they took the precaution of hoisting a white flag with a red cross, a symbol that the Blackfoot had promised to respect and that safeguarded the missionaries, their horses and possessions.[17] In 1869, Lacombe spent three weeks in a Blackfoot camp near Rocky Mountain House (Alberta) where, in addition to providing religious instruction, he studied their language.[18] Scollen and Doucet followed in the footsteps of Lacombe after his departure in 1872 and, the following year, they established Notre-Dame de la Paix on the Bow river west of Calgary, the first permanent Oblate mission among the Blackfoot. Notre-Dame de la Paix was to serve as a central mission among the Blackfoot and from there the Oblates could reach further south other members of that confederacy as well as minister to the needs of emerging centres such as Calgary and Fort Macleod.[19] These visits were in turn followed by the establishment of permanent missions in Alberta among the Peigan at Brocket in 1881 (Conversion de Saint-Paul), the Blackfoot at Cluny in 1882 (Sainte-Trinité) and the Bloods at Stand Off in 1899 (Saint-François-Xavier).

During this period, the Oblates also expanded the missionary frontier in southern Manitoba that they had abandoned after their initial encounter with the Saulteaux had proved so disappointing. Some ten years after they had withdrawn from the region the Oblates returned to the southeastern end of Lake Manitoba at Fond du Lac (Saint-Laurent) an important gathering place for the Métis, Saulteaux and fur traders.[20] Saint-Laurent became a Métis parish and served as the focal point of Oblate activity and subsequent expansion in the interlake region. Further east, Joseph Lestanc began to visit the Métis and Saulteaux at Fort Alexander at the mouth of the Winnipeg River on Lake Winnipeg in the 1860s but it was only in 1876 that a permanent mission was established.[21]

△ △ *First Oblate mission among the Peigans.* (PAA, OB 9832)

Fort Alexander also facilitated the evangelization of the Saulteaux near the Manitoba-Ontario border and the establishment of three missions in that region: Kenora, McIntosh and Fort Francis.[22] To the east in what is today southern Saskatchewan, Taché selected the site of Saint-Florent Mission (Lebret, Saskatchewan) in 1865 and, three years later, Jules Decorby became the first resident missionary among the Métis, Cree, Saulteaux, Sioux and Assiniboine of the Qu'Appelle valley.

With respect to the Métis, the Oblates also continued a ministry that had originated with their secular predecessors in Red River. This was the tradition of accompanying the hunters *à la prairie* and living with them and instructing them in their camps that the Oblates not only refined but, in the case of Lacombe, successfully adapted to the evangelization of the Cree and Blackfoot. Henri Faraud in 1847 and lay brother Louis Dubé in 1849 were the first Oblates to undertake this ambulant ministry.[23] After 1849 this practice was discontinued and only resumed in 1859 at the request of the Métis.[24] Between 1862 and 1882 Oblates from Saint Boniface, Lebret and Saint Joseph (North Dakota) accompanied the hunters and resided with them in their winter camps at Saint Joseph and Devil's Lake in North Dakota and in Canada along the Souris River, Wood Mountain, Fort Ellice, Cyprus Hills and the Milk River.[25]

The presence of numerous Métis south of the international boundary necessitated the maintenance of two missions, St. Joseph and Pembina in the North Dakota. As a result of problems with the fierce Sioux in that region, American authorities welcomed the presence of Oblate missionaries as intermediaries. In the period 1863–65, Alexis André was employed by the American military as a peace emissary among the Sioux. Although his peace mission ultimately failed, American officials continued to support Oblate establishments in the territory and proposed that the American government provide assistance to the missionaries.[26] With the disappearance of the buffalo and a shift northward in the Métis population it was decided, in 1876, to detach the St. Joseph and Pembina missions from the jurisdiction of St. Boniface.

As Lacombe and others discovered among the Cree and Blackfoot, the *mission à la prairie* or *mission ambulante* was in many ways much more effective than the seasonal contact made at a trading post or mission. In 1870, for example, Joseph Lestanc opted to remain at Wood Mountain (Saskatchewan) where he had gone to visit a sick person rather than return to Qu'Appelle because there he would have only a dozen Métis families whereas at Wood Mountain there were one hundred. Furthermore, the hunters had promised that there would be no drinking, that they would build him a house and chapel, look after his needs and provide him with transportation to visit other wintering camps.[27] Lestanc's residence in the camp enabled him to make optimum use of time to provide religious instruction and services.

René Rémas accompanied Cree hunters in the region between present day Calgary and Edmonton in 1860 and claimed that this three-month ministry was more effective than if he had remained at Lac Ste. Anne. After a successful hunt, the camp was not displaced and during that time he could hold a regular mission with mass, hymns, catechisms and instructions for all. During a move he could instruct the children when the caravan rested whereas adults were instructed at night.[28] Like the Métis of Red River, those of the plains built a residence-chapel for the missionary, fed him, provided transportation to other camps and buffalo robes as an honorarium.[29] In addition to spiritual comfort and protection, the presence of the Oblates among the Métis provided them with a mechanism to alleviate social tension and a means to facilitate the grouping of extended Métis households.[30]

The Indian missions, especially the more distant northern ones, provided very little material support to the missionary nor did they possess such a readily marketable and universal resource such as the buffalo. As a result of this and the limited resources available to the Oblates, each mis-

△ △ *The interior of St. Peter Mission, Reindeer Lake, 1912.* (AD)

sion in the interior had to strive to be self-sufficient in the basic necessities. The penury of the missionaries was accentuated further by the high
cost of supplies and difficulties inherent in transporting them into the
interior. In practice, however, not all missions became self-sufficient
despite prodigious labour and efforts nor did they all possess productive
potential with respect to agriculture and cattle. The case of Reindeer Lake
with its lack of arable soil provides an example of the incredible toil that
was entailed in cultivating a garden and raising a small herd of cattle and
the passage of time did not significantly alter these conditions.[31]

Although food was crucial for the maintenance of a mission, there
were other items that were equally essential but could not be acquired or
produced locally and the Oblates obtained these from agents in eastern
Canada, the United States, England and France. Such goods were very
expensive because of the high cost of transportation over long distances
and requests from individual missions had to be prepared at least one year
in advance to enable these items to reach their destination on time. For
the far northern missions orders had to be placed three years in advance.[32]
In preparing their annual budgets individual missions doubled the price
of goods purchased through their English agent as an accounting procedure to factor in the cost of shipping and transportation.[33]

While the high cost of transportation into the interior was a source of
constant concern to the Oblates, the complaints against the quality of

goods received were a source of even greater frustration.[34] More serious, and at times, life threatening situations arose when the goods that had been ordered did not reach their destination for various reasons. In the fall of 1875, for example, the packages destined for the Île-à-la-Crosse mission did not arrive. As a result of a misunderstanding, some packages had remained behind at Fort Carlton while others had been dispatched to another location. In the meantime, the mission had been fortunate to borrow what it required from the local HBC post but if its own supplies failed to arrive again it would not be able to return in kind what it had borrowed and would be forced to pay a high monetary price.[35] When the orders of the individual missions failed to arrive the potential for disaster was great.[36]

Annual orders for goods that were indispensable to the survival of the mission refer to a ubiquitous category identified as *butin* in mission documents. This designation included items such as tea, tobacco, sugar, powder, shot and calico cloth, which might be used by the Oblates themselves, but whose main purpose was to serve as a currency in the interior to purchase needed provisions and services from the Indians and Métis and to pay the services of guides and labourers. *Butin* was also used in missions to pay Indian women for washing clothes and performing other domestic services.[37]

Since *butin* was necessary as a medium of exchange, most missions had a "store" in which these articles were kept. In reality this was the mission's "bank" that paid *engagés* (employees) and purchased necessary supplies and services from local sources.[38] At times, the "store/bank" extended credit to individuals and the easiest way to discharge such obligations was to reimburse the mission with animal skins, the other universal frontier currency. Although necessary, this practice raised issues of delicate concern for the Oblates. To begin with, the HBC had received assurances that the missionaries would not engage in trade or purchase furs from the First Nations and the company would not tolerate violations of this agreement. The Oblates went to great lengths to respect this understanding.[39]

While the views of the HBC could not be ignored, the "store/bank" created a more significant moral dilemma for the Oblates in view of their vow of poverty. There were instances where the transactions resulted in a profit for the mission and this led to allegations that the missionaries were preoccupied with commerce. In 1883, Louis Soullier, the canonical visitor to Canada, found it necessary to denounce potential abuses in the commercial transactions of missions. Furs could be accepted in payment for debts where money did not circulate but the missionaries had to exercise prudence in marketing these furs and sell them only at a "modest price."[40] Some years later, another visitor was even more explicit and declared that merchandise could be given only as salaries and for the purchase of provisions and services used by the missions. The outright purchase or trade of animal skins was prohibited because it was a source of the complaint and scandal. He noted furthermore that the "stores," farms, mills and boats owned by the missions were sources of revenue and that they had been used by others, especially whites. The visitor foresaw the day when changing conditions would enable the missions to abandon such enterprises and, in the meantime, he too urged prudence and caution.[41]

Étienne Bonnald justified advances made to Indians from the mission's "store" on the grounds that it was the missionary's duty to help the temporal as well as the spiritual welfare of his charges. He claimed this temporal help was even more mandatory when the HBC issued orders that, henceforth, no presents or credits were to be given to Indians. In such circumstances, Bonnald claimed that the Indians had no place to turn to but the mission for the goods they needed to hunt or fish.[42] Others argued that the mission "store" made it possible for Indians to obtain goods at less expense and without having to travel long distances.

There is evidence to suggest that the fervour of Natives was sometimes directly proportional to the generosity of the missionary. Léo Balter decided to close the "store" at Saddle Lake (Alberta) because the Indians came to regard it as a source of welfare. This action had the desired effect of reducing the number of mendicants but Balter noted that it also terminated the conversion of Protestant Indians whereas the zeal of neophytes had decreased considerably.[43] Balter's experience demonstrates that over time the Oblates "discovered" that the response of Indians to Christianity was not necessarily motivated by spiritual considerations. Missionaries and their institutions were sources of welfare or a source of supply for indispensable articles that were difficult to obtain in the interior. Given the traditional Catholic view of charity to one's neighbor, the Oblates were placed in a difficult position when they refused to provide the necessary items and this situation was also exploited by Indians.

In an attempt to reduce the high costs and problems associated with supplying and transporting goods to their missions the Oblates adopted various strategies. There was an attempt to make individual missions self-sufficient through the establishment of gardens and farms such as those at Île-à-la Crosse and/or the procurement of supplies of meat or fish from local Indian or Métis sources. Surplus production or potential surplus production in one mission was sent to other missions to enable them to reduce costs and dependence on external sources of supply.[44]

The problems associated with the purchase of goods for the northern missions paled in comparison to the difficulties involved in transporting them to their final destinations. By using the HBC brigades to carry their goods the Oblates were able to concentrate their personnel and resources on evangelization but, consequently, they remained at the mercy of a commercial company for a vital service. As early as 1854, Taché announced that the Oblates had to overcome this dependency and, as a first step, he gave orders that a road be cut through the forest between the new mission at Lac La Biche and Fort Pitt to pick up the supplies brought up by the Red River brigades.[45] Notre-Dame des Victoires Mission at Lac La Biche not only occupied a strategic location between the Mackenzie and Churchill watersheds but its fertile soil permitted agriculture and the raising of cattle. Established in 1853, the mission's physical plant subsequently was enlarged to include warehouses, a large farm, cattle and a saw mill.

Notre-Dame des Victoires was in the Diocese of St. Boniface and, hence, under Taché's jurisdiction but he offered it to Faraud if it could facilitate the provisioning of the northern missions. The Vicar Apostolic of Athabasca-Mackenzie accepted the mission and established himself there to oversee its operations.[46] Consequently, from 1869 until 1889 the mission was the entrepôt for the northern missions, bringing in goods overland from St. Boniface that had been ordered overseas and then transshipping them northward from Lac La Biche via the Little La Biche River to the Athabasca River and then northward to Fort McMurray. In addition to this transportation function, the mission also grew and processed foodstuffs that were sent to the northern missions. These activities entailed the construction of warehouses, the maintenance of freight teams and carts, the building of barges and canals as well as the building of a road between the mission and the Athabasca River to eliminate problems with low water levels on the Little La Biche River. In the meantime, the HBC was evaluating different water routes for its own supplies and, in 1888, it signed a contract with Faraud to transport the supplies for his missions in the Mackenzie basin via Tawatinaw and the Athabasca River northward to the Mackenzie Basin missions.[47]

In the meantime, the Red River Insurrection of 1869–70 presented another challenge to the missions of the North West by threatening to disrupt the movement of goods from Red River into the interior. From Lac La Biche, Faraud advised Maisonneuve that rumours were circulating to the effect that next season the Provisional Government would prevent the shipping of goods bound for the north. Faraud expressed the hope that an exception would be made for the supplies destined for the missions.[48] Albert Lacombe warned *l'abbé* Noël-Joseph Ritchot of St. Norbert that if transportation from Red River were disrupted, no furs would be sent there from the Saskatchewan region. Anticipating the worst, Lacombe stated that HBC posts and Oblate missions were organizing caravans to obtain supplies from Fort Benton and Helena in Montana.[49] Faraud's agent in London was informed to be ready to ship what had been ordered via Red River or Fort Benton depending on the outcome of events in Red River.[50]

At the last moment, however, news from Red River were reassuring and the Montana project was shelved temporarily. Informing Maisonneuve of this turn of events, Lacombe warned that if the government did not hasten to improve communications between the North West and Red River, a supply route from Fort Benton would become a reality.[51] Seven years later, in 1877, the St. Albert mission sent a brigade of 15 carts to Fort Benton to obtain its supplies of flour. Although 118 bags of fine quality flour were obtained at a reasonable price, the voyage entailed more problems than had been encountered and no subsequent expeditions were undertaken.[52]

Although a purely temporal matter, transportation was a matter of ever present concern for the Oblates. While the arrangement Faraud concluded with the HBC in 1888 lessened the involvement of the Oblates in transportation and supply it did not provide them with a sense of security. The Oblates began to complain of exorbitant increases rates and of arbitrary decisions on the part of company personnel that had dire consequences for the missions. Furthermore, the company boats only stopped long enough to discharge cargo and this made extended visits impossi-

△ △ *Supplying the Mackenzie missions, Philip Thompson, P. Gillis and Brother Joseph Brodeur.* (Grandin Province Archives)

ble.[53] As a result of these problems, Émile Grouard, who succeeded Faraud as Vicar Apostolic of Athabasca-Mackenzie in 1890, embarked on the construction of steam boats to free his missions from dependency on the HBC transportation system. The first boat, the *Saint-Joseph,* was built and launched at Nativity Mission in 1893 for navigation on Lake Athabasca and the Athabasca River between Fort McMurray and Fitzgerald. In 1894 construction began at Fort Smith on another boat, the *Saint-Alphonse,* for navigation on the Mackenzie River from Fort Smith to Peel River. In 1902 Grouard had another steam boat constructed for navigation on the Peace River.[54] The tangible results of these maritime ventures were far reaching. To begin with, significant reductions in transportation costs were realized and these savings made it possible to establish new missions and institutions. In addition, the standard of living of northern missionaries was enhanced.[55]

In addition to transportation and supply, the scarcity of qualified workmen was another constant source of concern for the Oblate missions. The demanding conditions and hardship associated with the early missions was not conducive to the employment of secular personnel who found it difficult to accommodate themselves to such poverty. Many became discouraged and left.[56] Even in missions where conditions were superior, the wages demanded were prohibitive, engagements were seasonal and the missionaries were hard pressed to provide food and shelter

△ △ *Winter stockpile of firewood at Lac La Biche, Alberta.* (PAA, OB 4040)

△ △ *Sawing firewood at Grouard, Alberta.* (PAA, OB 10780)

for the employee's wife and family not to mention indispensable articles such as tobacco and cloth.[57] The local labour pool, the Métis, also were reluctant to work for others and they detested agricultural and construction work.[58] The predicament of the missionaries was appropriately described by Augustin Maisonneuve who equated the Oblates to starving individuals who possessed money and were attempting to purchase in a market where nothing was available.[59]

Problems associated with the shortage of workmen were accentuated during the winter season. Large quantities of fish had to be caught to feed the dog teams, mission personnel and missionaries. A considerable amount of labour was required to cut, haul and store the firewood that

△ △ *Fishing camp near Fort Chipewyan, Alberta, Brother Louis Crenn,*
Brother Henri Sareault and Philippe Mandeville.
(Grandin Province Archives)

was required to heat the mission premises during the winter. Where a mission had a larger physical plant as a result of a school, hospital or orphanage, the problems associated with an adequate supplies of food and fuel were compounded.

The need for labour varied directly with the size of the mission. A central mission such as Île-à-la-Crosse required the services of four to five *engagés* in addition to two lay brothers. Two of the former would be occupied with fishing throughout the winter to provide sufficient fish for the personnel at the mission and the twelve to fifteen dogs that were needed for winter travel.[60] Even in a central and less isolated mission such as St. Albert *engagés* were difficult to obtain and expensive. Grandin was forced to pay £28 per annum for the mission's *engagé* and, in addition to this sum, the mission had to provide food and *butin* for the man's wife and four children. Even at such prices and conditions, Grandin complained that it was impossible to obtain *engagés* at more remote missions such as Lac La Biche and Île-à-la-Crosse.[61]

Given the necessity for industrious and competent workmen, the Oblates resorted to extraordinary means to ensure that such individuals

△ △ *Gardening at Beacon Hill, Saskachewan.* (PAA, OB 86)

would remain in their service. From Nativity Mission at Fort Chipewyan, Isidore Clut implored Taché to send the wife of the *engagé*, Guillaume Bousquet, because this would guarantee the services of this precious individual for an extended period. Admitting that the cost of her transportation and keep would be high, Clut claimed that it would be money well spent because it would retain her husband in the mission's employ and she herself could be very useful.[62] Jean Tissot, the superior at Lac La Biche, informed Taché of the unusual measures that had to be adopted to maintain the services of labourers. One *engagé* had been admitted to the Oblates' table while two young Indian servants lived with the Oblates. Tissot claimed that the welfare of the mission required such departures from the rules of religious community life.[63]

At Pelican Lake (Saskatchewan), Étienne Bonnald raised two orphans and they assisted him in his work around the mission. Bonnald claimed that single servants entailed considerable expense and that married ones cost two to three times more because the mission had to supply food, lodging and firewood for the family. Maintaining a dog team was an additional expense because of the equipment (such as nets and canoes) that was necessary to catch the fish to feed the dogs. For his part, Bonnald dismissed his employees and got rid of the dogs and fishing equipment because it was cheaper for him to purchase the firewood and provisions and he had no fixed monthly payments to make. To facilitate travel in the winter he employed a young man and paid him a reasonable monthly sum.[64]

In the final analysis, however, not all missions were in a position to adopt Bonnald's policy with respect to employees and servants and other means had to be adopted. Although it was difficult to employ individuals in the interior there were some who were prepared to work for the missions and signed contracts to that effect. In 1862, for example, Georges Bourque contracted to work for the Lac La Biche mission for a period of two years for £30 per annum.[65] Other contracts were shorter such as that of Jos Cyr who was employed by the St. Boniface mission for a three-month period and was paid £4 per month.[66] Some, like Albert Lacombe, were able to find help but offered their *engagés* to missionaries with a more pressing need.[67]

What many of the *engagés* lacked in determination and good will was more than compensated by the altruism and perseverance of a class of individuals known as *donnés*. These were individuals who literally gave themselves and their labour to the missionaries for the duration of their lifetime in return for lodging, clothing care in their old age and education for their children. In terms of the duties they rendered, they have been appropriately described as Oblate lay brothers who had not taken vows.[68] One of these individuals was Louis Dazé, a French Canadian who served the St. Albert mission for many years. In November 1875, Dazé and two Oblates were accompanying a group of Indians hunting buffalo near the present location of Calgary. On a cold and stormy night the horses strayed and Dazé left the camp to look for them despite warnings from the Indians that conditions were too dangerous. Dazé never returned and his frozen body was discovered four days later on the banks of the Bow River.[69]

Given the reluctance of secular workmen to accept the demanding conditions and hardship associated with mission life and the small number of *donnés,* the responsibility for manual labour came to rest with the Oblate lay brothers. These individuals provided invaluable support for the missionaries, especially in the formative years of a mission, by liberating them from construction work and domestic duties thereby allowing the Oblates to devote more of their time to evangelization. In the post-establishment period the lay brothers operated printing presses, operated saw mills and flour mills, maintained large physical plants in schools and hospitals, built and navigated barges and steamboats. They were also farmers, fishermen, and hunters and active participants in the religious services and spiritual life of the mission. Without the services provided by lay brothers, the apostolic duties of the missionaries would have been curtailed seriously. Despite the pressing need for their services, there was always a shortage of lay brothers. In 1868, Bishop Grandin estimated that he needed 20 lay brothers to staff existing missions and, since he did not have that number at his disposal, he refused all requests for their services.[70]

In addition to the lay brothers, members of female religious communities such as the Grey Nuns rendered invaluable assistance to the Oblates, making it possible for the missionaries to devote more time to evangelization. These sisters accepted responsibility for educating the young, and caring for the elderly, the sick, the infirm and the indigent.[71] The presence of female religious communities and lay brothers introduced a division of labour that made it possible for missions to expand and enhance their activities while simultaneously allowing the Oblates to concentrate on their apostolic function. The fact that missionaries, lay brothers and nuns all belonged to religious communities bound by the vow of poverty meant that their labours were *gratis pro Deo* and this contributed significantly to enhancing the real value of the limited financial resources available to the Oblates.

Like the Oblates, the nuns who came to the missions of the North West were motivated by the same fervent desire to serve God and Church. This dedication made it possible for the sisters to endure the primitive conditions they found in the missions. One of the Grey Nuns who arrived at Lac Ste. Anne in 1859 informed her superior that the new community had no need for complex accounting procedures because everything was in common. If someone provided the sisters with food they ate, if there was firewood they warmed themselves, if there was none they went without. The parlour was an unknown institution and the only visits the sisters received were from individuals who were sick.[72]

In addition to their functions as religious auxiliaries the sisters reinforced elements of white civilization in the distant and isolated missions. In terms of cleanliness many of the missionaries had adapted only too well to the environment and the presence of nuns forced them to pay closer attention to personal hygiene and cleanliness.[73] The sisters also usually washed and repaired the missionary's clothing, assumed responsibility for the vestry, rang the church bell to announce prayers and services and assisted at mass as cantor.[74]

As a result of the Catholic Church's association of women with the temptress Eve, the presence of females in general created concern for the Oblates in the North West. Bishop Mazenod had wondered if the virtue of the missionaries had not been placed in peril as a result of contact with Indian women and was reassured by Grandin that such was not the case.[75] Joseph Fabre, who succeeded Mazenod as superior general, advised Taché that while sisters did much good in the missions, precise rules defining the relations between Oblates and sisters were necessary to eliminate problems that might arise from relationships that were "too frequent and intimate." Outside the confessional, an Oblate was not to converse with the sisters individually or alone by himself.[76]

The nature of relationships between Oblates and nuns was the source of extensive comment by Louis Soullier in the report of his canonical visit of the Vicariat of St. Albert in 1883. Soullier described the sisters as "*saintes filles*," the necessary complement to the activities of the Oblates. However, Soullier cautioned the Oblates to be discrete, dignified and edified in their relations with members of these female communities because they worked in a country where the majority of inhabitants were of different religions and did not believe in the virtue of the priest.[77] In agreement with Bishop Grandin, Soullier issued regulations concerning relations between missionaries and sisters. Contact between the Oblates and the nuns was limited to that necessitated by the ministry, charity or convention. Oblates who had to enter the kitchen, chapel or classrooms where the nuns were working were not to remain longer than necessary and were not to converse with the nuns. Oblates were to enter the classroom only to present religious instruction and at times agreed upon and suitable to the sisters. When the Oblate superior as principal exercised his right to visit the classrooms, he was to advise the mother superior beforehand and she was to accompany him if she deemed necessary.

Since the least indiscretion could have serious consequences for the Oblates, Soullier also commented on the proprieties to be observed with secular women. Women were not to be admitted alone into the mission or residence nor to the confessional after sundown. Women were not to be employed unless absolutely necessary whereas useless and frequent visits were to be avoided. Male housekeepers were preferred but if a female one had to be employed she was to be selected carefully and spend the night away from the Oblate residence. Furthermore, she was not to be permitted to have excessive visits from other females or her parents.[78]

In the missions of the interior the presence of sisters added another dimension to the personal rivalry and bitterness that characterized the first generation of missionaries. In 1863, for example, Julien Moulin informed Taché that Henri Faraud was spending too much time with the sisters at Île-à-la-Crosse and that Protestant ministers were spreading rumours to the effect that the Oblates were all married. As superior of the mission, Moulin informed Faraud that it would be improper for him to take English lessons from one of the nuns. Moulin had also voiced his reservations to Bishop Grandin when the latter advised the missionaries to teach Indian languages to the sisters.[79] Jean-Marie Caër complained to the superior general that ever since his arrival in St. Albert he noted that the superior had "frequent" and "unnecessary" communications with persons of the opposite sex especially the sisters and the girls in the kitchen. Caër also reiterated allegations that Albert Lacombe kept a young girl for long periods of time in his room, caressed her and sat her on his knees.[80] A few years later, Moulin alleged that Caër was visiting the nuns at Île-à-la-Crosse frequently. This was qualified by Brother Jean Pérréard who stated that Caër scandalized everyone by boating with the nuns and by clandestine walks with them in the woods.[81]

The Oblates were quick to recognize the significant assistance the sisters rendered to their missionary work and their contribution to the success of their Apostolate. At Île-à-la-Crosse Henri Faraud informed Taché that the sisters required "a strong dose of the love of God and one's neighbor" to be happy in the conditions that were to be found at the mission. To make life more bearable for the sisters Faraud had a part of the garden fenced off for their exclusive use.[82] A few months later, Faraud lamented the fact that the sisters had to work in a country where gratitude was unknown but he believed certain that their recompense would be even greater in heaven.[83] Seven years later, in 1869, Faraud then a bishop, claimed that the school directed by the sisters at Île-à-la-Crosse was becoming a source of glory and strength for the Catholic faith. He affirmed that their knowledge, candor, zeal and humility excited his admiration to the highest degree. In his estimation the sisters were all saints and, if he were pope, he would canonize them all.[84]

The presence of nuns, as members of a female religious community, produced a unique variant of the traditional conflict associated with gender roles. At St. Albert, for example, administrative difficulties arose between the sisters and Jean Tissot, the mission's superior. Bishop Grandin became quite alarmed because he feared that the situation might lead to the recall of the sisters by their superiors. Grandin reminded Tissot that the sisters were not servants and were part of an autonomous congregation such as the Oblates. While the sisters had agreed not to concern themselves with temporal matters, Grandin claimed that they had not renounced to being masters in their own house. The sister superior was to enjoy a certain latitude in disposing of the goods of the mission that were confided to her without having to secure the authorization of the Oblate superior. Grandin expressed his displeasure with the situation by declaring that neither he nor Tissot would allow the status of the sisters in St. Albert to exist within the Oblate order.[85]

In the final analysis, religious vows did not eliminate differences of gender or traditional perceptions of sex roles on the missionary frontier. In 1872, Émile Grouard was making his order for supplies for Providence Mission. He informed Roderick MacFarlane of the HBC that the 400 pounds of grease was "occasioned by the large quantity of soap which the sisters waste every year." According to Grouard, the nuns were "constantly washing" and seemed to have come to the mission for "nothing else."[86] A few years later, Grouard ordered a case of printing paper from Paris to print a book at Lac La Biche. He informed Bishop Faraud's *procureur* in St. Boniface that without the paper the printing of the book would be put off until next year. Grouard informed the *procureur* that if the box arrived in Red River in time for transshipment it was to be sent to Lac La Biche even if it meant leaving behind the baggage of a sister destined for that mission.[87] Grouard later qualified his decision by stating that it was unpleasant to go against the caprices of the sisters and thwart their desires but that the nuns had to learn to accord priority to the welfare of missions rather than the "minor bodily comforts of the sisters."[88]

Bishop Faraud was also perplexed by the sisters at Lac La Biche who insisted on having a male servant. Faraud had requested someone between the age of 40 and 45, who was reliable and willing to serve for a lengthy period of time but the sisters insisted on having a servant regardless of these criteria. Faraud smiled at the dismay of the nuns when a young man of 24 years of age arrived at the mission and there was little choice but to accept him. Faraud claimed that there was little use in dotting one's "i"s when those who read the message did not bother to put on their eye glasses. In a more serious vein, Faraud wondered how the young man could be allowed to enter the convent where, in addition to the nuns, there was a dozen strapping young girls who liked to display themselves.[89] The bishop, also condemned the constant traveling in and out of the interior by the sisters as very disruptive and expensive for the missions. Worse yet was the fact that those who remained in the missions desired "all sorts of fantasies." He cited the example of one sister who had 1200 pounds of "extravagant baggage" despite his formal orders. Faraud expressed relief that "this insupportable daughter of Eve" was being recalled and expressed amazement that the mission had put up with her for so long.[90] The superior general of the Grey Nuns also regretted the changes in personnel and the expenses they entailed. However, in the interests of harmony and the welfare of the mission concerned as well as the personal sanctification of the sisters, personnel were replaced when it was believed that this would have a positive effect.[91]

For his part, Laurent Le Goff ridiculed the "unimaginable" scale of the convent that was being constructed at Île-à-la-Crosse. According to Le Goff, the local population did not regard the 80' x 30' building as a *bâtisse* but rather as a *bêtise*. It was a magnificent polytechnical school but Le Goff lamented the fact that none of the students could perform basic mathematical functions. Since the sisters had insisted on such a structure, he claimed that one had to be built to ensure the welfare of the mission.[92]

Unlike established parishes in settled regions, the missions of the North West could not count upon the faithful for adequate financial support. The resources that were available came, in large part, from Catholics in France through the intermediary of two institutions: *l'Oeuvre de la Propagation de la Foi* and *l'Oeuvre de la Sainte-Enfance*. Founded in Lyon, France in 1819, *l'Oeuvre de la Propagation de la Foi* consisted of an association of individuals organized in groups of ten, one hundred and one thousand who made a small weekly contribution to a central fund. This money was then provided to Catholic missions according to their need.[93]

L'Oeuvre had its own periodical, *Les Annales de l'Oeuvre de la Propagation de la Foi*, to keep its associates abreast of the work being undertaken with their donations. Mazenod often sent reports of Oblate activities to the *Annales* to sustain this interest and stimulate greater generosity on the part of readers. Much of this information took the form of letters or excerpts from reports he received from Oblates serving in the foreign missions.[94]

Letters and reports from the missions of the North West not only stimulated donations from those associated with *l'Oeuvre* they also promoted vocations. Given these benefits, Superior General Joseph Fabre complained to Taché in 1864 that his missionaries were not writing "interesting letters" to the directors to thank them for their financial support. Consequently, Fabre instructed Taché to write an "edifying letter" once a year to *l'Oeuvre* describing what had been accomplished in the missions of the North West. Fabre indicated that without such publicity it would be impossible to send additional missionaries to Red River.[95] *L'Oeuvre* provided Oblate bishops and vicars apostolic in the North West with special direct allocations to support their ecclesiastical institutions as opposed to their missionary efforts that were supported by the general grant given to the Congregation. The annual allocation, however, while it offered a precious support, often was not sufficient to defray the costs involved especially those of the Diocese of St. Albert and the Vicariate Apostolic of Athabasca-Mackenzie within whose borders the main thrust of missionary activity was carried out after 1870. In 1865, Faraud claimed that he could not bring the sisters to Providence Mission because his special allocation would not even cover the annul deficit for the vicariate.[96] In addition to such shortfalls, there were instances when *l'Oeuvre*, acting on reports that the bishops had sufficient funds or had received substantial amounts from other sources, contemplated reducing the amount it provided.[97]

More serious, however, were the reductions in allocations resulting from international events over which the Oblates had no control. The Revolution of 1848 in France seriously undermined the revenues collected by *l'Oeuvre* with the result that there was not sufficient money available to pay for the goods destined to the Red River missions.[98] The military defeat of France in 1870, the subsequent fall of the Empire, the proclamation of the Republic and the occupation of the papal states by Italian nationalists presaged an even worse financial calamity for the missions of the North West.[99] In the end, however, there was only a slight and temporary decrease in donations in France and the pre-war level was quickly attained and surpassed.[100] These funds, while they represented only a small part of the total operating cost of the Oblate missions, nevertheless, were important and the Oblates interceded with *l'Oeuvre* to forestall potential reductions and to plead for additional funds.[101]

The other institution that provided funding to the Oblate missions in the North West was *l'Oeuvre de la Sainte-Enfance* founded in 1843 by Bishop Forbin-Janson, Primate of Lorraine. Its purpose was to provide money to missions in China to purchase, educate and maintain unwanted children who otherwise would be abandoned or killed by their parents. While the funds allocated by *l'Oeuvre de la Propagation de la Foi* could be used at the discretion of the missionaries in any facet of their apostolic work, that provided by *la Sainte-Enfance* could be used only to promote the baptism and education of infidel children.[102]

A subsidy of 3000 francs was given to Taché in 1861 but the directors expressed the fear that, given the high cost of education and the small number of children, the results would not be proportional to the commitment undertaken by *la Sainte-Enfance*. Needless to say, Taché was humiliated at being treated as an irresponsible functionary who had to be subject to close scrutiny and he riposted that each of his missionaries would have no difficulty in spending the allocation.[103] In 1864, funds from *la Sainte-Enfance* supported 22 girls and 20 boys in four schools and two orphanages. Ten girls were also employed in two workshops (*ouvroirs*) attached to the schools/orphanages.[104] Unlike the Orient where money from *la Sainte-Enfance* was used for the outright purchase of unwanted infants from their parents, the practice in the North West was to lease the children for a period of time and to place them in a residential school where they would be raised in a Catholic atmosphere and instructed in practical vocational skills. The transaction was consummated by providing a sum of money or presents to the parents during the period the children were in these school. The virtual purchase of an Indian infant by the Oblates was very rare.[105]

The amount provided by *la Sainte-Enfance* was always significantly less than the allocation of *l'Oeuvre* and both subsidies combined were never sufficient to cover the annual expenses incurred by the Oblates and their institutions.[106] While individual missionaries might cover their expenses during their ministry among the Métis, those who served among the Indian populations did not encounter this same spontaneous generosity. In 1894, Étienne Bonnald of Pelican Lake claimed that he had been the first in the country to ask Indians to make an annual contribution to the church. One-half of the adult males in his mission made an annual offering that Bonnald used to provide charity to the more unfortunate.[107] A quarter of a century later in Berens River (Manitoba), Bonnald had a different experience when the Indians "revolted" against the introduction of Sunday collection.[108] At Saddle Lake, for example, a collection taken at Christmas mass in 1906 was deemed to be such an "innovation" that the event was recorded in the mission's *codex historicus*.[109]

Since the missions could not provide an adequate level of revenue other exterior sources had to be found. Institutions such as *l'Oeuvre Apostolique de Paris* were asked to provide church ornaments, sacred vases and other religious objects for existing and newly built chapels on Indian reserves.[110] Individual missionaries also appealed to friends for assistance. Through the intermediary of a benefactress, Mélasyppe Paquette asked Catholics in New York City for assistance, and through the pages of the *Catholic News,* he asked for donations of clothing for the students at his school in Duck Lake (Saskatchewan).[111] Oblate missionaries and bishops returning to their native France for a visit took advantage of their voyage to preach in various churches and parishes to raise money for their missions. Albert Lacombe's reputation as an indefatigable traveler was excelled by his resourcefulness as a fund raiser. Lacombe undertook numerous trips to eastern Canada, the United States and Europe to raise money for his work and for the education of Indian children. Lacombe's appeal was irresistible especially when it was addressed to wealthy and influential friends. Responding to a request for money, William Van Horne appended a cheque for $100.00 as well as some sound advice to the venerable Oblate:

> I am sorry to hear that you are in debt. I suppose it worries you because you are not used to it as I am. I am nearly always in debt. It is the creditor who should be unhappy—not you. However, since you are not used to it, I send you a small chq [sic] toward helping you out.[112]

Be that as it may, there were limits to the largesse of the faithful and friends as well as the resources of the various Oblate jurisdictions in the North West. The expansion of the Oblates from the international boundary to the Arctic Circle within the space of 40 years was not only an impressive feat but also a very costly undertaking. The cost of maintaining Oblate missions and institutions would be expensive and would increase as their functions became more complex and comprehensive. In the early period of establishment the Oblates gathered abandoned orphans, the disabled and the elderly in their missions and provided the young with a modicum of education. The schools and orphanages of the post-establishment period were much more imposing institutions that imparted a basic education as well as practical vocational skills to Native children of both sexes.

Although somewhat *ad hoc* and rudimentary, these early educational initiatives demonstrated the value of a controlled environment to foster Christian values and western European norms. During the period of expansion and consolidation the Oblates increasingly became convinced that the success of their efforts was limited by the sporadic nature of the encounter with Indians. It was believed that a more extensive and frequent contact in a milieu more conducive to inculcating the Christian message would produce more tangible results. It was also observed that the young were more amenable to the changes that the Oblates sought, especially when the children were in the custody of the missionaries and removed from their nomadic background and traditions. Through practical education they hoped to continue and enhance their apostolic work and at the same time prepare the Native and Métis populations for the changes that were taking place in the North West.

The new missionary thrust envisaged by the Oblates was a radical departure from their early apostolic among Natives and Métis. These initial contacts had left Indian society largely intact because the Oblates had accommodated themselves to the Indian way of life and the dictates of the environment and the seasonal calendar. The ethnologist, James Axtell, has formulated categories to facilitate the study of cultural conflict in colonial North America. He suggests that "we should judge the European colonial cultures in *offensive* terms, as societies on the muscle." Indian cultures, should be judged "in *defensive* terms, largely because they were tolerant of other people and their religions and were, in fact, the targets of

European invasion."[113] Within this conceptual framework, the Oblates themselves recognized the strength of the "defense" mustered by Indians and the necessity of enhancing their own "offensive." This would be accomplished by opening up a second front in the form of schools whose object was to transform and restructure Indian spirituality and culture. This new strategy would significantly decrease the advantages the First Nations possessed.

△ △ △ △ △ △ △ △ △ △ △ △ △   **5**

INITIATION TO CHRISTIANITY

T he Oblate Apostolate in the Canadian North West had a dual purpose. There was an initial pioneer stage in which the Natives were to
be taught the fundamental truths of the Catholic faith. It was
believed that the Christian message was so powerful and compelling that
it would be accepted immediately by those to whom it was preached.
After being sufficiently instructed, Indians would be inducted into the
Christian community of believers through baptism. According to Catholic
missiology, baptism would rescue the individual from the clutches of Satan
and provide a "divine seal" in the form of an "indelible character" that
remained forever with the individual.[1] Baptism did not bring an end to
the process of evangelization because it was but a stepping stone leading
to Christianization, a greater spiritual maturity, that was the ultimate
objective of the Oblate missionary thrust. Christianization necessitated frequent contact with neophytes in order that the missionary might provide
the necessary encouragement and vigilance. In addition, neophytes had
to be provided with practical lessons on Christian life and transgressions
had to be identified and corrected quickly.[2]

In this later stage of evangelization the Oblates prepared their neophytes to live a truly Christian life, celebrate the sacraments and abide by
the moral precepts they had acquired.[3] Despite the alleged superiority of
Christianity, however, the Oblates realized that the attainment of this
greater spiritual maturity would be a difficult process. The challenges did
not come from the physical environment but from Native culture and

traditions that were deemed to harbour Satan and his nefarious influences. According to the Oblates, these alleged pagan vestiges and superstitions exerted a powerful countervailing influence and had to be eradicated. On this principle there could be no equivocation and, to ensure that the seed of Christianity would take root and flourish, the Oblates as proselytizers could not but become "exclusive and intolerant."[4]

Christianization also was characterized by a more profound knowledge and appreciation of the tenets of Catholicism and a determination to eliminate any contradiction between one's daily life and those principles. According to Albert Lacombe, Christianization was related to civilization because, in "civilizing" the Indians and elevating their morals, the missionary was reforming them and placing them in their proper perspective, that is, man made in the image of God.[5] Be that as it may, Axtell has demonstrated that the "shucking" of the old corrupted individual and the creation of a new person was a very dramatic and traumatic process for Indians. In discarding the "old self," Natives were being asked to "commit cultural suicide." The Indian "was expected to peel off his whole cultural being, his 'savagery' in order to prepare for whitewashing in 'the blood of the Lamb.' "[6]

As missionaries, the Oblates believed that a keen felt need to be redeemed was the only motive for conversion. Since Indians were a deeply spiritual people, there were some who responded positively and spontaneously to the proclamation of the Gospel by the Oblates. These "true" converts simultaneously reflected and reinforced the conviction of the Oblates that Catholicism was the only legitimate expression of Christianity. In the final analysis, however, this is a simplistic interpretation that does not consider other equally important reasons which determined Indians to become Christian. John Webster Grant has suggested that Indians attributed the superior power and technology of whites to their Christian religion and hoped to share in that power by adopting that spirituality.[7] He also argues that critical circumstances caused Natives to turn to Christianity because "the birds and animal spirits to which they had looked for illumination were no longer readily found in their accustomed places or seemed already to have fled from them." Grant also cautions that the acceptance of Christianity by Indians may very well have been "A Yes That Means No?"[8] For his part, James Axtell claims that the adoption of Christianity ensured the ethnic survival of Indians because they successfully used it for their own purposes.[9] The presence of disease, the need to have the missionary as an intermediary and the desire to obtain material benefits were also motives for adopting Christianity. Indians in different regions at different times were subject to different influences and these in turn fashioned their responses to the Christian message

The early Oblate missionaries had not received any special pedagogical training to assist them in their Apostolate among the Native populations of western Canada. As they resolved the problems associated with the establishment and maintenance of missions, the Oblates had to develop and refine a methodology and instructional techniques that were appropriate to communicating the Christian message in a meaningful form to an illiterate, uneducated audience. This process involved many components and was very complex because it went far beyond simply transforming the message to conform to the intellectual level of those that were being instructed.

In the Canadian North West, the Oblates began by proclaiming the Gospel, proceeded with more substantial religious instruction and ultimately, through baptism, led the non-Christian populations to spiritual regeneration and membership within the Christian community. To overcome barriers and establish a bond between themselves and those whom they were evangelizing, the Oblates observed certain ceremonial acts when they met Native or Métis populations. These rituals struck a responsive chord among the members of those communities who were sensitized culturally to elaborate ceremonials of welcoming. On the Pacific slope, the Oblates placed great emphasis on shaking hands when they met the Indians and they encouraged other external expressions of welcome such as the discharging of firearms to announce the arrival and departure of the missionary.[10] The Oblates of the Canadian North West also used these ceremonial acts of greeting but many also followed the example of Bishop Vital Grandin who, when he first met Indians and Métis, taught them to cross themselves. If the handshake denoted a fraternal bond between Indian and missionary, the sign of the cross was an even more salient symbol because it indicated a spiritual kinship.[11]

To attain their goal of a spiritual regeneration culminating in baptism the Oblates began by providing an elementary explanation of the basic tenets of Catholicism. This instruction could take various forms depending on the circumstances. A regular mission was organized when the

Natives gathered to trade or hunt and, because of its relatively lengthy duration, it was the most forceful mechanism for personal contact and effective instruction. At Île-à-la-Crosse, for example, there were two such missions, one in the spring when the Indians came to trade their furs and one in the fall when they returned briefly to obtain the necessary supplies for winter. The spring mission was more prominent and often was the only one and, hence, earned the name *"la grande mission."*[12] The regular mission included evening and morning prayers, public instructions and sermons, catechism lessons for the young and those about to be initiated into the faith, mass, penitential rites, Sunday observances, visits to individual households and to the sick.

Missionaries conducting a mission used the daily schedule of Indians to their advantage. Albert Lacombe, who accompanied the Cree on their buffalo hunts in the 1860s, quickly discovered that the most appropriate time to provide religious instruction was when everyone was in camp preparing and drying the meat taken during the hunt. In the morning, he gathered the women in the middle of the camp, instructed them and taught them prayers and hymns. When the women returned to their duties, Lacombe directed his attention to the sick. Afterwards, he sought out those individuals who had refused to be instructed and attempted to convince them by refuting the objections they had voiced. At mid-day Lacombe gathered the children, instructed them and sang hymns. Later in the afternoon, he sought out those Indians whom he had been unable to see earlier. In the evening, he instructed the men and afterwards, while smoking the calumet, discussed religious matters and answered questions that were put to him.[13] In evaluating the early Oblate apostolic work among the Cree, Grandin concluded that the best means of converting them was not to meet them at a trading post but to go out and live among them for part of the year. According to Grandin, Lacombe had demonstrated that this was possible and two other Oblates, Joseph Dupin and Constantine Scollen, were adopting the same strategy.[14]

Missions were also held at special times during the liturgical year to prepare neophytes for special religious observances. At Canoe Lake (Saskatchewan), for example, it was customary for the missionary to visit the Cree for a two-week period before Easter in order to prepare these individuals to celebrated Easter and to fulfil their paschal obligations of confession and communion.[15] Missions were also held when it was deemed that the behaviour of Indians was in serious need of modification to make it conform to accepted Christian values and standards. In later years, the payment of treaty money to the various tribes resulted in the presence of large numbers of Indians and missions were organized to coincide with these events.[16]

Initially, the Oblates favoured the extended or *grande mission* over missions of a shorter duration. It was believed that the *grande mission* made it possible not only to instruct a much larger number of individuals but also to do so more effectively. Furthermore, the extended mission was well suited to the seasonal activities of the Indians who came to the trading posts at regular intervals. Be that as it may, the *grande mission* had to be altered at times to suit circumstance. At Île-à-la-Crosse, the Oblates had established the practice of missions in the spring and the fall with the latter being held in the second half of September and lasting about twelve to fifteen days. This schedule was based on the arrival at Île-à-la-Crosse of the HBC supply barges from York Factory. The arrival of the barges was a great event for the region and many Natives gathered to obtain advances for their furs and whatever goods and munitions they required for the forthcoming season. The Oblates scheduled the fall mission to coincide with this Indian presence.[17] By 1875, however, the fall mission had lost its importance because the HBC no longer sent its supplies by barge via York Factory. Merchandise from England was being directed to Red River and from there to Green Lake with the result that barges were arriving at Île-à-la-Crosse at different intervals in the summer and fewer Indians came. Furthermore, those that did remained for only a short period of time because of other commitments. Consequently, the spring mission became predominant.[18]

Some of the positive attributes associated with the *grande mission* were, in time, deemed to be handicaps by some Oblates. In 1866, for example, the spiritual and religious exercises associated with the mission at St. Bernard (Alberta) lasted twenty days. Nevertheless, René Rémas believed that more satisfactory results could be attained if the Oblates organized more missions during the year and remained in the midst of the Natives for longer periods of time.[19]

In addition to differences of opinion concerning the most effective means of evangelizing the Native populations, there were variations in the methods used to transmit the Christian message. Valentin Végréville uti-

lized a technique that he claimed produced "brilliant results" because anyone who listened to one-third of his instructions could not resist being
converted. He structured his presentations on biblical/salvation history
and, chronologically, his exposition began with the present. From this
familiar starting point to his Native audience, he then worked backwards
through time to Adam and ultimately to God. Having arrived at God,
Végréville traced the common origins of all nations. He went on to discuss
eternity, the Trinity, the creation of angels, the universe, and humanity,
paradise and hell, the fall of humanity, the Ten Commandments and the
sacraments. Végréville developed 64 instructions to encompass this conceptual framework and claimed that at Reindeer Lake most of the Indians
whom he instructed reached the level of the sacraments.[20]

Végréville also used this method at Fort Pitt where he preached a mission in October 1865 consisting of catechism in the morning and evening
and two additional instructions, one in Cree and the other in French.
Sensing that his audience was lacking in perseverance, Végréville decided
to dispense with traditional fire and brimstone instructions because these
would have been too discouraging and he substituted "simple" but "solid
and practical" instructions dealing with faith, morality and the sacraments.[21] Given the level of sanctification that he deemed necessary,
Végréville announced that he intended to remain in Fort Pitt for two
months. This declaration met with a mixed reaction: some were overjoyed, others enraged and many remained indifferent. Végréville attributed the lack of spirituality to the fact that the Indians had seen few missionaries and only for very short periods of time. Furthermore, the
missionaries had scarcely known or understood the Natives and had not
been able to express themselves clearly because they had not mastered the
language. After nearly three months of effort, Végréville claimed that his
objective had been reached because the Indians were coming to confession and receiving communion.[22]

Gérasime Chapellière visited Waterhen Lake (Saskatchewan) in 1879
and his initial reception was so frigid and distant that he did not immediately begin to discuss religion for fear of alienating his audience. He
thought it preferable to slowly gain the esteem and affection of the
Indians. Those who came to visit him were motivated by curiosity rather
than a desire to be instructed in the faith and, realizing that this was the
case, Chapellière used an indirect approach by asking questions such as:

"Do you wish to pray?" "Do you wish to be instructed?" The answers were usually evasive and, when he referred directly to religion, the Indians became indifferent, disgruntled and uninterested.[23] He wished to baptize some infants but was told to ask permission from the elders. When Chapellière did so, he quickly discovered that they too were evasive. In the meantime, the young men decided that they would leave to go hunting.[24]

For his part, Étienne Bonnald affirmed that clear and simple instructions were superior to eloquent presentations and suggested that the effective missionary prepared and assimilated God's word before passing it on to the Native populations. According to Bonnald, the catechism, prayers, commandments and hymns had to be explained word for word and the daily gospel paraphrased. He recommended that this learning be reinforced by examples that appealed to the imagination of Indians. He urged the use of hymns because the Indians responded so positively to songs and music.[25] Bonnald profited from a voyage to France to purchase accessories such as statues and ornaments for his chapel. When he placed a lamp to illuminate the sanctuary, Bonnald noted an increased attendance at daily mass and heightened fervour among his Christians. He claimed that the frequent recitation of the rosary and the exercises of the stations of the Cross attracted Indians.[26]

It also became apparent to the Oblates that, regardless of the means adopted to transmit the Christian message, the primary instrument in the process was the missionary himself and, consequently, he required special skills. Jules Decorby described evangelization as a demanding and arduous task that required patience and courage. Many hours and countless repetitions were needed to enable an Indian to learn the basic prayers and articles of the faith. This was a "thankless task" but, nevertheless, one that had to be undertaken with great patience. A single, inadvertent word could ruin the progress that had been achieved because Indians quickly became discouraged.[27] Étienne Bonnald advised missionaries that, while traveling, they were to follow Christ's example and take what was offered to them by the Indians. In return, however, Bonnald cautioned missionaries to be prudent with their provisions and to give only tea and biscuits for fear of creating a group of individuals who were always hungry. Although, the missionary was to help widows and orphans who were in real need of assistance.[28]

Regardless of the attraction that Christianity and the missionary might have had for Indians, and the personal skills of the latter in dealing with the former, the Oblates quickly became aware that the process of conversion entailed serious obstacles. To begin with, the migratory nature of the western tribes made it difficult for the Oblates to establish and maintain the contact they believed was necessary to provide adequate and effective instruction as well as the paternalistic supervision that would ensure conformity to the precepts of Christian morality. Protestant ministers preferred to establish themselves in Bay posts rather than go out among the tribes and, hence, the Oblates were able to turn migratory habits to their advantage. The signing of treaties, while it made the tribes more sedentary, made the Protestants more meaningful competitors because they lost their trepidation and began to establish themselves on reserves.[29]

In the meantime, the fact that some of the fundamental tenets of Christianity ran counter to the grain of Native culture was a more important consideration for the Oblates. The concepts of monogamy and the indissolubility of marriage struck no responsive chord among the Indians and were not readily accepted. Julien Moulin affirmed that the Chipewyan of Green Lake were indifferent to Catholicism. They admitted that they did not despise prayer but were reluctant to pray with Moulin because they would have to renounce polygamy.[30] Vital Grandin admitted that the Chipewyan, despite their good dispositions for Christianity, were reluctant to enter into an indissoluble marriage. According to Grandin, they wished to have a trial period in marriage, a 'noviciate' so to speak, and many desired to remain novices indefinitely.[31] Some years later, when a Peigan chief introduced himself and his four wives to Grandin the latter exclaimed that if polygamy could be reconciled with Christianity, "the chief would soon be a son of the true Church."[32]

If conflicting views on the nature of marriage perplexed the Indians, denominational rivalries among the missionaries themselves were even more disconcerting. Joseph Lestanc affirmed that differences in religion among whites were a serious obstacle to the conversion of the Cree and Saulteaux near Ste. Angèle Mission (Saskatchewan) because the Indians were not able to overcome the confusion engendered by these conflicting claims.[33] Leonard Van Tighem predicted that the Assiniboines of Lac La Nonne (Alberta) would someday become good Catholics. In the meantime, however, he complained that their evangelization entailed difficulties. The majority had been baptized by Protestant ministers and while they assisted regularly at Catholic services, received instruction and even went to confession, they were reluctant to abjure and be baptized into the Catholic faith. When asked to do so by Van Tighem the Assiniboines left and only returned to the mission some weeks later.[34]

On the other hand, Henri Faraud claimed that missionary efforts were impeded by sickness among Indians. Faraud claimed that, among Christians, sickness was a warning from heaven and an agent of conversion whereas among Indians illness was a source of discouragement and a frequent cause of the loss of grace. When Natives became convinced that disease still persisted after baptism, they turned to their traditional practices such as magic and sorcery for protection.[35] With respect to the Blackfoot, Lacombe claimed that their pride was a significant barrier to the acceptance of Christianity because they would not admit to being sinners. Like the Pharisees, the Blackfoot were convinced that they were good hearted individuals and that their conduct was irreproachable. In addition to this serious fault, Lacombe alleged that the Blackfoot were being corrupted and demoralized by contact with whites who possessed neither moral nor religious principles. Furthermore, the Blackfoot were polygamous and the establishment of Mormons near their reserve was regarded as unfortunate.[36]

It was in their comments on the society of the First Nations that the Oblates truly reflected the exclusive and intolerant nature of Christianity. As missionaries, they were so convinced that Catholicism was the only true spiritual expression that they were profoundly surprised if not shocked when Indians turned a deaf ear or returned to their traditional practices and spirituality. The Oblates could not accept that there numerous reasons why Indians embraced Christianity. Furthermore, Grant's assertion that "for most Indians the profession of Christianity was a subtle but effective way of rejecting it" was foreign to the missionaries.[37] The Oblates were unable to comprehend the social and economic foundations of polygamy in traditional societies and, hence, they passed a moral judgment on that institution based on what was acceptable in their own cultural and religious background. Similarly, as mighty warriors of the Plains, the Blackfoot were naturally proud of their heritage and accomplishments and not necessarily hypocritical and self-righteous as Lacombe alleged. What was a virtue to the Blackfoot, their reluctance to adopt

European values and habits quickly became a sin and evidence of obstinacy to the missionaries.

Since the Catholic Church taught that it was the sole instrument of grace and that baptism was a prerequisite to salvation, the object of initial Oblate missionary efforts was to prepare neophytes to receive this indispensable sacrament. Thus, individuals were given instruction that provided them with the knowledge of Catholicism deemed necessary for baptism and *ipso facto* admission into the Church. With respect to healthy adults, the Oblates insisted that those who wished to be baptized should believe in Jesus Christ, express a genuine desire to become Christian, be repentant and promise to avoid temptation and sin. Aspirants also had to abandon their old traditions such as polygamy, divorce, sorcery and gambling. They were not only to substitute Christian values and morality for the old ways but also to conduct themselves in accordance with these new precepts.[38] Neophytes were given instruction on the nature of God, the story of Adam and Eve, heaven, purgatory and hell as well as mysteries of the faith such as the Trinity and Incarnation as part of their preparation. They were also taught to recite the Apostles' Creed, Our Father and Hail Mary, the Ten Commandments, the sacraments and the ordinances of the Church.[39] The candidate received baptism when the missionary was satisfied that he was sincere and well disposed and had demonstrated a sufficient knowledge of the faith.

Since baptism was deemed to be a prerequisite to salvation and a mark of membership in the Church, the Oblates went to considerable effort to administer the sacrament on individuals. The unusual experience of Bishop Taché in ministering to a Native woman at Île-à-la-Crosse in 1855 is evidence of this determination. The woman was seriously ill and had confessed to Taché but constant vomiting prevented her from receiving communion. As her condition worsened, Taché administered Extreme Unction and confirmed her. She died shortly after having been granted absolution and as she was six months pregnant, Taché was confronted by a "most delicate and difficult task." He asked a woman who was present to perform the necessary operation to expose and baptize the child contained in the dead woman's womb. The woman was very reluctant but religious motives persuaded her to do what Taché has asked. The child was alive when baptized but died shortly thereafter and Taché informed his own mother that the Native woman and her child were now in heaven and he expressed the hope that they were praying for another mother and another child to whose separation they perhaps owed their eternal happiness.[40]

Some Oblates were more demanding than others in admitting Natives to baptism and other sacraments. On the Pacific slope, the 1858 directory for missions affirmed that those who presented themselves for baptism had to be put to the test and that this trial should last for a minimum of one year. The directory recommended a more rigorous examination for adolescents, young adult women and married women of child bearing age.[41] In the Canadian North West, the sacrament of baptism was administered with a minimum of instruction and without a rigorous examination to infants, the elderly and those threatened by death. The Oblates readily baptized infants who were brought to them by parents especially if the parents consented to the ceremony. The young were baptized with few preliminaries because of the high rate of infant mortality among Native populations. Furthermore, baptism established a link between the Oblates and the families of those who received the sacrament. Prolonged instruction was also waived in the case of those who were very sick and, in some cases, Indians claimed to be ill in order to be admitted to baptism.[42] The religious training of the young and the ill was limited to making the sign of the cross and comprehending that they had been baptized. These individuals could not recite prayers such as the Our Father. The very old who had been baptized also had very little knowledge of religious matters nor were they in a position to enhance their knowledge afterward.[43]

The requirements, the length of instruction and the severity of the examination varied with the circumstances and the individual missionary. At Fort Chipewyan in 1851 Henri Faraud was demanding in admitting adults to baptism. While the Natives there desired to be inducted into the Church, Faraud was in no hurry to baptize them and they continued their instruction until they received the sacrament.[44] A few years later at the same mission, Isidore Clut admitted that at first he had baptized only a small number of Indians because he had difficulty in speaking their language. As he became more fluent he baptized those who were "sufficiently instructed" and well disposed to Catholicism because he was concerned that many were dying without being baptized. Some of Clut's neophytes were so well instructed that they in turn instructed other Indians and also taught them to pray. Clut established a rendezvous with the latter group and promised to baptize those who were reasonably well instructed.[45]

At Pukatawagan (Saskatchewan) Étienne Bonnald refused to baptize some adults until he could provide them with additional instruction and put them to the test.[46] Bonnald also related an unusual incident involving an Indian at Fort Nelson who offered him his son to baptize on the condition that the boy be brought up in the Protestant faith. Bonnald refused but he often had baptized the children of Protestants if the parents did not impose any conditions.[47] Some time later at Pelican Lake, Bonnald met a Protestant family who had a newborn child. The minister had been asked to come and baptize the infant but had not done so. Relatives prevailed upon the infant's father to have the Oblate perform the ceremony. Bonnald agreed and justified his actions on the basis that the boy could die at a very young age.[48] In 1883, Léon Doucet visited a Blackfoot boy whose health was declining steadily. Doucet spoke to him of religion and even made him pray but waited until the boy's health worsened to suggest baptism because he doubted the individual's sincerity.[49]

Despite its importance, baptism was, nevertheless, but a first step towards full incorporation into the Church and those who received it were not automatically admitted to the other sacraments. Certain practices such as gambling, drinking and dancing were deemed to be serious *désordres* by the Oblates and were not tolerated. Games of chance were seen as a particular evil and Grandin initially excommunicated the Chipewyan who habitually took part in such activities. Grandin advised Léon Doucet, who was wintering among the Métis in 1874, not to tolerate gambling in their camp and, if their desire to gamble persisted, Doucet was to leave and return to St. Albert. Grandin was willing to tolerate games of chance for recreational purposes but prohibited those activities where large stakes were involved and in which losses entailed hardship on the losers or their families. Such individuals had to promise that, henceforth, they would abstain from gambling before being admitted to the sacraments. In 1875, Grandin advised Julien Moulin at Île-à-la-Crosse that habitual gamblers as well as those who lost or won large sums were to be denied the sacraments.[50]

Despite his severity on the matter of gambling, Grandin was very moderate and practical in admitting Métis and Natives to the sacraments whereas some of his clergy were much more demanding. In 1869, the requirements imposed by the Oblates at Lac La Biche were so demanding that the missionaries were accused of being tainted with Jansenism.[51]

Grandin, argued that because of their past and traditions, the Métis and Indians in the North West who became Christian were very different from European Christians. Furthermore, this fact had to be taken into account when evaluating the behaviour of Métis and Indians and establishing meaningful expectations of morality for these individuals.[52] Steps also had to be taken not to offend or alienate neophytes from the Church.

In missions where there were permanent Indian populations, Grandin established a cycle of regular confessions four times a year for children.[53] The elderly and perhaps senile who had been baptized and who knew very little about the faith and were incapable of learning more were instructed when they came to confession and the missionaries made them discharge their penitential obligations before they left the confessional.[54] Grandin did not follow the practice of bishops in France and Canada of confirming individuals only after they had made their first communion because it was customary for Catholic Indians in the North West to be admitted to communion some time after their marriage had been regularized by a priest. Consequently, Grandin preferred to confirm prior to the first communion because he believed that confirmation not only strengthened the newly acquired faith but also prepared the recipient to receive communion.[55]

With respect to communion, the initial practice of the Oblates in the North West was to be very demanding and admit only a few Indians mostly the elderly to communion. Bishop Mazenod was astounded when Taché informed him of this policy. Mazenod affirmed that without communion it would be impossible to Christianize the Native populations and Taché promised to overcome the reluctance of his clergy to admit Indians to communion.[56] On Taché's subsequent visit to Nativity Mission (at Fort Chipewyan), more than one hundred adults received communion and were confirmed. Grandin recalled later that it was only after this event that the mission began to progress and the Indians became Christianized. Nevertheless, the Oblates proceeded with caution and at first admitted to communion only those whose marriage had been regularized in the eyes of the Church. A few years later, children were admitted to first communion especially in those missions where the Oblates had the assistance of female religious communities to prepare the children to receive the sacrament.[57]

In 1883, Louis Soullier, the representative of the superior general and canonical visitor to Canada, also expressed concern with the practice of allowing only those Indians whose marriage had been regularized to receive communion. According to Soullier, this requirement was excessive and not consistent with the principles of justice and charity. Since Indians wished to receive communion and frequently asked to be admitted, he affirmed that their faith was intense and their knowledge of religion generally was adequate. Consequently, he believed that there no longer existed any valid reason to refuse them communion to such persons when they were of an age when they could most benefit from that sacrament.[58]

The recommendations of Mazenod and Soullier contributed to relaxing the requirements for admission to communion. However, certain idiosyncrasies within the Native community could not be resolved by authoritative regulations and were left to the discretion of the missionaries in the field. In 1862, for example, Grandin qualified the longing of Indians at Nativity mission to receive communion by stating that they had "too great a desire." He cautioned that some of these individuals were motivated by pride rather than by love of God.[59] Some time later, Grandin encountered the opposite phenomenon at Île-à-la-Crosse where the Indians did not want to receive communion because they felt unworthy to do so and feared that they would sin afterwards. Despite his reassurances Grandin could not convince these individuals that a Christian received communion in order to lead a good life.[60]

If the admission of Natives to baptism and the sacraments proved difficult, the application of the Christian rules of marriage presented even greater and, at times, seemingly insurmountable obstacles for the Oblates. The concept of an indissoluble and monogamous marriage was culturally foreign to most Indians and this repugnance was complicated by the fact that the Oblates at first regarded non-Christian Native couples as unmarried and, hence, living in concubinage because, in the eyes of the Church, no contract existed between the partners. Such a contract was deemed necessary for a valid marriage to have taken place.[61]

As could be expected, this regulation produced hardship for both Natives and missionaries especially in those instances where one spouse wished to convert while the other refused to have their marriage regularized by the clergy. In a letter to Bishop Taché and Albert Lacombe, Grandin described a situation that was not uncommon in Native communities. A woman desired to convert to Catholicism but her husband, while making no attempt to prevent her from embracing the faith, refused to be married by a priest. Since the woman had children she did not wish to leave her husband.[62] In the circumstances describe by Grandin, the spouse who intended to convert could not admitted to the Church. Thus, it became the practice to baptize only couples in order that they might enter into a monogamous and indissoluble marriage as Catholics. A mixed marriage between a Catholic and non-Catholic Indian was tolerated only if it was impossible to prevent the union. Grandin advised his clergy to grant absolution to the Catholic partner in a union where the other spouse refused to have the union regularized.[63]

As a result of these difficulties, Grandin brought the matter of traditional Indian matrimonial customs to the attention of the Sacred Congregation of the Propaganda in Rome. Grandin admitted that Indians did not enter into a formal marriage contract but lived together in a provisional union and could continue to so for the remainder of their lives although they did not consider themselves to be married to one another as did Christians. If the woman was unhappy or if the alliance produced no children after a few years the union would be terminated. If the union lasted for seven or eight years, and if it resulted in children, Grandin felt certain that the couple would not separate.[64] He added that there were many Indians who had been living together since they were young and who would not separate because they loved each other and had children. Furthermore, these individuals would experience great anxiety and hardship if their unions were regarded as invalid and they had to separate as a consequence.[65]

The Congregation of the Propaganda was unable to provide a general rule to be applied to every case but, nevertheless, it provided directives to guide the missionary clergy in the North West. Each case involving the validity of a Native marriage was to be examined carefully. If, after scrutinizing the circumstances and the manner in which the union was entered the missionary concluded that it was nothing more than concubinage, the couple had to be separated before being admitted to baptism. On the other hand, if the union were deemed to be a valid marriage, the couple were to be baptized. In the event that one partner wished to convert and the other refused, the one that desired to become Catholic could be baptized. According to Propaganda, it was necessary to baptize to ensure the continuation of a valid marriage because to do otherwise would be to go against justice and morality.[66]

The directive from Propaganda made it possible to admit spouses who desired to become Catholic into the Church on the understanding that he/she would not enter into another marriage in the event of being abandoned by his/her actual spouse.[67] A further complication arose when, in the past, those who desired to convert had been married to different spouses. In such instances, the Oblates were not authorized to determine the validity of previous marriages but to marry those who had been baptized with their current spouses.[68]

Even after being instructed on the essence of a Christian marriage and being baptized some Indians returned to their old tradition of abandoning their legitimate wife in order to cohabit with another woman. Those who did so were excommunicated and not allowed to enter the Church or the missionary's residence. Ostracism and the fear of excommunication were powerful means of ensuring that the Natives conformed to the Christian concept of marriage but these measures sometimes produced unexpected consequences. Some women, realized that Christianity had enhanced their status and, aware that their partners could not expect to receive baptism if they deserted or abandoned them, sought revenge for the poor treatment they had received from their partners prior to the arrival of the missionaries. Consequently, there was a temptation among those males preparing to be admitted to the Church to change their partners at the slightest provocation.[69] In preparing couples for marriage the Oblates stressed the fact that marriage was a sacrament that adults entered into voluntarily and that both contracting parties were equal. To the stupefaction of those present, some women refused to consent to marrying those whom they had been living with because they had been forced by tradition and circumstances to enter into these unions.[70]

Polygamy was another obstacle to the conversion of Natives and, as in the case of indissolubility, the application of this Christian value also conflicted with ancient traditions and brought hardship to some. The Oblates insisted that the male rid himself of surplus wives but this worked hardship on the women involved as well as on their children. For their part, male Indians agreed to do this with great reluctance and usually insisted on remaining with the youngest of their wives rather than the first one as the Oblates insisted. The Oblates devoted much of their time to marital matters not only because the precepts of Canon Law had to be upheld but also because transgressions provided too tempting an example for neophytes to imitate. In 1870, for example, Hippolyte Leduc of St. Albert was so indignant at the conduct of a woman who went to live common law with a man who had left his legitimate wife that he forcibly went to separate the couple and even administered a few lashes to them. A few weeks later the couple had reunited and Leduc asked Alexis André who happened to be in the vicinity to intercede. André's "powerful arguments" had the desired effect and the couple separated permanently.[71]

Since marriage was such an important cornerstone in the Apostolate of the Oblates in the North West, Grandin urged his missionaries to closely scrutinize matrimonial matters because he was convinced that good marriages created good families. Grandin set the example by marrying the young man who had been his traveling companion for ten years to an orphaned girl that had been raised by the nuns at Île-à-la-Crosse.[72] Unfortunately, not all of Grandin's nuptial arrangements were constructed on such solid foundations. In 1866, he informed Taché that an individual had married his first cousin in a fit of madness. At first, Grandin had forced the couple to separate but, since they were unable to find other partners, they reunited. In desperation, Grandin provided the necessary ecclesiastical dispensation and married the couple. Grandin indicated that he had refused three times to marry another couple in similar circumstances but felt that eventually he would be obliged to marry them.[73]

At Fort Chipewyan, Isidore Clut complained that his charges did not comprehend "the severe and rigorous laws of marriage" while others seemed to ignore them despite the fact that they constituted the main thrust of his instructions. Clut remarked, however, that the marriages of younger Indians were much more stable than those of older individuals.[74] Nevertheless, Clut had to inform Valentin Végréville at Reindeer Lake of the identity of some young individuals from Nativity Mission who persisted in living in concubinage and who had departed for Reindeer Lake in order to conceal the fact. Since some of the Reindeer Lake Indians were frequenting Clut's mission at Fond du Lac, Clut asked Végréville to identify those whom he had excommunicated for concubinage.[75]

In addition to emphasizing the Christian concept of marriage and the family, the Oblates also closely scrutinized the morals of their flock with particular emphasis on the "delicate subject of impurity." René Rémas claimed that sodomy was more common among young Indians than was commonly believed. On the other hand, onanism was rarer but he found no one who would admit voluntarily to these two acts without being interrogated. Confronted by this state of affairs Rémas affirmed that a missionary had to act with great prudence and sometimes it was better to put the question directly to the individual: "When an evil thought suddenly enters your mind, do you derive pleasure from this experience?" "In sharing these impure thoughts and desires with another male and in touching yourselves, did one of you imagine the other to be a female?" "Did you commit sins of impurity with an animal?"[76] Louis Dauphin's Cree catechism had a series of questions dealing with impurity: "Did you experience pleasure while entertaining impure thoughts?" "Do you desire to commit impure acts with anyone?" "Were the individuals you desired male or female?" "Were they related to you or to your spouse?" "Do you commit impure acts on your body?"[77] Dauphin also included a special thirteen-page supplement to the Sixth Commandment in his Cree catechism. It consisted of special questions addressed to young girls, married men, married women with marital problems and young men who came to be confessed prior to being married.[78]

The behaviour of the Indians themselves could complicate the Christian state of matrimony envisaged by the Oblates. In Fort Cumberland, a new convert decided to go to Red River to seek a wife who had been brought up by nuns. He indicated that in the event that the nuns would not or could not provide him with such a spouse he would remain a bachelor.[79] In Winterburn (Alberta), the missionary complained of a young man who was so ashamed to marry that he refused to do so even though the girl was probably pregnant. He added that such a state of affairs was common on the reserve.[80]

After the signing of treaties and the creation of reserves the Oblates often turned to the secular state for assistance in enforcing the tenets of Christian marriage. The Oblates hoped that the power of the state would be used to eradicate scandalous and provocative practices such as concubinage but if the act of cohabitation was not complicated by other factors the authorities usually did not intervene to separate the individuals.[81] The state was also reluctant to prosecute those who took children as wives. The deputy minister of Justice did not advise prosecution if the husband of the child did not have another wife.[82] The Oblates were more successful in obtaining the assistance of the authorities in cases involving bigamy. Since bigamy presented a serious scandal as well as a source of temptation the Oblates urged immediate and severe punishment for the guilty party.[83]

There were instances when government policy created hardship for Indians who had entered into a Catholic marriage and the Oblates voiced a strong protest. The Department on Indian Affairs wished to prevent Indians from moving about reserves and local Indian agents did not issue rations to those who changed their domicile. In 1892 Grandin brought to the attention of Edgar Dewdney, the minister of the Interior, the case of a young man married to a girl of his reserve but living in a different village because the parents of the girl, in consenting to the marriage, insisted that the couple reside near them. The agent refused to issue rations to the young man despite the fact that the missionaries supported his case because they feared that the couple would be forced to separate.[84] Grandin requested that when an Indian presented proof of having been married before a clergyman, that individual should be allowed to pass to the reserve of his wife or *vice versa* without loosing any of the benefits granted under the Indian Act. Grandin had taken the matter up with officials of the Department but had not been able to convince them that a lawful Christian marriage was sufficient reason to move about on a reservation. In frustration, he cautioned Dewdney that if he could not remedy the situation:

> I must inform you that I consider myself, my missionaries and our Christians obliged to obey God rather than man and consequently we cannot submit to a law or ordinance absolutely opposed to the law of God.

Grandin also hinted that if the situation did not change his letter would be printed and sent to members of Parliament.[85]

While government policy with respect to Indian marriages disappointed the Oblates, their attempt to promote Christianization was at times a frustrating experience because of the Native community's negative response. Léon Doucet complained that he held prayers as usual but that few children and even fewer adults bothered to attend. The few young people who attended seemed to be present only to make a mockery of the prayer service. Doucet attributed this indifference to the fact that the

Indians now were accustomed to the missionary and, hence, lost their interest in religion because it was no longer novel.[86] At Pelican Lake, Étienne Bonnald complained that the religious knowledge of children was not impressive. One day when they were asked where God lived one of them replied that He inhabited an island on the lake. When asked who created fishes another replied that it was his mother.[87]

In the final analysis, the difficulties inherent in Christianization presented problems of a greater magnitude than those that had been associated with the initial establishment of missions and the evolution of a missionary strategy appropriate to conditions in the Canadian North West. As pragmatists, the Oblates were always experimenting and adapting their techniques. This can be seen in their initial preference for *la grande mission* because it afforded a more extensive contact with the Indians. As time passed and *la grande mission* was found wanting, variants in the form of shorter but more frequent missions or visits to Indian encampments were substituted depending on local circumstances and the preferences of individual Oblates in the field. The rich liturgy and ceremonies of the Catholic Church also appealed to the Native and Métis populations.

The missionaries also demonstrated great ingenuity and flexibility in the development of instructional aids. Albert Lacombe, transformed the Catholic ladder into "a small masterpiece of pedagogy." The Catholic ladder had been perfected by missionaries in the Pacific North West and it represented a return to the older method of the Apostles of proclaiming "the saving events in which God entered into human history" as opposed to the contemporary method of expounding on complex moral and dogmatic truths.[88] While preaching to the Blackfoot in 1865, Lacombe supplemented his instruction with drawings made in the sand. Noticing that this visual presentation appealed to his audience, he later suspended a buffalo robe between two poles and used it to draw figures and symbols to present biblical history. Upon returning to St. Albert, Lacombe used ink and paper to prepare more elaborate versions of his prototype. In 1872, the Sisters of the Congregation of Notre Dame in Montreal prepared a definitive coloured edition and it became the most popular of all Catholic ladders.[89]

Lacombe's Catholic ladder served the objectives of both missionary preaching that entailed the initial proclamation of the Gospel and cate-

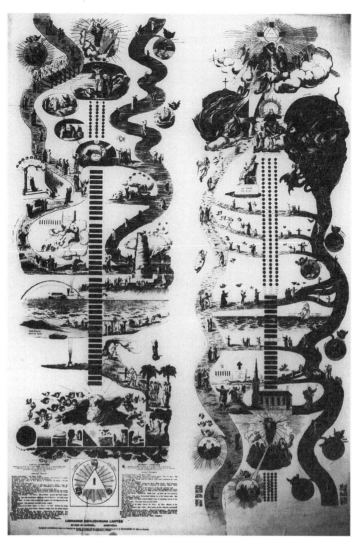

△ △ *Father Albert Lacombe's Catholic Ladder. This is a 1941 reprint by l'Institut de Missiologie, Université d'Ottawa. In actual use the bottom of right half of this reproduction would be placed on the top of the left half.* (AD)

chetical instruction directed at those who had been exposed to the faith. The Trinity was at the base of Lacombe's ladder surmounted by Creation and the Creator. Forty horizontal black bars represented the 40 centuries before the birth of Christ and the most significant historical events in that era were depicted. The mystery of Christ was located at the centre of the

△ △ *Sister teaching catechism class using Lacombe's Catholic Ladder.*
(PAA, OB 9516)

ladder. Two points above the crucified Christ represented the two nights prior to the Resurrection, 40 others the 40 days prior to the Ascension. Red horizontal bands represented the centuries after the birth of Christ and again the most important historical events were illustrated. At the summit of the ladder was to be found the judgment that awaited each individual.[90] The uniqueness of Lacombe's ladder was that it presented two paths. To the right was that of evil illustrated by evidence of idolatry, paganism and the presence of the seven capital sins. To the left was the path of righteousness represented by the Old and New Testaments, and the virtues and sacraments of Christianity. Because of the clear and uncomplicated manner in which they presented history, dogma and morality, the Catholic ladders, especially Lacombe's with its graphic colours and illustrations, provided invaluable assistance to the missionaries.[91] It is interesting to note, however, that most of the Indians depicted on Lacombe's ladder were on the path to perdition.

Lacombe's other contribution to the Oblate Apostolate was an illustrated Cree language catechism and an illustrated catechism for instructing Indians. The illustrated catechism was more detailed than the ladder and was meant to be used by those who were familiar with the rudiments of the Catholic faith. Lacombe believed that images were to the illiterate what writing was to the literate and, hence, the illustrated catechism would be invaluable to instruct adults quickly.[92] The Cree catechism contained prayers, hymns dealing with various themes and an elaboration of the verities of Catholicism. Over one-half of the Commandments were illustrated with transgressors who had been chastised for their behaviour. Only the first six of the ordinances of the Church were included and the seventh, dealing with the responsibility to tithe, was omitted because it would be redundant in the western missions. No attempt was made to make a similar adaptation with the illustrations that reflected Christian life in France.[93]

Despite these positive attributes and the zeal and determination of the Oblates, it became apparent to those involved in missionary work that serious obstacles impeded Christianization. There was also resistance on the part of Indians to the acquisition of this greater spiritual maturity and after an initial positive response to the Christian message, many Indians grew lukewarm, if not opposed to further indoctrination. As Indians became aware that "shucking" the old man meant giving up their identity or as their aspirations in adopting Christianity failed to materialize, they reverted to their ancestral traditions because these offered greater comfort and satisfaction. For their part, the Oblates did not understand the function and value of these cultural traits and summarily dismissed them as vestiges of paganism that posed a serious threat to their objectives.

In the final analysis, however, Christianity was a force far more powerful than the Oblates ever imagined. Cornelius Jaenen has succinctly summed up the challenge presented to the culture of the First Nations when he stated:

> The intrusion of Christianity, together with other components of European cultural contact, undermined traditionalistic native belief systems, challenged their world view and their harmonious integration of religion to the ecosystem. Conversion inevitably destroyed the unity and homogeneity of native communities, set off conflicts within families, bands and tribes and finally threatened the authority of the *shaman*. This essentially destructive aspect of missionary work was emphasized by the evangelistic and exclusive message of the Gospel which required not just intellectual assent and belief, but also repentance, reincarnation and rebirth so that the convert might aspire to spiritual regeneration and "the resurrection of life."[94]

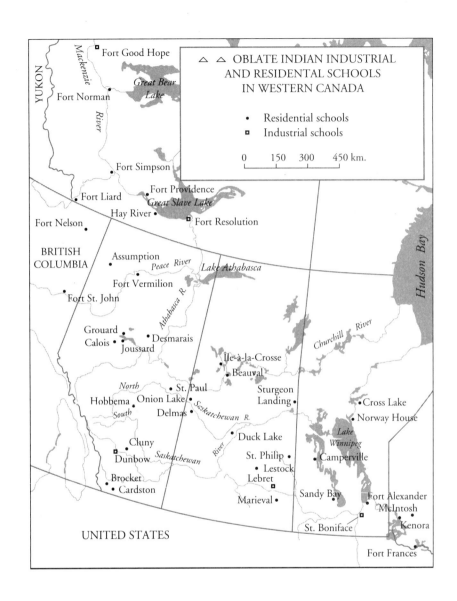

YUKON

Fort Good Hope

Mackenzie

Great Bear
Lake

Fort Norman

River

△ △ OBLATE INDIAN INDUSTRIAL
AND RESIDENTAL SCHOOLS
IN WESTERN CANADA

• Residential schools
▫ Industrial schools

0   150   300   450 km.

Fort Simpson

Fort Providence
Fort Liard   *Great Slave Lake*
Hay River •   ▫ Fort Resolution

Fort Nelson •

BRITISH
COLUMBIA   Assumption
•   *Peace River*   *Lake Athabasca*
Fort Vermilion
• Fort St. John

Athabasca R.

Grouard •
Calois •   • Desmarais
Joussard

Churchill River

Île-à-la-Crosse
• Beauval

North   • St. Paul   Sturgeon
Hobbema • Onion Lake •   Landing •
South   Delmas •   *Saskatchewan R.*

• Cross Lake
• Norway House

*Lake
Winnipeg*

• Cluny   • Duck Lake
Dunbow   *Saskatchewan*   St. Philip •   • Camperville
• Lestock   Lebret
Brocket •   • Cardston   *River*

Marieval •   Sandy Bay •   Fort Alexander
McIntosh

UNITED STATES   ▫ St. Boniface   Kenora

Fort Frances

Hudson Bay

△ △ △ △ △ △ △ △ △ △ △ △ △ △   **6**

EDUCATION

An Extension and Enhancement of Mission

Although the Oblates were a primarily a missionary order the nature of their apostolic work among non-Christians, especially children, involved them in educational ventures. Bishop Mazenod's *Instruction* (1851) enjoined the Oblates to establish schools in their missions in order to instruct the young in the fundamentals of Christianity and simultaneously provide them with a practical education to prepare them to live and function within a sedentary, civilized society, that is, one that reflected the traditions and values of western European civilization.

To the Oblates, the school became a key instrument with which to lead neophytes towards a more meaningful understanding of religion as well as the determination to make one's behaviour conform to these precepts.[1] Thus, mission and school were an apostolic and pastoral outreach to the First Nations and integral parts of the Oblate frontier "parish." The school would enhance, consolidate and strengthen the Christian notions implanted by the initial contact with the Oblates. Furthermore, its carefully controlled environment would not only strike a decisive blow against alleged pagan superstitions but also against migratory hunting traditions that allegedly were preventing Indians from attaining material success.[2]

As in the case of missions in the North West, the Oblates were not the initiators of Catholic pedagogical efforts among aboriginal populations but they quickly became the dominant participants in that venture. In

Red River, Bishop Provencher had established schools for Métis children in the hope that some could be prepared for an indigenous priesthood and he subsidized the schools because the parents were unable to pay fees. Provencher's coadjutor and successor, Alexandre Taché, also made sacrifices to provide for the education of Métis children. The Oblates expected great things from the Métis, "the first born of the faith in the West," who, by that very fact, were regarded as the bridge between the worlds of the Native and that represented by the Oblates.[3] It was to enhance this role of mediator that Taché in 1858 sent three young Red River Métis (Louis Riel, Louis Schmidt and Donald McDougall) to study in the seminaries of Quebec. Unfortunately, Taché's proposal to create an indigenous priesthood never materialized as all three protégés abandoned their studies before being ordained.

In the interior the Oblates often adopted Native and Métis orphans out of charity, or to have someone to teach them the language and provide assistance around the mission. At Fort Chipewyan, for example, Henri Faraud adopted a young orphan whom he named Lamisère. When Grandin arrived at the mission in 1855 he taught Lamisère catechism and the latter in turn taught him the Chipewyan language. Out of curiosity, Lamisère attended classes when Grandin taught French to the Métis children and his knowledge of that language quickly surpassed that of many of the regular students. Grandin admitted Lamisère to the classes and taught him how to read. Lamisère was later sent to Quebec to attend school but soon became ill and died there. A short while later, at Île-à-la-Crosse, Grandin adopted two young orphans and, on his way to France to be consecrated bishop in 1859, Grandin brought them to Saint-Boniface College in the hope of preparing them for the clergy. A short while later, however, they withdrew from the institution.[4]

In the meantime, schools were started in many missions in the interior. In 1861, René Rémas began teaching approximately 30 children in Fort Edmonton.[5] At St. Laurent (Manitoba), Laurent Simonet spent the winter of 1863 in a house rather than in his chapel because the former was better suited to the operation of a school. He reported that children, even very young children, came every day for lessons. In the evening, he taught a few adolescent boys and men.[6] At St. Laurent de Grandin, in the territorial district of Saskatchewan, a regular school was opened in 1881.[7] Shortly after his return to Alberta in the winter of 1883, Albert Lacombe

△ △ *Catechism class at Fitzgerald, Alberta, Julien Duchesne and*
Louis Dupire. (PAA, OB 727)

taught school to 40 students in Fort Macleod and to older persons who came in the evening.[8]

Even a remote and destitute mission such as St. Peter's at Reindeer Lake started a school in 1870. Seventeen students were present on 20 June to participate in the solemn ceremonies to mark the opening. The mission's bell was rung and parents and students entered the chapel singing the *Veni Creator* and other hymns in Chipewyan.[9] As was the case in most missions the school also functioned as an orphanage. One week after the school opened, the mission accepted its first orphans, two young Chipewyan boys, who were about six years of age. A short while later, the missionaries took in ten-year-old Cree boy.[10] Ovide Charlebois opened a school at Fort Cumberland in 1890 and taught the children four hours a day. In addition to its function as an instrument of acculturation, Charlebois hoped that the school would generate a small revenue for the mission through government subsidies. He requested a grant from the lieutenant-governor of the Northwest Territories but was told that no money was available.[11]

Schools in the larger missions were more impressive institutions especially when they were staffed by nuns. Social class was apparent in the organization of the school at Île-à-la-Crosse that encompassed a "*pensionnat supérieur*" comprising the children of the HBC officers and a "*pensionnat inférieur*" consisting of the children of the HBC servants as well as the Indian orphans attached to the mission.[12] An attempt was made later to establish a day school for those who were unable to attend as boarders but the practice was abandoned because it was believed that it created too many inconveniences. In 1871, the school had 36 boarders and the last ones to be admitted attended on the condition that their parents supplied the necessary food to nourish them.[13]

The Lac La Biche mission also had a school-orphanage and, in 1862, the Grey Nuns assumed responsibility for that institution. Despite the facilities and services available, the Oblates complained that it was impossible to make parents understand the necessity of having their children educated and, hence, missionaries had to implore parents to enroll their children. This inability to comprehend the benefits of education was deemed to be a serious obstacle to the progress of the school. Furthermore, the Métis preferred to live isolated from one another at some distance from the mission and this made it difficult for children to attend school. The only way the Oblates could obtain students was to assume all costs associated with the education, boarding and lodging of the children the parents consented to send.[14]

Prosper Légéard noted a similar negative attitude to education among the Métis of Île-à-la-Crosse. Reporting on the progress of the school in 1873, he claimed that the Métis attached little importance to education and were not convinced when the Oblates stressed its value. The Métis, however, were impressed by important people who spoke French and so the Oblates took advantage of the passage of high ranking officers of the HBC and had these individuals visit the school and examine the students. These examinations contributed to the glowing reputation of the Île-à-la-Crosse in the North West. In 1873, W.S. Christie, Inspecting Chief Factor for the Northern Department, and his entourage were so impressed with the exam that they visited the sisters afterward and Christie donated £5 to the orphans.[15]

Not every school, however, obtained such positive results and even Île-à-la-Crosse experienced frustrating results. In 1872 Légéard complained that the school had not lived up to its reputation because, in the absence of adequate supervision, the boys had acquired corrupt practices.[16] At Fort Edmonton, René Rémas complained that two-thirds of his students had disappeared and the remainder were often absent.[17] Shortly after beginning to teach on the Blackfoot reserve, Léon Doucet came to the conclusion that the Blackfoot were no better disposed to education and religion than the Bloods and the Peigan. In the beginning, there was a large number of students because the school was new and the students were interested. As the novelty wore off, attendance dropped and Doucet claimed that if he had not provided tea and biscuits he would have been the only one left in the school.[18]

In this early period everyone agreed that the school had to provide religious instruction and create an atmosphere that would promote acculturation, but there were conflicting views on the language of instruction that was to be utilized. In keeping with the apostolic tradition and as a pragmatic expedient, religious instruction was provided in the local Native language. With respect to subsequent instruction, Valentin Végréville suggested that students at Île-à-la-Crosse, especially the children of HBC officers, should learn to speak French and that they should be discouraged from speaking Cree. He believed that a system of rewards and constant supervision would ensure that French prevailed. Once a core of French speaking students was created, Végréville affirmed that new students would conform readily to this model without resistance and with very little effort on the part the missionaries. He claimed, furthermore, that the children of HBC officers had to learn more than the local Indian language if they were to succeed in the company's service.[19] At Fort Edmonton, Constantine Scollen, then a lay brother, taught religious instruction in Cree and provided "a bit" of instruction in French. Scollen chose to teach English because he believed a sound knowledge of that language was necessary to hold a "good position" in the HBC's service.[20]

Despite limited resources at their disposal and a lack of appreciation on the part of students and their parents, the Oblates did not abandon their educational efforts. By 1870, there were eleven schools within the boundaries of the civil province of Manitoba and three outside its limits. While some of these schools, such as those in St. Boniface and Fort Garry accommodated whites, the majority were for Métis and Natives.[21] The Diocese of St. Albert cared for 58 orphans and had 45 Indian children in its schools in 1876 and, in 1880, it was educating 200 Indian children.[22] Grandin was pleased with the results of the schools especially those at Lac La Biche, St. Albert and Île-à-la-Crosse, which were operated by the Grey

Nuns. As early as 1872, he claimed that the Indian orphans brought up by the nuns and the mission could no longer be considered "primitive" because they had been instructed in and understood the rudiments of the Catholic faith and many could read and write French. As soon as they were old enough, orphans assisted in the sowing and harvesting of crops and performed other duties depending on their age and sex. When the boys were about 15 years of age, they came under the exclusive supervision of the missionaries and lay brothers who provided them with vocational training. The girls remained with the sisters and perfected their knowledge and skills in the domestic arts. During this time, Native children became "civilized," that is, they were weaned away from their ancestral traditions and adopted a more mature European lifestyle.[23] This higher stage of social development was characterized by a Euro-Christian work ethic, agriculture and sedentary settlements, and Christian family relationships. While religion was the dominant civilizing force, Grandin was convinced that its thrust had to be seconded by the schools.[24] According to the bishop, religion was indispensable to the process of "civilization" because, in the absence of a religious infrastructure, civilization in terms of the acquisition of European values and norms, would be nothing more than a thin veneer.

In addition to the influence exercised by nuns in their schools and orphanages, Grandin believed that the presence of Métis children in these institutions would assist in changing the lifestyle of Indian children who were present in larger numbers. Indian children would benefit from contact with the Métis who were higher on the spectrum of social development and organization because the migratory tradition was weaker. Thus, the Métis became the bridge, the *trait d'union,* between the "primitive" and "civilized" elements. Where Indian children mingled with Métis children in schools and orphanages, Grandin claimed that the latter adopted the ways of the former and that it was difficult to distinguish between the two. He noted the same phenomenon among Indian children who had been adopted by Métis families and Indian girls raised in Catholic orphanages and schools and married to Métis.[25]

While Grandin regarded the Catholic religion as the dominant civilizing force he was also aware that one had to provide Indians with a good example to imitate. From a spiritual point of view, Catholic Métis were an excellent Christian role model but material considerations could not be overlooked by the missionaries since the ability to work and earn a living was deemed to be central to the concept of civilization. Since the buffalo, the mainstay of Métis society, was quickly disappearing the Métis would have to exploit other resources. The Oblates thought that agriculture would provide greater security and long-term prosperity than the hunt and through the farms and herds of cattle attached to missions such as St. Albert they hoped to convince the Métis of the benefits that sedentary agriculture had to offer.[26]

With regard to the Indian populations, Grandin proposed to establish a model farm at Onion Lake (Saskatchewan) in 1873. This model farm was to be a more sophisticated institution than Albert Lacombe's earlier initiative among the Cree at Saint-Paul des Cris (Alberta). Under the supervision of Oblate personnel, Indians who demonstrated the best dispositions would be taught to sow and harvest crops and to build homes for themselves. The object of this venture was to make Indians self-sufficient and productive entities, in other words, "civilized" individuals who readily would be incorporated into the mainstream of society.[27] The initiation into agriculture through the large Oblate farm at St. Albert or a model farm such as that proposed by Grandin was a powerful instrument of evangelization and apostolic influence.

Unfortunately, however, the high hopes Grandin entertained for the model farm were not realized and the Indians did not substitute sedentary agriculture for their traditional migratory habits. In 1877, the federal government began to distribute seed and implements to reserves and appoint farm instructors as part of its attempt to transform Natives into farmers. Like the Oblate farm in St. Albert, the instructors' farms on reserves were to be "the practical exemplification to the Indians of the manner in which farms should be managed. . . ."[28] The government also was confident that Indians would adopt agriculture and the reserves and their residents would become self-supporting. In less than ten years, however, the government closed the instructors' farms because the Indians had not responded positively by adopting the model that had been presented to them.[29]

Louis Soullier, the Oblate canonical visitor to Canada in 1883, reiterated Mazenod's recommendation that Natives had to be initiated to and practice a lifestyle that was more favourable to their temporal welfare. Turning to the establishment of instructors' farms by the government,

Soullier claimed that this venture profited primarily Indians who resided on reserves where Protestant missions had been established. Catholics did not possess sufficient resources to duplicate the St. Albert farm in other areas. He claimed that the St. Albert farm had made agriculture more progressive and had provided an excellent work experience for the orphans attached to the mission.[30]

Soullier's comments on the value of the practical experience acquired by the orphans housed at the St. Albert mission is indicative of the subtle change that had taken place in Oblate thinking since Grandin had first proposed the establishment of model farms a decade earlier. The Oblates still maintained their belief in the value of agriculture as an instrument of "civilization" and a powerful aid to evangelization. Experience, however, had demonstrated that it was virtually impossible to "civilize" and Christianize adults. Consequently, the attention and efforts of the Oblates came to focus on Native children.

For his part, Grandin realized that these children had special needs. He was aware that there was a tendency for these children to die when they were removed from their traditional environment, confined in a building and forced to eat a different diet. In contrast to this radical transformation that often brought death to those whom it was attempting to "civilize," Grandin proposed to carefully wean the children away from their traditional culture. Under the care and direction of the missionaries and nuns, these children would be fed their customary food, allowed outdoor recreation and made to work outdoors.[31] Through religious instruction and a practical education, Grandin's initial objective was to create individuals who were half "civilized" and for whom the traditional lifestyle would no longer be possible. He argued that while the normal process of transformation would be detrimental to Indians, the method used in mission schools and orphanages would eradicate the "primitive" elements in the character of Indians and, in fact, save them from extinction. Describing his proposals to "civilize" Native children to Colonel J.F. Macleod of the North West Mounted Police, Grandin affirmed that the missionaries instilled such contempt for ancestral traditions that the children were humiliated when they were reminded of their origins. The results with Native children in mission orphanages had been so dramatic Grandin predicted that, if he had ten such institutions to look after 1000 Native children, the entire race would be redeemed quickly.[32]

Grandin was convinced that compelling hunters to exchange their bows and arrows for ploughs and hoes would be equivalent to condemning them to death because they did not possess the necessary skills to make the transition. An Indian chief had informed Grandin that his people could never become farmers because they knew nothing other than how to hunt and fish. The chief went on to state that if Indians were to be saved from starvation and extinction, fathers must be able to teach their children to farm and to construct homes like the whites did.[33] Experience with Native orphans in Oblate institutions demonstrated that it was possible to alter behaviour patterns among the young and thus bring them to a higher level of social and economic maturity, in other words, to "civilize" them. The mingling of Native children with Métis families and children had also resulted in the former adapting the more "civilized" ways of the latter.

Based on these observations and experiences, Grandin evolved a plan to "civilize" the Native populations through the intermediary of their children and, as early as 1879, he began to make recommendations to the federal government regarding the work that had to be done to "civilize" the Indians and save them from extinction. He claimed that the only effective means of saving Indians from destruction was to focus all efforts on their children. He predicted that education would not be an effective instrument if the child continued to live with his/her family because attendance at school would be irregular and there would be a reversion to old ways that were harmful. Grandin suggested that the only way to ensure success was to remove children from their parents and make them lead a different life. To lessen traditional influences and the possibility of reverting to ancestral traditions, these children would be kept by the school until they reached the age of majority or they married. The end result of this process would be a "civilized" Indian who had the potential to become a productive and self-supporting individual and Grandin urged the authorities to provide such persons with additional animals and implements to encourage them.[34]

Grandin claimed that Indian parents would consent to the removal of their children because they were aware of the dreary future that was in store for the younger generations. He affirmed that it was the parents who were asking the Oblates to take their children and prepare them for a better destiny. Much as the Oblates were willing to accede to this request,

△ △ *Page from Bishop Vital-Justin Grandin's journal.*
(PAA, OB 10051)

they could only accept a small number of children because of their limited resources. Grandin stated that the Oblates currently were raising 100 Indian children at considerable expense and sacrifice and were proving that it was possible to "civilize" Indians through their children. The greater the number of Indian children the missions could assist, the larger the number of useful and productive citizens that would be produced. For his part, Grandin wanted to open three or four more schools in order to respond positively to those Indian parents who wanted to give up their children.[35]

Since this projected increase in the number of schools entailed resources the Oblates did not have, Grandin impressed upon the government the necessity of assisting him in "civilizing" of Indian children. As an experiment Grandin suggested that the government allow the Oblates to accept children who were five years old and retain them in their schools or orphanages until these individuals were 21 years old or married. He asked the government to pay half the cost ($40.00/year) of boarding students between five and 16 years of age. For the remainder of the time, these students spent at school the government would put aside half of the cost of their board in a trust account. This sum would be given to students when they married and they could use it to establish themselves on farms. Grandin claimed that the initial cost to government would be more than compensated by future savings because these Indian children and their progeny would not require subsequent assistance because they would be useful and productive citizens.[36]

While Grandin's proposals were directed toward Natives who lived in areas where agriculture was possible, he also made recommendations to government concerning those who inhabited nonarable regions. Grandin feared that, under the influence of numerous traders, Indians in these regions would hunt and trap indiscriminately and eventually bring about their own destruction through poverty and misery. To prevent this from happening, Grandin suggested the creation of a monopoly in which a single company would be allowed to trade in these areas under strict government control. While making a large profit, this company would also provide benefits to the Indians and reduce the cost to the state. The company would have to purchase furs at a reasonable price, support schools and maintain establishments where orphans, the sick and elderly could be cared for. It should also adopt measures to prevent the destruction of fur bearing animals upon which the Indians relied. Grandin justified these conditions on the grounds that those who enriched themselves at the expense of the Indians should also have to assist them.[37]

A short while later Grandin informed Prime Minister John A. Macdonald that he had abandoned his earlier recommendation concerning a trading company with monopoly privileges in favour of a superior proposal. Grandin now urged the government to assist Indians who inhabited nonagricultural land and not abandon them because they could not be farmers or because they lived outside existing treaty limits. According to Grandin, Natives in the portions of his diocese unfit for cultivation were having a very difficult time and the authorities could do nothing for them because they had not signed a treaty. Grandin urged the prime minister to provide them with the same assistance as that given to treaty Indians. Furthermore, they should be assisted to relocate on arable land and those who did not wish to move should be given substantial assistance.[38]

Grandin also impressed upon Macdonald the necessity of supporting Oblate efforts to "civilize" Indians through the intermediary of their children. While the government had spent a large sum of money attempting to civilize Indians, Grandin claimed that the results were dubious. He claimed that his method of acculturating the young worked well and produced phenomenal results. Grandin affirmed that children brought up in Catholic establishments lost all their Indian traits by the time they left and they did not want to receive the grants given to Indians because they wished to live as whites and were able to do so. Macdonald was asked to use his influence to obtain governmental grants for Oblate educational efforts among Indians and to exempt goods used in missions from custom duties. Since missions, schools and orphanages were supported by charity, Grandin believed that it was unjust for the government to profit from part of the resources used to civilize Indians through customs duties.[39]

In 1883, Grandin again petitioned the federal government in his name and on behalf of the Catholic population of the Northwest Territories. He asked that annual grants be paid to teachers in Catholic schools for Indians and that subsidies be provided to charitable institutions to support orphaned children. He also recommended that students who did well in school be emancipated from treaty when they married and that they be given a sum of money and a free piece of land. To accommodate such students, the government should reserve a township of land as close as possible to the school. He urged the government to assume responsibility for health services provided to Indians and recommended that special assistance be provided to widows and orphans as well as the sick and infirm. He reiterated his earlier request that Indians be provided assistance to move to more productive land and suggested that Métis who had been forced by want to accept treaty be allowed to withdraw without having to reimburse the government for what they had received. Furthermore, the government should assist the most destitute of Métis to establish themselves on farms.[40] Grandin's request for assistance was supported by a petition from the Catholic hierarchy of Quebec that urged Macdonald to provide the necessary funds to establish schools, workshops and model farms under the direction of the Oblates to facilitate the transformation of Indians into useful citizens.[41]

In the meantime, Henri Faraud also approached the government for funds to sustain and enhance his educational efforts in the Mackenzie basin. He had established an asylum for orphans at Providence Mission (Northwest Territories) and, in 1866, the Grey Nuns arrived to assist in this venture. Faraud claimed that since the sisters had opened their school it had an average attendance of 28 students. Given the dispersal of the Native population and the small white population attached to the HBC post, a day school was not practical. Faraud claimed that the mission had to accept as boarders all who were interested in being educated and this was a heavy financial burden. The success of this institution convinced him in 1875 to open another at Fort Chipewyan where the Grey Nuns were teaching 18 students. According to Faraud, his limited resources prevented him from taking in more students and he asked the government to provide assistance for these schools.[42]

Like Grandin's recommendation concerning Indians who inhabited nonarable areas, Faraud's request for assistance also created a predicament for the authorities. In a memo to his superior, deputy superintendent of Indian Affairs Lawrence Vankoughnet stated that Faraud's request involved Indians who resided outside existing treaty limits. Vankoughnet believed that whatever action would be taken in this instance would set a precedent for dealing with similar applications in the future. The deputy minister of the Interior, E.A. Meredith, appended a note to the memo indicating his conviction that a "dangerous precedent" would be set if the government agreed to provide assistance by means of an annual allowance.[43] Faraud was subsequently advised that, although the government appreciated the efforts he and the Grey Nuns made on behalf of Indian orphans, no funds were available to assist Indians outside of treaty areas. Furthermore, the moneys that were available were for the "benefit of Indians exclusively."[44]

The only assistance that the Oblates received came as a result of the intercession of Lord Dufferin, the governor-general, who convinced the federal government to exempt articles destined for use in orphanages and schools from customs duties. A few years later, this privilege was suspended and Faraud protested that not only were new articles subjected to duty but that used clothing collected by Catholics in Europe for use in orphanages was subject to the same rates. He also complained that if his institutions were too far removed from treaty limits to receive government funding the authorities should not impose additional hardships that might prevent him from sustaining his schools and orphanages.[45]

The question of state aid to Catholic institutions was again raised in 1882 when the assistant superior of the Grey Nuns in Montreal petitioned Prime Minister Macdonald for financial assistance to continue their work. Sister Charlebois stated that four institutions in St. Albert, Île-à-la-Crosse, Fort Providence and Fort Chipewyan were responsible for the care and education of 164 Métis and Indian children. She added that in view of the current financial situation consideration was being given to closing down the establishments in Fort Providence and Fort Chipewyan.[46] A marginal note in the draft reply to Sister Charlebois requested the commissioner of Indian Affairs to include in his estimate for schools an item for special grants to schools outside treaty limits.[47] In the meantime, Bishop Taché met with officials of the Department of Indian Affairs to discuss the subject of assistance and he strongly supported the claims of the Grey Nuns. According to Taché, although the government was not bound by treaties in the Athabasca and Mackenzie regions, it was still responsible for educational facilities because the area was part of the Dominion.[48] In a memo to Macdonald in February 1885, Vankoughnet stated that schools in St. Albert, Lac La Biche and Île-à-la-Crosse received a subsidy of $300.00 a year. No grants had been made to areas outside treaty limits and Sister Charlebois's petition again brought the matter of assistance to such institutions to the fore. He added that the Anglican Bishop of Moossonee also sought aid for schools on the shores of Hudson's Bay and had been informed that the government was not funding education in areas where treaties had not been signed.[49]

Since adequate funding was critical to the success of the civilizing venture envisaged by the Oblates, other potential sources of revenue had to be exploited by them. The closure of Saint-Paul des Cris in 1871 was demoralizing for Grandin as a religious and ecclesiastical administrator and heart breaking for Lacombe who had established this mission. Worse yet, Grandin's revenues were such that he could not provide additional funds to extend Lacombe's initial apostolic work among the Blackfoot. To alleviate this penury, Grandin proposed to undertake an extended foreign tour to seek alms for his work. His missionaries, especially Lacombe, did not approve because they believed that Grandin's absence would create far more serious problems. Instead, Lacombe proposed that he would embark on a preaching tour of Canada and the United States.[50] In commenting on the opposition to his departure Grandin informed Taché that he had no doubt that Lacombe could make a profitable tour on behalf of the Blackfoot and Cree missions. However, as bishop Grandin was responsible for more than these two tribes and he feared that Lacombe would want to keep the money he collected on the pretext that it was destined for the Cree and Blackfoot missions.[51] A short while later, Grandin agreed to Lacombe's tour and declared that if Lacombe succeeded in raising enough money for his Cree and Blackfoot missions it would be a boon to the diocese.[52]

In 1877, Grandin returned to France for medical treatment and profited from this enforced sojourn to promote the welfare of his missions but he confided to Augustin Maisonneuve that the results were not encouraging. To begin with, there was a limit to the amount Frenchmen could donate since they also had their own Catholic institutions to support. Furthermore, the presence of numerous missionaries and bishops from Canada, each asking for assistance for their missions had a negative effect on potential contributors. Instead of openly soliciting alms Grandin preferred "to make his needs known" to Catholics and he spoke only in those parts of France where he was not known in order not to bore his listeners.[53]

Ten years later, the situation had not changed only the venue. Returning from the 1887 meeting of the General Chapter in Rome, Grandin decided to preach and solicit donations in the eastern United States. Despite a letter of recommendation from the Cardinal Prefect of the Sacred Congregation of the Propaganda, Grandin was not accorded a warm reception. The Bishop of New York, for example, initially appeared sympathetic but later refused to allow Grandin to make a collection in churches on the grounds that the faithful were already burdened with the establishment of parochial schools and should not be subjected to additional levies or collections. Only French Canadian priests provided a warm welcome to a frustrated Grandin who informed Bishop Laflèche of Three Rivers that the English-speaking clergy avoided him as much as possible and at times refused to meet him. According to Grandin, only his departure pleased these individuals.[54]

More disturbing, however, was Grandin's allegation that Taché would not share with him the proceeds of a collection in favour of Catholic schools in the North West.[55] Some years later, in 1900, Grandin dispatched Lacombe on a long voyage to Europe to promote Catholic immigration and to solicit contributions. The financial component of Lacombe's mission was not successful and when he discussed this critical issue with Leo XIII, the pontiff replied that the request for financial assistance had to be made to the bishops of Canada who were obligated to assist Grandin and his schools. Based on this recommendation and given his precarious finances Grandin made an impassioned plea for assistance to the Canadian hierarchy.[56]

This preoccupation with financial considerations to ensure the success and continuation of Oblate educational efforts among Indian and Métis populations in the North West caused Grandin to create a special institution, which he designated *l'Oeuvre de la civilisation des Sauvages par les petits enfants.* Given the importance of the school as an instrument of "civilization" and Christianization and the insufficient allocations made by *l'Oeuvre de la Propagation de la Foi* and *l'Oeuvre de la Sainte-Enfance,* Grandin could only provide the necessary supplementary funds at the expense of moneys destined for his missions.[57] Grandin made his proposal known to prominent Catholic laymen and clergy in Canada and Europe but their response was no more positive than his appeals to the faithful at large for donations.[58] Grandin complained that with the exception of Louis Veuillot, the French ultramontane writer, no one offered to support or assist him in establishing this institution. Even Taché did not share Grandin's views and the latter was so demoralized that he thought that only God was willing to listen to his project.[59]

For its part, *l'Oeuvre de la Propagation de la Foi* was suspicious of Grandin's venture, which it regarded as a competitor. He had to reassure the directors that it was not and that its purpose was only to adopt Indian children to save them from certain physical and moral death. The children raised and educated in Catholic institutions were no longer primitive individuals because they could earn their living and function within the mainstream of society. Given the limited resources available only a small number of children could be rescued and he added that the funds provided by *l'Oeuvre* supported the missions and not orphanages.[60]

In discussing the matter of government assistance to orphanages, Alexander Morris, the treaty negotiator, declared that the authorities could only provide $25.00 per year for the support of orphan children of tribes who had accepted treaty. Morris suggested that the Oblates imitate the practice of the British in India where orphans were supported by respectable families. At Grandin's request, Morris agreed to become the first foster parent by adopting an orphaned Indian girl and paying for her board. Thus, Grandin affirmed that his project did not conflict or compete with *l'Oeuvre* and that it would establish in England a mechanism whereby Indian orphans in the various dioceses in British North America could be adopted, "civilized" and transformed into productive members of society. According to Grandin, this would complement and complete the work that *l'Oeuvre* had begun by making possible the conversion of Indian orphans.[61]

In letters to potential benefactors Grandin stated that, while the destruction of Native society was imminent, experience had shown that it was possible to "civilize" and save Indians through the intermediary of their children. Proper facilities would be needed not only for orphans but for those children whose parents consented to confide them to the Oblates. Grandin estimated the cost of educating and boarding a child at $80.00 per year and, undoubtedly to dispel opposition from *l'Oeuvre*, he stated that France could not be expected to establish a society to provide funds for the schools of the North West. Since the First Nations were British subjects and France already had furnished missionaries, English Catholics should contribute to promote the advancement of Indians. Grandin suggested that many English Catholic families could adopt a child from the time it entered school until it left to be married. When the child married he would have to be provided with a sum of money to enable him to build a small house and establish himself as a farmer.[62]

L'Oeuvre de la civilisation des Sauvages par les petits enfants was to be established in Scotland, Ireland, England, Canada and the United States to enable English-speaking Catholics to contribute to the education of

Native children. Since it would not be possible for all Catholics in these countries to adopt an Indian child, they could, nevertheless, contribute according to their means and, collectively, these funds could accomplish a great deal.[63] Grandin envisaged three different categories of membership in this society. Those who contributed the entire cost of boarding an Indian child ($80.00), would be given the privilege of bestowing their family name on their protégé. Individuals or families could join together to contribute to the cost of adopting a child and in such cases a draw would be made to determine who would provide the name for the adopted child. A third category included those who gave one dollar a year.[64]

Despite Grandin's declarations and explanations *l'Oeuvre de la Propagation de la Foi* insisted that his association was a competing religious institution and that it would undermine its own activities. The French association persisted in its opposition and, in June 1878, Grandin capitulated and abandoned his plan to establish his organization in Europe.[65] *L'Oeuvre* then indicated that it had no objection to the establishment of Grandin's institute in Canada and, consequently, he approached the members of the Canadian hierarchy and asked them to become patrons in their respective dioceses. Grandin claimed that he was reluctant to impose another charity on the bishops of Canada but that the opposition of *l'Oeuvre* left him no alternative. Furthermore, a charitable society such as he proposed to establish did not exist in Canada and it was a wonderful opportunity for Canada to attract God's blessings through a noble cause.[66]

Bishop Edouard Fabre of Montreal and Archbishop Joseph Duhamel of Ottawa advised Grandin to obtain the authorisation of the Archbishop of Quebec to have *l'Oeuvre des Écoles du Nord-Ouest* incorporated as a charity within ecclesiastical provinces rather than individual dioceses in order to accord it more prestige and ensure its success. When Grandin acted on this suggestion, Archbishop Elzéar-Alexandre Taschereau did not refuse but neither did he give his permission. Speaking of the work that had to be done in Quebec, the Archbishop informed Grandin that he managed the affairs of his archdiocese without Grandin's assistance and, hence, Grandin should do the same.[67] Be that as it may, the bishops of the Ecclesiastical Province of Quebec signed a pastoral letter on 3 April 1883 committing their support for missionary activities in the North West by designating that each year one Sunday collection would be taken up in all churches and chapels in Quebec for Native schools and education. The proceeds of this collection would be divided among the western bishops who were involved in Indian education. The Quebec hierarchy described the Oblate Apostolate in the North West as an activity that was *"patriotique, civilisatrice et chrétienne."*[68]

Grandin also approached the federal government for grants to the schools and orphanages that had been established in his diocese. In 1873, an Order-in-Council appropriated $300.00 for the education of Indian children in St. Albert and a year later another Order-in-Council made the same sum of money available to other schools attended by at least 25 students.[69] The first payment, however, does not appear to have been made until 1875 when Grandin received a cheque for $300.00 as a grant for the St. Albert school and subsequently was advised by Minister of the Interior David Mills that requests for assistance for schools and orphanages should be addressed to the local authorities. With respect to Indians, Mills stated that, when their lands were ceded to the federal government, they would be entitled to receive the same benefits as those who had signed treaties. In the meantime, the government was allocating $300.00 to assist in supporting Indian children being educated in St. Albert. Other schools designated by Grandin would be entitled to a similar grant if the average attendance was at least 25 Indian pupils but grants of land would not be provided to orphanages and model farms.[70]

Needless to say, Grandin was pleased to receive the grant for the St. Albert school but he reminded the deputy minister of the Interior that the average attendance was not 25 but closer to 60 and sometimes 70 students. The schools at Lac La Biche and Île-à-la-Crosse were attended by at least 25 students and Grandin asked that they be accorded the same allocation as that given to St. Albert.[71] In late 1876, Mills recommended that $300.00 be given to the St. Albert school and that an additional $300.00 be allocated to the schools at Lac La Biche and Île-à-la-Crosse as Grandin saw fit. A short while later, Grandin was informed of the grant and reminded that the Department could provide assistance only for the education of Indians.[72]

While the question of Indian education weighed heavily on Grandin's mind, he was also concerned with initiating policies that promoted the spiritual and temporal welfare of Natives. Grandin was convinced that, left in their traditional surroundings, Native children had few opportunities and incentives and, as a result, lacked the means to establish themselves adequately when they married. Consequently, in 1880 he suggested to Lieutenant Governor David Laird that if a work ethic were to be inculcated among Indians they would have to be withdrawn from their traditional surroundings at a young age and kept in school until they married or reached the age of maturity.

Another means of accomplishing this same goal would be to place Native children in Christian homes but Grandin was quick to point out that families who took in Indian children would have to be reimbursed for their sacrifices and the children would have to remain in their custody for an extended period of time.[73] To this end, Grandin sought the passage of special laws dealing with the adoption of Indian children. He recommended that institutions that adopted Native children be given absolute paternal authority over them until they were 20 years old. Furthermore, he asserted that institutions should benefit from a part of the labour of their charges and that the proceeds of the remainder should contribute to their support and to the creation of a fund to assist them in establishing themselves once they married. To enable institutions to be more generous, Grandin suggested that the government provide financial assistance and dowries to Indian children. He also asked that these same privileges be accorded to individuals who agreed to adopt Native children when it was demonstrated that these children had not been mistreated and had been given a good education with a view to making them productive citizens.[74]

Equally important to Grandin was the fact that children raised by Christian institutions and families would constitute important role models whose Christian values and work habits would be emulated by others and perhaps even by adult Indians. Grandin was so convinced of the necessity of extending the "civilization" of Indians through the intermediary of their children that he channeled all his effort and energy to promote that objective. He was so inspired by what had been accomplished in St. Albert, Lac La Biche and Île-à-la-Crosse that he wanted to duplicate the schools and farms elsewhere and acculturate an even greater number of children. It was on these redeemed children that Grandin placed his faith for the future of the Indian race. When they married, they would raise Christian families and become veritable pioneers within their tribes. Grandin predicted that within a hundred years the Indians would disappear as migratory hunters and be replaced by a civilized and productive element integrated within the mainstream of society.[75]

Grandin was convinced that white civilization, as represented by the advancing agricultural frontier, would destroy the Indian within a short period of time. The only means of avoiding this catastrophe was to transform the children into individuals who no longer could lead a nomadic lifestyle and who could adapt to the new order.[76] If Native children were to be means through which the larger Indian community was to be redeemed, the Oblates and their institutions were the agents *par excellence* to effect this transformation. The work that had been done at St. Albert, Île-à-la-Crosse and Lac La Biche demonstrated that the metamorphosis was possible but it was only a modest beginning. Grandin wanted to increase the number of Oblate schools and orphanages in the North West to accelerate the transformation and to more solidly entrench the new values and lifestyle among the young and through them to the larger Native community.

In addition to a multiplication of facilities, Grandin envisaged a carefully controlled learning environment in these institutions. To begin with, the institution had to have absolute authority over its charges for a considerable period of time because those who left after a short while and returned to their homes reverted to the nomadic traditions of their families. Not only were these individuals not "civilized" but the Oblates had wasted valuable resources in the process. Grandin also wanted children to be admitted to Oblate schools at an early age, preferably between four and eight years because he believed that at ten years of age it would be too difficult to bring about the modification that was envisaged. The students would be divided on the basis of sex whereby boys came under the jurisdiction of the Oblates and lay brothers while nuns supervised the girls. Grandin even envisaged the establishment of a facility for physically and mentally handicapped Indian children.[77]

Grandin found a tangible expression of the educational experience he envisaged for Indian children while visiting a reformatory prison for young offenders in Citeaux, France, in 1878. His observations led him to conclude that the sentence of the prisoners was rendered "almost pleasant" and that it made better Christians of them. He was delighted by the musical entertainment and performances the young detainees provided visiting clergy. The manual work they performed in the institution's shops was even more impressive to Grandin who observed them working and studying according to their abilities.[78] Grandin's observations of institutional life in Citeaux, the Oblate philosophy and experience in the North West, contributed to the formulation of his concept of the industrial school as a carefully controlled and disciplined environment to bring about the social transformation of Native children. The graduates of these institutions would be useful, industrious, progressive individuals, ready and able to earn their living and raise Christian families.[79] As an extension of mission, the school would facilitate religious instruction and provide it on a regular basis. Children would be more predisposed to attend religious services and this would facilitate the evangelization of their parents.

The Oblates and their auxiliaries, the female religious communities, were ready and willing to establish and staff institutions such as orphanages and industrial schools but assistance had to be obtained from other sectors. Grandin had predicted that it would be easier to find persons willing to work in these institutions than it would to find persons willing to contribute the necessary funds.[80] His experiences with Catholics at large, the church hierarchy, his encounters with *l'Oeuvre de la Propagation de la Foi*, his attempt to establish an independent organization to obtain funds, all attest to the difficulties and frustrations that he faced in attempting to support his schools and orphanages.

When the financial resources of the Catholic community proved insufficient, the Oblates, out of necessity, turned to the Canadian government, which had jurisdiction over Native populations in the North West. The alliance between church and state was facilitated by the fact that there were similarities in their goals. Both groups desired to wean the Indian and Métis populations away from their traditional nomadism. In addition, church and state believed that residential schools with their carefully disciplined and controlled environments "were the great crucibles in which young Indians would shed their ancestral ways."[81]

Despite these similarities, the alliance between church and state proved to be tenuous at best. To begin with, the Oblates did not have a monopoly on Indian residential education and they had to compete with Protestant denominations. This denominational rivalry heightened the problems associated with Indian education. Furthermore, government policy with respect to Indian education and the desires of the Oblates were often contradictory. Equally important was the fact that Indian students were a captive audience and the schools really did not serve their needs.

△ △ *Dunbow Industrial School hockey team.* (PAA, OB 535)

△ △ △ △ △ △ △ △ △ △ △ △ △ △

INDIAN INDUSTRIAL SCHOOLS

A Promising Oblate Venture

In addition to their apostolic duties among the Indian and Métis populations of the North West the Oblates had to assume auxiliary obligations such as the establishment of schools, orphanages and hospitals
because the area initially lacked such institutions. Through education the
Oblates sought to bring about a moral, social and economic regeneration
of Native society and traditions. This radical transformation was deemed
to be a prerequisite to Indians becoming self-supporting citizens in the
new order that was emerging on the prairies.[1] The attempts of the Oblates
to transform the society of the First Nations were motivated by a sincere
conviction that Catholicism was the only valid expression of religious
spirituality and that the adoption of a sedentary lifestyle would reinforce
Christian values as well as provide a superior material status for those who
made the transition.

The schools, orphanages and hospitals established by the Oblates
required more financial resources than that which could be marshalled by
the Catholic community or the congregation. The federal government,
because of its treaty obligations with respect to the education and welfare
of Indians, was both the obvious and logical source of funding available
to religious denominations such as the Oblates. To fulfil its obligations,
the federal government established day schools after the Indians began to
settle on reserves. Many of these institutions were conducted by religious
denominations subject to the inspection of the Department of Indian

Affairs and its agents.[2] These day schools, however, were not entirely successful and many had to be closed because of low and irregular attendance and the difficulty of obtaining and retaining qualified teachers as a result of low salaries. In addition, the poverty of Indians, the isolation of reserves and the late school entry age were deemed to be further handicaps.[3]

In 1879, the federal government sent Nicolas Flood Davin, M.P. for Assiniboia West, to Washington, D.C., to study the operation, cost and effectiveness of industrial schools established for Indians in the United States. Davin reported that day schools had not been successful because they had not been able to overcome traditional influences. As a result, the Americans had turned to industrial schools, which became the principal feature in their policy of "aggressive assimilation" to quickly enfranchise Indians.[4] The Canadian government proposed to adopt similar institutions to achieve the same objective. In the House of Commons, Prime Minister Macdonald compared the Indians to the ancient Egyptians because they were migratory, deprived of property and doomed to wander the continent. He asserted, however, that through education, the "nature of the animal" slowly would be eradicated by altering the environment.[5]

While Ottawa was examining alternatives to day schools on reserves, the Oblates were slowly formulating their own views on what they believed to be the most appropriate education for Natives. The experience of the Oblates in establishing schools in missions, raising orphan children in their institutions and Vital Grandin's observations at Citeaux led them to advocate an institution in which children would be admitted at a young age and remain for a considerable period of time. These children would be fed, clothed and lodged by the Oblates and given an education that was practical and academic and which reinforced Christian values and traditions. The carefully controlled environment in these institutions would be enhanced by the fact that students were "continually under the moral and civilizing influence of devoted teachers."[6] For its part, the Canadian government believed that, as a result of training in industrial trades, Indians could raise their standard of living and be integrated more readily into the larger society.

Grandin, with the assistance of Albert Lacombe, was the architect of Catholic Indian residential education policy in the North West but the concept of providing a practical education and basic vocational skills to aboriginal populations was not unique to these two individuals. It is found in the writings of Bishop Mazenod and in the early Oblate experience in Lesthos (1862) and British Columbia (1868).[7] Grandin had made numerous representations to government concerning the education and welfare of Indians and Métis and, in the process, he and Albert Lacombe developed the concept whereby the government would build and retain ownership of the schools but religious denominations would be responsible for their actual administration of the institution.[8] Both Grandin and Lacombe began to petition the government and had influential friends make representations on their behalf.

In 1882, Grandin went to Ottawa to discuss the education and welfare of Indians with the federal authorities and, after six months, he became frustrated at the length of time required to transform verbal promises into written ones.[9] While Grandin had not succeeded in having the government agree to all his requests, he was consoled by the fact that the authorities had accepted the industrial school project and agreed to build one in his diocese for the education of the Blackfoot. Mindful of his previous negotiations in Ottawa, he asked Macdonald that a decision with respect to this establishment be made as soon as possible and that Lacombe be empowered to select a suitable site between Fort Macleod and Calgary. Grandin also alleged that the United States was more generous than Canada in its treatment of Indians and he expressed the hope that Macdonald would do as much for Natives in southern Alberta as the United States government had done.[10]

On 19 July 1883, an Order-in-Council appropriated funds to establish three industrial schools in western Canada. Two of these, Dunbow in Alberta (St. Joseph) and Qu'Appelle in Saskatchewan (Saints-Anges), were entrusted to the Catholic Church while the third, at Battleford, also in Saskatchewan, was under the direction of the Church of England. While Grandin readily ratified the appointment of Lacombe as principal of the Dunbow school, he was less reassured by other proposals and stipulations. Grandin confided to Taché that the government was not well disposed to the presence of nuns in the school because this would ensure the success of the venture and intimidate Protestants. Grandin also reiterated his lack of confidence in Macdonald by affirming that the prime minister only seemed interested in trifling with the Oblates.[11]

Grandin also made his reservations known to Sir Hector Langevin, the minister of Public Works, and commented on the differences between the Blackfoot and other tribes in the West. According to Grandin, the Blackfoot were more barbarous and, hence, the most difficult of the western tribes to "convert, instruct and civilize." Grandin claimed that he would do everything in his power to accept the government's conditions because he wished to save and civilize the Blackfoot. Nevertheless, he believed that the school could not accept children over six years of age unless they were exceptionally well disposed and claimed that nothing could be done with Blackfoot boys between eight and ten years of age. The school would have no need of a farmer or carpenter to instruct children because he wanted nuns to be the only teachers. Construction plans developed by the government were unsatisfactory because everyone would be under one roof. This was unacceptable to sisters who insisted on having their own building and who did not want to teach boys. Grandin found it difficult to believe that the school would only accept boys and he argued that the Blackfoot could not be "civilized" without first "civilizing" future mothers. He insisted on having two separate houses: one directed by nuns for girls and the other for boys under the supervision of priests.[12]

In a subsequent letter to Langevin, Grandin claimed that government stipulations seemed to have been made to ensure the failure of an industrial school among the Blackfoot. Grandin asserted, however, that the school would succeed if he were free to implement a more practical policy based on the experience of the Oblates as missionaries. He suggested that a start be made with eight to ten boys between the ages of five and six. When these boys were accustomed to discipline, a few more could be taken in and assimilated and more added as time passed. At some distance from the boys' establishment there would be one for girls under the direction of nuns. The sisters would begin by taking in eight to ten girls and gradually increase the number. The nuns would be responsible for cooking and washing and Native girls would become acquainted with duties appropriate to their sex.[13]

Grandin also objected to the stipulation that all school personnel other than the principal were to be lay people to ensure that the schools would be immune to criticism by fanatics. Grandin claimed that while three institutions in his diocese had always been under the direction of priests no one had ever called them noviciates. He also affirmed that the government did not want to assist these schools and that while a grant of $30.00

per child had been promised for the St. Albert school as a result of Langevin's intercession, he had never been able to obtain that promise in writing and the money had never been paid. Grandin then turned to liberty of conscience, a matter that would become a source of dispute in future years.[14] Since it was not clear whether children attending a Catholic industrial school would all be Roman Catholic he declared that Catholic children in a Protestant institution should not be compelled to abandon their faith but should be free to visit the priest or that a priest be permitted to provide religious instruction for these children. He asked that these same privileges be accorded to Protestant children in Catholic schools.[15]

The government's decision to build and confide two industrial schools in the west to the Oblates was interpreted as a significant milestone in the congregation's apostolate among the Native populations. Louis Soullier, the canonical visitor to Canada, claimed that the goal of the industrial schools was to hasten the social transformation of Indians by providing their children with a practical education. Within this context, the Dunbow school was very important because it would be a crucial adjunct in the evangelization of the Blackfoot. Dunbow was to be a powerful bulwark of "Christian influence and social prosperity" and its success would encourage the Oblates to establish additional similar institutions at their own expense. Soullier urged Oblates in Grandin's vicariate to make whatever sacrifices were necessary to ensure the success of this venture because the honour of the Church was at stake.[16]

The importance of the school as an instrument of proselytization was not lost on Oblates serving in the field. In a lengthy report to the Superior General, Hippolyte Leduc, Vicar General of St. Albert, described the problems that had impeded the evangelization of the Blackfoot. Leduc argued that there was hope in redeeming them if the Oblates could occupy themselves seriously with their children. He cited government statistics to the effect that there were 1980 children of school age among the four tribes as well as the government's intention to build schools on the reserves. There was no doubt in Leduc's mind that the school had become a matter of life and death for the Oblates. He stated that if the Oblates found the resources and personnel to manage these schools the Indians would embrace Catholicism. If they failed to seize this opportunity, Indians would not convert.[17]

Although the government had authorized the construction of two Catholic industrial schools, the Oblates were frustrated by the inactivity that accompanied the Order-in-Council. In late January 1884, Taché urged Macdonald to act immediately so that the construction material could be readied in the winter. A month later, he was again pressing the prime minister for a decision and declaring that he was coming to Ottawa for an answer.[18] St. Joseph's Industrial School, Dunbow, opened in November 1884 in the midst of what Lacombe described to Macdonald as "many difficulties and contradictions."[19]

The recruitment and retention of Indian children proved to be an acute problem for industrial schools in general and Dunbow in particular. The first Blackfoot boys were brought to the school on 5 November by Jean L'Heureux, an errant French Canadian who had lived among the Blackfoot for many years and who served as government interpreter on their reserve. The school's register noted that some of the boys were too big and too well acquainted with the Indian way of life and hinted that they would not want to remain in the institution. L'Heureux returned from Blackfoot Crossing on 20 November with three more boys and on 27 December with two more.[20] On 15 November, less than two weeks after the arrival of the first students, an entry in the register recorded that Indians had arrived at the school and created trouble by attempting to demoralize boys and create a disturbance. The next day, three boys left in the company of these same Indians. Two weeks later, another boy was removed by his brother and the school had to expel another because he was too difficult to manage.[21] A few months, later police from Calgary had to be called in because the principal wanted to expel older boys and required the police to prevent them from leaving with younger students.[22]

In the meantime, the Oblates attempted to convince the Indians to send their children to Dunbow but were not successful. Among the Bloods, the institution was suspect and some, out of a spirit of hostility, spread rumours unfavourable to the school. For their part, the first contingent of students were unhappy with their stay at Dunbow and made additional disparaging remarks when they returned to the reserve and this further alienated the Native community. Lacombe visited the reserve with Hayter Reed, the assistant Indian commissioner, and spoke of the benefits of education but the audience led by Chief Red Crow avoided the subject of the school despite Reed's insistence that education be discussed.[23]

Six months after the school had opened, Lacombe admitted to Edgar Dewdney, Indian commissioner for the Northwest Territories, that despite all their efforts the Oblates had not succeeded in making Indian children like the school or preventing them from deserting. He attributed this state of affairs to the fact that the boys who were sent to the school were too old and too big and the absence of any means to compel students to remain at the institution. Lacombe had even offered presents and money to parents to dissuade them from removing their children but to no avail.[24] While the authorities co-operated with the Oblates in their efforts to recruit children, they were reluctant to adopt drastic measures to compel attendance. Dewdney informed Lacombe the government could not refuse rations to Indians who did not send their children to school and justified this stance by affirming: "You know they have nothing else to depend upon, except what they get from us and we cannot deprive them of it altogether." He stated, however, that luxuries such as tea and tobacco, which were given in small quantities, might be withdrawn from those who did not send their children to school "and we might be more liberal with those who did."[25]

In an attempt to reverse the losses caused by desertion, Dunbow began to recruit beyond the Blackfoot reserve *per se*. Early in 1885, L'Heureux had brought nine boys from the Blood and Peigan reserves but the register noted that some were older and would not likely remain.[26] Even with his knowledge of and intimacy with the Blackfoot, the recruitment of potential school children proved to be a difficult and demanding task for L'Heureux. To prevent parents from reclaiming their children, L'Heuruex had to guard the children, gather them in the evening and leave the reserve quickly thereafter. When he was camped for the evening L'Heureux had to amuse and entertain his charges until they feel asleep and then maintain surveillance while they slept. At daybreak he departed for Dunbow as quickly as possible.[27]

For his part, Lacombe made representations to the Indian commissioner to enforce attendance and discipline. Lacombe wanted to prohibit Indians from camping near the school because of the nefarious influence this contact had on students. He insisted that the government would have to coerce parents to send their children to school by means of threats and withholding of rations. Parents who sent their children to school should receive a reward. He also suggested that, if necessary, the police should return deserters by force. Furthermore, Lacombe insisted that children sent to the school should not be more than eight years of age. To facilitate the learning of English, Lacombe recommended that a few white boys and Métis who spoke English should be enrolled at the school. In addition, Dunbow should be allowed to admit destitute Cree children. It was thought that the Blackfoot would be easier to manage and would lose their solidarity if they were mingled with children of other groups.[28]

The authorities were not willing to admit a limited number of white and Métis children unless their parents agreed to pay the cost of tuition, board and clothing.[29] However, the government authorized the admission of children belonging to tribes other than the Blackfoot. Consequently, in the fall of 1885, Lacombe visited Cree missions in the hope of recruiting children and he returned with 18 students.[30] By April 1886, most of the 32 students enrolled at the school were Cree and, with one exception, all of the original Blackfoot students had left. Lacombe made numerous efforts to obtain Blackfoot children especially young ones but he was not successful.[31]

Recruitment problems at Dunbow were compounded by administrative difficulties resulting from the fact that Lacombe was a nonresident principal. The Oblates recognized that this was "an anomaly of the first magnitude" and rectified the matter by appointing another member of the congregation, Charles Claude, to replace the peripatetic Lacombe.[32] While the appointment of a resident principal improved the general administration of the school it could not address the outstanding issues of recruitment and desertion. Various new methods were tried to obtain students. In 1888, for example, a Blackfoot signed a formal witnessed contract undertaking to leave his daughter at the school for five years in return for the sum of twenty dollars. During this period of time, the girl would become a ward of one of the teachers. A few days later, the girl's mother appeared at the school and demanded the return of her daughter. When the principal refused, she removed the child and another young girl.[33] For his part, L'Heureux enhanced his recruitment activities by establishing a sort of kindergarten in his residence to prepare Blackfoot children for St. Joseph's. Unfortunately, L'Heureux's activities on behalf of the school had aroused the animosity of the Reverend J.W. Tims, the Anglican pastor at Blackfoot Crossing. In October 1891, Tims complained to the Indian commissioner that L'Heureux was "practicing immorality of a most beastly type" with Indian boys in his home. Allegation of L'Heureux's homosexuality had been voiced in the past and had been reiterated by the Oblates themselves. Consequently, he was dismissed and Dunbow lost its most active recruiter and supporter.[34]

The passage of time did little to improve Dunbow's reputation among the Blackfoot and recruitment was always difficult and necessitated constant visits to homes on the reserve. Dunbow's problems were complicated by the fact that the school was located some distance from the Blackfoot Reserve as well as the Blood and Peigan Reserves. This meant that parents were not likely to see their children for some time once they were enrolled at the institution. Consequently, Indians promised to send their children but when the missionaries came to get them they were confronted by excuses and sometimes outright refusal. A small minority, however, were faithful to their word and brought their children to the mission. In recording one such instance the *codex historicus* of St. Francis Xavier Mission on the Blood Reserve noted that the parents had been courageous and that tears had not made them change their minds as was often the case.[35] There were also instances where children had agreed to go and seemed happy to do so but later changed their minds and complained that they were being forced to attend.[36] When students were recruited they were usually taken to Dunbow as quickly as possible because experience had shown that a delay, even a short one, was often dangerous.[37]

Since they had placed so much faith in Dunbow as an instrument with which to "civilize" the Blackfoot, the results were a bitter disappointment to the Oblates. It was only natural that they deflected the responsibility for this state of affairs to government administrators and policy. In his 1901 report on the school to the superior general, Maurice Lépine accused the majority of local Indian agents of being fanatics and of seeking only to hinder the Oblates as much as possible and preventing the recruitment of children for Dunbow. He contrasted this with the experience at Qu'Appelle where children from the industrial school had been kept away from other Natives and were doing well under the direction of the Indian agents and the clergy.[38]

When industrial schools were first established, the government assumed all operating costs. A short while later, the Oblates complained that in order to reduce expenses, the government substituted a per capita grant and made the congregation responsible for all administrative costs.[39] Under the system of per capita operating grants, low enrolments produced disastrous consequences and these, in turn, necessitated equally drastic measures. In an attempt to remain solvent, Dunbow had to reduce wages and rations and lay off staff. The acquisition of vocational skills was reduced to work on the farming operations that produced the food consumed by the school and a surplus that could be sold for much needed revenue. Dunbow had fewer problems increasing the size of its herds than the number of students, which peaked at 120 in 1895 and then declined afterwards.[40]

While the government was not prepared to provide additional funds or increase the per capita grant, officials attempted to provide assistance by other means. In 1901, for example, the Indian Commissioner attempted to transfer surplus students from the Crowfoot Boarding School at Cluny (Alberta) to Dunbow to relieve congestion in the former institution and fill the void at the latter.[41] Changes in personnel did not make an appreciable difference to the deficit or the low number of students. Henri Grandin, the Oblate provincial, was also concerned with recruitment but he alleged that the problem was due to the Department and some of its agents. Members of the Sarcee band were willing to send their children to Dunbow but Grandin claimed that the Department was opposed to this. He also alleged that the agent on the Blood Reserve would not help with recruitment or assist in returning deserters.[42] As a result of Grandin's allegations, the Department instructed to agents to make a special effort to recruit for Dunbow. Grandin was also informed that the agent on the Blood Reserve reported that parents there objected to having their children sent to Dunbow because they had no faith in the institution. According to the deputy superintendent general, orphans from the Blood Reserve could be sent willingly to Dunbow if good works were being done there but, in the present circumstances, the strong arm of the state was needed to send them there. The bureaucrat informed Grandin that if the school was to be successful, radical administrative changes would be required and concluded with a blunt declaration: "and I have to request that you will give this matter your earnest consideration."[43]

As time passed, the Department became convinced that Dunbow's allocation could be used more profitably on other schools in the region although the Oblates would not entertain closing the institution.[44] Two factors accelerated the final demise of Dunbow. In 1912, John T. McNally was appointed first Bishop of Calgary and he also had the distinction of being the first English-speaking Catholic bishop in western Canada. McNally soon became embroiled in controversies with French religious orders in his diocese including the Oblates whom he deprived of their parish in Calgary. In addition to the friction caused by this new ecclesiastical jurisdiction, WWI accentuated many of Dunbow's perennial problems especially those related to finances and student enrolments. In January 1919, Deputy Superintendent General Duncan Campbell Scott advised McNally that there were only 36 students at Dunbow and a staff of eleven. Scott affirmed that serious consideration should be given to closing the school, which had been built for the Indians of southern Alberta and which only had two children from the Blood Reserve in attendance.[45] A month later, Scott again wrote the bishop to reiterate grievances surrounding the operation of Dunbow and again suggest the closing of the institution. Scott also insisted on the employment of teachers who were qualified to provide instruction in English. It would appear that Scott was well versed in the family quarrels of the Catholic hierarchy in Canada. He suggested to McNally that if one of the bishop's own English-speaking priests were in charge of Dunbow:

> we would postpone definite action to close the institution and would co-operate with you in endeavouring to increase the attendance and make the school a vital factor in Indian education.[46]

McNally sent a copy of Scott's letter to Augustin Dontenwill, superior general of the Oblates, with his own evaluation of the situation at Dunbow. McNally stated that he did not want to ask Grandin to remove the school's current principal for fear of offending the provincial and straining their relationship. The bishop asked the superior general to write to Grandin explaining the situation "and asking him to hand over the institution to the Bishop of the Diocese, so that the latter may, by meeting the Department's wishes, save a Catholic school from being closed."[47]

In the meantime, Grandin pressed McNally to make known his wishes on the school and the improvements that the Department requested. The bishop's desire to assume direction had diminished because he had not succeeded in having the superior general and his advisers order the transfer of the administration of the institution to the Diocese of Calgary.[48] In the face of McNally's continued procrastination, Grandin again wrote the bishop on 7 April 1920 asking for a clear and prompt answer on the status of Dunbow: were the Oblates to close the school, continue its operation or transfer control to the diocese?[49]

The following year, in 1921, the Oblates informed the deputy superintendent general that, in view of proposals to build a large Catholic Indian school near Claresholm, Alberta under McNally's jurisdiction, it would be preferable to close Dunbow as soon as possible. Scott was informed that, if the Department so requested, Dunbow could be closed within a few months subject to a satisfactory financial settlement.[50] Given the principals and the issues involved, a decision would not be made quickly. In April 1922, Grandin reported that McNally did not want to make the decision to close Dunbow for fear of creating the impression that he was persecuting the Oblates and by default the Oblates would have to assume that initiative. Grandin stated that the continued operation of Dunbow would require considerable renovations and upgrading and the Oblates would not continue without adequate funding from the Department. According to Grandin, McNally now feared that his school at Claresholm might not be built and, hence, desired to keep Dunbow open.[51] On 16 May 1922, Grandin made an official request to the Department on behalf of the Oblates for the immediate closing of Dunbow because of recruitment difficulties and the dilapidated condition of the physical plant.[52] In view of the reasons presented, Scott had no objections to the "an early closing" of Dunbow and in October 1922 the school was closed.[53]

It is ironic to note that although Bishop Grandin was the architect of Catholic Indian residential education in the West, the most successful of the original industrial schools was the one located in the Archdiocese of St. Boniface. Situated at Lebret, the Qu'Appelle school was to serve the

Cree, Assiniboine, Saulteaux and Sioux reserves in region. It was close to these reserves but was not located on one of them and, while the distance was not great, it nevertheless served to reinforce the non-Indian nature of the institution. Within the context of Indian residential education, however, the adjective "successful" is a very relative term. The first student arrived at Lebret on 23 October 1884 but the principal, Joseph Hugonnard, and the Indian agent were forced to scour eight reserves over a radius of 70 miles to obtain others. Thus, in March 1885, there were only 25 students and it would take another half year before the quota of 30 students was reached despite the fact that there were 300 eligible students on the neighbouring reserves. In later years, when the combined efforts of the Oblates and agents proved ineffective, police were used to force children to attend the institution.[54]

As at Dunbow, the government initially had made no provision for the education of Native girls at Lebret school but the Oblates nevertheless managed to recruit some which they housed in the attic.[55] Hugonnard took the matter up with Commissioner Dewdney asserting that if the purpose of Indian education was to engender "a reformation more or less of the tribes," the girls also had to be educated. If they were left out of the process it would be difficult to make the next generation respectable or law abiding. Furthermore, Hugonnard remained convinced that girls would be easier to train because they had been brought up to be workers for their people. He predicted that under the control of nuns, Indian girls "would make noble women and good mothers and live a happy and respectable life." He stated that the school should be able to accommodate 75–100 girls and suggested to Dewdney that a separate building be erected to house the girls.[56] A short while later, in 1886, the government authorized the construction of an addition for girls.

The Indians of the Qu'Appelle valley, like the Blackfoot, were very reluctant to send their children to the industrial school. Hugonnard alleged that parents refused to send their children because they would be too lonesome without them, parents felt that the Oblates would make their children work too hard and would inflict corporal punishment on them. There were fears that Indian children would be given medicines that whites consumed, that baptism would kill Native children, that children would be forced to blow into long tubes (musical instruments). It was felt that children who adopted white ways would be separated from their parents in the afterlife. The Saskatchewan Rebellion of 1885 accentuated hostilities towards the school as parents believed that their children would be safer at home. Others believed that the school would transform their children into soldiers because of the custom of making children walk in pairs in the school.[57] Consequently, some parents insisted on certain conditions before allowing their children to attend the school. Some stipulated that their children were not to become Christians, not to be made into soldiers, not to have their hair cut or be sent to other countries.[58]

The difficulty in obtaining students for the school precluded any careful selection of children and some who were not in good health were admitted in an attempt to meet the institution's quota. The industrial school environment with its strange food, confinement and stuffy buildings affected the health of students and those whose health was not strong to begin with died quickly.[59] In 1886, for example, five students died at the Qu'Appelle school and a sixth died early in 1887. Although none of the children had contracted a contagious disease, parents attributed the deaths to life and conditions at the school and some came to retrieve their children. Fifty Indian students died in the first eight years of the school's existence and it is estimated that half of the students did not live to benefit from the education they received.[60] Contrary to what the Oblates had anticipated, these deaths had not terrified the Native community but rumours persisted from time to time.[61]

Hugonnard had to go to great lengths to recruit students for his school. To begin with, he had to obtain permission from the reserve's chief before recruiting on that reserve.[62] Even when permission was obtained, it was often very difficult to convince parents to part with their children. It took Hugonnard three years to persuade Chief Piapot to send his children to the school.[63] Convincing Piapot to send his children to the school was a significant victory for Hugonnard because if an important personage such as Piapot allowed his children to attend it was an indication of support for the institution and it would be easier to convince others to enrol their children.

In August, when the Indians came together to receive payments from the government, Hugonnard visited the reserves with students from the school. He celebrated mass in their midst, the children sang and he spoke of the school. He claimed that the Indians admired the behaviour of the students and finally realized that the students were not in a prison. In the evening, Hugonnard attracted the Natives with a display of fireworks and the students once again performed but no one would agree to send their children to Lebret although there were 40 who were of school age.[64] Although its difficulties associated with recruitment and acceptance by the local Native community were similar to those at Dunbow, the Qu'Appelle school fared much better. Beginning with 25 students when it opened in 1884 attendance grew steadily: 81 in 1886, 140 in 1889, 194 in 1892, 238 in 1895, 226 in 1904 and 280 in 1914. In the period 1884–1961, 3,380 Indian children attended the institution.[65]

In the early years of the Qu'Appelle industrial school Hugonnard, like Vital Grandin, lamented the fact that the personnel were lay people. He asserted that the farmer, bookkeeper, school teacher baker, carpenter, blacksmith received $3,000 annually in salaries from the government and argued that if members of the congregation occupied these positions that sum of money could be made available to the missions. However, Hugonnard was quick to point out that the Oblates who accepted these positions would have to speak English, be proficient in their trades and possess some aptitude to teach children.[66]

The St. Boniface Industrial School in Manitoba was the third such institution administered by the Oblates in the West. Although it was not one of the original schools authorized by the 1884 Order-in-Council it was, nevertheless, built and maintained at government expense. The St. Boniface school had been established by Taché in 1890 for the purpose of educating Indian girls. This institution was directed by the Grey Nuns and a separate school for Native boys was opened in 1891 under the direction of a secular priest. Four years later, in 1895, the two institutions were merged and placed under the administration of the Oblates.[67]

Louis-Philippe-Adélard Langevin, the Oblate who succeeded Taché as Archbishop of St. Boniface in 1891, waxed eloquent on the school in a report on his vicariate. He was impressed with the progress of Indian children in learning to read and write, their ability to learn vocational skills and their remarkable talent for music. Their spiritual dispositions, however, were even greater sources of consolation for the missionaries. Langevin reported how a dying Indian child informed the nun who was caring for him that he was offering his life for the archbishop's schools.

Another allegedly asked for a pass so he could return home to convert his mother whose conduct left much to be desired. According to Langevin, such examples were proof of what education had done for the Saulteaux who previously always had "rebelled against salvation."[68]

Unfortunately, Langevin's optimism was not shared by government officials. Concerned about mounting expenses, the Department decided to close the industrial school for girls and replace it with a boarding school. The boy's school was maintained as an industrial school with an authorized enrolment of 80 pupils at an annual per capita grant of $110. Needless to say the Oblates were not happy with the demotion of the girl's school and the enrolment limits placed on in the boy's school.[69]

The problems associated with making the St. Boniface Industrial School more cost efficient were related to enrolment and were aggravated by the government's policy of paying only half the per capita rate for students under ten years of age. St. Boniface experienced difficulty in obtaining older males as students and made the authorities aware of this dilemma. The government's view was that the responsibility rested with Church authorities and that the difficulty would be overcome if the Church could establish an adequate system of transferring pupils from the smaller and more numerous boarding schools to industrial schools.[70] In 1903, for example, the St. Boniface industrial school had only 73 students and the principal stated that it was impossible to recruit others, especially older ones. The institution's financial problems were heightened by the fact that it did not possess sufficient land to keep a herd of cattle, to grow crops to feed the students or to teach boys to become farmers.[71]

Confronted with inadequate recruitment and constant debt, the Oblates agreed to transferring the students of the St. Boniface industrial school to three new boarding schools to be built on reserves at Fort Alexander, south-east of Lake Winnipeg; Sandy Bay on Lake Manitoba and Fort Pelly. In approving the proposal, Langevin informed the minister of the Interior that the boarding schools would be more satisfactory and provide a better education. The reluctance of parents on distant reserves to have their children educated would be reduced. Furthermore, the Indians on these reserves had asked for boarding schools because day schools had not been properly attended.[72] The government transferred ownership of the buildings and property of the St. Boniface industrial

△ △ *Qu'Appelle Industrial School at Lebret, Saskatchewan.* (AD)

school to the Oblates and in return they agreed to build the three boarding schools valued at $12,000 each.[73]

The Qu'Appelle Industrial School with its 509-acre site represents the
epitome of the co-operation between church and state to create an artificial environment designed to create the progressive "godly generation" of
assimilated Indians. The location of these schools away from and off
reserves was significant because because the coercive power of the state
could be used to negate or reduce Native cultural influences. Indian
agents were used to recruit students for schools and permits signed by
these officials were required for travel off the reserve. Government could
also be pressured by missionaries to enact legislation, such as compulsory
school attendance regulations, that promoted assimilation.[74] The industrial school was to missionaries and government bureaucrats what the
foreign compound was to diplomats, an artificial, cultural creation
unwanted by the local majority but maintained by the power and influence of the alien minority. The industrial school would replace the family
as the agent of socialization and acculturation and the missionaries and
nuns would become surrogate parents.[75]

It was by means of this "cultural greenhouse" and through the application of the proper nutrients and adequate cultivation that the Oblates
proposed to produce the desired hybrid. The proper nutrients included

religious instruction that was regarded as indispensable to civilization. The programme of studies authorized by the Department of Indian Affairs provided for religious instruction and at Qu'Appelle one-half a day was devoted to this subject during regular school hours. In addition to traditional religious services on Sundays and Catholic feast days, there were common prayers in the morning and evening and a hymn sung before bed time. Hugonnard reported to the Department in 1901 that during the winter months he held a daily class for the whole school in which he provided one hour of religious instruction outside regular school hours. Students also attended chapel in the morning and at night on a daily basis and the Lebret church in the morning and afternoon on Sundays.[76] However, Hugonnard did not advise the authorities that he held catechism classes in Cree and Sioux for students.[77] Every year a retreat was preached to students in Saulteaux "to revive their faith and purify their consciences." In addition to being pious, the students were reported to enjoy receiving the sacraments, praying and singing hymns in their own language.[78] As a result of this careful spiritual nurturing and cultivation the majority of Native children admitted to the school were baptized once they were sufficiently instructed and prepared. Only ten of the first one thousand children who attended the Qu'Appelle school were not baptized.[79]

The spiritual noviciate that the children underwent through the intermediary of instruction, baptism, confirmation, communion was complimented and paralleled by a temporal apprenticeship designed to civilized them and ensure their material well-being.[80] The curriculum in industrial schools was designed to provide students with a basic academic education and useful vocational skills to prepare them to live and function in the larger European-Christian community. Children were divided into three groups based on sex and age: boys and girls under twelve years of age, senior boys and senior girls. The "half-day system" applied to the senior students and they spent half the day studying academic subjects while the other half of the day was devoted to learning trades and doing manual work under the supervision of instructors. At Qu'Appelle, senior boys learned vocational skills by working with the blacksmith, carpenter, shoemaker, baker, tinsmith, and painter and by assisting with work on the farm and the large garden. The senior girls were prepared by the sisters for their future roles as Christian mothers and housewives and they learned traditional domestic skills and assisted in the laundry, kitchen and sewing room.[81]

Hugonnard also used other means to ensure and promote the Christianization of Indian children. To begin with, he asked sisters who had the necessary linguistic skills to teach pupils first in Cree and then provide instruction in English. Furthermore, he also developed and used bilingual English-Cree primers.[82] Hugonnard's actions were not in conformity with the policy of the Department of Indian Affairs that insisted on English language instruction but they were consistent with the Oblate practice of using the language of those whom they were evangelizing. Furthermore, although not born in Canada Hugonnard, as a French-speaking Oblate, did not remain oblivious to the ubiquitous debate over language, nationality and religion in Canada. Within this context, the French not only associated the English language with Protestantism but also contended that the loss of one's mother tongue through assimilation would quickly lead to the loss of the Catholic faith.[83] Thus, the preservation and enhancement of Indian languages was a bulwark against Protestantism and the local dialect was usually used for presenting religious instruction in schools. The French-speaking Oblates were interested only in weaning the Indian of the North West away from their former traditions and spirituality, not in depriving them of their language and culture. This is in sharp contrast to the twentieth century experience in British Columbia where English-speaking Oblates did not master the Indian languages and insisted on the exclusive use of English in their schools.[84]

At the Qu'Appelle school Hugonnard also deviated from government policy on the matter of parental visits to the institution. The Department's view was that these visits should be limited because they facilitated the retention of Indian languages and customs. Hugonnard sought to use visits to promote the conversion of parents. He was also conscious of the close family links in Native society and these reminded him of his own background and he was sensitive to Indian culture. He interpreted governmental regulations that allowed only "parents" to visit students he gave a much broader interpretation to include relatives as well as the biological parents.[85]

Various other expedients were used by Hugonnard and other Oblates to facilitate the proselytization and civilization of Indian students. Brass bands and team sports were deemed to be civilizing influences as were excursions to fairs or band tours as well as participation in traditional celebrations such as Christmas and Dominion Day.[86] Children from Qu'Appelle and other industrial schools attended the Columbian Exposition in Chicago in 1893 and demonstrated their intellectual and vocational skills and greatly impressed spectators.[87] Hugonnard, who was aware of the influence of the environment on the formation of values and character, also realized that graduates of Qu'Appelle were in a precarious position when they completed their studies and returned to the reserves. He feared that there would be a return to traditional ways because the influence of the traditional milieu was still strong and enticing especially after the highly structured and restricted atmosphere of the industrial school. As a means of keeping students under the supervision of the school for a longer period of time, providing them with an opportunity to practice what they had learned in school and exposing them to more civilizing influences, the Qu'Appelle school began to apprentice graduating pupils to settlers. In 1892, 18 girls were hired out as domestic servants and 17 boys as carpenters and farmers. These students were under Hugonnard's supervision and it was he who arranged the terms of their employment, received their wages and kept in contact with them. It was thought that this apprenticeship programme would make it easier for students to establish themselves as self-sufficient individuals.[88]

The establishment of the File Hills colony on the Peepeekisis Reserve near Lorelie, Saskatchewan was another means of extending the training and values acquired in schools in the Qu'Appelle valley. Hugonnard and other Oblates had envisaged the establishment of a special reserve for male graduates who would go there when they left the institution at 18 years of age. There, they would prepare a plot of land for farming and build a house and, after a couple of years, they would return to the school to choose a wife from among the female students.[89] The File Hills colony was begun in 1901 by W.H. Graham, Indian agent at Qu'Appelle, who was also concerned with graduates reverting to old ways and traditions. Each graduate who settled on the colony was given an 80-acre plot of land, a pair of oxen and a plough, money to build a house, the loan of two or three cows and 300 dollars[90] The File Hills colony was an "experiment in radical social engineering" under the watchful supervision of church and

state. Those who settled there were not allowed to visit each other frequently and no couples could live there together unless they were legally
married. Dances and other forms of tribal ceremony were forbidden
because they were deemed to be an impediment to progress and civilization but these prohibitions were not always observed by the residents.[91]

The purpose of industrial schools as envisaged by the Oblates was to
transform Native life and society by raising a generation of devout progressive Christians by means of what anthropologists call a "directed
acculturation situation."[92] Everything in these institution—location,
design, curriculum, activities, teachers—promoted and reinforced that
objective. In addition, government agencies and policies presented a powerful stimulus and ancillary support to Oblates efforts. Children were to
be placed in these industrial schools at a young age before they had been
thoroughly socialized by the Native community and adopted habits that
were incompatible with the Christian ideal held by the Oblates and the
level of civilization desired by the government. Since environmental
influences were deemed to be so important it meant that the life and
activities of students would be regulated closely in such institutions.
Discipline and a well ordered life were other characteristics that denoted a
"godly generation."[93] The function of the industrial school was similar to
that of the public school in the larger white community. Both institutions
were agents of cultural conformity. The public school was to assimilate
the European immigrant to Anglo-Saxon norms and traditions and bring
about "the pure gold of Canadian citizenship,"[94] whereas the industrial
school would produce "civilized," progressive, Christian citizens among
the Indians.

Industrial schools became a powerful second front in the overall
Christian "offensive" against Indian culture and traditions but they never
achieved the total victory envisaged by missionaries and bureaucrats.
Despite the serious challenge presented by these institutions, Indian society was not completely deprived of the initiative and was able to mount a
strategic defence that reflected an adjustment to new circumstances and
conditions.[95] In the early years of the treaty era, Indians welcomed the
establishment of schools on reserves and asked that their young be educated. At the signing of Treaty 6 in 1876, Chief Poundmaker had spoken
in favour of education in order that Indian children might enjoy a good

life like white children.[96] As in their initial contact with Christianity, Indians believed that there was power in education and that through the learning process they could share in that power and prepare themselves for the new ways. There was even a connotation of magic with writing becoming known as the "talking paper."[97] Indians very quickly realized, however, that industrial schools were not a product of the society they served, that parents had no voice in the educational process and that these institutions were designed not to enhance a lifestyle but replace a traditional one with another. The "defence" mounted by Indian parents is evident in their reluctance to send their children to industrial schools and, hence, recruitment for these institutions was always plagued by difficulties. Other parents, actually attempted to subvert schools by sending only females, the sick or orphaned. Indians would array one denomination against another as well as manipulate Indian agents to seek the removal of their children or prevent them from being sent to school.[98]

There is no doubt that attendance at an industrial schools produced a frightening experience for Native students as well as a sharp contrast with the world which they had known. Chief Dan Kennedy recalled that at the age of twelve he was "lassoed, roped and taken to the Government School at Lebret." Having never seen the inside of house he was "thrust into a new world called civilization." He lost his tribal name was given a new one that could be pronounced and written in English. As a further step on the road to civilization his long braids were cut and Kennedy wondered whether his mother had died since the cutting of hair was a sign of mourning in the Assiniboine culture. To add to the confusion, the curriculum often contradicted traditional teaching. Kennedy's "defence" was to escape three times but each time he was captured and returned to the school. Like many other Indian children he resigned himself to becoming part of a captive audience.[99]

As a joint venture between church and state, industrial schools established a pattern of association that would bind Oblates, Indians and bureaucrats for the next three-quarters of a century. The initial financial arrangements would be altered by a parsimonious government and there would be changes in policy but the rational for Indian education remained unchanged. The government, through the intermediary of the Oblates, co-opted the socializing influence of Catholicism to produce "civilized," progressive, Christian citizens. Whatever benefit the alliance between church and state may have had for the Oblates at the time it would be negated later by the conviction shared by many Natives that, through its schools, the congregation willingly assisted the government in promoting a policy of cultural genocide.

△ △   *Graduates of Hobbema Residential School, 1940.* (PAA, OB 2551)

△ △ △ △ △ △ △ △ △ △ △ △ △   # 8

INDIAN RESIDENTIAL SCHOOLS

A Frustrating Oblate Experience

The residential school was to the Indian missions what the parochial school was to the regular white parish. Thus, school and mission became a single entity and the school was considered as forming part of the Indian "parish" entrusted to the care of the Oblates. As a means of Apostolate the school had two objectives. Its most important goal was to inculcate Catholic ideals and morality to its charges. In addition, the school was to promote and enhance the material welfare of its pupils by providing them with the skills necessary to survive after they left the institution. The residential school also provided the Oblates with utilitarian advantages. Those who attended the schools could contribute to the evangelization of their parents and tribe or at least encourage the latter elements to adopt a more regular practice of Christian precepts and traditions. The Oblates were convinced that, through the prayers of students, many heretics and infidels had been redeemed and saved.[1]

While the collaboration of the federal government in the educational process undoubtedly stimulated the optimism of the Oblates, the overall policy of that government vis-à-vis Indians provided an even greater source of encouragement. Where missionaries argued that Christianity would result in the substitution of a new and regenerated individual for the previously corrupted Indian, the federal government believed that the adoption of agriculture would "assuredly dispossess the Indian of his nomadic habits and the uncertainties of the chase, and fix upon him the values of a permanent abode and the security of a margin of surplus."[2] Furthermore, agriculture would impose a mastery over nature, instill the concepts of private ownership, competition, thrift, diligence and proper family life.[3] Hayter Reed, who rose through the ranks of the Department of Indian Affairs to become deputy superintendent general, was motivated by a grand design to transform Indians into "a self-supporting peasant class" in which poverty on reserves would be banished by hard work.[4] Another deputy superintendent general, Duncan Campbell Scott, declared in 1920 that he wanted "to get rid of the Indian problem" and that his department would continue its efforts "until there is not a single Indian in Canada that has not been absorbed into the body politic."[5]

Residential schools were an important instrument in bringing about the desired transformation of Indian society sought by church and state. As in the case of the Oblate Apostolate that had to be altered from time to time to respond to changing conditions, the educational policy of the federal government also underwent change. At first the government built large industrial schools such as those at Lebret, St. Boniface and Dunbow and paid all of the operating costs. The government later became concerned with costs and decided to pay an annual per capita grant from which all operating costs had to be met. Smaller institutions known as boarding schools were established later on or near reserves. These boarding schools received an annual per capita grant and were managed and maintained by religious denominations. Given the proximity to the reserves they were designed to serve, these schools were more popular with the Indians than the more distant industrial schools.[6] Boarding schools served as feeders for industrial schools and, initially, the former provided education in agriculture rather than vocational training.[7] In 1923, the government abolished industrial schools as a distinct category and the industrial schools that were still operating and boarding schools collectively became known as residential schools.

The passage of time also brought significant changes in curriculum and administrative policy. The goal of industrial schools had been to prepare students to take their place in the larger white community as tradesmen or farmers. After 1896, however, the bureaucrats became disillusioned with the results as few Indian students graduated and fewer still found employment. To save money, the government opted for boarding schools and improved day schools and the emphasis was placed on "vocationally oriented teaching and education for citizenship" to provide skills that were immediately useful on reserves.[8]

The process of socialization in residential schools ran counter to the traditional methods used by Native society to achieve the same objective. Indian society socialized children and controlled adults through techniques that taught individuals to avoid behaviour and situations that could result in shame and ridicule and result in collective disapproval and shunning by the larger community. The school, with its rigid rules, strict discipline and notions of guilt, presented a sharp contrast to the techniques of a "society of shame." Consequently, Indians tended to regard the personnel in residential schools as cruel individuals who sought only retribution. For their part, missionaries viewed Indian society as "hopelessly indulgent of children."[9] Indians were quick to ascertain the objective of missionary schools and also realized that attendance in residential schools would result in a loss of parental influence over the children who attended. There was a fear in the Indian community that children who became Christian could no longer be healed by medicine men, would become white in their ways and, hence, separated from their parents in the afterlife.[10] The resistance of Indian parents was not so much against education, that is, the acquisition of skills necessary to function in society, but the fact that the schools were substituting acculturation for this desired objective.[11]

Life in a residential school was highly regimented and closely supervised by the Oblates and members of female religious communities. At St. Michel's school in Duck Lake, for example, students arose at 6:00 A.M., attended mass at 6:30, studied at 7:00 followed by breakfast at 7:45. Afterwards, the younger students had recreation while the older ones performed manual labour prior to attending classes at 9:00. There was a 15-minute recess prior to the resumption of classes at 10:45 followed by another 15-minute recess before lunch. Classes resumed at 1:00 P.M. and lasted until 3:30 when there was another recreation period and manual work for older boys. Classes resumed at 4:30 followed by a recreation at 5:00, religious instruction at 5:30, supper at 6:00, recreation at 6:30. There was singing a few times a week at 7:30 followed by recreation at 8:00 and bedtime at 8:30 P.M. From April to November the older boys were occupied continuously with agricultural work or construction. From November to April the boys were in class for one-half day. Three meals were served daily at 7:15 A.M., 12:00 and 6:00 P.M. Those who were afflicted with tuberculosis were fed separately and given meat, eggs and milk four to six times a day.[12]

Residential schools operated on what was known as the half-day system in which students were occupied for half the day in normal scholastic activities and the remaining half day in learning vocational skills. Girls aged 17, if they were sufficiently advanced in their school work, usually did not attend classes and spent their school day learning to sew, to make garments and to cook. Those aged 15 and 16 spent half the day learning sewing and knitting and the younger ones learned sewing and knitting between 2:30 and 4:00 P.M. each day. All girls knitted in the evening between 7:30 and 8:00 P.M. There were no classes on Saturdays and the boys, with the exception of the younger ones, did outside work until 3:00 P.M. During this time the girls did the housework and mended clothes. There was an obligatory bath at 3:00 P.M. followed by a recreation until 8:00 P.M.

With respect to the spiritual life of students at St. Michel's there was the customary religious instruction supplemented by ceremonies marking the first communion of pupils, and the exposition of the Blessed Sacrament and mass in the boys' room. Various religious confraternities such as the Children of Mary, Children of the Guardian Angel and Children of the Infant Jesus were organized to promote religious training and the spiritual well-being of the students. There were also annual pilgrimages to the shrine at St. Laurent de Grandin. The principal, Ovide Charlebois, encouraged the Apostleship of Prayer and communion as reparation on the first Friday of the month. He also gave religious instruction to the younger pupils in Cree.[13] The favourite sport of boys was football followed by baseball, archery, running and spinning tops. Girls preferred croquet and ball.[14]

Given the nature and objective of residential schools, the Native community entertained suspicions about these institutions and was reluctant to confide its children to their care. The problems associated with recruitment, however, were not limited to the larger schools such as Dunbow and Qu'Appelle but common to all residential schools. In 1903, for example, the school at Saddle Lake was a source of concern because it was difficult to recruit children, to have them admitted and, afterwards, to keep them in the institution. Parents were opposed to being separated from their children until the latter reached the age of 18 because they were deprived of the services or work the children could render. There were complaints that once at school, children no longer loved their parents, were arrogant and disobedient when they returned to the reserve, demonstrated no useful work skills and spoke only a few words of English. Illness and the deaths of students at the school were other problems at Saddle Lake as well as in many other similar institutions.[15] In other schools there was a dislike of particular Oblates or nuns. The Oblates admitted that the reasons put forth by Natives for not sending their children to school were not entirely unfounded.[16]

All Oblate principals were forced to travel to reserves to identify and recruit potential students for their institutions. Such initial visits were followed up by others from time to time but especially prior to a new school term. Even the resourceful Joseph Hugonnard experienced difficulties recruiting for the Qu'Appelle school and had to camp in the midst of the Indians to obtain students. While on a recruiting tour of one reserve in 1909, for example, a woman lunged at him knife in hand while her two children who were in the house broke a window and escaped into the woods.[17]

Other means of obtaining students included the purchase of wardship over a child for a specified interval. At Onion Lake (Saskatchewan), a father signed a contract confiding his three children to the mission. For its part, the mission agreed to raise and educate the children and return them when they reached the age of 16.[18] Regardless of how desperate they were for students, the Oblates were forced by circumstances to honour the promises they had made to parents to obtain their children. Julien Thomas had sent a boy from Norway House to the Qu'Appelle school. The father had consented to allow the boy to go for a two-year period but wanted him back because his health was failing and the boy could be of assistance to him. In exchange, the father would send a younger child to the school in Cross Lake (Manitoba).[19] It would appear, however, that Hugonnard was having his own problems with recruitment at Qu'Appelle and was reluctant to allow the boy to return. Confronted with this procrastination, Thomas warned that if the boy was not returned, Indians in the region of Norway House would mistrust the missionaries and the Oblates would be unable to obtain students for the school they proposed to open at the mission. The boy's return to Norway House was deemed to be so crucial that another Oblate was prepared to go to Qu'Appelle and return him.[20]

Recruitment was complicated by the fact that, initially, the Oblates had very little to use other than moral suasion to obtain students. In 1894, however, the Indian Act was amended to include a school attendance clause to assist industrial schools in maintaining adequate enrolments. Although it would take another quarter of a century before more comprehensive legislation was enacted to include all Indian children between the ages of seven and 15, the Oblates now could seek the assistance of the local Indian agent and, if need be, the police.[21] In 1915, there were 15 cases of police intervention to force children to attend the Qu'Appelle school.[22] In 1919, Qu'Appelle had more than 40 truant children and some of these had been absent for two years. The new principal, Joseph Léonard, toured all of the neighbouring reserves and advised Indian agents to return the truant children. In this instance, the outcome was fruitful and Léonard believed that the success of the venture outweighed the effort and fatigue involved.[23]

Despite the passage of time, recruitment continued to be a serious problem affecting Oblate residential schools. In some schools, Indians were paid a small sum to compensate for the expenses incurred in bringing their children to the institution. Those who took their children to the school in Delmas (Saskatchewan), for example, received three dollars for each child brought in the first month following the opening of classes and one dollar for each child brought during the rest of the school year.[24] At Sturgeon Landing (Saskatchewan), the distance between the school and reserves caused problems. One hundred students attended the school but recruitment necessitated paying the expenses of students who came from 100–150 miles to attend the institution. In addition to the expense involved, Indians did not like to send their children that far especially if they were ill.[25]

If recruitment was difficult, keeping Indian students in residential schools proved to be an equally vexing problem for the Oblates. In 1903–04, for example, the Saddle Lake school was plagued by the frequent desertion of students. An attempt had been made to transfer the deserters to an industrial school but Department would not permit this unless the boys were likely to remain there for at least two years. Boys who were not yet 16 and in good health could be sent to an industrial school but the principal was advised that threats were not to be used because the government did not want to create the impression that industrial schools were prisons.[26] The students who had escaped were punished but principal Léo Balter believed that kindness was the best means of managing the children and he was opposed to physical punishment because he was convinced that it would serve no useful purpose.[27]

Reflecting on the errors committed at Cross Lake, which had an effect on student morale, Pierre Lecoq asserted that admitting older girls between 16 and 18 years of age had been disastrous because they were only interested in pleasure and exerted a bad influence on the younger students. He claimed that allowing students to return to the reserve on the first Sunday of the month and later on all Sundays was another error. The students returned to the school in an excited state and the sisters were vilified. When these "dangerous excursions" were terminated, the parents encouraged their children to desert with all the clothing that had been provided by the school. As a pretext for escaping, the children alleged that the sisters were beating them. Within a short time, the school retained only five of its original 14 students. Lecoq claimed that more students could have been retained if students had been allowed to go home on Sundays and holidays or whenever parents wished, and if parents and friends had been invited to eat with the children at school.[28] Similar problems had been encountered at Qu'Appelle but, at Pine Creek (Manitoba), students visiting their homes on Sundays did not generate the problems described at Cross Lake. At Pine Creek, the parents were described as "good Christians" who lived close to the school and who brought their children back prior to the evening meal on Sundays.[29]

At Brocket (Alberta), Jean-Louis Le Vern took a dim view of the Indians coming to camp at the mission. He claimed that they installed themselves as if they were at home and went to take their meals at the school as if this was their right. Needless to say there was great resentment when Le Vern attempted to put an end to this "abuse."[30] As in other schools the presence of female students in Brocket created additional problems. Le Vern took exception to the custom of young males coming to spend an evening at the school in the girls' recreation room with the permission of the supervising sister on the pretext that one of the boys was a brother of one of the girls at the school. Le Vern affirmed that, as a result of these visits, the girls had become infatuated and were writing love letters. He took advantage of his sermon to demand that such visitations cease, to scold the girls and enlighten the nun who was responsible for the girls.[31]

In some cases, the character and competence of the personnel at the school heightened the traditional dislike of the institution by the students who had to attend. In the early 1920s, the situation at Lestock alarmed Oblates associated with that school. Hercule Émard regretted that the fire, which had destroyed St. Boniface College, had not ravaged the school at Lestock as long as there would have been no loss of life. He was convinced that the children would be better off at home given the conditions at the school.[32] This critical assessment was supported by that of Philippe Geelen who complained of the school's large debt and the fact that the accounting was very haphazard. He expressed his embarrassment that the pupils were dressed in rags and had to go home for the Christmas holidays in that manner. The morale of the children suffered as a result and the Indians were no longer coming to church and they had not received instruction in their own language for some time.[33] A few days later, the Department was no doubt pleased to hear from the Manitoba provincial that the Oblate principal had been removed because of failing health.[34]

At Pine Creek, the Oblate brother was unable to manage the pupils who took advantage of his good nature and escaped. The situation worsened and had a negative impact on the recruitment drive undertaken by the principal. Joseph Brachet informed his provincial that there was little use in recruiting students who were more difficult to manage when it was not possible to retain the more docile ones who were already at the school. A lay person could not be employed to replace the brother because experience had demonstrated that Indian parents had little faith in lay personnel and would keep their children at home.[35]

As a result of the difficulties encountered in recruiting and retaining Indian pupils and dealing with the Department of Indian Affairs, not every Oblate looked forward to the obedience that appointed him principal of a school. In 1919, Paul Bousquet informed his provincial that the difficulties experienced at Fort Alexander, Manitoba. Native students were deserting, parents wanted to protect them and felt that Bousquet was too harsh. Bousquet stated that when a more lenient Oblate could be found to accommodate the Indians he would gladly relinquish the reins of authority.[36] Three years later, in 1921, Bousquet complained that he was fatigued, morally and physically, by his administrative duties and the perpetual problem of desertions. Alleging that he required medical attention, Bousquet indicated that he wanted turn his responsibilities over to someone else. He added, furthermore, that after 19 years he did not care who replaced him so long as he was no longer associated in any way with Indian schools.[37] Unfortunately, Bousquet's wish was not granted and he would serve another seven years as principal at Fort Alexander, six at Fort Frances, Ontario and one at Camperville, Manitoba before terminating his long association with Indian schools.[38]

The introduction of more vigorous school attendance legislation in 1920 affecting all Indian children between the ages of seven and 15 did not bring an end to the problems associated with recruitment and desertion. From Fort Alexander, Bousquet informed his provincial that when students deserted and were not returned by their parents he now could call on the assistance of the police. However, there was a lengthy interval before the police could begin their search and the students had an enjoyable holiday during this interval. When the deserters were returned, they were reprimanded and confined for a few days before joining the other students. These same students would often desert again for no obvious reason. The return of deserters in a police automobile contributed to increasing desertions as other students desired the same lavish treatment.[39]

As a solution, Bousquet recommended to Indian Affairs that habitual deserters be transferred to another institution and, in 1920, two students had been transferred from Fort Alexander at government expense. This action had a salutary effect on the remaining students and their parents. Students did not leave the school without permission and later when desertions resumed, parents immediately assisted in searching for and returning their children because they did not want them to be transferred to a distant institution. However, when parents became aware that deserters were no longer being transferred, their efforts to locate and return truant children diminished considerably. In 1926, Bousquet asked to transfer one student to Qu'Appelle but was informed that permission would be granted on the condition that he transport the student at his expense. He claimed that the per capita grant was not sufficient to warrant such an expense and, furthermore, the student in question would not willingly accompany the principal to Qu'Appelle without trying to escape. Bousquet complained that the authorities did not provide sufficient assistance to principals to maintain order in their institutions. At the moment Bousquet had two deserters who were being encouraged by parents and he feared that others would be encouraged by this example.[40]

In October 1928, Joseph-Arsène Brachet reported that eight boys had escaped from the Camperville school and five had been captured. Another had returned half dead but the remaining two were not to be found even with the assistance of the police. In the meantime, four girls had escaped and were being pursued. Brachet was troubled by these desertions and argued that the discipline and regimentation would have to be relaxed. He claimed that it was difficult for children to remain silent or in the same position for long periods of time.[41] At the same time, Fort Alexander experienced similar problems but with more tragic consequences. In July 1928, two new students and one senior one escaped and stole a boat and headed across the lake. They were presumed to have drowned the following day.[42]

There were four desertions at Qu'Appelle early in 1936 but the principal put an end to evasions by expelling those who deserted and rewarding those who remained "magnificently" with games. In his assessment of the situation he recorded that some Indians were happy while others complained somewhat, as was the prerogative of every "self-respecting Indian."[43] The following year, in 1937, the reputation of the school and its programme spread and Natives wanted to enrol their children. When the school had its quota an attempt was made to have parents send their children to the school in Lestock but they did not want to do so. The opening of classes on 29 August witnessed an "extraordinary event" in the arrival of 162 students accompanied by their parents who were attracted by a field day organized by the Oblate seminarians. With the exception of one reserve, all students arrived within four days. Another field day in 1938 to mark the opening of the school year was characterized by the same success.[44]

The school leaving age also created problems for principals and their schools. Mathias Kalmès of Fort Alexander suggested that it should be 18 years and argued that the principal be given the authority to discharge students at an earlier age if he deemed necessary. Confronted with additional desertions, Kalmès wanted the police to assist in returning students who were not yet 18 but was informed that this was not possible. In the

△ △   *Qu'Appelle Residential School Band (c 1930).* (PAA, OB 8006)

circumstances, he felt that the school would soon be half empty.[45] One month later, some 16-year-old girls had deserted and the principal sought the assistance of the police but they would not intercede because the girls were 16 years of age and could legally leave the institution. Kalmès related how one Indian parent came to the school and demanded the return of his daughter since she was of age. This experience left little doubt in Kalmès's mind as to the determination of parents who were aware of the terms of the Indian Act and would not be put off.[46]

For its part, the Department did not insist that students be discharged when they attained 16 years of age but principals had to apply to the Department for permission to keep children who were over 16 but under the age of 18.[47] In some instances, it was the parents who sought to keep their children, especially females, in school for a longer period. In applying to the Department to keep four girls who had reached the age of 16, Edmond Pratt of Hobbema stated that one was to be married next year and her parents wanted her to remain at school in the meantime "to protect her from any accident." In the case of another girl, the parents insisted that she remain until she married because another of their daughters had "an accident" and they did not wish this to happen again.[48]

Ensuring the chastity of young Indian girls was obviously very important to the Oblates from the point of view of Catholic morality but there were other considerations that were equally important. There would be great embarrassment for the Oblates if a female student in a residential school became pregnant not to mention the adverse effects that parental disenchantment would have on future recruiting. Consequently, it was not surprising that the Oblates carefully supervised their female charges. In Hobbema, Pierre Moulin reported that young men were coming to the school in an attempt to seduce the girls. Three girls had run away with these males and Moulin had them arrested and they were given a one-year suspended sentence. After the trial one boy returned to the school and was writing and speaking to one of the girls. Moulin asked the Department to authorize the local agent to have the individual removed from the reserve and, if he persisted, to have him charged with trespassing.[49]

Despite perennial problems associated with the recruitment of students for residential schools the Oblates had to be very careful in accepting female students. Parents were known to hide the fact that their daughter were pregnant, allow them to be recruited by residential schools and then when the female's condition became obvious, blame the institution for what had happened. To prevent such an event, visits were restricted to the parlour where only the mother and father were allowed to see their children after class. Furthermore, females were not allowed to go to the parlour alone and visits in the evening were not allowed without a special permission from the principal.[50]

The state of health and death of students in schools were other factors that affected recruitment and desertions. The reluctance of Native parents to part with their children forced the Oblate schools to accept children that were very young or old and at times some whose health was poor. The consequences were predictable: 50 pupils died in the first eight years of operation of the Qu'Appelle school. Given the poor state of health in the Native community at large, 50 per cent of the pupils did not live to use their education.[51] In 1902, Jacques Riou reported that it was impossible to recruit students at Blackfoot Crossing (Alberta) because over 30 children had died in the last two months as a result of disease.[52] Given the fear and aversion of death among the Blackfoot, the Oblates had to take their precautions. When a young Franciscan nun who served as an auxiliary at Dunbow died, news of her illness and demise was kept from the students and their parents and the body was removed at night because it was felt that the Blackfoot would no longer consent to their children remaining in the institution if they knew the truth.[53] In 1903, the high death rate on reserves near Saddle Lake deflected adverse comments on the death rate at the school itself.[54] The death of four children at Onion Lake in one year made it virtually impossible to convince parents to send their other children to that school.[55]

The question of what to do with sick Native students perplexed the Oblates and at times created delicate situations. At Saddle Lake, a student was taken ill and her parents who were also sick were unable to visit her. Léo Balter visited the parents with news of their daughter's health. When her health declined, he again went to inform the parents but they reproached him for not having told them sooner. According to Balter, the parents were convinced that the missionaries were prophets who could predict the future.[56] On another occasion, Balter had refused permission to a sick student to return home and the sadness caused by this decision was interpreted by Natives to be the very cause of the illness. When two other children were taken ill, Balter notified the parents who immediately came to the school and set up their tent next to the mission. They expected to be fed during their stay and were quite upset when this antic- ipated charity was not forthcoming.[57] In another instance, the health of a student who had been at death's door had improved since he had been returned to his parents and the principal concluded that it would be "more reasonable, charitable and diplomatic" to return sick children when requested to do so by parents. Balter felt that the parents would be impressed and the students would want to return to the school when they recovered.[58]

At Qu'Appelle, Joseph Léonard informed his provincial of his opposi- tion to sending tubercular children to the sanitarium because it rendered recruitment impossible. To begin with, parents did not want their chil- dren confided to that institution and the Oblates were unable to over- come this resistance. Léonard also alleged that a doctor was recruiting for the sanitarium by sending children there that had been pronounced healthy by the school's own official doctor.[59] The introduction of nurses in residential schools was viewed with some suspicion by the Oblates. These nurses were dubbed "envoys of the king" and there were allegations that they insisted on the ridiculous and impossible, lacked discretion, occupied themselves with matters outside their jurisdiction and spied on the Oblates.[60]

The mingling of students from different tribes, often used as a last resort to attain the authorized pupillage, also created problems for recruitment and the general administration of a school. Chipewyan children had been sent to the Saddle Lake school but they did not mix well with the dominant Cree children. The Chipewyan were ridiculed and ostracized, became demoralized, refused to take part in recreation and succumbed to disease. Needless to say, the Chipewyan sent for their children upon hearing that they were dying at the school. The principal remarked that, in these circumstances, there was little chance these students would be returned to the school but he added that the institution was not anxious for their return in view of the problems their presence had generated.[61] Chipewyan children also attended the school at Onion Lake but their parents complained that they returned home imbued with the superstitious ideas of the Cree and, hence, were reluctant to send them back.[62]

The presence of the Métis on or near reserves provided the Oblates with an opportunity to satisfy their moral obligations as missionaries and to balance their budget as school administrators by admitting Métis students to maintain the pupillage authorized by the Department of Indian Affairs. At Crooked Lake, for example, Théophile Campeau informed Archbishop Langevin that there were ten nontreaty Métis children who could attend the boarding school if the government provided for their education.[63] From the Blood Reserve, Jacques Riou informed the superintendent general that there were several mixed blood children living with Indians and who received rations and treaty and he asked that the mixed blood children living on the reserve be admitted to the boarding school as if they were treaty Indians.[64]

While the Department adopted the ruling that mixed blood children in the western provinces and Northwest Territories were not to be admitted to Indian schools as grant earners, it was more sympathetic to the category of mixed blood children described by Riou. The Department conceded "that all children, even those of mixed blood whether legitimate or not, who live on an Indian reservation and whose parents on either side live as Indians, even though they are not annuitants, should be eligible for admission to the schools."[65] The Oblates were happy with this policy but they wanted the government to do more for the Métis. Henri Grandin, the Alberta-Saskatchewan provincial, advised the deputy superintendent, that the Métis were the wards of the government and, hence, the state had to assume responsibility for their education. Grandin claimed that when many of the Métis chose scrip they made a mistake and this should have been opposed by the government. Grandin would not accept that this error freed the authorities of all responsibility for the Métis and he urged the Department to "help us as much as possible in our efforts to educate the half-breed children, and to make of them useful citizens." [66]

The Department, however was not willing to extend its responsibilities to the general Métis population as Grandin had suggested. This is evident from events at the Qu'Appelle school where Métis children had been accepted as students to maintain the pupillage and the Department had been asked to sanction these admissions. In 1913, the school had been given one year to remove these students from the roll but the Oblates claimed that they could not recruit a sufficient number of Indian children to replace the Métis. [67] The Oblates were advised that the one-year extension was not to be taken "as an endorsation of a policy favouring the admission of halfbreed children to Indian schools." [68] The following year, the Oblates advised the Department that a honest effort had been made to recruit Indian children during the year but that discharges had been abnormally high. Consequently, the school was not filled and while the names of 15 Métis children had been removed from the roll 36 still remained. The Department was asked to provide another one-year extension for these children. [69] The Department agreed but on the distinct understanding that all mixed blood children were to be discharged by 30 June 1915. Joseph Hugonnard was informed by Assistant Deputy Superintendent J.D. McLean that the school was to be conducted exclusively for Indians and "in the future this policy will be strictly carried out." [70] Needless to say, the Department was not happy when its inspector reported on 7 August 1915 that two-thirds of the Métis children were still in residence. [71]

In 1918, Pierre Moulin applied to have two Métis children admitted to the Erminskin school in Alberta. He did not object to the Department's refusal but to the insinuation that he had been recruiting outside the reserve for students. The father of the children had given a resident of the reserve full custody of the children prior to the request. In addition, Moulin believed that it was necessary to protect these two children from other members of the family who had been arrested for theft and vagrancy. [72] A few years later at Crooked Lake, the government refused to pay for the education of Métis children who lived off the reserve but the Oblates were convinced that the grant could be obtained if the children lived on the reserve and if their lifestyle were no different than that of the Indians.[73]

With respect to Métis pupils in Indian residential schools the Oblates were confronted with changes in government policy. In 1927, Jules Le Vern asked the Department for permission to admit a few Métis children from the Pincher Creek area to the Brocket school. Le Vern claimed they were as poor and destitute as orphans and their parents consented to allowing them to remain on the reserve and get married after they left school.[74] The deputy superintendent replied that favourable consideration would be given to admit orphan and other Métis girls who would remain on the reserve after graduation. This was contingent upon the Indians consenting to the admission of these girls to band membership. Le Vern was advised that this special consideration did not extend to male Métis.[75] Seven years later, in 1934, when Le Vern made a similar request for the admission of Métis to the school and band membership, he was informed that "absolutely no half-breed children can be admitted to our schools."[76]

Holidays presented a problem for the Oblates and their residential schools and, hence, they were reluctant to grant them. Vacations, especially extended ones, lessened the impact of the school as students returned home to their parents and the pattern of life on the reserve. Holidays also increased the tendency for truancy among students. Indian parents, who were very fond of their children, naturally wanted to have them home especially for Christmas and New Year's. Such was the case at Saddle Lake in 1905 when parents demanded the return of their children for New Year's. The principal, Léo Balter, advised the Indians that he could not let their children leave without granting a similar leave to all students. He claimed, furthermore, that in the past when leaves had been granted, there had been abuses as some students returned late while others did not behave well after their return. Balter's reply seemed to have satisfied the parents who made the request.[77]

Regardless of how the Oblates felt about holidays, the policy of the Department also had to be considered. In 1925, the Department decreed that it would allow pupils an annual leave of up to 43 days with grant. These holidays were to be taken consecutively during the September quarter and the practice of giving leave at Christmas was "considered unwise." Henceforth, the Department would not pay the grant for unauthorized holidays during the festive season. Principals were not to allow annual leave to children who had to return to the school under escort from a previous vacation.[78] In 1937, this policy was changed to grant up to two months leave to pupils and this was to be taken in July and August. Vacations taken at other times were to require the Department's permission. It was felt that this extended holiday would eliminate the need for weekend holidays or Christmas holidays "for which no authorization can be given."[79]

While departmental policy on vacations accorded with the views of the Oblates on the subject, in some schools it created a serious problem. Jules Le Vern reported that the residents of the Blood Reserve were furious and insisted that their children be given a Christmas holiday. According to Le Vern they protested so strongly that the Indian agent and school inspector became alarmed and supported the request. On the advice of the agent, Le Vern lent his support to the request but was dismayed to learn that the Department authorized a four-day holiday at Christmas but without the payment of the grant. Le Vern was convinced that the Bloods would have removed their children by force in any event and affirmed that the school had been punished unjustly by the loss of the grant.[80]

As could be expected, the association between church and state did not always bring about the results that the two parties anticipated. Gustave Fafard, principal at Marieval (Saskatchewan), complained that the Indian agent had given permission to students to absent themselves from school and suspected that it was the Oblate principal who brought the matter to the attention of W.M. Graham of the Qu'Appelle Agency. In the meantime, the children had not returned and Fafard believed that he would have to go looking for them. His task would be rendered more difficult because the agent allegedly told the parents that they should blame Fafard for being deprived of the assistance and pleasure of their children.[81]

The Department and its officials also had their complaints against the Oblates. Indian Commissioner Hayter Reed complained to Lacombe about Joseph Hugonnard's management at Qu'Appelle. Reed claimed that the school was not run as economically as possible and that Hugonnard did not pay attention to the directives of the Department. The Commissioner cited examples of instances where the principal went "diametrically opposite to such expressed wishes." Hugonnard had erected a waiting room and dining room for Indians visiting their students. It was the Department's policy to discourage such visits and the provision of food in the dining room and sending it to their lodges encouraged Indians to disregard the pass system. Agents also complained that Indians whose rations were cut for not working on the reserve quickly rushed to the school where Hugonnard fed them. Hugonnard also was accused of discharging students on dubious pretexts.[82]

In the Battleford Agency, the agent complained that the principal of the school at Delmas was creating considerable trouble because children were allowed to go home every time it was reported that a relative was sick. The agent alleged that these children did not return to the school for considerable periods of time and he wanted the practice to cease. Joseph Angin was warned that no child was to be excused without an order from the agent or the medical officer.[83] For his part, the principal of the school at Kenora was accused of carrying students on the roll that were not actually at the school. There were suggestions that too many white students were mixed with the Indians at that school.[84]

Other schools were criticized for exceeding the authorized pupillage and, hence, Oblate provincials advised principals not to take in more students than that allowed by the Department. The provincials feared that officials would take a dim view of the larger number and come to the conclusion that the per capita grant was too generous because the school could afford to lodge, clothe and nourish the surplus students. In the case of the Blue Quills school, the provincial instructed Léo Balter to take in only between five and ten students above his authorized pupillage to avoid conflicts with the Department and increasing the school's deficit. Furthermore, Balter was advised to make a careful selection of recruits, to give priority to those who were in need and avoid selecting very young children as much as possible.[85]

Given the nature and slowness of the federal bureaucracy, it is not surprising that Oblate principals became frustrated when making submissions for their schools. At Fort Alexander, Pierre Bousquet required a kneading machine for the school's bakery but he informed his provincial that it would be useless to ask for one because the Department had not yet replied to the request he had made the previous year. Bousquet claimed that he had written 15 letters asking for a metal oven and finally succeeded in getting a reply asking what size of oven he required. He had sent the tenders for the installation of electric lighting at the school but hinted that it would be quite some time before it was actually installed. A frustrated Bousquet exclaimed that, in their relationships with government, angels would sin through impatience if in fact they could sin.[86]

In addition to contention with the Department that was external to the Oblates, there were two potential internal sources of discord in residential schools. The delegation of authority between the principal and his associates such as the spiritual director, the bursar and teachers had not been clearly established. In some instances, principals interpreted the concept of ultimate responsibility for the institution to mean that they were absolute masters. The notion that the principal was the absolute master of the school was later denounced as a "false concept" by the Oblate administration.[87] A far more serious and widespread internal conflict involved the relations of Oblates in residential schools with the female religious communities who assisted them in these institutions. Traditional gender roles were central to these differences but the disputes they engendered were heightened by jurisdictional disputes that again revolved around gender, that is, a mother superior responsible for a female religious community within the school and a father superior responsible for the male community and the general administration of the school.

Sisters from various religious communities accepted to provide instruction and to perform other duties in these institutions. For administrative purposes the Department of Indian Affairs came to insist that an Oblate assume the title of principal and exercise overall responsibility for the school. This individual was also the superior of the Oblates who worked at the school or were attached to the local mission.[88] The Oblates entered into a contract with the nuns. In the case of the 1924 contract signed between the Oblates of the Alberta-Saskatchewan province and the Sisters of the Assumption at Delmas, the Oblates designated the principal who was to receive a salary of $300 per annum and free room and board at the school. The principal remitted the school grant to the sisters who were responsible for the day-to-day operations of the school. Missionaries or brothers who were not directly employed at the school but who resided there permanently paid $150 monthly for board and room. The sisters also did the laundry and mended the clothing of the principal and those

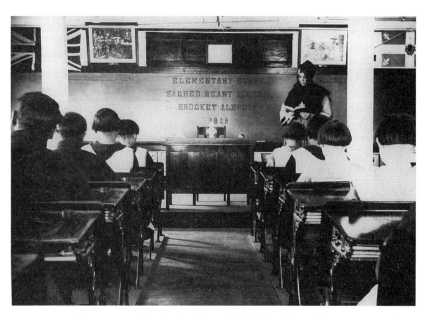

△ △ *Classroom at Brocket Residential School conducted by Grey Nuns of Nicolet, 1929.* (PAA, OB 188)

who paid board and room. They also cleaned the mission once a week and were responsible for the cleaning of the church and sacristy.[89]

Similar contracts were signed in Alberta with the Grey Nuns at Brocket, Cardston and Saint Paul, the Sisters of Providence in Cluny and in Saskatchewan with the Sisters of the Assumption at Onion Lake. An extensive examination and study of these documents reveals that it was not the division of labour or the financial arrangements that engendered difficulties between the Oblates and the sisters.[90] Problems arose in the actual operation of the school, a grey area in which responsibility and jurisdiction overlapped. The Oblates did not object to the nuns receiving the entire grant accorded to a school but they insisted that the nuns operate their schools in the best possible manner with respect to nourishing and clothing students. Oblate provincials also believed that the nuns should listen to and apply the wise advice they received from Oblate principals. Since these principals were responsible to the Department it was believed that their advice should be considered and adhered to as far as possible.[91] Conflicts of jurisdiction did not arise in the case of hospitals because the government confided the direction of those institutions directly to the sister superior and the Oblate superior attached to the local mission had no administrative function. With respect to schools, however, the Department came to insist that the Oblates assume total administrative responsibility.[92]

In addition to difficulties arising from overlapping functions personality conflicts, differences of opinion concerning pedagogy and the disciplining of students provided other avenues of contention between Oblates and members of female religious communities who collaborated with them. At the Saint Eugene Residential School in Cranbrook, British Columbia, relations between the Sisters of Providence and a succession of Oblate principals deteriorated to the point where the sisters became demoralized and withdrew from that institution in 1929.[93] In Cluny, where the same community worked in the school, Jacques Riou insisted that the sister superior respect his authority and threatened to leave if she did not. Riou also reminded the sisters of developments in Cranbrook and used this as a veiled threat.[94]

The school at Crooked Lake was plagued by a serious imbroglio involving the sisters and the principal. The controversy reached such proportions that Archbishop Langevin of St. Boniface became involved. The archbishop informed Théophile Campeau that relations between himself as principal and the sisters had to improve. Matters at the school were further complicated by the fact that the sisters were a cloistered community. Langevin's great fear was that if the sisters left as a result of problems emanating from differences of personality and philosophy between the principal and the mother superior, no other religious community would want to become involved with the school.[95] A short while later, Langevin informed Albert Lacombe that the principal and sisters were still at odds and that the school was facing bankruptcy. While Langevin believed that both sides were at fault he remained convinced, nevertheless, that the principal should be able to get along with the sisters.[96]

During an inspector's visit to the Blue Quills School at Saddle Lake in 1903, it became apparent that a student registered at the school had, in fact, been occupied at manual labour for the previous month and this had been done without the knowledge of the inspector or the principal. To complicate matters, another sister had placed some students in higher grades without notifying anyone to spare the students the shame associated with failing a grade. As principal, Léo Balter was called upon by the inspector to provide explanations and he rebuked the sisters for these uni-

△ △ *Construction of Blue Quills Residential School, St. Paul, Alberta.*
(PAA, OB 8607)

lateral actions.[97] On another occasion, Balter lamented the fact that as a
result of a quarrel with the sister superior, an Indian completely had
abandoned the practice of the Catholic religion.[98]

Oblate provincials were acutely aware of the necessity of harmonious
relations between missionaries and sisters in residential schools. Henri
Grandin, the Alberta-Saskatchewan provincial, informed Julien Moulin
in Hobbema that he should not hesitate to do what the sisters asked and
advised him to pay half of the cost of the stove they had requested.
According to Grandin, the interior painting at the school could be
delayed for some months without inconveniencing anyone whereas an act
of charity that provided assistance to the sisters would please them
immensely.[99] A few months later Grandin informed Moulin that he
regarded as "very reasonable" the sister superior's request that the Oblates
provide assistance in order that the students not suffer as a result of the
high cost of provisions. According to Grandin, the sisters would not be
able to properly nourish the children on the $72 per capita grant they
received. Moulin was advised to delay all repairs for the present time and
use the funds that has been saved to decrease the school's deficit to maintain food at adequate levels.[100]

At Lestock, the principal, Alphonse Dugas, discussed with his provincial the $100 per month salary requested by the nuns. Dugas stated that
the cost was not significant if one compared the salaries that would have

to be paid to lay persons. However, the principal complained that the superiors of the sisters paid little attention to the needs of residential schools when dispatching personnel. He claimed that they often sent to Indian schools sisters who were sick or who were not wanted elsewhere. One or two very proficient nuns were sent out to maintain appearances but the remainder were mediocre. To substantiate his contention Dugas described the *maîtresse de salle* as "the greatest nonentity that could be found under heaven's canopy."[101] The nuns had asked that the school provide their habits and Dugas expressed the concern that this request would open a Pandora's box. Furthermore, the nuns came with a very small trousseau and he was forced to provide them with garments. As for the sick sisters, Dugas claimed that the schools would be forced to purchase the tonics necessary to restore their health.[102]

The government's insistence that English be taught in Indian schools was reflected in the correspondence of many Oblate missionaries and became a source of contention between the missionaries, nuns and departmental officials. Discussing the need for sisters at the school he was establishing at Fort Pelly (Saskatchewan), Jules Decorby stated that it was imperative that at least one sister be capable of teaching English and that the community be acceptable to the Department.[103] On the Blood and Peigan Reserves, Joseph-Jean-Marie Lestanc alleged that children were not learning English because only one nun, the superior, knew the language but, unfortunately, she had little contact with the students outside regular class hours. He had given a talk to the sisters on the necessity of learning English and working to ensure the success of the school.[104] His colleague, Jean-Louis Le Vern, recorded in the *codex historicus* of St. Paul's Mission (Alberta) that the sisters at Stand Off were incapable of teaching English. According to Le Vern, the Department had complained of this state of affairs in 1898. The students were aware of this and discipline suffered. In 1905 after receiving the inspector's report, the Indian commissioner notified the school of the teacher's lack of English and asked that she be replaced by an English-speaking sister.[105]

The complaints of the Oblates and departmental officials had been brought to the attention of the mother house of the Grey Nuns in Nicolet but, as far as the Oblates were concerned, the situation did not improve. In 1922, the school inspector visited the school and indicated that the teacher was incompetent and suggested that she should take a few lessons from the sisters who operated the convent in Pincher Creek. Le Vern encouraged the local superior to agree to this recommendation and the teacher in question spent two weeks in Pincher Creek studying pedagogy with the Daughters of Jesus who operated a convent in that town.[106] When the sister superior on the Peigan Reserve was transferred to the school on the Blood Reserve, Le Vern at first pitied his colleague Eugène Ruaux. However, Le Vern soon regretted his initial reaction and alleged that the sister had been replaced by one whom he described as a "complete nullity." He also claimed that the sister who was responsible for the boys hated them and was in turn detested by the students. As a consequence, Le Vern was plagued by "a series of continual desertions" and he was at a loss as to how to remedy the situation.[107]

Nine years later, in 1933, François Blanchin, the new provincial of the Alberta-Saskatchewan province visited the Peigan Reserve. In the *codex historicus,* Le Vern noted that the most critical matter on that reserve as well as that of the Bloods was the inability of the sisters to provide adequate English language instruction. In the complaints raised by the Department on this matter Blanchin saw an underhanded persecution of the Oblates and their work. He also recognized that there was a lack of good will on the part of the sisters' mother house that obstinately refused for more than a quarter of a century to prepare qualified teachers despite the complaints that had been made by the Oblates.[108]

The competency of the sisters to provide instruction in English was also a problem at Pine Creek in 1902. When the sisters accepted to conduct the school, the matter of a nun who could teach English having responsibility for the boy's class had not been raised. The school had a nun who was able to teach English but she was sent elsewhere and replaced by an auxiliary sister who was unable to provide instruction in English.[109] The principal, Paul Bousquet, asked the superior general of the congregation to at least send an auxiliary sister who could teach English because such instruction was necessary in residential schools.[110]

Although English had to be taught in residential schools, Oblate provincials also insisted that missionaries attached to the school also learn the local Indian language. Thus, when Avila-Nectaire Ruelle was sent to Pine Creek as principal in 1905, he had to learn Saulteaux as well as teach English to the children.[111] With respect to the sisters, they were encouraged to study both Saulteaux and English but the emphasis was placed on the latter because it was believed that students would not make satisfactory progress without a knowledge of English. Thus, Ruelle insisted that English only be spoken in the school. The nuns received instructions from their provincial to speak only English to the children and she indicated her intention to provide a certified sister who could teach English.[112]

In Fort Alexander, the Grey Nuns did not have enough personnel to staff their hospitals and desired to be replaced as teachers in residential schools. Philippe Geelen claimed that, as a result, they had to be tolerated along with all their caprices. As principal, Geelen warned the Oblates at Fort Alexander to be on their guard and not to engender difficulties with the nuns. Geelen claimed that when he was at Lestock, the sisters had used sacramental wine to prepare medicinal tonics.[113]

On a more serious vein, Joseph Brachet of Pine Creek complained to his provincial in 1927 that the Benedictine Sisters were unable to continue at the school. According to Brachet, their main complaint was that they could not beat the girls as often as they wished. He cited the example of one nun who assisted another in inflicting corporal punishment on a girl for some alleged insignificant offense. This unwarranted punishment antagonized the other female students who attempted to escape en masse. In the night, they succeeded in breaking and opening the windows that Brachet had nailed shut as a precaution. Although the girls had been prevented from escaping, Brachet warned that they were still very agitated and that he expected more problems.[114]

In 1924, Jacques Riou wrote a lengthy report to Bishop McNally outlining the reasons for the lack of success in the evangelization of the Blackfoot. He claimed that one major obstacle had been the lack of mutual support between sisters and principal. He attributed this to the spirit of independence among the sisters who wanted to direct things their own way. According to Riou, the sisters had to recognize the fact that residential schools were not orphanages, that pupils in these institutions were wards of the government and had a right to an education. The principal was responsible to the Department and, to simplify matters, finances had been left in the hands of the sisters. According to Riou, sisters, like all other employees, were subject to the principal and this was the source of the problem. The sisters wished to be independent not only in regards to the per capita grant but also in the general management of the school. They wanted complete authority over students and the utilization of class time.

Riou affirmed that this lack of cooperation had disastrous results because the Indians complained their children learned nothing in school whereas the Department expected more for the funds it had expended. The sisters did not respect missionaries and did everything to promote their own self-interest. They could not expect to make pupils speak proper English when they continued to speak French in their presence. The sisters had lost the confidence of pupils, as well as that of former students and this lack of popularity created difficulties for recruitment. According to Riou, the only remedy was to replace the sister superior at the school and then clearly explain to the others what was expected of them and identify the areas outside their jurisdiction.[115]

The partnership between the Oblates and the government to provide education for Indians did not put an end to earlier attempts by the missionaries to establish schools on a more modest basis. At Fort Cumberland, for example, Ovide Charlebois began teaching local children four hours a day in November 1890. He sent a report on the activities of his school to the lieutenant-governor of the Northwest Territories and asked for a grant but this request was refused.[116] Circumstances on some reserves caused the Oblates to put aside their advocacy of residential schools and support the establishment of a day school when the latter appeared to be the only alternative to not having a Catholic school of any kind. In 1914, Louis Dauphin urged the establishment of a day school at Le Goff, Alberta. Despite the disadvantages presented by that type of school, Dauphin believed that it was the only way to gather the children for catechism. Furthermore, local Natives were reluctant to send their children to the school at Onion Lake because it was too distant.[117] At Portage La Loche, in 1922, Jean-Baptiste Ducharme conducted school on a seasonal basis in the period November to June when hunters left their wives and children close to the mission. In the morning he taught an hour of catechism, in the evening syllabic script, mathematics and singing.[118]

If the association of the government was necessary to the Oblates in their educational endeavours, the participation of the Native population was an even greater imperative. There were features within Native society, however, that made the establishment of schools difficult and impeded

△ △ *Jean-Baptiste Ducharme teaching catechism to a group of*
Dene children at Portage la Loche, Saskatchewan, 1939. (AD)

the educational process. On the Peigan Reserve, the Indians lived in small groups of four or five lodges spread out along the Old Man River and this dispersal made it very difficult for the Oblates to reach the children and get them to attend classes.[119] In the region of Rivière Qui Barre (Alberta), the Oblates were confronted with a another demographic problem in that Catholic Assiniboines were dispersed among different reserves and they attempted to convince them of the advantages of grouping themselves in one reserve.[120]

The chief and councilors of the Alexander Reserve met with the Oblates and asked them to secure the establishment of an industrial school on their reserve. The Indians also wanted the school to be staffed by nuns who would educate and nurse the children. The Assiniboines did not want to send their children to the Oblate facility in St. Albert because it was not a *bona fide* industrial school nor did they wish to send them to Dunbow. For their part, the Oblates had no choice but to attempt to convince the Indians to send their children to their existing establishment in St. Albert.[121] At Blackfoot Crossing, a Protestant boarding school was built at a short distance from the Oblate mission in 1894. Albert Lacombe had promised the Blackfoot earlier that a Catholic school would be built and, with the establishment of the Protestant institution, the Natives were upset with the Oblates for not keeping their promise and, hence, they allowed the minister to recruit their children.[122]

The Oblates entertained high hopes for their educational institutions but, on the whole, these objectives were not realized. To begin with, the vision of the perfect Christian that would be fashioned by these institutions was defective. Residential schools worked on the principle of directed cultural change, that is, the replacement of a traditional culture by a modern one in a carefully controlled environment and in a short period of time. "Cultural replacement" was rejected overwhelmingly by Indians who would have preferred "cultural synthesis" whereby they could have been free to borrow and adapt elements of the modern culture to suit their own needs and ensure their own identity and survival.[123]

Since this latter option was not possible, Indians adopted various defence mechanisms to resist being transformed into Euro-Canadians with darker complexions. As in the fur trade era, Indians demonstrated great resiliency and learned to exploit market factors to their advantage. Practices established in the early fur trade and missionary periods became institutionalized in the era of residential schools. Like the trading post and the mission, residential schools were an avenue of welfare for Indians who were able to exact certain conditions as a prerequisite to the admittance of their children. Parents could insist on being housed and fed while visiting their children even if this ran counter to the regulations of the Department. In Kenora, for example, some Indians who sent their children to that institution did so on the express condition that their children not be baptized by the Oblates.[124] Indians were also quick to exploit the presence of a mission or school belonging to a rival denomination or to seek the intercession of the Indian agent to promote their own ends. For their part, students could escape and, in some instances, they adopted the ultimate form of resistance by setting fire to the school and destroying it. In Pine Creek, one student made three attempts to set fire to the school.[125] Not all attempts were unsuccessful and, in the case of Pine Creek, 13 persons lost their lives in the conflagration of 25 February 1929.[126]

In addition to transmitting a radically different culture and values, residential schools were physically alien to Native society. In terms of architecture, the large rectangular structures cannot be said to have blended in with the landscape nor did the buildings reflect forms that were familiar or meaningful to the Indians they housed. In addition to being unattractive, the schools reflected a restrictive and highly structured milieu. The food was strange, the surroundings unfamiliar, family and friends were distant and the language was different. The limited capacity of residential schools also served to undermine Oblate objectives.

Once these children left the school, the Oblates did not have the resources or personnel to maintain frequent and close contact with them and when they returned to their reserves there was a pronounced tendency to return to traditional and familiar cultural and spiritual practices. The Oblates lamented this tendency and to counter it, principals sought to maintain contact with former students by means of visits to reserves and the inauguration of associations of graduates.[127] Both the visits to reserves and the alumni associations were designed to at least sustain and, if possible, enhance the Christian traditions previously inculcated by the school. For its part, the federal government was also frustrated with the results produced by schools and this disenchantment was reflected in administrative changes. The per capita grant system was introduced to reduce expenses and the curriculum was altered as defects in the original vision became apparent. The government increased and centralized its control by acquiring ownership of residential schools in the 1920s and introducing compulsory school legislation.

If the earlier period of missionary activity sometimes produced "tobacco Indians," that is, Natives who converted because of the material goods provided by missionaries, residential schools often produced a sterile, outward conformity to Christian values and traditions. By the 1930s, however, many Oblates were expressing concern with the results of their missionary efforts in general and that of residential schools in particular. They came to realize that their missions and schools had been, and remained, artificial creations that had not been incorporated successfully into the Native milieu. If these basic institutions were foreign elements, how firmly entrenched was the Christianity they had implanted? What was the essence of that Christianity?

The answer to these fundamental questions required a critical examination of Oblate missiology, activities and objectives. This evaluation and subsequent directives designed to transform Christianity into a more meaningful and expression of spirituality for Natives were provided by the canonical visit of northern and western missions by Superior General Théodore Labouré in 1935–36 and the recommendations contained in his report.

△ △ △ △ △ △ △ △ △ △ △ △ △ △ △

9

THE OBLATES AND
THE FEDERAL GOVERNMENT

A Tenuous Relationship

The association between the Oblates and the federal government to provide education to Indians brought about a significant change in traditional relationships in the North West. Prior to this collaboration, the Oblates had interacted primarily with the Hudson's Bay Company and, in general, this relationship had been amicable and produced strong bonds of trust and friendship because Oblate and trader shared a similar lifestyle and worked in the same environment with and were dependent upon the First Nations. Although mission and trade post each had a distinct sphere of influence, the efforts of one contributed to the welfare of the other. In the early stages of the Oblate establishment, the relationship between the Oblates and the federal authorities was distant and minimal. Individual bishops made requests to the government to provide assistance in various forms to the schools and orphanages that had been established in the larger missions. The most significant bureaucratic threat to Oblate interests was a proposal in 1879 to end the duty-free exemption for goods destined for missions. Informing a friend of this change in legislation, Bishop Alexandre Taché of Saint Boniface said that it was "very painful" to learn that the return to power of "friends" had engendered new problems for the missions.[1]

After 1880, however, such concerns paled in comparison to new ones that emerged as a result of the assumption of increased responsibilities by the Canadian government after the acquisition of the North West and the signing of treaties with the Native populations. While there was a similarity of interests between the government's attempts to "civilize" the First Nations by attempting to transform them into sedentary farmers and Oblate efforts to Christianize them, it did not produce an amicable relationship and a sense of trust. To begin with, the Oblate missions and the federal bureaucracy were separated by distance, class and culture. Furthermore, as legal guardians of Indians the federal government enjoyed a status and a prestige superior to that of the missionaries.

The Oblates were not the only contenders for the favour of the federal authorities and, as time passed, there was a growing suspicion in their minds that the authorities were discriminating deliberately against their missionaries and institutions and catering to the interests of Protestant ones. Some of the frustrations and suspicions of the Oblates were due to the fact that, initially, they were overly optimistic concerning the beneficial consequences of the treaties on their apostolic work. Vital Grandin hoped that the treaties and establishment of reserves would foster the evangelization of the Indian tribes by weaning them away from the hunt. Consequently, to facilitate the evangelization of Indians in the Treaty 6 area, the establishment of a mission was proposed near Fort Pitt where it would be possible to serve the bands living on the six reserves located between Île à la Crosse and Fort Pitt. After the mission was built, the Indians no longer came because the authorities would not allow them to leave their respective reserves. In effect, these regulations precluded the Oblates from gathering the Indians in camps as had been done in the past. To continue their apostolic work the Oblates would have to establish themselves on the reserves.[2]

In the meantime, Protestant missionaries were also aware of the importance and advantages of locating themselves on reserves. Problems did not arise when the Oblates or Protestant missionaries established themselves on a reserve but after the initial establishment that, in effect, created a confessional monopoly for one group. As bishop, Grandin believed responsible for the spiritual welfare of Catholic Indians on reserves where the Oblates had not established themselves in a permanent manner. As could be expected, conflict and controversy arose when Grandin extended this responsibility to include the Catholic minority on reserves where there was a Protestant establishment.[3] For its part, the Department of Indian Affairs preferred to divide reserves among the different denominations and, given the problems associated with separate schools in the larger Canadian community, did not look too kindly on the prospect of competing missions or schools on any reserve. The policy of the Department was to allow missionaries as much freedom as possible in the exercise of their duties but, in the final analysis, the Department was bound to respect the wishes of the Indians in all matters dealing with their reserve.

Be that as it may, Grandin interpreted the attitude of the authorities as an anti-Catholic sentiment. He stated that there had to be a good entente between church and state and that he had done everything in his power to promote that objective and asserted that the authorities had not demonstrated the same good will. Grandin felt that he could make no additional compromises and had to make a firm stand on the question of liberty of conscience of Indians.[4] As a witness to the signing of Treaty 6 at Fort Pitt in 1876, Grandin contended that Indians had been told they were free to have whatever missionaries they pleased and, furthermore, once they were settled on their reserves, they would receive whatever schools they requested.[5] He claimed that, rather than abide by this fundamental principle, the government decided to divide reserves among the different denominations regardless of the wishes of the inhabitants of the reserves in question. According to Grandin, when Indians requested that he send missionaries to their reserve, the authorities invited rival Protestants on the pretext that Catholics already had numerous missions. In cases where Protestants were already established on a reserve, Grandin claimed that he was refused permission to send missionaries even if Catholics were in a majority on that reserve. Grandin defended the right of Natives to choose their missionaries and he alleged that neither the government nor its bureaucrats had any say in the matter. Furthermore, a majority, regardless of its size, had to respect the rights of the minority.[6]

As a result of difficulties with officials and the desire to obtain more support for his institutions, Grandin went to Ottawa in 1883 to present a petition to the prime minister and his associates. After four months of waiting, Grandin was becoming disenchanted with Macdonald's promise that action would be forthcoming and that matters would be attended to by Lieutenant-Governor Dewdney of the Northwest Territories. Through his intermediary, Hippolyte Leduc, Grandin let it be known that he was tired of polite phrases and promises.[7] Even more frustrating to Grandin was that he had no written confirmation of verbal promises made to him by Macdonald a month earlier. After six months of waiting in vain for that written declaration Grandin decided to return to the North West and he implored the prime minister: "For God [sic] sake don't disappoint me."[8]

Despite reassurances received on the eve of his departure, Grandin's problems with bureaucrats not only continued but escalated. Consequently, two years later, in 1885, the bishop was again in Ottawa requesting an interview with Macdonald "on any day that may be found convenient."[9] The following year, in 1886, Leduc and other Oblates were requesting an appointment with Macdonald and the minister of the Interior.[10] In the meantime, a frustrated Grandin wrote to Taché seeking the archbishop's support to save Catholic missions on Indian reservations. Grandin complained that government policy was making it impossible for him to establish missions on reserves. Grandin alleged that once a mission was built, the authorities moved the Indians and the establishment served no useful purpose as was the case at Lac Ste. Anne, Lac La Nonne and Muskeg Lake (Saskatchewan). In other instances, Indians on reserves had been allowed to take scrip and were *ipso facto* outside the reserve while the Oblates were left with the expenses and the teachers they had recruited in central Canada for these reserves.[11] Grandin also sent a detailed memorandum on outstanding issues to Sir Hector Langevin and it was forwarded to Macdonald.

Finally, on 9 December 1886, the prime minister replied to Grandin agreeing that the religious liberty of Indians should be respected and protected and that no Indian would be denied advantages given to others because of religious affiliation. Macdonald also agreed that missionaries should be free to exercise their ecclesiastical functions without interference from the Department of Indian Affairs and its officers. Indians were also to be free to embrace the religion of their choice and should not be compelled to abandon missions that had been established for them. Macdonald also agreed that officials were not to insist that Indians send their children to a school that did not reflect their religious affiliation.[12]

Despite the assurances contained in the prime minister's letter, events in the diocese convinced Grandin that the discrimination against and persecution of Catholics had not ceased. One year later, Grandin complained that the government had not understood a crucial factor, that is, that under the treaties Indians had a right to confessional schools determined by the religion of the majority on a reserve. According to Grandin, in overlooking this principle the government had occupied itself with dividing the reserves among the different religious groups. He proposed that before building a school the Department should undertake a census to determine the religion of the majority and designate the school accordingly. The religious minority would be entitled to a separate school if its numbers warranted.[13] Grandin also approached federal Conservatives from Quebec such as Sir Hector Langevin and Adolphe Chapleau and, while they seemed well disposed, he was not impressed with their efforts.[14] He described French Canadian cabinet ministers as small boys who answered "amen" to everything Macdonald said. According to Grandin, Macdonald was a crafty person who put people off with fine words but, in reality, accorded the least possible.[15]

Grandin interpreted the appointment of Edgar Dewdney as minister of the Interior and superintendent general of Indian Affairs in 1888 and that of Hayter Reed as Indian commissioner as a slight to Catholics. Dewdney allegedly had declared himself against Catholics as the end of his term as lieutenant governor of the Northwest Territories and had supported Reed's harassment of Catholics.[16] When Dewdney entered politics Catholics had campaigned for the appointment of a co-religionist as Indian commissioner or as assistant commissioner. For his part, Reed was keenly aware of the delicate nature of these appointments and he suggested that Amédée Forget, then clerk of the territorial Council should be named assistant commissioner to placate the Catholic element.[17]

Forget's appointment, while it was a practical diplomatic measure, did not significantly alter Grandin's conviction that Catholics were being discriminated against. As time passed and redress for Catholic grievances was not forthcoming, Grandin became convinced that Catholics were the victims of a Protestant conspiracy and that drastic measures were necessary to remedy the situation.[18] In December 1889, Grandin informed Dewdney that, despite years of complaints, the grievances and abuses were still evident. The bishop believed that orders to discriminate against Catholics were being issued from the upper echelons of the department and Dewdney had to accept the responsibility since he was its head.[19]

In the meantime, Grandin prepared a lengthy memorandum on his difficulties over the years with the Department of Indian Affairs. After studying the document Deputy Superintendent General Lawrence Vankoughnet reported to his superior that the Department and its personnel were bound by a policy of strict neutrality in religious matters on reserves. Not only did the Department not interfere in religious affairs, it gave missionaries every possible latitude to establish themselves on reserves so long as the Indians did not object. Vankoughnet was very critical of Grandin's allegations that Protestant agents had discriminated against Catholic missionaries and their institutions and suggested that the bishop should provide specific examples of the government's failure to maintain neutrality. According to Vankoughnet, the suggestion that departmental personnel conspired against Catholics to please their superiors was another "gratuitous allegation." He also advised his superior that replacing Protestant agents by Catholic ones would not guarantee impartial treatment to Protestant Indians and missionaries.[20]

While Grandin was not convinced by Vankoughnet's analysis and comments he, nevertheless, would have been surprised to learn that Protestants also had their grievances against the Department and its policy. Cyprian Pinkham, the Anglican Bishop of Calgary, complained to Commissioner Hayter Reed that the Oblates had invaded Anglican territory and built a school on the Blood Reserve. Although he was of the Anglican persuasion, Reed was scrupulous in his efforts to be both diplomatic and neutral in the controversies that embroiled Catholic and Protestant missionaries. In his reply to Pinkham, the Commissioner stressed that the school first had been offered to the Anglicans but the Bloods would not agree to this and the Department was obliged to respect their wishes.[21] In all probability, Pinkham found this explanation as reassuring as those received by Grandin.

In the meantime, the secretary of the Church Missionary Society drew Reed's attention to another flagrant violation of the Anglican Church's status this time on the Thunderchild Reserve. The Anglicans had been the first to establish themselves on that reserve and the Oblates were now attempting to establish their own school and he wondered how Anglicans could "be expected to promote our work if the Papists are granted everything they demand." The secretary went on to allege that Anglicans had been forced out of the Sweetgrass Reserve because the Department saw fit to support Catholic claims.[22] When Archdeacon Mackay of Prince Albert was advised that the Indian Act allowed the establishment of a separate

school such as that on the Thunderchild Reserve, he urged Reed to protect the Indians from becoming the pawns of "narrow minded bigotry
and sectarian animosity." Mackay reminded the commissioner that the
Anglican Church has always worked "faithfully and loyally" with the
Department and had always abstained from establishing itself on reserves
where other denominations were already present.[23]

Administrators such as Reed had to exercise "the most judicious application of diplomacy" in dealing with "temperamental ecclesiastics."[24] Not
only were they confronted with bitter prejudices and rivalries between
denominations, there were instances where it was difficult, if not impossible, to discern the true views of the residents of a reserve with respect to
confessionality and its corresponding impact on education. In the case of
the Thunderchild Reserve, the Department contended that the chief and
a majority of the residents were opposed to the establishment of a
Catholic school and, hence the Department could not authorize one.[25]
For his part, Grandin argued that Catholic Indians on the reserve had
never been asked whether they would support a Catholic school nor had
they ever voted on the matter in an assembly. He claimed furthermore
that Catholics were in a majority on the reserve and that a minority was
depriving them of a school of their choice.[26]

Consequently, in August 1890, Grandin went to Ottawa in a final
attempt to put an end to the long standing controversy and to present
Dewdney with a summary of complaints against the Department.[27]
Grandin insisted on a rigorous observation of Macdonald's promises to
protect the liberty of conscience of Indians and allow missionaries to
exercise their duties freely. As a refinement of these principles, Grandin
wanted the Department to prevent Catholic children from being admitted to Protestant schools, to place Catholic children under the supervision of Catholic inspectors, to observe neutrality in religious matters and
to appoint civil servants professing the same faith as the Indians they
served.[28] The bishop sent a copy of his memoir to Macdonald and
affirmed that if the substance of the prime minister's letter of 9 December
1886 had been obeyed there would be no problems between Catholics
and the Department.[29]

While the question of liberty of conscience was a central concern for
Grandin, other related issues surfaced and troubled the Oblates. On
numerous occasions Archbishop Taché had drawn Macdonald's attention

to what he regarded as blatant discrimination against Catholics within the Department of Indian Affairs and suggested that a word from the prime minister "would smooth many difficulties and remove much unpleasantness."[30] With respect to the complaints of the Catholic hierarchy against the Department, Taché alleged that Catholics were excluded from the Regina office, there was no Catholic Indian agent in the North West and there were difficulties in establishing schools as a result of the poor disposition of the Department. According to Taché, officials in the Department sympathized with those of their own faith and Catholics were disadvantaged because they had no one in positions of authority. He claimed, furthermore, that the low salary paid to teachers in Indian schools "works more severely against us than against others."[31]

In 1889, on behalf of the bishops of the Ecclesiastical Province of St. Boniface, Taché lodged a formal complaint against the Department of Indian Affairs before the governor-general in Council. He argued that Catholics were being discriminated against because most of the Department's employees were Protestant. There were only a few Catholics among the 40 officials and employees in Ottawa, two among the 18 employees in the Indian Commissioner's office in Regina and only two Catholic Indian agents among the 25 in treaty areas one to seven. Taché concluded his memorial with a reminder that when Canada assumed jurisdiction over the North West the six bishops in the Ecclesiastical Province collectively had 114 years of service in the West and had exercised a salutary influence over the Indian population and prepared the way for the extension of Canadian authority over the region. The bishops were humiliated that they had been dealt with "as if we were men against whom it is necessary to guard, even in the interests of Indians."[32]

As a result of these long standing grievances and Grandin's memoir, Indian Commissioner Reed sent a circular to all employees and agencies on 31 October 1890 clearly stating that the Department insisted on "strict neutrality" in religious matters "and will not tolerate any difference of treatment based directly or indirectly upon Denominational prejudice." Officers and employees were also reminded that all missionaries were to be free to exercise their ministry among the Indians and that any request to erect buildings to be used for religious purposes were to be sent to the commissioner with a statement indicating whether or not the Indians were in favour of the proposal.[33] Indian agents were instructed to make a complete report of any admission of children of one denomination admitted to schools operated by another in order that each case be dealt with individually.[34] Dewdney went over the issues raised in Grandin's memoir and informed the bishop that when cases of "unfair or unjust treatment" of Catholics were brought to his attention, "the Department will see that the wrong done is promptly rectified."[35]

Although the circular and other communications clearly spelled out the Department's neutrality in religious matters, accusations of discrimination continued. In 1895, Théophile Campeau complained that the government was falsifying its statistics to declare three reserves Protestant. He alleged that an attempt was made to silence him by declaring his reserve to be Catholic.[36] The following year, Joseph Lestanc complained that he had been advised by the Indian agent on the Sarcee Reserve that he could no longer hold religious services on the reserve because it created problems for the agent. Indian Commissioner Amédée Forget informed Lestanc that the agent had acted improperly and, in so doing, had contravened the Department's policy of strict neutrality. Obviously aware of the delicate nature of the situation, Forget expressed the wish "to see a cordial feeling existing among the different denominations and a desire on the part of each to refrain from entering small fields already occupied by others."[37]

While the Oblates succeeded in having the Department commit itself to a policy of neutrality to protect the liberty of conscience of Indians, the attempt to secure the employment of more Catholics within the Indian Affairs bureaucracy would prove far more difficult. However, given the importance the Oblates attached to Catholic employees within the bureaucracy, they were prepared to press the matter. In 1888, Taché and Grandin along with other prominent western Oblates and Catholic laymen petitioned Macdonald to appoint Angus McKay, an Indian agent in the Manitoba superintendency, to the position of assistant commissioner. McKay was described as a good and honest agent in addition to being of mixed blood and Catholic. Macdonald was reminded that there were no Catholic Indian agents in the North West, only three Catholic farm instructors and only one Catholic employee in Regina.[38] As a result of difficulties on the Alexander Reserve the government agreed in principle to the appointment of a Catholic agent but nearly two years were to pass before the appointment was made.[39]

Grandin also believed that many of the problems associated with Catholic reserves could be resolved and to some extent eliminated if such reserves employed Catholic officials and, furthermore, if Catholic schools on reserves were the jurisdiction of Catholic inspectors. In 1887, Grandin had informed Thomas White, then minister of the Interior, that the main source of conflict between the government and himself was because most of the government employees in his diocese were Protestant. Grandin requested that more Catholic agents should be employed at least on those reserves where the majority of Indians were Catholic. White recognized the necessity of employing Catholics and was willing to appoint a Catholic inspector on the condition that the person was not a clergyman. At this juncture Grandin was somewhat embarrassed because, after having made the request, he did not have a candidate to put forward and he sought Taché's assistance in finding one.[40] White had given Grandin assurances that this inspector, while being a representative of the Department, would also relate to the bishops to ensure that Catholic rights in educational matters were respected. A Catholic inspector was appointed but, in the meantime, White died and, according to Grandin, the assurances provided by the minister "had been buried with him."[41] Much to Grandin's dismay, the appointment of a Catholic inspector did not produce the anticipated results. To begin with, Joseph Hugonnard, of the Qu'Appelle Industrial School in Saskatchewan, declared that he had no use for such an individual. For his part, Grandin claimed that he did not know where the inspector was or what he was doing. Worse yet, the number of complaints against the Department and its officials had increased rather than decreased since the inspector's appointment.[42]

In their dealings with the federal authorities the western Oblate bishops were aware that they were disadvantaged by not having a spokesman to represent them in Ottawa. Consequently, they could not act collectively but individually with the result that their actions were uncoordinated and lacked a central thrust. Albert Lacombe had suggested that the Oblates establish an institution similar to the Bureau for Catholic Missions in Washington, D.C., which represented and promoted the interests of Catholic Indian missions in the United States. Lacombe believed that such an institution would do an immense good for the Oblate missions of the North West and spare the bishops of having to travel to Ottawa.[43] Grandin suggested a less expensive undertaking that would involve one or two Oblates in Ottawa being designated grand vicars of the western bishops.[44] In the meantime, Henri Tabaret, rector of the University of Ottawa acted as Grandin's representative in the national capital. Tabaret died in 1886, and was replaced by Edmond Gendreau, another Oblate professor at the same university. In May 1888, Gendreau had a long interview with Macdonald on the subject of Grandin's complaints. Macdonald claimed to be confused because the information provided by the Department contradicted that furnished by the bishop. Gendreau suggested that the prime minister appoint a trustworthy person to undertake an inquiry into the legitimacy of Catholic grievances. Macdonald indicated his complete confidence in Gendreau and asked him to undertake the investigation.[45]

Gendreau's superiors were at first reluctant to allow him to undertake the inquiry but finally consented. Gendreau began by presenting the documents dealing with Catholic grievances in English to Macdonald. With the death of Thomas White, Macdonald had assumed responsibility for the Indian Affairs but Gendreau claimed that nothing had been gained because he preferred to deal with the late minister.[46] In July 1888, Gendreau began to visit reserves in the diocese of Saint Albert but admitted his investigation was more officious than official. Very little resulted from his visit and the Oblates who were serving in the missions thought that it was all window dressing to placate Catholics and make it possible for the perpetrators of injustices to continue.[47] According to the report published in the Oblate periodical *Missions,* Gendreau was able to establish the validity of Oblate grievances against the Department and wanted to present a written report of his investigation but he was only allowed to make a verbal one with the result that his mission had little or no effect.[48] Albert Lacombe described Gendreau's visit of the western missions as a comedy and a farce because he was nothing but the puppet of the government and the congregation in the province of Quebec.[49]

Be that as it may, Gendreau continued to represent the western bishops. In January 1889, he was present at a meeting between Taché, J.H. Pope and Macdonald in which the archbishop presented his own grievances concerning the Department of Indian Affairs.[50] Cognizant of his precarious status, Gendreau informed Alexandre Blanchet that if the Oblates were aware of how difficult it was to obtain something from the government for the western missions they would be more lenient in their judgment of him. Gendreau claimed that it was difficult to obtain justice from the government let alone a favour but he did not despair. He reminded Blanchet that the Oblates had to deal with a Protestant administration and with Dewdney whom he described as "the most fanatic of all."[51]

In the meantime, the western Oblates continued to press the congregation to regularize Gendreau's status and asked the superior general to appoint him their *chargé d'affaires* to the federal authorities. In 1891, Gendreau was named the official representative of the western bishops vis-à-vis the federal government and the Department of Indian Affairs.[52] Lacombe, who had been critical of Gendreau's 1888 visit because the envoy lacked an authoritative status, was pleased with the appointment.[53] Grandin believed that he needed the services of a younger enterprising priest such as Gendreau because he and the other missionaries were old and burdened with routines that were difficult to change.[54]

Unfortunately, Gendreau's appointment did not put an end to all the outstanding issues between the Oblates and the federal authorities. A few months after Gendreau's appointment, Lacombe informed him that there was trouble between Dewdney and himself over the hospital on the Blood Reserve. Lacombe thought that the government wanted to deceive him and, if that were the case, he promised to do everything in his power to publicize the matter.[55] In 1894, Grandin informed Gendreau of the death of the Catholic farm instructor on the Poundmaker Reserve. With the death of this individual, there were no Catholic employees on the reserve and it was imperative to replace him with another Catholic. According to Grandin the agent was opposed to Catholics and his subordinates shared his views.[56]

Gendreau continued to act as the official representative of the western bishops until 1898 when the government sent him to investigate Indian reserves in the Yukon.[57] After Gendreau's departure, the western Oblate bishops negotiated with the federal government on an individual basis and there was a considerable delay before another representative was named. In the meantime, while the Oblates lacked an official voice their views still carried considerable influence in administrative circles. Early in the twentieth century the federal government was considering abolishing industrial schools because of high operating costs. A member of the Missionary Society for the Canadian Church, Samuel H. Blake, had been appointed to chair a committee investigating Anglican Indian missions and he challenged "the correctness of pleasant reports" sent to the MSCC by its missionaries. Blake believed that Indian schools were too costly and inefficient and argued that the government should assume more responsibility for their cost and administration.[58] Blake enlisted the support of the missionary secretaries of the Methodist and Presbyterian Churches and corresponded with Frank Oliver, the minister of the Interior. While the latter appeared to support the concept of secularization of Indian education, Blake was informed that the government would not proceed to implement that objective because of opposition from Catholics. In actual fact, Blake was a voice crying in the wilderness because neither Anglican, Methodist nor Presbyterian "were really anxious to dismantle their educational programs."[59]

In view of the critique made by Blake and the importance of Indian residential education to the Oblate Apostolate, the Oblates were keenly aware of the necessity of having a representative to make their views known to the federal government and to protect their vested interests. The appointment of a career civil servant, Duncan Campbell Scott, as deputy superintendent of Indian Affairs in 1913 marked a turning point in the management of the Department that, henceforth, would be more cost effective and centralized. Finally in 1920, Joseph Guy was appointed to replace Gendreau but not in an official capacity because his superiors feared that his duties would become too time consuming.[60] While this was not to the liking of some of the western Oblates, Guy was not concerned. He claimed that, in being allowed by his superiors to continue his work, he was doing no less than if he had been given an official title by the Oblates. More important, Guy claimed that the Department regarded him as an official representative and treated him accordingly.[61]

For their part, Oblate principals such as Jacques Riou in Cluny were convinced that an official representative in Ottawa was needed to publicize the work of the schools and to ensure impartial treatment by the Department. Riou contended that it was better to deal directly with the superintendent general rather than by written submissions that were not understood or acted upon by subordinates. It is not known whether Riou was aware of the true status of Guy's position but, nevertheless, he thought that in Guy the Oblates now had someone to communicate with and who could personally present their requests to the superintendent general.[62]

Within the congregation and its missions and residential schools in the North West, Guy's appointment was indicative of a degree of administrative maturity and a professionalization of function. As their representative in Ottawa Guy not only brought the concerns of the Oblate principals to the attention of the authorities, he also prepared detailed instructions on how to prepare their submissions especially matters related to budgets and expenses. Budgets were to be prepared in October; they were to be carefully itemized in appropriate categories, justified and prioritized. Current expenses were to be discussed with the local Indian agent but Guy suggested that a copy of the relative correspondence should be sent to him to allow him to supervise matters and provide information as the need arose.[63] Guy claimed that in general the Department was well disposed to Oblate schools and recognized that the administration of those schools was superior to all others. Guy placed himself at the disposal of the principals to maintain that status and to ensure that the Oblate schools received the grants to which they were entitled. In turn, principals could assist him by heeding his suggestions on how to prepare their requests and by providing accurate information.[64]

As the representative of the western Oblates, Guy preferred diplomacy and tact to direct confrontation. He advised principals who had complaints against the Department or its officials to attempt to resolve these differences amicably. If this did not produce the desired result, Guy would use his official position to register a formal complaint. He advised principals to formulate their grievances in a "clear and concise manner." Most important, he cautioned that violent or insulting letters should never be addressed to the Department. If such comments deserved to be made they were to be expressed verbally.[65]

While Guy's philosophy was to avoid direct confrontation, he was not afraid to act decisively if the situation warranted such measures. There had been a long standing confrontation between Indian Commissioner William Graham and other religious denominations and, in 1924, Guy informed the Manitoba provincial that the Oblates had to support a resolution seeking the removal of Graham from office. Guy added that the Anglicans and Methodists were also dissatisfied and would support the resolution.[66] In the meantime, Graham resolved his problems within the Department and insisted that Guy put an end to the agitation in Ottawa to have him removed from office. Oblate principals thought that it would be preferable if the Oblates ceased their opposition to the commissioner. Otherwise, it was feared that Guy would be the victim of Graham's reprisals and his influence as representative would be negated.[67] For his part, Graham advised Deputy Superintendent General Scott not to inform Guy and representatives of other denominations of the appropriations voted by Parliament for residential schools but Scott refused to withhold such information from Guy and the other denominations.[68]

While it was impossible to conciliate Graham, Guy's tact and diplomacy facilitated his function as intermediary between the Department and the Oblates. Informing Pierre Moulin of Hobbema that he had been unable to secure the grant that had been requested for certain pupils, Guy stated he had discussed the matter in detail with two officials. When it became apparent that the Department would not agree, Guy dropped the matter because to persist would have done more harm than good.[69] But, Guy was quick to inform principals that if they refused too often to do the Department's bidding, they would expose their own requests to total refusals. Guy informed Paul Bousquet of Fort Alexander that his attitude was straining the good relations between the officers of the Department and the Oblates. Contrary to what other principals did, Bousquet believed that construction and reparations at the school were to be undertaken uniquely at government expense because the school was the property of the state. Bousquet was advised to contribute to such expenses because experience had demonstrated that in helping oneself much more could be obtained.[70] Guy's prestige was such that he was asked to visit the Province of Alberta-Saskatchewan in 1925 to assist the provincial in organizing residential schools for the purpose of establishing better relations with the Department.[71] The following year, in 1926, Guy was asked to visit the Mackenzie district where the Oblates were experiencing difficulties with the Department concerning the establishment of a school and hospital. Given Guy's influence in government circles, it was thought that if he came to evaluate the situation he would be in a better position to defend and present the requests made by the Oblates.[72]

At the same time that Guy was professionalizing the role of Ottawa representative and making that office more influential, Oblate principals began to adopt procedures used by their secular counterparts. In 1924 the Oblate principals of Indian schools held their first convention in Lebret. The purpose of this meeting, which, henceforth, would be held annually, was to unify administrative practices in schools, and improve the education given to students. The principals also wanted to familiarize themselves with the educational goals of the Department and cooperate more efficiently with the bureaucracy.[73] The 1925 convention passed resolutions requesting the establishment of a special programme of studies for Catholic residential schools, the designation of one Oblate school as a centre of higher education and another for vocational education, and the continued supervision of the progress of former students when they returned to their reserves.[74] In the case of these resolutions, the greater professionalization and efficiency on the part of the Oblates was not matched by that of the authorities who procrastinated despite Guy's insistence on a prompt reply. This delay caused Guy to inform a colleague that "the dilatoriness of the federal bureaucracy could envy that of Rome."[75]

The conventions also dealt with matters of immediate concern for principals and Indian schools. The 1926 meeting recommended the replacement of the Butler catechism by McVeigh's. In some schools there were three different catechisms in use and the principals thought that religious instruction suffered as a result.[76] In 1934, the convention of principals in the Oblate Province of Alberta-Saskatchewan made recommendations on the language issue in Indian residential schools, an issue that was creating problems with inspectors who insisted on the use of English. The Oblate principals passed resolutions favouring the use of Native languages in morning and evening prayers and in religious instruction. Some principals argued that it was cruel to insist on the use of English during recreation.[77] The principals also recommended that an indirect supervision be maintained over graduates after they left school. The principals also regarded marriage between graduates as the crowning point in the school's programme and these marriages were a guarantee for the future. In these circumstances, the school provided the trousseau for the bride. Given the importance the Oblates attached to marriage, the separation of spouses was regarded as a veritable scourge on reserves. Since the Department had no regulations curtailing separations, the principals wanted each band to pass a law condemning them.[78]

The 1934 convention also dealt with issues of a very practical nature that in the past had created difficulties and, if left unresolved, could heighten tensions between the Oblates and officials of the Department.

The principals acknowledged that teachers in residential schools had to be qualified to discharge their duties and that the congregation would have to offer a reasonable salary to obtain such personnel. Other members of religious communities who interacted with the pupils had to possess a sufficient knowledge of English. With respect to the superior of the nuns, the least the Oblates could ask was that she too be equal to the task, that she be able to speak English and be able to welcome officials of the Department.[79] Continuing on this theme, the 1942 convention recommended that summer school courses be organized for teachers in residential schools. Another resolution at these sessions called for the appointment of a special inspector for residential schools to coordinate academic and vocational instruction.[80]

The admission of Catholic students into Protestant administered schools was another contentious issue that had been raised by Grandin. It was closely related to the larger question of liberty of conscience and the Department's position was made clear in the circular sent to agents, inspectors and principals on 31 October 1890. Children were not to be placed in any industrial or boarding school conducted by any denomination other than that to which the parents belonged without the express consent of the parents. Commissioner Hayter Reed suggested that it would be preferable to have such consent in writing and a full report on each admission was to be made to him.[81] In 1897 Clifford Sifton, as minister of the Interior, reiterated the rule that no Catholic child was to be placed in a Protestant institution and *vice versa.* He insisted that all schools receiving government assistance abide by the regulation and ordered that all Catholic children in Protestant schools or Protestant children in Catholic ones be discharged. In the event of a dispute concerning the religion of a child, the Indian commissioner was to make a ruling.[82]

In addition to the vigilant supervision of the state, Catholic and Protestant clergy monitored each other's admissions and were quick to act on violations.[83] The confessionality of students was complicated by the actions of parents, who for various reasons, sometimes chose to place their children in schools operated by a denomination different than that in which the children had been raised or baptized. At Qu'Appelle, a Catholic mother decided that her son should be transferred to the Protestant Indian school in Regina. The pastor of the Regina school accompanied the woman when she secured the authorization of the

Indian commissioner. The mother came to the Catholic school to get her son and had a letter signed by the Indian commissioner as well as the support of the local agent. The child was not released and the woman vowed to return with more documents.[84] In Hobbema, a Protestant parent placed his daughter in the Catholic school. The local Protestant minister came to the school accompanied by the police to obtain her release but the principal, Pierre Moulin, refused to discharge her and referred the case to the Department for a final decision.[85]

In 1921, the Department decided to adhere more strictly to its policy of not allowing children to attend a school conducted by a different religious denomination and ruled that "children from Protestant and Roman Catholic homes would be considered eligible for admission respectively to Protestant and Roman Catholic homes only." Wards of the state would be admitted only to institutions administered by the church to which their parents belonged. In cases where the religion of the home could not be identified by the Department, the child's father would decide. The superintendent general thought that this directive would minimize difficulties in the recruitment of students but he did not want it to provoke requests to transfer a child from one school to another.[86]

When asked by Scott to comment on the new policy, Guy congratulated the Department for attempting to resolve a difficult matter but he could not accept entirely the directive that had been adopted. According to Guy, the ruling would admit children from Catholic and Protestant homes respectively to Catholic and Protestant schools and this was contrary to the Indian Act that referred to child rather than home. Furthermore, Guy claimed that the ruling would paralyze missionary efforts and that the religion of the child had to be the determining factor. He recommended that dubious cases were to be resolved by sworn declarations before a magistrate and two witnesses.[87]

As a result of criticisms by Protestant clergy, the Department submitted its interpretation of the Indian Act to the deputy minister of Justice who expressed the opinion that a Protestant child was one whose parents were Protestant and that a Catholic child was one baptized as such or whose parents were Catholic. He added that the father had the right to determine which faith his children would be raised and that the father's wishes had to be considered. A Protestant father could have his children raised in the Catholic faith but would have to sign an affidavit to that effect for the Department's protection.[88]

This legal ruling removed a crucial ambiguity and Guy was very happy. The matter had been decided in favour of the Oblates who were permitted to admit Protestant children to their schools as long as the father signed a sworn declaration permitting their children to be baptized and educated in the Catholic faith.[89] Despite this favourable ruling, Guy counseled Oblate principals to be prudent in recruiting Protestant children for their schools. Informing Pierre Moulin of Hobbema that the Department had ruled in his favour in the admission of Protestant students at that institution, Guy reminded Moulin that a victory in Hobbema would be offset by loss suffered by another Oblate principal. Guy's comments on the neutrality of the Department were a far cry from that of Grandin's a few decades earlier. According to Guy, the Department detested confessional conflicts and attempted to eliminate them. Furthermore, he claimed that, in the last few years, official were "very just" vis-à-vis Catholics.[90]

Despite the Department's attempts to provide regulations, problems related to the admission of students of one denomination being admitted to school of another continued to emerge. In Hobbema there was friction with the Methodists in 1926 and Joseph Guy advised Pierre Moulin to contact him in the event of difficulties. Guy described the actions of Methodists as "a war to the death" and advised Moulin to defend his interests while he took the matter up with the bureaucrats in Ottawa.[91] The Department continued its policy of being extremely reluctant to admit Catholic children to Protestant institutions and vice versa but in cases of "extreme difficulty" it was prepared to depart from this "usual practice."[92] For his part, Moulin claimed that when the family was Protestant he did not ask them to send their children to his school. When the parents demanded that he accept their children, he did so on the condition that the children become Catholic. He insisted, furthermore, that the parents would have to cooperate to keep the children in the Catholic faith after they left the school. According to Moulin such parents usually decided to become Catholic themselves and he admitted them to the sacraments after a probationary period.[93]

In 1928, Mathias Kalmès of Fort Alexander informed Guy that a pupil whose mother was Catholic while the father was Protestant was enrolled

△ △ *Bishop Joseph Guy of Grouard with early snowmobile, 1935.* (AD)

at the school. The boy had been baptized in the Anglican faith but Kalmès affirmed that the mother wanted him raised as a Catholic. When the Protestant minister heard of this he contacted the agent and the latter insisted that the boy be removed from the school because his registration had not been sanctioned by the Department. For his part, Kalmès claimed that he would not give in so readily. According to Kalmès there were at least 13 baptized Catholic children whose parents were Catholic attending the Protestant residential school on the Gordon Reserve and the authorities were doing nothing to have them removed.[94]

In 1927 Guy received an obedience appointing him rector of Mathieu College in Gravelbourg, Saskatchewan. Two years later, he was named Vicar Apostolic of Grouard, a position he maintained until being transferred to the Diocese of Gravelbourg in 1937. In the meantime, he continued to look after the interests of Oblate residential schools but obviously in a reduced capacity given his ecclesiastical responsibilities. The position of representative of the western Oblates took on additional importance as a result of the activities of Gabriel Breynat, Vicar Apostolic of Mackenzie, who was building Catholic hospitals in the North. As events were to prove, the venture into denominational health services for Natives would create as many difficulties and contentions as had denominational residential education.[95]

Thus, by the mid 1930s, the Oblate Apostolate had become increasingly complex and diversified and the problems that were emerging transcended those associated with facilitating relationships with the federal authorities. While the maintenance of a good rapport between the Oblates and the government and its bureaucracy was still a priority, other equally challenging issues had appeared on the horizon and required attention. Much had been accomplished with respect to the establishment of missions, schools and the provision of health services but it became apparent that this had been done by individual Oblates and bishops who used methods that differed widely. It was also evident that there was no common front against problems facing all missionaries regardless of where they were in the western and northern regions of Canada. Furthermore, there was no formal mechanism to unite and bring those Oblates involved in Indian missions, schools and hospitals together and provide them with a medium to discuss and study their problems and adopt the best solutions.[96]

In addition to these internal concerns, the Oblates believed that it was necessary to critically examine their mandate as missionaries to the Native population in view of the changes that had taken place in the North West. Administrative concerns and the need to reassess institutional objectives coincided with the canonical visit of western and northern missions between June 1935 and July 1936 by the Congregation's superior general, Théodore Labouré. Labouré was concerned with reasserting Oblate missionary objectives, promoting unity of action and cooperation within Oblate ranks and bringing about an integration of all apostolic efforts relating missions and schools.

△ △ △ △ △ △ △ △ △ △ △ △ △   **10**

THE OBLATES AS
"FATHERS, GUIDES AND PROTECTORS"
OF ABORIGINAL COMMUNITIES

A s Christians and as pastors the Oblates could not remain indifferent to the predicament of the First Nations peoples of the North West especially after 1870 when the old order based on the buffalo hunt was fading away. In an era when the larger white community was hardly aware of Native peoples, let alone sensitized to their needs, the missionary, was indeed a voice crying in the wilderness. On the other hand, as guardians by default of the Native element in the North West, the Oblates became society's conscience and admonished those who dealt with the Native community to abide by the principles of justice and equity. The Oblates did not actively seek this function of advocate, it was forced upon them by circumstances. On the remote fringes of the Canadian North West, the missionary was the only countervailing force to the fur trader. Within treaty areas, the Oblate also became the logical intermediary between Indians and an impersonal and often uncaring bureaucracy.

Prior to 1870, the presence of fur traders and their posts presented certain problems for missionaries and their apostolic efforts but the commercialization of the fur trade produced relatively minor changes in Native life and culture. Despite their different objectives, the Hudson's Bay Company and the Oblates had been able to accommodate one another. The Bay, despite its commercialization of the fur trade, nevertheless, introduced an element of stability in economic relationships. The

Oblate presence presented a potential threat to the Bay but the missionaries contributed to the *status quo* by stressing that, as Christians, Indians were morally bound to respect and honour their obligations. The arrival of free traders threatened the very nature of relationships between the Bay, Oblates and Indians not to mention exposing neophytes to nefarious influences. Thus, it is not surprising that, in their representations to the authorities concerning the welfare of Indians, the Oblates recommended that the fur trade be conducted by a single company, the HBC. In the event that free traders established themselves in a region, mission personnel remained neutral in order not to provoke either party. However, the mission insisted that Indians pay their debts to the HBC.[1]

The fact that the Oblates favoured the HBC as opposed to free traders, however, did not mean that they approved of company policy at all times. In 1894, for example, the Indians at Reindeer Lake complained that the company was offering them absurdly low credits for the coming season and they asked Alphonse Gasté to intercede on their behalf. Gasté agreed to speak to the company inspector who was currently visiting the post and suggested that the credit offered to the Indians be increased. Furthermore, Indians from Churchill were not given credits and told to return to that post to trade. According to Gasté, Natives from Churchill were free to go where they pleased so long as they honoured their obligations to the company.[2]

The departure of disgruntled Indians from Reindeer Lake posed a threat to the stability of the mission and Gasté decided to organize a system of transportation independent of the HBC to bring the furs of mission Indians to market.[3] At neighboring Pelican Narrows (Saskatchewan), Étienne Bonnald also denounced the parsimonious attitude of the Bay and the company's attempts to discredit the missionaries who were assisting the Indians by accepting their furs in exchange for the items needed for hunting or fishing.[4] Gasté also feared the low credits given at Reindeer Lake were but the first step in another attempt to close the post and force Indians to trade at other posts where expenses were not as considerable. He went to Prince Albert to discuss the position of the mission with his religious superiors and to inform free traders of the opportunities for trade. As a result of his efforts, the Bay faced competition and had no choice but to keep its post open.[5]

While the Oblate hierarchy in principle preferred the HBC to free traders, the views of missionaries in the field were dictated by local circumstances. At Fort Dunvegan, an American free trader, the famous "Twelve Foot Davis," treated Christophe Tissier liberally with culinary delights. After preparing an epicurean meal Davis would hoist a flag as a signal and Tissier would quickly appear.[6] This familiarity earned Tissier the displeasure of his superiors and a reprimand.[7] For his part, Joseph Letreste admitted that free traders had rendered real services in the Peace River region by causing an increase in the price paid for furs and decreasing the cost of merchandise. Letreste claimed that free traders had brought in large quantities of tea and matches and that prior to their arrival tea was reserved for "the mouths of gods and high dignitaries."[8]

At Île-à-la-Crosse the mission and the HBC post were at odds and, as a result, the mission's supply of food was threatened. A calamity was averted by the presence of a Catholic free trader in 1897 who provided the mission with all it required and rendered many services and assistance to the missionaries. When this trader received an unexpected high price for his furs, he purchased equipment for the mission and had it shipped to Île-à-la-Crosse at his own expense.[9] Even Bishop Émile Grouard, who was a staunch company supporter, admitted that a Catholic free trader at Sturgeon Lake facilitated the conversion of Indians in that area. Constant Falher had visited the region for ten years but had not been able to remain for any length of time because he lacked the necessary resources and had no assistance to construct an adequate chapel. The free trader allowed Falher and other Oblates to use his own residence while they conducted their mission.[10]

While relations between the Oblates and the Bay were generally good and a rapprochement was possible with some free traders, the presence of other elements in the North West was viewed with deep suspicion by the missionaries. The transfer of Rupert's Land to the Dominion in 1870 and the subsequent signing of treaties with Indian tribes marked the beginning of a new era in the history of the North West and this transformation troubled the Oblates. As early as 1864, for example, Albert Lacombe was lamenting the presence of white miners in the Edmonton region the majority of whom he described as "rabble."[11] A few years later, Lacombe admitted that it was impossible to stop the flow of whites in the West. He claimed that they were ruining the country by their insatiable greed and, as an example, he cited the slaughter of 30,000 buffalo in the winter of 1869 between Fort Carlton and Rocky Mountain House. Lacombe argued that Indians would need special protection to cope with the presence of whites and he suggested that the government allow only one company to trade with the Indians. Although, missionaries were to be allowed complete freedom to carry on their work among Native populations.[12]

Within a short period of time, the intrusion of whites was noted further north in the Athabasca region. In 1882, Émile Grouard informed his friend Roderick MacFarlane of the HBC that a prospector had departed from Lac La Biche for Fort McMurray in search of exploitable resources.[13] The following year, Grouard informed MacFarlane that surveyors had surveyed three townships around Fort Dunvegan. This activity produced a "land fever" and speculators had already "picked up the most beautiful places in the whole North West."[14] While Grouard feared the commercial repercussions of the white presence, he was quick to note another danger it presented. The newcomers were in majority Anglo-Protestant, and as such, presented another threat to the Oblates and their work. In 1911, Grouard, as Vicar Apostolic of Athabasca, informed a relative that a large part of his vicariate had been invaded by Anglo-Protestant colonists and that civilization was accompanying them and the region would soon have railroads and telegraphs. He feared that such progress would engender much physical and moral misery.[15]

The presence of whites while it may have presented a moral dilemma for the Oblates was also accompanied by other more immediate consequences that had serious repercussions on Native society. In 1864 Isidore Clut recorded that the arrival of the brigade from Peace River had brought an epidemic to Nativity Mission. While the members of the brigade became ill and recovered, local Indians died of the disease. Clut buried eleven Indians and claimed that the death rate would have been much higher without the assistance provided by the Oblates and the Bay. On the positive side, Clut affirmed that he had never seen such fervour among the Indians since his arrival at the mission and he claimed that the pestilence had even rendered fervent those who had been indifferent.[16]

The incidence of disease would become a recurring theme in the correspondence of missionaries in the North West. In 1869 Henri Faraud identified measles, scarlet fever and *"la maladie napolitaine"* following one another and sometimes acting simultaneously to destroy one-third of the Native population. Contrary to Clut who believed that the epidemics were a catalyst on conversions and spirituality, Faraud feared that disease would wipe out the converts.[17] A short while later, smallpox ravaged St. Albert on the eve of the buffalo hunters leaving for the fall hunt. In less than a month two-thirds of the hunters were stricken with the result that there were often not enough men to raise camp and to hunt.[18] In St. Albert itself one-third of the population died and Vital Grandin recorded up to seven funerals a day. Famine was anticipated because the crops failed and there was little farm work that could be done. The Oblates rendered whatever services they could but Grandin admitted that most of those who were ill lacked basic care.[19]

In 1885, Alphonse Gasté accompanied a brigade from Cumberland to Reindeer Lake and was occupied caring for those who were stricken by disease. Gasté was sent ahead by the bourgeois to inform the Chipewyan that some members of their tribe had died as a result of the contagion. In the meantime, other Chipewyan came into contact with the brigade, contracted the disease and returned with it to their camp.[20] The Cumberland region itself was ravaged by measles and the mortality rate was very high. Ovide Charlebois reported that it was not unusual to find four to six sick persons in a hut and one dead child.[21] During one winter at Île-à-la-Crosse, Laurent Le Goff was called upon to make 14 visits to sick Indians. Three of these were to Portage La Loche and one was 60 miles beyond that location. He estimated that these four voyages necessitates 1000 miles on snowshoes and that the remaining visits accounted for another 1500 miles of travel.[22]

In addition to disease, the decline of the fur trade, the disappearance of the buffalo and the advance of white settlement in the North West had serious repercussions for the Native population. As a result of the treaties it had negotiated, the federal government assumed responsibility for the welfare of Indians and, hence, the Oblates turned to the federal authorities to ensure the welfare of the Native and Métis communities. The plight of the Blackfoot after the signing of Treaty 7 was brought to the attention of the authorities by Constantine Scollen. In 1878, as some 4000 Blackfoot gathered near Fort Macleod to receive their annual payment, Scollen enlightened Edgar Dewdney, lieutenant governor of the Northwest Territories, on the grievances and discontent of the Indians and was able to avert an open confrontation.[23]

The following year, Scollen wrote to Major Irvine of the North West Mounted Police and declared that the Sarcee, Bloods and Peigans had not understood the implications of the treaty they had signed because of the absence of competent interpreters. He claimed that the Indians had signed because previously they "had been kindly dealt with" by the authorities and they were convinced that this precedent would provide them with food and clothing as the need arose. Scollen contended that outside influences also were brought to bear on the Indians and he reiterated that "they were not actuated by any intuitive comprehension of what they were called upon to do."[24] He stated that the Indians were now depressed and demoralized, reduced to eating dogs and wolves and forced to scatter in search of food. They could no longer live in big camps under the authority of their chiefs. Begging and stealing cattle alarmed the settlers and Scollen predicted dire consequences if there was another difficult winter. At the request of the Blackfoot, Scollen had petitioned the lieutenant governor for a plough and potatoes but this had been refused. Scollen claimed, furthermore, that the Peigans had not received the implements and seed promised in the treaty. According to Scollen, "this is too much procrastination at a time when the Indians are in extreme need."[25]

For his part, Bishop Faraud urged the government to assist Indians who lived outside treaty areas.[26] Archbishop Taché petitioned the Department of Indian Affairs on behalf of Indians on reserves near Lakes Winnipeg and Manitoba who occupied land that was of poor quality. Indians at Duck Bay had applied to have their reservation moved from the island to the mainland and, at the request of the Oblates who served there, Taché recommended that the transfer be granted.[27]

Such advocacy and intervention, however, dictated diplomacy and prudence. In 1883, Louis Soullier, the canonical visitor to Canada, remarked that in cases of Native grievances against abuses of civil authority the Oblates, as their "fathers, guides and protectors," could not refuse to provide advice and assistance. However, he reminded the Oblates of the delicate nature of such involvement and the serious consequences that could result from "rash initiatives."[28] A short while later, a similar caution was expressed by Albert Lacombe in a letter to Henri Grandin. The experienced Lacombe advised Grandin to exercise prudence in dealing with matters affecting Indians and their agents. According to Lacombe, one should not act impetuously because that would result in more harm than good for the Indians as well as the Oblates. Grandin was cautioned not to believe everything the Indians alleged against their agents and not to become implicated in their complaints. Grandin's sole motive was to promote the interests of the Catholic religion and he was to do as much good as possible on the reserves.[29]

As events were to prove, such cautions were indeed opportune because of the complex nature of relationships between Indians, missionaries and the personnel of the Department of Indian Affairs. In addition, the volatile issue of confessional rivalries was always in the background. In 1888, Indians at Rivière Qui Barre sent a telegram to Prime Minister Macdonald complaining that they were starving and asking for a commission of inquiry. Alexandre-Marie Blanchet advised Bishop Grandin of the situation and suggested that there was an absence of good will on the part of certain Indian agents. Blanchet reported that the Indians wanted a Catholic agent in whom they would have confidence and, since all the Indians were Catholic, Blanchet supported their request.[30] As a result of his advocacy in favour of the Indians, Blanchet was accused of inciting them, an accusation he denied in a letter to the Indian Commissioner Hayter Reed. Blanchet claimed that he had counseled the Indians to be prudent and exercise care. He affirmed, however, that, like all citizens, the Indians were entitled to justice. Reed was informed that the Indians had held a meeting and unanimously decided to publish a letter in the Edmonton *Bulletin* denouncing him and their agent.[31]

The health of the Native population continued to be a source of concern for the Oblates and, after the signing of treaties, they made numerous requests to improve health services. As could be expected some of these requests created friction between the missionaries and the bureaucracy. In 1887, for example, Alexandre-Marie Blanchet asked for a resident doctor at Rivière Qui Barre because of the high mortality rate among Indians. When this was refused, Blanchet took the matter up with the lieutenant governor because the agent would not assist the Indians. A reply from the Indian commissioner suggested that a visit by a doctor had not revealed a significant amount of sickness whereas the agent reported that no complaints had been made against him. Blanchet wanted to formally deny these allegations but was forbidden to do so by his superior.[32]

In 1896, Henri Grandin had asked that a doctor be sent twice a year to attend Indians living around Lac La Biche. He was informed by Indian Commissioner Amédée Forget that the local agent had been contacted and had recommended that medicines be sent to the Oblates along with instructions for dispensing them. Forget's reply to Grandin was typical:

> In view of this, and of the Agent's statements, and considering also the large expenditure which according to his estimate would be necessary, I have not felt that I could recommend to the Department that a doctor be sent in.[33]

In his 1908 report on the Vicariate of St. Albert and Saskatchewan, Grandin expressed the fear that the Native population was on the verge of extinction as a result of the numerous epidemics and diseases that had decimated its ranks.[34]

Even after the establishment of industrial schools the Oblates still continued to make representations to the authorities to promote the welfare of the Indians. In 1889, Lacombe wrote to Edgar Dewdney outlining various proposals to ameliorate life on the reserves. Lacombe recommended the establishment of shoe manufactures, bakeries, individual landowning and stores on reserves and recommended that Indians be employed by the North West Mounted Police. Dewdney agreed with the suggestion to establish shoe manufactures on reserves and provide the necessary instruction in that trade because this would allow Indians to utilize the hides of animals they killed and contribute to making them self-sufficient. Concerning employment, Dewdney believed that the government should do more to increase the number of Indians employed by the NWMP.[35]

Some of the Oblate requests ran counter to government policy and, hence, were not accorded. In 1892, for example, Henri Grandin advised the minister of the Interior that a small band of Cree near Lac La Biche were being forced to abandon their reserve and go elsewhere. According to Grandin, it would be preferable if they relocated in Saddle Lake but they refused to leave. He claimed these Indians received no help from the government and he believed that this was unjust.[36] The Indian commissioner affirmed that it was the policy of the government to allow hunting

Indians to remain hunters so long as there was sufficient game to support them. When the hunt failed to sustain them, they were brought to a reserve where they were supervised by an agent and a farm instructor. In the case of the Indians alluded to by Grandin, they derived from a band of mixed bloods who had left the treaty. Hence, they never had a reserve and the commissioner believed that it would be a waste of money to provide them with assistance to establish themselves as farmers where they were currently located.[37]

In 1894, Bishop Grandin supported the complaints of residents of the Blood Reserve concerning the scantiness of rations. He affirmed that the allowance of one pound of meat per day was insufficient. While he did not suggest any motives for this policy he, nevertheless, stated that intermittent fasting was injurious to health and hunger and encouraged Indians to kill their cattle. As a solution, the bishop recommended that the meat ration be increased to one and one-half pounds per day and that rations be distributed more frequently.[38]

For his part, Bishop Émile Legal supported a petition from the Chipewyan of Onion Lake who sought to have the size of their reserve extended. Legal affirmed that these Indians had been supporting themselves for some time and were intent on doing so in the future. He claimed that the reserve was already too small and cited the fact that the hay needed to winter cattle had to be cut outside the boundaries of the reserve.[39] Gustave Simonin supported the chief of one of the bands on the Hobbema Reserve who contested the HBC's claim to one section of land situated in the middle of the reserve. The Indians feared that they would loose this land and did not wish to part with it at any cost and Simonin was asked to intercede on behalf of the band.[40] Indians from the Long Lake band asked Henri Grandin to support their request to have their agency divided into two parts. Grandin advised the deputy superintendent general that the request would be advantageous for all parties because it would overcome problems associated with distance, neglect and aged agency personnel.[41]

The Oblates also interceded on behalf of individuals. In 1892, Bishop Grandin threatened to use publicity to secure the readmission of an Indian and his wife to the Ermineskin band and the restitution of their treaty rights. Upon receiving a telegram from Dewdney to this effect Grandin informed Taché that, when confronted with publicity, the authorities became accommodating and pleasant.[42] In 1898, Émile Legal asked the Indian commissioner whether a member of the Saddle Lake Agency who had participated in the North West Rebellion and who had since lived in exile in the United States could return to his reserve without being molested. Legal was informed that under the terms of a general amnesty granted in 1886, rebels who were not guilty of murder could return without fear of retaliation. In the case presented by Legal, however, the individual had lived in a foreign country for more than five years and hence under the terms of the Indian Act, had forfeited all treaty rights and could be reinstated only with the consent of the superintendent general.[43] Further south among the Assiniboines, the chief had not received any recompense in 1886 although he had not taken part in the North West Rebellion. Since the others who had remained neutral had received gifts, the Assiniboine chief complained to the agent but a definitive answer was not forthcoming and Alexandre-Marie Blanchet alleged that confessionality was involved.[44] For his part, Janvier Danis petitioned the Department on behalf of a destitute family of four orphans. The mother was a treaty Indian who had passed away a few weeks earlier, the father was serving a life sentence and the children required assistance. Danis asked that the children be admitted to the Crowfoot Boarding School.[45]

The establishment of schools provided the Oblates with the opportunity to make representations on behalf of pupils. In 1914, Pierre Moulin, urged the Department to assist a former pupil at Hobbema. This graduate had done well since leaving school, had married recently and wished to establish himself on the reserve. Moulin described the individual as one of the best pupils and suggested that he be provided with a good plough and disk harrow.[46] Some years later Moulin asked the superintendent of Indian Education to pay the board and tuition for two students who had successfully completed their grade eight exams. Since the school did not provide instruction beyond that level Moulin wanted to send them to another school.[47] For its part, the Department wished to assist deserving students but wanted to know whether the parents were "sufficiently interested" to pay at least part of the cost.[48]

The authorities were aware of the esteem in which the Oblates were held by the Indians and, hence, sought the services of the missionaries to promote government policy. Albert Lacombe and Constantine Scollen were used as interpreters during the negotiation and signing of treaties to convince the Indians that the Dominion did not want to deceive them but enhance their welfare. In 1883, the Blackfoot stopped surveyors from staking out the CPR line on their reserve. Lacombe immediately advised Lieutenant Governor Dewdney of the incident and called a meeting of the chiefs at the mission. Lacombe distributed sugar, tea, tobacco and flour and counseled the chiefs to allow the surveyors to continue their work and promised that Dewdney would come and reach an agreement with them.[49]

Two years later, in the midst of the North West Rebellion, the government wished to ensure the loyalty of the Blackfoot and Dewdney asked Lacombe to be present at a meeting at Blackfoot Crossing for the purpose of reassuring the Indians. In the presence of Lacombe and Dewdney, Chief Crowfoot declared that the government had nothing to fear from the Blackfoot. The good news was telegraphed to Macdonald who announced it to Parliament.[50] Constantine Scollen met with the chief and headmen of the Peace Hills Reserve and using "the strongest language," advised them to control their people.[51]

While the Oblates insisted that Indians uphold duly constituted authority, they were not prepared to contribute to the spoliation of Indian interests. In 1905, a rancher near the Blackfoot Reserve wished to rent part of that reserve to pasture his cattle. The agent was in favour of the proposal and tried to enlist the support of Jacques Riou by stating that the rancher's wife was Catholic and would be generous towards the mission. Riou refused to lend his support to the venture because it was in the interests of the Indians to keep their best fields of hay.[52] In 1924, Jean-Louis Le Vern denounced the renting of part of the Peigan Reserve to a political friend of the government despite the unanimous opposition of the residents. Le Vern claimed that the Peigans were correct when they declared that the government had acted like a highway robber in this transaction.[53]

In addition to their concern for the material welfare of the Indian population, the Oblates also attempted to safeguard and promote those of the Métis whose condition was even more precarious. With the disappearance of the buffalo and the advance of settlement in the North West, the socio-economic status of the Métis decreased significantly. The Oblates began to make representations to the authorities to halt this decline. Bishop Grandin urged the government to extend privileges granted to the Manitoba Métis to those of the Territories. He also advocated the enactment of hunting laws to prevent the destruction of the buffalo and providing assistance to those Métis who agreed to abandon nomadism and became farmers.[54] In an attempt to protect the Métis against the destructive influence of the ever-increasing white presence in the North West, Grandin and the Oblates suggested that the Métis opt for reserves rather than individual homesteads. In this way, the Oblates hoped to avoid the experience of the Manitoba Métis who had chosen scrip and later abandoned their lands when they found themselves at the mercy of speculators, acquisitive white farmers and the controversy and confusion surrounding land claims under the Manitoba Act.[55]

Despite the efforts of the Oblates to intercede on behalf of and protect the Métis, the problems encountered in Manitoba followed the Métis as they sought a new life in the District of Saskatchewan. There were difficulties in having Métis lands surveyed into traditional river lots and in confirming ownership of these lands. Métis who had left Manitoba encountered problems in obtaining the land they were entitled to under the Half-Breed Grant. As in the case of Manitoba, Métis in the Territories sold their scrip for cash and this profoundly distressed the Oblates who preferred to see the Métis as sedentary farmers. The Oblates did not comprehend the Métis desire for "immediate cash" and, although they were motivated by the best of intentions, the missionaries did not understand the "complexities of the situation" that existed on the eve of the Rebellion and, hence, were not able to provide the best of advice.[56] In the end, the impatient and frustrated Métis rejected the Oblates whom they regarded as too closely associated with the procrastinating authorities and turned instead to Louis Riel.

Grandin was convinced that the Métis had committed a serious error in asking Riel to return from exile and champion their cause and interests and he and his missionaries became increasingly suspicious of the Métis leader's motives as time passed. In the midst of a volatile situation, the Oblates were attempting to preach moderation to the Métis and maintain them in state of obedience while urging the federal government to redress the legitimate grievances of the Métis.[57] As the defenders of orthodoxy and legitimate authority, the Oblates energetically denounced Riel's leadership and the armed rebellion that erupted. Nevertheless, the Oblates admitted that extenuating circumstances had provoked the Métis to take up arms. Grandin alleged that English-speaking residents had attempted to steal Métis lands by means of illegal activities and that in purposely overlooking these tactics the government had further exasperated the Métis.[58] Another Oblate suggested that the government's refusal to employ the Métis on reserves or as interpreters was responsible for the disenchantment. The Métis were fully qualified to serve as agents and farm instructors and would not require the services of interpreters to carry out their duties.[59]

With respect to Riel's role and leadership in the Rebellion, the Oblates found it impossible to identify any mitigating elements and their views were very critical and hostile. In assuming the mantle of the prophet Riel presented a direct challenge to the legitimacy and function of the Oblates as the authoritative representatives of the Church. Thus, the Oblates countered by affirming that Riel was a false prophet who had usurped their priestly function. More significant than the challenge which Riel may have presented to the Oblates and their ministry was the fact that his creative doctrines had succeeded in indigenizing the Christian message and presenting it in a form that was meaningful and relevant to the Métis and the crisis their society was facing.

The success of Riel, the prophet, alarmed the Oblates who, as a result of their orthodox convictions, were unable to recognize or accept his prophetic role as a supplementary and legitimate expression of the Catholic faith. To the traditionalist Oblates, Riel was a threatening religious outsider and he was accordingly denounced in no uncertain terms. Riel was described as an apostate, a heretic, a fiendish instrument of Satan who deceived and deluded the gullible Métis. Riel's religiosity was denounced as theatrics and many Oblates convinced themselves that Riel was insane.[60] Insanity proved to be a convenient Oblate explanation for Riel's actions because it was unequivocal and could be comprehended readily by all. Insanity made it possible for the Church to readmit Riel to the fold because he had not been responsible for his actions during the Rebellion. More important to the Oblates, however, was the fact that as an interpretation insanity relegated Riel's religiosity to the rank of an inadvertent and temporary aberration from the one true Catholic faith.

To further minimize the extent of Riel's influence over the Métis, the Oblates declared that very few of them had been actively involved in the Rebellion and understood the consequences of their actions.[61] In their petitions to the authorities after the Rebellion on behalf of the imprisoned Métis, the Oblates declared that the Métis had been forced or duped into taking arms by Riel or by others who had incited them to promote their own interests. Consequently, the Oblates urged the government to impose the slightest possible penalty on those who had been imprisoned.[62] Grandin asked the government to reprieve Métis prisoners and to grant an amnesty to those who had fled to the United States. Grandin also used his influence on the minister of the Militia to secure the release of Maxime Lépine, a member of the Exovedate, the provisional government established by Riel.[63]

In the years following 1885 there was a growing estrangement between the "first born of the faith in the West," and the Oblates, their traditional pastors. In some areas the Métis were purposely avoiding meeting the missionaries while in others they were alleging that the Oblates were deceiving them or that the Oblates had provoked Riel into rebellion to lessen his influence over the Métis.[64] In 1898, Grandin remarked that the estrangement of the Métis was still very evident and that their prejudice against the Oblates led them to believe any accusation against the missionaries.[65] Reports that some Métis had confided the education of their children to a Protestant minister so disconcerted Grandin that he implored God "to forgive the Métis and remember their previous good dispositions."[66]

In addition to the spiritual impoverishment noted by the Oblates, the material well-being of the Métis also declined after 1885. There was widespread poverty among the Métis and this was complicated by the alienation of their lands. According to Grandin, the Métis who lived around towns quickly succumbed to terrible vices such as drunkenness and immorality. Others were leaving the settled areas to avoid white civilization and continue their traditional lifestyle. While this was preferable to the experience of the urban Métis, Grandin believed that, sooner or later, white settlers would invade those frontier areas and again dispossess the Métis.[67]

Given the importance of discontent associated with land claims as a factor that had contributed to the Rebellion, the Oblates urged the authorities to quickly resolve land claims when the Scrip Commission began its hearings.[68] The Oblates assisted Métis claimants by acting as interpreters, providing documentation from mission registers and records and interceding with the authorities. Given their own preferences for a sedentary Métis community, the Oblates attempted to convince them to accept land scrip. The Oblates urged the Métis not to sell their land scrip but often this advice was not heeded.[69] Problems arose even when the Métis accepted land scrip. In the Cumberland district, Ovide Charlebois reported that, in opting for land scrip, the Métis gave up their right to live on land set aside for Indians and since there were no other unoccupied lands in the region the Métis decided to leave and go elsewhere. With their departure Charlebois estimated that the mission lost three-quarters of its population.[70] In Pelican Lake in 1909, the scrip buyer had succeeded in purchasing seven of the eight scrips given to the Métis by offering alcohol as an inducement.[71]

Given their concern over the alienation of Métis lands the Oblates supported the government's proposal to offer a block of land to the Métis of Duck Lake to establish a special colony under the administration of the Métis residents. Three Oblates were present at a meeting in Batoche in 1890 to study the plan and there were insinuations that they favoured the proposal in order to divert Métis lands to French Canadian farmers. Vital Fourmond reassured the Métis as to the motives of the Oblates and, at a second meeting, a majority voted for the establishment of the colony. However, at a general meeting of the Métis in the district the motives of the Oblates were again questioned. These innuendoes and allegations that the colony would be nothing more than an Indian reserve contributed to the defeat of the proposal.[72]

While the government's proposal to establish a Métis colony at Duck Lake was not accepted by the Métis, the Oblates remained confident that sedentary agriculture would provide a solution to the distress and poverty facing the Métis community. In 1895, Albert Lacombe sent a memorial to the federal government describing the plight of the Métis in the North West. To improve their well-being Lacombe asked the government to grant four sections of land to the Episcopal Corporations of St. Albert, St. Boniface and Prince Albert for the purpose of establishing a religious settlement and an industrial school for the Métis. In addition, the government was asked to lease four townships to the bishops for subdivision into plots and distribution to Métis families to enable them to become self-sufficient farmers under the direction of managers appointed by the clergy.[73]

The government shared Lacombe's concern over the Métis and since his proposal involved no financial obligation on its part, the plan was accepted and land was set aside for the colony at St. Paul, Alberta.[74] Lacombe announced his proposal in an open letter to the Métis of the North West. He promised the Métis that they would become happy and self-supporting if they were once again willing to heed the advice of "the priest who is your true friend."[75] Grandin encouraged the Métis through a pastoral letter in June 1897 that urged the Métis of St. Paul to have confidence in themselves and reminded them that they were equal to any other. The bishop declared that, if the Métis were courageous and energetic, St. Paul would become a model colony and its residents worthy of admiration.[76]

The St. Paul colony was administered by Adéodat Thérien who believed that the residents were to live by the fruit of their labours and not expect the colony to support them like Indians on a reserve. Thérien categorically denied allegations that he had no choice but to feed the impoverished Métis at St. Paul.[77] In the meantime, the colony's expenses continued to mount and this alarmed Lacombe who insisted on retrenchment. For their part, the Métis did not appreciate Thérien's parsimonious ways and they alleged that he was allowing large sums of money destined for the use of the colony and its residents to stagnate in the bank.[78]

A short while later, Thérien admitted that the Métis no longer had confidence in the Oblates and were seeking other leaders because they suspected the motives of the missionaries. He thought that the material status of the Métis could not be improved without gaining their confidence and convincing them that it was necessary that they unite with the clergy.[79] As could be expected, Grandin was very saddened by the defiant attitude of the Métis and the sordid motives they attributed to his missionaries. He reiterated that the Oblates were not attempting to employ panaceas to alleviate the status of the Métis but provide them with effective assistance to ensure a better future for them and their children.[80]

In the meantime, the colony struggled on and the Oblates hoped the government would provide an annual subsidy to allow them to continue its operation. Unfortunately, this grant was not forthcoming and special collections undertaken for the benefit of the colony were not enough to meet current obligations.[81] There were also problems associated with the shortage of skilled personnel to erect and maintain mills in the colony that destroyed the little faith the Métis had in the Oblates as managers.[82] Then on 15 January 1905, students who no longer wished to attend the boarding school set fire to the building and destroyed it with the loss of one life. The Oblates continued to support the colony as best they could but four years later, on 10 April 1909, they withdrew and the colony was opened to French Canadian settlement. The admission of French Canadian farmers together with earlier allegations that the Oblates had profited at the expense of the Métis at St. Paul intensified the disenchantment with and alienation of the Oblates that had been growing since the Rebellion and Riel's execution.

Disenchantment was also voiced by the Métis of Saint-Laurent de Grandin (Saskatchewan) who, in 1896, petitioned the superior general of the Oblates and complained about the dismemberment of their parish. The Métis stated that when the Oblates came to establish the mission they built the church and heeded Bishop Grandin's advice to establish themselves around the mission. With the spread of immigration new parishes were established, and this was to the detriment of St. Laurent's interests. In the end, Bishop Émile Pascal decided to dismember the parish despite an earlier promise not to do so. The residents no longer had a resident clergyman and had to travel long distances to perform their religious duties. They predicted that spiritual ruin would be accompanied by temporal ruin. The Métis accused the principal of St. Michel's School and other Oblates of unduly influencing the bishop and they asked the superior general to give them justice. The 75 petitioners indicated their determination to take the matter before Leo XIII if necessary.[83]

As events were to demonstrate, the Métis would be confronted by problems far more serious than the dismemberment of the parish of St. Laurent de Grandin. In his report to the 1908 General Chapter, Henri Grandin wrote that Métis missions that had few contacts with whites were holding their own whereas in those that did, the economic well being of the residents declined and lost the piety inculcated by the pioneer missionaries.[84] Nevertheless, the Oblates were prepared to continue ministering to the Métis. In 1921, Grandin asked Joseph-Amédée Angin to visit Wolf Lake and evaluate the possibility of visiting this mission on a regular basis. The Métis were to build a chapel and were to be informed that if Angin were to visit and instruct them they in turn would have to demonstrate good will and furnish whatever they could to assist him.[85]

In the twentieth century, the plight of the Métis worsened and the Oblates were hard pressed to alter this state of affairs. In 1924, Adéodat

Thérien wrote to the government of Saskatchewn to alleviate the plight of the Métis at Onion Lake. He also advised his provincial of the "lamentable condition" of the Métis of Alberta and Saskatchewan and their dismal prospects for the future. The former director of the ill-fated colony at St. Paul des Métis was hard pressed to offer a solution. He claimed that experience had demonstrated the futility of giving land to the Métis because they quickly alienated or abandoned their farms. Their efforts as farmers were mediocre because they lacked initiative and had no sense of husbandry. Thérien claimed that the Métis should have been given reserves with agents, instructors, residential schools to initiate them to agriculture and sedentary life. However, the Métis did not want this and Thérein alleged that the lure of the old ways negated their efforts and those of their missionaries.[86]

Thérien complained that the federal government would do nothing for the Métis whereas provincial governments seemed disposed to act but, in fact, did little. Confronted with this inactivity Thérien suggested that the government set aside a block of land where the Métis could settle. He also recommended that Métis who married Indian women should be free to join his spouse's reserve. Thérien claimed that marriages between the Métis and Indians would be to the advantage of the latter who were declining as a result of consanguineous marriages. According to Thérien, children from marriages between Métis and Indians were more numerous, more robust and better formed than those of unions between Indians. He also suggested that a Métis who had given his daughter in marriage to an Indian should be able to live on the reserve with his son in law in his old age.[87]

Concern over the plight of the Métis was raised in the 1931 report on Oblate missions among Native populations in Canada. The section of the report on the Alberta-Saskatchewan province lamented the fact that the Métis were disappearing as a result of absorption into other ethnic elements as a result of inter-marriage or incorporation into the Indian community because of a similar lifestyle. The Oblates noted a parallel spiritual decline among the Métis and attributed this in part to their migratory habits. Other factors which contributed to the loss of spirituality were "godless schools," the spectacle of immoral whites and the temptations offered by their society. Worse yet, was the fact that governments cared little about the fate of the Métis. This disinterestedness was condemned and the Oblates argued that the Métis should not be placed on the same level as other groups in the West. The Métis had to be accorded special treatment to make the transition to a sedentary life and that this status was well merited would have contributed to making the Métis a "race of honest and useful citizens."[88] In addition to the disinterestedness of governments, the scanty resources of the Oblates imposed serious limitations on the work that they could undertake among the Métis. Within the Alberta-Saskatchewan province Indian and Métis missions were not self-sufficient and funds from other Oblate sources had to be used to offset the annual deficit.[89]

In the meantime, the Métis were becoming increasingly conscious of their identity and heritage and no longer ashamed of Riel's leadership. They began to speak out against those Métis, like Louis Schmidt, who had been assimilated into the French Catholic community and had denounced Riel and his movement.[90] The Métis also condemned clerical influence over their affairs and rejected traditional Catholic interpretations that were critical of Riel. This nationalistic consciousness and militant sentiment culminated in the creation in St. Vital in 1909 of the *Comité Historique de l'Union Nationale Métisse* that later commissioned a journalist and author, Auguste-Henri de Trémaudan, to compile a more accurate representation of Métis history and the role of Riel especially in the Rebellion of 1885.[91] As de Trémaudan began his research, the *Comité Historique* took exception to the *Histoire abrégée de l'Ouest canadien* written by the noted Oblate polemicist, Adrien-Gabriel Morice. In February 1925, the *Comité Historique* prepared a report on errors it had identified in Morice's book and asked the author to correct them.[92] When Morice did not reply, the *Comité Historique* asked the *Association d'Éducation Canadienne Française du Manitoba* to cease purchasing the book for use in schools and awarding it as prizes. The *Comité Historique* also refuted Morice's interpretation of the events of 1885 in a lengthy letter published in *La Liberté.*[93] This communication provoked an equally extensive reply from Morice and, in the month that followed, the protagonists exchanged their missives through the intermediary of *La Liberté.*[94]

The final chapter in this controversy was written some ten years later when de Trémaudan's *Histoire de la nation métisse dans l'ouest canadien* was published posthumously. The author died before completing a special chapter on the events of 1885 and the *Comité Historique* decided to publish the results of its own research and interviews of eyewitnesses at Batoche as an appendix to the volume. In this 45-page document, the *Comité Historique* categorically refuted allegations that the Rebellion had been ill advised and premeditated, that the Métis had occupied and profaned the church at Batoche, that missionaries and nuns had been held prisoner at Batoche and that Riel had apostatized and created a new religion. The Appendix also suggested that in 1885, the Oblates had acted as informants for the authorities, approved of the actions taken by the government and tacitly agreed to sacrifice Riel's life.[95]

Morice, who regarded the St. Vital Métis as insolent, amateur historians, found many things to criticize in de Trémaudan's book. He suggested that de Trémaudan had been ill when he wrote the book and that he had relied on Métis gossip rather than critical sources. Nearly half of Morice's 92-page critique was devoted to the Appendix that he regarded as a personal insult. Morice claimed that the only valid historical sources were the letters of contemporary missionaries and the evidence they gave under oath at the trials of the rebels. He went on to defend the actions of the Oblates in 1885 by alleging that they were opposed to Riel's movement because they foresaw its disastrous consequences. Morice dismissed allegations that the clergy had not attempted to secure clemency for Riel by declaring that it would not have been wise for them to do so because this would have aroused and intensified the fury of the Orange Lodge and nullified the influence of petitions for clemency.[96]

The polemic between Morice and the *Comité Historique* is indicative of the growing estrangement between a significant segment of the Métis community and the Oblates after 1885. In the events of 1885 the *Comité Historique* and its supporters discovered a glorious past and traditions as well as individuals who had promoted and defended Métis interests. Thus, 1885 became a source of pride to the Métis because it represented their legitimate aspirations as a nation led by indigenous leaders who shared the same ideals. In the twentieth century, the Métis had become of age and were no longer willing to accept being amalgamated and, consequently, marginalized within the larger French-speaking Catholic community.

With respect to the Oblates and the Native community, the parting of the ways was not as evident or as dramatic as it had been in the case of the Métis. There had been messianic and prophetic individuals who had appeared among the Chipewyan and other northern Indians in the period 1859–1889. The Oblates were aware of the potential threat presented by indigenous prophets and, as the representatives of orthodoxy, they responded accordingly. The individual who appeared at Île-à-la-Crosse in 1859 claiming to be the "Son of God" was ridiculed along with his teachings in an attempt to undermine his stature and influence among his followers.[97] To the Oblates, these prophetic impulses were aberrations from the true faith and inspired by Satan. The prophets were deemed to be "unfortunate visionaries" whose pride had been manipulated by demonic influences. According to Taché, the "Son of God" and other prophets were insane individuals because they believed in the deification of humans, rejected the greatness of God and purported to understand matters that were beyond the competence of humans.[98] The indigenous prophets became "religious outsiders" within the mainstream of Catholicism and hence were identified as heretics by the Oblates who could neither recognize nor accept the prophetic impulse as a legitimate expression of spirituality.[99]

As the representatives of orthodoxy, the Oblates judged devotion and piety by rigid criteria. Religious enthusiasm aroused the suspicions of the missionaries. Émile Grouard noted the presence of a fervent convert at Sturgeon Lake who exceeded the customary limits of devotion by imitating the missionary's costume and actions. This behaviour amused other Indians who referred to this individual as "pope." According to Grouard, naïveté and idiosyncrasy had been responsible for this person's zeal and he identified a potential danger in unrestrained enthusiasm.[100] The Oblates also perceived a threat in the activities of Jean L'Heureux, an errant French Canadian who lived among the Blackfoot and engaged in catechetical activities. L'Heureux gathered the Blackfoot for prayer, instruction and singing of hymns that he had translated and this earned him the title of "false priest." L'Heureux was still suspect by the Oblates despite the services that he rendered to the missionaries especially as a recruiter for the Dunbow Industrial School.[101]

Despite the appearance of prophets and other "religious outsiders" the challenge to the Oblate from within the Indian community came not in the realm of spirituality but that of politics. Following WWI, Indians who had served in the armed forces took the lead in organizing a movement to improve their status and to protect their interests. In 1919, Frederick

Ogilvie Loft, an Ontario Mohawk, founded the League of Indians of Canada for the purpose of giving Indians a greater voice in determining their destiny and the disposition of their lands. Loft's agitation displeased the Department of Indian Affairs and it placed him under police surveillance and sought to silence him by stripping him of his Indian status.[102]

For their part, the Oblates also were suspicious of these attempts to unite Indians because lay movements presented a potential challenge to the influence of the Church. In 1920, a circular written by Loft inviting Indians to join the League reached reserves near Fort Frances, Ontario. The principal of the residential school had prohibited Indians from joining this allegedly "socialist" organization and, when fire destroyed the local church, it was deemed to be an act of vengeance against the opposition of the Oblates to the League.[103] When the League met on the Thunderchild Reserve in 1921, Henri Grandin, the Alberta-Saskatchewan provincial, asked some of his missionaries to attend the proceedings. He informed Joseph Guy that the meeting had generated much discussion on the best means of educating children. While "nothing too exaggerated" had been said against the Department, Grandin wondered who was behind the movement to unify Indians but he took comfort in the fact that a Métis Oblate, Patrick Beaudry, had been elected Alberta president of the League.[104]

The following year, Grandin advised Henri Delmas that the Oblates had to be prudent in their response to the League. Grandin had been advised by Deputy Superintendent General Scott that the League was systematically opposing the Department and that Loft was regarded as the enemy of the Department. Grandin suggested that the Oblates should not become involved on behalf of an individual they did not know and they should not alienate the Department.[105] Grandin's concern had been heightened by the actions of Jean-Louis Le Vern who had written to Loft and sent money collected for the League on the Peigan Reserve. Le Vern also complained to Loft about the manner in which Department personnel were treating residents of the reserve.[106] Loft in turn sent a copy of this communication to Scott and the latter, in describing the former as an "agitator," was surprised that Le Vern collected money for the League and blamed Department personnel for "certain alleged inattention." Scott warned Grandin that harmonious relations were not promoted when the principal of the school was in "hostile correspondence with an outside person."[107]

In 1930, the Alberta and Saskatchewan sections of the League adopted the name, League of Indians of Western Canada. On the Thunderchild Reserve, John Tootoosis traveled and organized on behalf of the League to provide better education for Indian children. He was told by Ernest Lacombe that little good would come out of such efforts because too many persons already were unemployed as a result of the Depression.[108] Although a Roman Catholic, Tootoosis had been critical of the Indian residential school system and the role of the clergy and he continued his organizational work on behalf of the League and later the Union of Saskatchewan Indians. His activities and criticism irritated Théophile Bouchard in Delmas, Saskatchewan, who warned parishioners in his Christmas sermon that Tootoosis should be excommunicated for his opposition to the Church.[109] Some years later, on behalf of Saskatchewan Indians, Tootoosis prepared a brief for the Joint House of Commons and Senate Committee on Indian Affairs, which met in the period 1946–48. At this time, another Indian organization, the Queen Victoria Treaty Protective Association, was started on the neighbouring Poundmaker Reserve. Tootoosis suspected that Bouchard was the driving force behind the association and that its objective was to divide the Indian movement and defend Oblate interests in residential schools.[110]

Thus by the 1930s, the First Nations were expressing their discontent with the status quo and they resented the paternalism and tutelage inherent in the grand design that church and state sought to impose on them. It is indeed ironic to note that Indians initially demonstrated a keen interest in Christianity and the establishment of agriculture on reserves. With respect to the latter, Sarah Carter has demonstrated that government policies "made it virtually impossible for reserve agriculture to succeed because the farmers were prevented from using the technology required for agricultural activity in the West."[111] If the circumstances facing most farmers in the West left much to be desired, government policy made the situation worse for Indians. In the end, Indians were willing to use the new technology and ways of whites to allow them to overcome the loss of the hunt but they resisted all attempts aimed at undermining their culture.[112]

Indians also welcomed Christianity and education because of their inherent power and potential. As in the case of reserve agriculture, there was a disparity between theory and reality and initial optimism gave way to the "Onset of Doubt" described by John Webster Grant.[113] For the majority of Indians, Christianity had produced neither a liberation nor true and equal membership in the Christian community of believers. For its part, the educational process was not rooted in the needs and aspirations of the First Nations. Residential schools were to assimilate the young to a new culture and to depreciate Indian traditions and values. This too was unacceptable to Indians and while they were initially on the "defensive," they later found the resources to adopt a stronger "offensive" position through the organization of their own institutions such as the League of Indians. In this "offensive" stage Indians from the residential schools used the skills acquired in those institutions to begin the revolt against paternalism and colonialism. The disenchantment between Native and Oblate would reach its apogee in the third quarter of the twentieth century as a consequence of a collective conviction within the Indian community that the Oblates, through their activities and residential schools, had participated in a programme of cultural genocide aimed at depriving the First Nations of their language, traditions and identity.

11

△ △ △ △ △ △ △ △ △ △ △ △ △

THE CANONICAL VISIT OF
SUPERIOR GENERAL T. LABOURÉ

The Precursor of a New Missionary Orientation

A s the First Nations were beginning to question and challenge the system
that church and state had created to assimilate them, the Oblates
were evaluating their accomplishments as missionaries. In the twentieth century the western Oblates could reflect upon an impressive record
of accomplishments but, as time passed, the gap between the pioneer
Oblate past and the twentieth century experience widened. The older
optimistic view that Christian instruction and education were sufficient to
transform migratory hunters into progressive, sedentary citizens clashed
with the reality of life and opportunity on a reservation. Concern also
was raised over the degree of spirituality among Indians as the Oblates
noted a return to traditional spirituality among some and a rejection of
Christianity among others. Once again the high aspirations of the past had
to be modified by the existence of a religiosity that conformed outwardly
to accepted Catholic patterns but that lacked spontaneity and fervour.

In their attempts to resolve the problems that confronted their ministry the Oblates were not free agents because they had to function within
existing ecclesiological structures. At this time, the object of missionary
activity was to implant the Roman model of the Catholic Church and the
extent to which this was successful was determined by measuring conformity to the parent institution. Thus, while the Oblates were concerned
with making Christianity a more spontaneous and meaningful experience
for the First Nations, the essence of the Christian message and the struc-

ture of the church being established would continue to be defined by agents and institutions from the outside.

The advance of white civilization and the increase of settlement also imposed new demands on the Oblates who were called to minister to many of the Catholic newcomers in the West. This created an internal conflict within the ranks of the Oblates. There were some who wished not only to continue but also refurbish their missionary tradition among the First Nations. There were others who felt that demographic patterns in the West necessitated a different strategy. In addition to the conviction that immigrants and colonization were valid endeavours for the congregation, there was a feeling that Oblates serving in the Indian missions and schools had become complacent. Progress and technology had breached the isolation of distant missions, reduced hardship and enhanced the comfort of mission personnel. Unfortunately, as the quality of life in missions improved, there was a feeling that the Indian missions were loosing their appeal among the Oblates.

Some of these tensions were evident in the 1898 report of the Vicariate of St. Boniface. Unlike the other vicariates that had been critical of the advance of settlement, St. Boniface did not appear concerned, perhaps because the influence of whites there had been felt earlier and was more dominant than in other parts of the North West. Its report for that year stated that, while Indian missions were a worthy institution, the future did not belong to these "enfeebled races" but to the Europeans who were settling and exploiting the fertile plains. The conversion of Natives had been a noble venture but it was no less worthy and glorious to lay the solid foundation for the extension of Christ's kingdom in the North West by becoming involved in colonization ventures. The report suggested that colonization would not harm the reputation of the Indian missions that still occupied the majority of Oblates working in the religious vicariates and even in the diocese of Saint Boniface.[1]

With the exception of urban centres and some established parishes where the secular clergy were established, the presence of whites in the North West entailed additional work for the Oblates who were called upon to minister to the Catholic element. Saint Lazare Mission in Saskatchewan, founded by Jules Decorby in 1875, initially served only Métis and Indians. The first white families arrived in the area in 1880 and were ministered to by Decorby. The fertile Qu'Appelle valley attracted many European immigrants and Decorby's ministry necessitated the knowledge of so many languages, Indian as well as European, that he became known as the "Little father who spoke all languages." In 1888, it was noted that Decorby was studying German, his tenth language.[2] Many missions became multicultural entities. In 1923, for example, Sainte Rose de Lima Mission in Saskatchewan consisted of 10 white families (two Belgian, two French Canadian and six English/Irish), 27 Métis families and 25 Cree families.[3]

From Notre-Dame de la Paix Mission near present day Calgary, Oblates visited Medicine Hat and went down the CPR main line as far east as Maple Creek (Saskatchewan).[4] The presence of the North West Mounted Police in Fort Macleod (Alberta) attracted entrepreneurs and settlers and the growing Catholic population was served by Oblates attached to the Blood and Peigan Reserves. The discovery of coal at Lethbridge (Alberta) and the construction of a narrow gauge railroad to meet the CPR mainline at Dunmore resulted in another Catholic nucleus that required ministering. In the meantime, Pincher Creek (Alberta) also developed and its Catholic population built a chapel and soon demanded a priest. Initially, Pincher Creek, Fort Macleod and Lethbridge were visited by Oblates serving on the nearby Blood and Peigan Reserves.[5]

In addition to increasing the pastoral duties of the Oblates, the presence of white Catholics created tension within existing missions where facilities had to be shared between the Native and white communities. In Lestock, for example, there was no church on the reserve and the chapel at the residential school was used for religious services by both Indians and white settlers in the region. This arrangement led to all sorts of difficulties. To begin with, the white population was dispersed and there was little sense of belonging to a parish. Since half the seats in the chapel were reserved for Indians, white "parishioners" were not overly enthused about honouring their financial obligations to the parish. Those responsible for the mission argued that a parish church should be built in the village of Lestock to serve the white population.[6]

In 1925, a formal request was made to the Manitoba provincial to build a church in Lestock. The 128 Catholics in the village had no means of transportation to the chapel at the school located four miles away. In addition, the chapel was too small and some Indians felt overwhelmed by whites who attended. Other Natives were too embarrassed to appear next to whites because the Sunday best of the latter contrasted sharply with the poor attire of the former.[7] With the building of a church in the village Mathias Kalmès, who preached a retreat to the school children and residents of the reserve, felt that the moment was opportune to attract the Indians to the chapel. They were poor and badly dressed and many would not attend services if whites still came to their chapel.[8]

A similar situation developed at Crooked Lake (Saskatchewan) where members of the reserve complained that there was not sufficient room in the church to accommodate everyone. The reserve insisted on having two masses, one for the Indians and another for the Métis and French Canadian settlers. The proposal was acceptable to the missionary but some of the French Canadians were not too happy.[9] At Saint Philip (Saskatchewan), Paul-Émile Tétreault informed his provincial that only three or four Indian families attended mass on Sundays. He cited numerous reasons for this state of affairs including the fact that, because of their poverty and shabby dress, they did not want to come to mass if whites were present. Tétreault stated that the Indians should have their own church located in the centre of the reserve.[10]

By 1935, the Oblates had 90 years of experience in the missions of the Canadian North West. While the main thrust of their efforts were still devoted to the Indian and Métis missions, some Oblates began to lament the fact that the enthusiasm of the pioneer era for this Apostolate was waning and, perhaps worse, was lacking. While canonical visits had been made from time to time in the past, they had focused on internal administrative and religious matters and had ever examined the very essence of the congregation's work among Native populations of the Canadian North West. Furthermore, among many active missionaries there was a feeling that their apostolic and educational efforts had not yet produced the desired generation of devout, practicing Christians.

Within this context, the canonical visit of 1935 was a significant watershed in the history of Oblate missions in the Canadian North West. The Oblate administration desired a comprehensive overview of the work of missionaries engaged in all aspects of the evangelization of Indians in Canada. The superior general, Théodore Labouré, informed provincials and vicars of missions that he could not undertake this crucial visit and, hence, he would appoint Gabriel Breynat, Vicar Apostolic of Mackenzie, as canonical visitor. Breynat was to examine the spiritual and material

Superior General T. Labouré visiting Fort Vermilion. (PAA, OB 9021)

welfare of missions and residential schools as well as all Oblate residences attached to these missions and schools.[11]

The announcement of this unusual visit naturally caused concern among the western Oblates but anxiety levels increased significantly when it became known that the superior general, in fact, would undertake the inspection. Ubald Langlois, the Alberta provincial, was of the opinion that it would be preferable to have it conducted by Breynat or Joseph Guy. The Indian missions and schools were special institutions whose complexity could be comprehended only by someone who was thoroughly familiar with them and their problems. Furthermore, Langlois believed that an experienced missionary was necessary to relate to the personnel who functioned in schools and missions, as well as federal bureaucrats and ecclesiastical authorities. According to Langlois, this was "an extraordinary special visit, the first of its kind," and it would become a "veritable inquiry" rather than a "simple rectification" of existing problems. It would have to determine the precise status of the congregation with respect to the bishops and civil authorities and it would have to negotiate with the bishops.[12]

Langlois's correspondent, Anthime Desnoyers, assistant general of the Oblates, replied that the "famous visit" indeed had provoked a lot of commentary. In a later letter, Desnoyers declared that everyone was satisfied with the superior general's proposed visit. Desnoyers contended that the "fruits" would be produced slowly and would be contingent upon the formation of personnel who could be incorporated into the new impetus that would be engendered by the visit. Desnoyers declared that there were some Oblates who would find it difficult to change their ways and that the superior general was aware of this. The assistant general claimed that it was crucial to obtain from the bishops and the Holy See a legal status that was advantageous and secure for Oblate missions and schools. If their future status remained uncertain, there would be less enthusiasm for apostolic efforts.[13]

The status of the Indian missions among the Native and Métis populations was addressed by Labouré in his 1935–36 visit to Canada. One of the sources of concern was that, with the passage of time, the original Oblate vicariates of the North West had been transformed into five archdioceses and five dioceses. In these newer administrative units, the Oblates continued to be responsible for Native missions with the tacit approval of the bishops. Labouré believed that this resulted in a precarious and ambiguous status for the Oblates and that a greater stability was required for their apostolic work. Far more menacing, however, was the fact that some bishops had indicated that they intended to confide the administration of Indian education in their dioceses to secular clergy and limit the Oblates to ministering to reserves and missions. Labouré made it very clear that if residential schools were taken away from the Oblates, their apostolic work on the reserves would be rendered impossible. Furthermore, the schools were indispensable to financing missionary efforts and the subsistence of the missionaries themselves. According to Labouré, the threat of dispossessing the Oblates of their schools was equivalent to suspending the sword of Damocles over their heads.[14]

Consequently, Labouré asked the bishops to formally grant the Indian missions to the Oblates subject to the approval of the Holy See. The superior general justified his request on the basis of growth and development in the North West and the fact that the bishops were preoccupied with immigration and the establishment of new parishes and could not devote the proper attention to ministering to Native populations. Since the Oblates also had become involved in immigration and ministering to whites, questions were raised concerning the disproportionate amount of personnel and resources they continued to devote to a decreasing number of Indians.[15]

Beneath these logistical problems, however, lay a more significant menace to the stability of Oblate Indian missions and the hegemony of

French-speaking Catholics within the hierarchy. In 1911, Olivier-Elzéar Mathieu was appointed Bishop of Regina thus becoming the first non-Oblate prelate in the western provinces. The nominations of an English-speaking bishop in Calgary in 1913 and an English-speaking archbishop in Winnipeg in 1915 were more threatening because they were indicative of a conflict for domination within the Canadian hierarchy. Shortly there-after, western sees once administered by Oblates bishops (Edmonton) or French-speaking prelates (Regina) received "Irish" or English-speaking incumbents.[16] Thus, Labouré's offer to have the Oblates assume the entire responsibility for Indian missions and his proposal for the creation of a special Native vicariate in the western and northern regions of Canada had a dual purpose. To begin with, it would have provided security for the missionaries themselves who, henceforth, would no longer be exercising their apostolic ministry at the pleasure of the bishop in whose diocese they were working. More important, however, was the fact that if the proposal were accepted the Oblates could not be dispossessed by an unsympathetic "Irish" prelate who replaced a French-speaking one.[17]

The secular bishops initially gave their assent to Labouré's project but, as a result of the opposition of three of the English-speaking prelates of western Canada and pressure brought to bear by the *Chargé d'Affaires* of the Apostolic Delegation to Canada, that support waned. The *Chargé d'Affaires* then recommended to Rome that the Indian vicariate suggested by Labouré encompass all of Canada. For their part, the Oblates sent Bishop Gabriel Breynat, Vicar Apostolic of Mackenzie, to Rome to defend the interests of their western missions. In an interview with Pius XI, Breynat reminded the pontiff that it was His Holiness who first had suggested the establishment of an Indian vicariate for the Canadian North West. Breynat also gave assurances that the Oblates supported the establishment of this vicariate because it offered guarantees of greater stability for their apostolic work. Pius XI appeared well disposed to the measure and so were the Prefects of the Congregations of the Propaganda and the Consistory. However, the Consistory placed the question before the bishops in such a vague manner that they were not certain what they were asked to approve. In the end, the pope decided to pronounce the final word on the matter himself and a solution was delayed.[18]

While the legal status of Oblate missions and schools was of crucial importance to the congregation, Labouré was also determined that his visit should refurbish the spirit of the early Oblate missionaries in the North West, encourage contemporary Oblates and inculcate in them a love of and pride in working with Native populations. The admiration of Pius XI, "the great Pope of missions," for the work of the Oblates in the North West had reawakened the missionary spirit within the congregation and a new era was in the making. The Oblates would have to reorganize their apostolic efforts to be part of this new missionary thrust.[19] The inclusion of a detailed questionnaire addressed to Oblate superiors, directors of residences and principals of residential schools was a notable departure from the procedure of previous canonical visits. These individuals were asked detailed questions on indigenous vocations, on the activities associated with their visits to Indian camps, the language used in their ministry, the establishment of an association to maintain contact with former pupils and the extent to which the Indians contributed to the support of the missionary and the church.[20]

Labouré identified some current tendencies that had to be altered in order to reawaken the missionary spirit of the Oblates. To begin with, missionaries would have to resume the study of Indian languages and abandon their erroneous believe that as a result of the schools a knowledge of English was sufficient. Missionaries had to be encouraged to study Indian languages and become the skillful linguists their predecessors had been. Labouré declared that the *status quo* was no longer a satisfactory state of affairs for Oblate missions some of whom were in a state of decay because they had not been developed. He also denounced the tendency not to establish new missions, to concentrate efforts on residential schools and, in the process, abandon Indians who lived on reserves.[21]

As a first step in the development of Oblate missions, Labouré insisted that missionaries re-establish contact with Indians by living in their midst on reserves. The previous policy of centralizing Oblates in larger residences in order that they might enjoy the benefits of religious life was appropriate in white parishes but Labouré asserted that it was a disaster for those who ministered among Indians. Furthermore, improvements in the means of transportation had not overcome the problems caused by having missionaries live at some distance from their flocks. Labouré urged a return to the older policy of having missionaries live in the midst of those whom they evangelized to ensure frequent and continued contact, to facilitate knowing neophytes individually and share their lifestyle. If the Oblates were to gain the confidence of the Indians the former would have to have intimate knowledge of the latter.[22]

Since contact with neophytes was deemed crucial to the success of the Oblate Apostolate, Labouré provided specific instructions to guide the missionaries. Each Sunday the missionary was to provide a well prepared instruction based on doctrine, morality and the gospel of the day. Catechism was to be presented every day to children and adults whose knowledge of religion was imperfect and the method of presenting the catechism would vary depending on the audience and its level of comprehension. The object and parts of the mass were to be explained clearly to the faithful. Indians were to be encouraged to sing hymns in their language during mass and religious services.[23] Missionaries were to make themselves available to hear confessions and provide the necessary spiritual direction. The faithful were to be exhorted to receive communion frequently and, when a sufficient number of individuals did so, the Oblates were urged to offer the prayer of thanksgiving with them. Labouré urged missionaries to assiduously visit families and those who were ill. He claimed that the success of evangelization depended on a missionary's influence and, hence, the Oblate had to know and love his flock and in turn had to be known and loved by them.[24]

Since Labouré was so convinced that contact with and knowledge of neophytes was a *sine qua non* to a successful ministry, he regretted the virtual disappearance of the annual mission. He recognized that changing circumstances no longer made it as mandatory for Indians to gather in a central location such as a trading post but, nevertheless, he affirmed that the Oblates had been negligent in organizing such missions. He declared, furthermore, that in many locations it was possible to organize annual missions as had been done in the past. Where Indians did not congregate on an annual basis Labouré recommended that the Oblates organize one to coincide with the visit of the bishop for confirmation. Provincials and vicars of missions were urged to restore the tradition of the annual mission to its previous status.[25]

In addition to the annual mission, the superior general decreed that camps and chapels on reserves had to be visited by missionaries. Furthermore, missionaries had to live in a central location on the reserve to be able to make these visits. Longer visits were preferred to frequent shorter ones because Labouré believed that more positive results would be produced by the former. When the missionary arrived in a camp, Indians were to be gathered for prayer and confession. In the morning there was to be prayer followed by mass and an instruction. Later in the morning the children would be gathered for catechism and to be taught how to read, write and sing. There would be another catechism for children in the afternoon. After the evening meal there would be prayers, hymn singing, recitation of the beads and an instruction. The day would culminate with confession and a visit to the sick and elderly.[26]

As a second prerequisite for a successful missionary policy, Labouré advocated a mastery of Indian languages. In the past, the intimate knowledge of Native dialects had contributed to the success of Oblate missionaries over Protestant ones and Labouré cited the dictum of an old Oblate to the effect that a missionary who did not understand the language of those whom he was evangelizing was like a soldier without a gun. Labouré alleged that the multiplicity of languages, a preference for ministering to whites and a overzealous desire to assimilate Indians were the main reasons for neglecting the study of Indian language. The superior general denounced the use of interpreters that had resulted in "painful and ridiculous experiences" and he made it clear that one could not claim to be an Oblate missionary without taking the trouble to learn the necessary languages to practice one's ministry.[27] Labouré also denounced efforts made in the name of progress that sought the assimilation of the Indian to white customs and traditions. Expressing ideas that were ahead of his time Labouré insisted that an Indian could be a good Christian without adopting European ways and without abandoning his/her language. The Oblates were reminded that it was not the intention of the Church to assimilate those who were being evangelized and that without a knowledge of Indian languages the Oblates could not successfully discharge Christ's commission.[28]

Labouré addressed the language question directly in the report of his visit of the Oblate missions. He recalled that the success of Oblate missionary activities in the North West had been due in large part to the success of the missionaries in mastering Indian languages. However, with the passage of time and the encroachment of white civilization, the superior general noted certain tendencies that contributed to the abandonment of Indian languages in school and apostolic work and affirmed that if these continued the efforts of the Oblates as missionaries seriously would be undermined. He saw fit to remind Oblates of the function of Native education and to re-affirm that residential schools were not to be transformed into academies where Indians were to be made into whites. The objective of Indian education was not to "de-Indianize" children but to transform them into good Christians. Thus, the Oblates were to strive to eliminate defects of character and maintain in the hearts of Indian children a love of their race and language.[29]

In conformity with the wishes expressed personally to him by Pius XI, Labouré ruled that, henceforth, all religious instruction in residential schools would be provided in Indian languages. Hinting that this question had been the source of disagreement in the past among Oblates, the superior general left no doubt as to the direction of future policy. Provincials and principals were reminded that this decision was not subject to discussion and had to be obeyed.[30]

In addition to the utilization of indigenous languages for religious instruction, Labouré decreed that where the principal was not fluent in the local Indian language, the provincial would send a missionary who was to provide religious instruction to the students in their language as often as possible. If there were more than one language spoken in a school each was to be used in turn to provide religious instruction. Since the shortage of missionaries had been identified as one of the factors contributing to the abandonment of Native languages, Labouré committed the congregation to recruiting devoted and competent missionaries for service in the missions.[31]

Labouré recognized the importance of syllabic characters as an instrument to facilitate evangelization and decided that the use of syllabics would not only be continued but that they would be used in all schools. The superior general hoped that the Department would allow the Oblates to include a period of weekly instruction in syllabics on the programme of studies for residential schools. If this request were refused, Labouré declared that Oblates and sisters in schools would teach syllabics after regular class time or during the period of religious instruction.[32]

The superior general also announced that, as a result of directives issued by the Sacred Congregation of the Propaganda, the General Administrative Council of the Oblates had ratified a proposal to establish three schools in western Canada to facilitate the study of indigenous languages by missionaries. Cree was to be taught at Grouard, Alberta,

Chipewyan at Beauval, Saskatchewan and Saulteaux at Fort Alexander in Manitoba. Furthermore, all missionaries who wished to serve among the Native populations would have to spend one year studying at one of these schools. In addition to studying Native languages, Oblates who attended these institutions would receive practical advice on their ministry among Native populations.[33]

Labouré was also concerned with the abandonment of Christian traditions by students once they left school and he attributed this state of affairs in part to excessive discipline and regimentation that had produced outward conformity rather than true Christian convictions. Labouré's recommendations were designed to overcome the adverse effects of compulsory observances. Pupils, for example, were to be encouraged to go to confession prior to mass but would not be obliged to confess themselves. It was only in the confessional that the children were to be provided with spiritual direction. Children were also to be encouraged to receive communion frequently and even daily but they were not to be cajoled or compelled. Furthermore, those who opted not to receive the sacrament were not to be reproached for their actions. The Oblates were not to force children to attend mass on a daily basis; they were to invite the pupils to do so but attendance was to be a voluntary act. Simple prayer books reflecting the different parts of the mass were to be prepared for the students in the appropriate Indian language. To ensure the proper nurturing of the Christian traditions acquired at the school, Labouré instructed missionaries to maintain contact with the children after they returned to their homes. The Oblates were to inculcate in former pupils a love of the school that had formed them. He suggested that a meeting or two per year accompanied by a celebration and banquet would attract the graduates.[34]

To eliminate situations that gave rise to immorality Labouré recommended that children of opposite sexes should be given the opportunity of meeting one another in the parlour or in recreation areas "under the open but discrete supervision of a sister." Labouré noted that in some schools the personnel lacked the dedication required to fulfill the role of supervisor. Consequently, students were left alone in rooms or dormitories with predictable immoral consequences.[35] Labouré was very much concerned with inadequate or uncertain supervision by males and, after reflecting on the matter, he recommended that the older male students be supervised and disciplined by "zealous, dedicated and competent nuns" who would strive to maintain piety and morality among their charges.

With respect to the administration of residential schools, Labouré deemed it necessary to reaffirm the authority of the Oblate provincial over such institutions within his province. The government confided the jurisdiction over residential schools to the Oblates and, since the provincial was the congregation's representative at the regional level, the government discussed matters affecting these schools with the provincial. Some principals, however, seemed unaware of the provincial's ultimate authority and regarded themselves as agents of the government and responsible only to that authority.

In re-affirming the authority of the provincial, Labouré eliminated any ambiguity concerning respective functions of provincial and principal. Principals represented the congregation in the administration of the school but their authority was delegated to them by the provincial. To confirm the authority of provincials, the government was asked to send all funds destined for residential schools directly to the provincials. They, in turn, would verify the sums received by means of reports prepared by the principals and would then credit the schools' bank account with the appropriate sum.[36]

The delegation of authority by the provincial had resulted in some controversy between principal and other Oblates in the school. To resolve these jurisdictional disputes Labouré clearly outlined the duties and responsibilities of principals. Like a *curé* in a parish, the principal was given authority to ensure the "ordinary" direction and administration of the institution. With respect to "extraordinary" matters, the principal had to seek the approval of the provincial. The principal was provided with assistants such as a spiritual director, a bursar and teachers and, although the principal was responsible for the day-to-day administration of the school, Labouré dismissed as false the concept that the principal was the absolute master of the institution. According to Labouré, the principal had to be the first to respect the rights of others and to abide by the rules that governed the conduct between Oblates and members of female religious communities. For their part, bursars were authorized to deal with "ordinary" expenses that had been approved without securing additional approbation. "Extraordinary" expenses could not be incurred by bursars without the approval of the superior. Labouré established categories of expenses that principals were authorized to incur without the permission of the provincial and those that required that permission.[37]

Labouré's report expressed concern with the location of the residences of Oblates and lay brothers who were attached to residential schools especially when their quarters were in the midst of pupils or in proximity to the domicile of nuns. Labouré asserted that it was not necessary for the good conduct of the school that the principal reside in proximity to students and sisters and oversee every aspect of the school's operation. He suggested that, in schools where principals left initiative and freedom of action to the nuns, the conduct of the school often was enhanced. He ruled that, where it was possible, the Oblates were to have their residence separate from the school premises and that the principal's office should be in the Oblate residence rather than in the school. Furthermore, principals were to take their meals with the Oblate community rather than with the pupils.[38]

The superior general observed that furnishings in the schools were too sumptuous and superfluous and this state of affairs was difficult to reconcile with religious life and the vow of poverty. He described some parlours as resembling those of the very rich with their massive and expensive couches and chairs. The offices of some principals on the other hand, could rival those of a bank director or a statesman. Labouré would not accept as a justification that the school was a government institution and had to be furnished accordingly. He ruled that the expensive furnishings be replaced as quickly as possible and, henceforth, there was to be no furniture in the office of principal or the rooms of the Oblates that contravened the spirit of religious life and the rules of the congregation.[39]

Labouré's report also commented on a delicate matter, the relationships between Oblates and members of female religious communities. He asserted that, as the assistants of the Oblates, sisters had to be treated as such and with the respect and deference accorded to members of a religious community. Principals were not to enter the residence of the sisters without the permission of the sister superior and only in the company of the latter. Since the part of the school reserved for the sisters was their convent, only the sisters had the right to regard themselves at home in those premises. If a principal had matters to discuss with the nuns, he would be received in the parlour or in the sisters' community room. Labouré emphasized that good relations between the Oblates and the sisters was necessary to ensure the success of the school. In consultation with the sister superior, the principal would formulate directives for the conduct of the institution in accordance with government regulations as well as for the spiritual and moral education of the pupils. He urged principals to second the authority of the sisters and provide them with all the necessary support and encouragement to discharge their duties.[40]

Labouré's report also addressed the question of indigenous religious vocations and this was a crucial concern to the Oblates. Despite the efforts of bishops such as Taché and Grandin and as well as those of individual Oblates, there had been very few vocations among the Aboriginal populations of the North West. Edward Cunningham, the first Métis Oblate, was ordained in 1890 and the second, Patrick Beaudry, was ordained eleven years later in 1901. Napoléon Laferté, a Métis from the Northwest Territories, was ordained in 1923 while Patrice Mercredi was ordained in 1934. At the time of Labouré's visit, however, no Indian had entered the Oblates. The value of an indigenous clergy was not lost on the Oblates and, hence, the failure to recruit one was a great disappointment. The virtual absence of priestly vocations was also a reflection of the shallow roots Christianity had made among the Métis and Indian populations.

In August 1935, the secretary of State for the Vatican had invited the Oblates to establish a seminary for Natives and Métis in the North West.[41] This was the first time that a distinct and special seminary had been proposed to encourage vocations and an indication that the previous method of training Native and Métis aspirants with white candidates for the priesthood had not been successful. During Labouré's visit, Oblate superiors and directors as well as principals of residential schools had been given a detailed questionnaire. With respect to vocations they were to comment on: (1) the possibility of vocations among Indians, (2) the proposal to establish an indigenous seminary, (3) how to ensure its maintenance and success and (4) whether the candidates should be admitted to the regular or secular clergy.[42]

Labouré admitted that there were "extraordinary difficulties" that had to be surmounted prior to preparing an indigenous clergy. Nevertheless, action had to be taken because Indian children had indicated an interest in the priesthood and four had been admitted to secondary education. However, the replies to the questionnaire suggested that the indigenous seminary proposed by the Vatican would not be in the best interests of a future Native clergy. The respondents argued that training the Indian and Métis aspirants apart from other white students would result in these elements considering themselves isolated from the other clergy and engendering and inferiority complex in their minds. Convinced that indigenous vocations had to be stimulated, Labouré proposed to open a small apostolic school in the midst of the tribes that were better disposed to providing vocations. This school would provide the traditional classical secondary education for students and simultaneously test their desire to become priests. After a few years, those who gave signs of being "serious vocations" would be sent to a seminary to continue their studies for the priesthood. According to Labouré, Indian and Métis candidates would thus complete their "social education" through contact with other future priests with whom they would associate when their studies were completed.[43]

In terms of problems confronting Oblate missions and schools the superior general's canonical visit was timely. By 1935, the missionary thrust begun 90 years earlier had reached its apogee. The missiology that had guided this pioneer stage was characterized by the implantation of a western European variant of Catholicism and its corresponding cultural values and traditions. The acceptance of this spirituality at first only implied the acceptance of its accompanying cultural attributes. In time, however, the civilizing dimension became explicit especially as a result of the venture into residential education and later the settlement, development and exploitation of the North West and its resources by non-Natives.

In the period of initial contact with the Oblates Christianity appeared as an impressive and powerful spirituality to the First Nations but, as John Webster Grant has pointed out, much of that appeal faded for subsequent generations.[44] For some, Christianity may have failed to facilitate the achievement of personal aspirations while for others, the residential school experience was devastating. Other students may have found it impossible to reconcile the liberation promised by Christianity with the poverty and lack of opportunity found on reserves. Some resented the fact that the acceptance of Christianity necessitated giving up their Indian identity. Those who became Christian faced a lonely experience as they lived in an in between world where they were not quite Indian but far from white.

The church implanted by the Oblates was not a living, dynamic church, rooted in the social and cultural traditions of those whom it served. Like all missionary churches, it was a foreign, colonial institution, a clone of its West European parent. Consequently, Christianity became very much a one-way street as far as many members of the First Nations were concerned and it is not surprising that many felt that it no longer represented a meaningful form of spiritual expression and reverted to traditional forms. Confronted with this indifference and, at times hostility, some Oblates began to question the effectiveness of their missionary efforts as well as value of the product it fashioned.

Within this context, the canonical visit of 1935 forced the Oblates to reflect on their apostolic efforts and Labouré's report provided a mechanism by which the Oblates were able to confront a missionary frontier that had changed dramatically. Most of his recommendations were rooted in the Oblate past but others anticipated the ecumenical spirit generated by Vatican II. First and foremost, Labouré stressed the need for a unity of objectives and methods. In addition, he desired to integrate all Oblate efforts in education, health services and missions. To this end, it was necessary to ensure the collaboration and cooperation of all constituent parts: missionaries, lay brothers and members of female religious communities.

With respect to the Christian message and its reception and adherence by neophytes, Labouré's insistence on a spontaneous response on the part of the believer rather than casual or mediocre conformity was a significant departure from the traditional view of what constituted a successful missionary effort as demonstrated by statistics relating to confessions, communions and baptisms. Be that as it may, Labouré's report did not transform a one-way street into a two-way street in which Natives shared equally in defining and practicing spirituality because neither time nor circumstance were appropriate for such a change. Nevertheless, in the next decades Oblates openly admitted that their missionary effort had been a tragedy for Native peoples because, while they had accepted Christianity, it had not accepted them or recognized their language and culture in the liturgy of the Catholic Church. Worse yet, was the fact that few within the Aboriginal community had experienced true Christian charity from other Canadians.[45]

THE OBLATE APOSTOLATE

One Hundred Years Later

The canonical visit of 1935–36 and the recommendations made by Superior General Labouré facilitated the transformation of a missionary institution that was nearly a hundred years old. As a result of the profound changes that had taken place in the western and northern regions of Canada, the Oblates were forced to examine their apostolic activity, re-evaluate their objectives and adopt methods that reflected changing times, circumstances and philosophies. The Oblate involvement in residential schools necessitated a close association with the government and its highly centralized bureaucracy. In view of the role that such schools were to play as adjuncts of missions and the revenues they generated, their continued existence could not be ensured uniquely by the efforts on individual principals and provincials. Consequently, Superior General Labouré called upon all Oblates involved in missionary activity and Indian education to work as a team committed to pursuing a common objective.

Labouré's extensive report contained the first official directives for the establishment of a permanent Oblate agency in Ottawa to represent, defend and enhance the interests of Oblate missions and schools in Canada. This agency was responsible for overseeing the status of missions and presenting requests for grants to the government for the construction, operation and maintenance of residential schools. A permanent representative resident in Ottawa was appointed by the Oblate General

Administration to act as intermediary between the vicars apostolic and provincials of the North West and the Department of Indian Affairs. The agency, initially known as *Missions Indiennes des Pères Oblats,* later assumed the name *Commission Oblate des Oeuvres Indiennes et Esquimaudes* [COOIE] (Indian Welfare and Training Oblate Commission). Its first officers were Gabriel Breynat, Vicar Apostolic of Mackenzie, president; Émile Bunoz, Vicar Apostolic of the Yukon and Prince Rupert, vice-president; and Joseph Guy, Vicar Apostolic of Grouard, secretary-treasurer. Omer Plourde, who had discharged the duties of a semi official representative of the western Oblates since Guy's elevation to the episcopacy in 1930, was named the agency's official representative in Ottawa.[1]

The first meeting of COOIE's management committee was held on 17 January 1936 in Ottawa when it was decided that the representative of the western Oblates would receive the official title of superintendent and provisions were made for his salary and expenses.[2] Unfortunately, the nomination of an official representative formally approved by the congregation did not put an end to the problems associated with that position. Initially, bishops and provincials continued to submit their individual budgets for schools under their jurisdiction to the authorities and there were also difficulties with collecting the money from the bishops and provincials to fund the bureau and pay Plourde's expenses.[3] In addition, his other occupation as director of Canadian Publishers Limited, an Oblate enterprise in Winnipeg, which published Catholic newspapers, made it impossible for him to take up permanent residence in Ottawa until 1942.[4]

Despite these initial organizational difficulties, COOIE was not inactive in promoting Oblate and Catholic interests. At its first meeting on 17 January 1936, it affirmed the principle of confessionality in Native hospitals and informed the Department that this recommendation had the support of the Catholic hierarchy.[5] In the event that the Department would not recognize the principle of confessional health care for Natives, COOIE later insisted on the employment of Catholic personnel in neutral hospitals in proportion to the number of Catholic Indians in the locality.[6] In pointing to the absence of Catholic functionaries in the Department of Indian Affairs, COOIE took up an issue first raised a half century earlier by Bishop Grandin. COOIE sent a special letter to Cardinal Joseph-Marie-Roderigue Villeneuve and all members of the Catholic hierarchy affirming that, since 50 per cent of the Native population was Catholic, Indian agencies where Catholics were in the majority should have Catholic personnel and this prerequisite should appear in civil service announcements for agents, inspectors and farm instructors. In an effort to promote good harmony and cooperation, the Department was asked to notify COOIE when such positions became vacant or at least request a list of potential Catholic candidates.[7] While this contentious issue was not likely to be resolved to the satisfaction of all, others lent themselves to a solution that was acceptable to the interests of both parties. In 1936, for example, COOIE asked the Department to authorize the use of the Butler catechism in all residential schools. For its part, the Department desired the adoption of one single catechism for all the its schools operated by Catholics.[8]

As individual missionaries had done in the past, COOIE, interested itself in promoting and enhancing the welfare of Indians. After the control over natural resources was returned to the provinces, COOIE became concerned that the provinces would exploit these resources without regard of the repercussions for Indians and, hence, deprive them of their own means of subsistence. Breynat contended that, in ceding their lands, Indians had not given up their right to hunt and fish, nor their lifestyle or traditions. Furthermore, many verbal promises had been made to Indians and these had never been kept. Breynat had made the authorities aware of the gravity of the situation and their responsibilities to Natives. Immediate action had been promised but nothing had been done to protect and rehabilitate Indians who were being threatened by resource exploitation. Breynat suggested that COOIE meet with the prime minister and his associates, inform them of the immensity of the problem and convince them to adopt an efficient plan of action to rehabilitate the Native population.[9] Thus, in 1939, COOIE passed resolutions calling on the government to restore exclusive hunting and fishing rights to Indians on the lands they occupied in order to provide them with a means of subsistence. The federal government was also asked to provide old age pensions to Indians because they were more destitute than the whites or Métis who received this allocation.[10]

As could be expected, COOIE's main concern was with missionary institutions such as schools and hospitals and, consequently, it used every opportunity to reiterate Oblate views on the provision of education and health services to Natives. In 1940, it presented a brief to the government supporting the principle of confessionality in the establishment of hospitals.[11] When it became aware that administrators within the Department were becoming opposed to residential schools because of their high cost and alleged impractical curriculum, COOIE affirmed that where Indians were still migratory hunters or dispersed, the residential school was the only institution that could educate them, restore the health of those ravaged by tuberculosis and inculcate the adoption of better mores.[12]

In 1941, the federal government's proposal to reduce the operating grant to residential schools resulted in a meeting between representatives of the Catholic, Anglican, United and Presbyterian Churches with T.A. Crerar, the minister of Indian Affairs. All denominations were quick to denounce the cavalier and unilateral manner in which the government had seen fit to reduce grants without consulting the parties that would be most affected by that decision.[13] The minister was advised, furthermore, that Indian education was acquiring more importance in missionary work because the Native population was increasing significantly with each passing year. Indians were not disappearing as had been anticipated previously and school budgets had to reflect this demographic pattern in order to provide adequate facilities. After the interview, the churches formed an Indian Co-operating Committee to lobby the government and urge it to pay a cost of living bonus for residential schools.[14] For their part, the Oblates predicted that disastrous consequences would result if the construction of new schools was stopped because of the war and if there were not sufficient funds to educate the existing school population.[15] As a result of this interdenominational pressure, the government agreed to provide a supplementary grant to cover cost of living increases.

In announcing this good news to the principal of the Duck Lake school, Plourde suggested that principals should write and thank the minister and use the opportunity to advise him of the financial difficulties occasioned by the war and thus lay the groundwork for the requests COOIE would make for the 1942–43 fiscal year.[16] When the government convoked a meeting of principals and first class teachers of Indian schools in Winnipeg in 1942 to study curriculum, Plourde advised Oblate principals that, in addition to studying the vocational programme, attention should also focus on a programme of studies that reflected the social and economic needs of Indians. If the curriculum were left unchanged it would be unjust to teachers and students because there would be an insistence on achieving standards set for whites but without providing the appropriate time to meet these objectives.[17]

Plourde also advised the Department that Oblate principals were very concerned with the lack of programmes to assist children after they left residential schools. He claimed that when children were dismissed from school at the age of sixteen they were too young to have acquired a trade nor had they received suitable training to enable them to earn a living whereas white children received training. Ubald Langlois, Vicar Apostolic of Grouard, had established a training centre for young girls at his own expense in 1939 and Plourde claimed that it had produced commendable results.[18] For its part, the Department was aware of the keen shortage of skilled labour but indicated there was little hope for additional funds to provide the training suggested by Plourde.[19]

The concerns raised by Plourde relative to post-school programmes and vocational training reflected the dissatisfaction of Oblates with a system that was not providing Indian children with an education that would enable them to earn a living and contribute to the amelioration of their social and economic status.[20] The Oblates believed that vocational instruction would have to acquire a more important status in residential schools and they complained that it was given too early in the school programme and that it was difficult to establish such courses in small schools with low enrolments. The Oblates suggested the establishment of an Indian technical high school at Qu'Appelle where pupils from all over Saskatchewan would be admitted and they argued that it was neither practical nor desirable to place Indian children in technical schools in urban areas. Furthermore, the Oblates stressed that vocational education should emphasize agriculture because it was the main economic activity on the prairies and it would permit graduates to earn their living on a reserve. The Oblates contended that the previous attempt to teach vocational trades to Indians had failed because they could not compete with white tradesmen and returned to their reserves where they found little to do.[21]

Despite Oblate efforts to make education a more meaningful and rewarding experience for Indian children, recruitment continued to be a serious problem affecting Oblate residential schools. In 1942 hardly any school had a full enrolment of students when classes began in September and principals complained that Indian agents were not cooperating with them for purposes of recruitment. According to the Oblates, this lack of cooperation resulted in principals expending considerable effort and spending significant sums of money to transport children whose parents refused to send them at the beginning of the school term. As a result of complaints from the Oblates, the Department promised greater cooperation and principals were advised to send the list of children to Indian agents in mid-August. The Department would advise agents to accompany the principals on each reserve and assist them in collecting the children and thus avoid numerous voyages. Agents could invoke compulsory attendance legislation whereas the Oblates would not dare to do so. According to Plourde, Indians had a "reverential fear" of agents and would obey them in instances when they would not do so for a principal.[22]

While the power of the state could be used to promote Oblate interests in the case of school attendance, there were instances where government policy was deemed to impact negatively. In 1945, Plourde congratulated the federal government for having brought Indians under the provisions of the Family Allowance Act. He claimed that this was a great step forward and, furthermore, it would demonstrate that there was no discrimination between Indians and whites.[23] However, Plourde expressed regret that under the terms of the legislation, financial benefits would not be provided to parents whose children were attending residential schools. He hinted that there would be a temptation for parents to keep children at home to receive benefits and recommended that the Act be altered to safeguard the right of Indians to have their children educated in residential schools and simultaneously allow them to receive benefits. Plourde suggested that the money paid to students attending residential schools should be placed in a trust fund that would be administered by the Department for the benefit of the children after they left school.[24]

Henri Routhier, the Alberta-Saskatchewan provincial, expressed similar concerns to T.A. Crerar, minister of Mines and Resources. Routhier contended that the exclusion of boarders in residential schools from benefits would produce tragic results. Parents would refuse to send their children to school to obtain benefits and he predicted that this would be the death of residential schools.[25] Crerar reassured Routhier by stating that the government would exercise care in the administration of family allowance benefits and cancel payments to parents who refused to send their children to school. According to the minister, this policy would result in a larger and more regular attendance in both day and residential schools for Indians.[26]

In the meantime, Superior General Labouré's injunction to the Oblates to find inspiration in their past and re-animate their ministry to inculcate a vibrant and dynamic Christian spirit among Natives struck a responsive chord within the ranks of the Oblates. Over the years, significant changes had taken place in the Oblate mentality. The altruism of the pioneer period had been replaced by a more mature viewpoint that concerned itself more with the process of conversion and the finished product rather than conversion as an objective in itself. At the same time, there was a growing conviction that a missionary had to do more than convert individuals; he also had to win the heart of those whom he evangelized. Bishop Ovide Charlebois advised one of his young missionaries that this could come about only if the missionary truly loved the members of his flock because love diminished faults and enhanced inherent qualities. In addition, the missionary had to be good, amiable and always prepared to be of service to his flock.[27]

These new tendencies were evident at the Qu'Appelle Residential School that had been destroyed by fire in 1932. While the fire had been a great tragedy for the Oblates, the interim measures that had to be adopted between 13 November 1932 and 23 March 1936 to house the students and continue their education produced unexpected positive results. The Oblates had established a scholasticate at Lebret in 1926 but, prior to the fire, pupils at the school and the scholastics had gone about their respective lives as perfect strangers. With the destruction of the school, pupils were housed in the scholasticate and shared a common room for recreation with the seminarians and both elements began to interact. To further promote the attraction and affection that was engendered by this contact, games and other activities were organized for both groups during their free time. The Oblates felt that contact with the seminarians provided pupils with an exemplary model of Christian virility and strength and they formed an association to promote these values. Two Native students who indicated a desire to become priests were sent to the Oblate juniorate at St. Boniface.[28]

Since the superior general had made it known that he could not tolerate inactivity or a lack of attention at chapel, Oblates at Qu'Appelle were confronted with the prospect of interesting the children who attended chapel or sending them out to play. The scholastics formed a liturgical committee and a programme of activities designed to fashion a "truly eucharistic mentality" and win the hearts as well as the souls of the students. As a result, every second morning the pupils sang in their own language in different groups and at the benediction of the Blessed Sacrament. All of the children sang at high mass and, during the service, the ritual of the mass was explained to the children by a scholastic. An Oblate also was at the disposition of pupils who wished to confess themselves. In addition, children were taught to serve mass and to play the organ in order that they might continue to exercise those functions when they returned to their reserves. The sincerity and devotion of the scholastics reassured the pupils while the former were rewarded by the love and friendship of the latter.[29]

In addition to promoting the spiritual welfare of its charges, the Qu'Appelle school also attempted to enhance their material well-being by sending three students to St. Boniface to study mink ranching. In the fall of 1938, the school built cages and bought 50 mink with one thousand dollars borrowed from the Department for this purpose. Mink ranching was seen as an ideal occupation for Indians and it was hoped that the project at Lebret would result in the creation of an industry that would provide an income for many. One student was placed in charge of the mink but lost nine as a result of feeding them too much meat. In the fall of 1939 it was decided to liquidate the mink because of losses and the low prices for the pelts. This had been an expensive venture for the Oblates and they were cautious about embarking on another.[30]

The need to make the missionary thrust a more dynamic and meaningful experience had also been voiced within the Church and had resulted in the creation of the *Unio Cleri*, an organization of the missionary clergy in 1917.[31] Several congresses were held in Italy and France under its auspices and, in 1934, it was decided that meetings would be held in Canada to study matters of concern to missionaries. At the request of Cardinal Villeneuve of Quebec, the *Union Missionnaire du Clergé* in Canada became the patron of these proceedings. Villeneuve regarded the UMC as a "normal school" for the preparation of a missionary clergy and he affirmed, furthermore, that "fraternal meetings" of those involved in missionary work were needed to define and enhance Catholic apostolic activities. These Canadian meetings, the *Semaines d'études missionnaires,* would contribute to a more critical and detailed knowledge of missionary matters.[32]

As a result, the first *Semaine d'études missionnaires* was held at the University of Ottawa, 6–9 October 1934. Most of the proceedings revolved around the fundamental theme of missiology in an attempt to identify and resolve problems associated with missionary work. Misssiology was becoming a popular term in missionary vocabulary and this is indicative of a more reflective attitude among active missionaries as well as an attempt to enhance their Apostolate by incorporating knowledge from disciplines other than theology. During the Ottawa sessions, Albert Perbal described missiology as "the science of missions" and affirmed that it consisted of critical and scientific approach to the study of the propagation of the Catholic faith its principles and its practical norms.[33] The second *Semaine d'études missionnaires* was held at Laval University in 1936 and had as its general theme problems associated with the conversion of non-Christians.[34]

The need for a more rational and unified approach to apostolic work was reflected in the publication of *Directives missionnaires* in 1942 by Martin Lajeunesse, Vicar Apostolic of Keewatin.[35] Lajeunesse's purpose was to provide his collaborators with guidelines to unify their work and to enable them to fulfill their obligations as missionaries. These directives reflected the views of his predecessor, Ovide Charlebois, on Christian virtues and the ministry as well as circular letters and other instructions published by other Oblates such as Cardinal Villeneuve, Archbishop Émile Legal of Edmonton and Superior General Théodore Labouré. Lajeunesse also included the methods and instructions of former missionaries in the directives. The observance of the directives was compulsory for all missionaries in the vicariate beginning on 29 June 1943.[36]

The growing importance of and interest in the science of missions was reflected in the publication of Joseph-Étienne Champagne's *Manuel d'action missionnaire* published in 1947. Professor of Missiology in the Faculty of Theology at the University of Ottawa, Champagne prepared this comprehensive manual to assist in the training of missionaries and to inculcate a new view, that of cooperation between different missionary institutions to achieve a common goal.[37] Champagne was instrumental in establishing the Institute of Missiology at the University of Ottawa the following year. The purpose of the Institute was to facilitate apostolic efforts by adopting a more effective missionary methodology that incorporated the latest scholarly knowledge. Champagne was convinced that an institute would prepare superior candidates to provide direction and leadership and make it possible for Catholic missionaries to enhance their reputation and be equal to the task facing them.[38]

As the Oblates were reflecting on their past and attempting to enhance the effectiveness of their activities, the missionary frontier had undergone significant change. The penetration of white civilization into the northern regions continued at an accelerated pace and the Oblates were very concerned about the consequences of this presence. In addition to the fatal attraction that the presence of whites presented to the Native community, the Oblates were responsible for ministering to the Catholic population in these new settlements. In 1939, one missionary was given responsibility for Catholics who lived along the rail line between Le Pas and Churchill.[39] In the Vicariate of Mackenzie, the discovery of gold on the shores of Lake Athabasca necessitated the establishment of a mission at the embryonic town of Goldfields in 1935.[40] The pernicious influence of white miners on Indians also was noted but the vicariate's report claimed that frequent visits by missionaries attenuated and prevented many abuses.[41]

The Oblates, however, were powerless to counter the economic and social effects of the recession of the 1930s. While the Depression created hardship for all Oblate missions in the western provinces, those in the north suffered more because they were dependent on charitable donations that were more difficult to obtain. The report of the Vicariate Apostolic of Keewatin for 1936 indicated that the poverty of Indians was caused by the cataclysmic drop in the price of furs that provided their only income. Consequently, the Indians were reduced to eating boiled fish and the Oblates complained that they could not provide them with used clothing because Catholics were donating it to the unemployed in the settled areas. The vicariate lamented the fact that, in such circumstances, Indians would be the last to receive charity.[42]

Métis education in the vicariate was threatened by the reduction in financial support provided by the governments of Manitoba and Saskatchewan. Teachers salaries were reduced significantly and, since the Métis had nothing to contribute, the vicariate had to provide the funds to keep the schools open. The vicariate also denounced the government's policy of selling licenses for commercial fishing in areas such as Pelican Lake. It was argued that the small revenue generated by the sale of these licenses undermined the interests of the Indians who had been urged to locate their reserves adjacent to these lakes. In addition, government regulations prohibited the killing of beaver, the only fur bearing animal present in the woods that year. The Oblates were pressing the authorities to provide assistance for Indians and Bishop Breynat of Mackenzie had gone to Ottawa to lobby the federal authorities.[43]

A dismal picture of the status of the Métis in the Portage La Loche region of Saskatchewan was painted by Jean-Baptiste Ducharme at in 1939. He claimed that hunting, fishing and trapping no longer provided a livelihood for the Métis because the payment of relief caused them to abandon their former self-sufficient ways to live at government expense. In the process, the Métis became convinced that they had a right to demand what they needed from the state and the consequences were disastrous because they no longer felt responsible to look after their aged parents or widowed mother.[44] He claimed that the only reasonable solution was to provide assistance only to those who were in extreme need and who had no one to assist them. Ducharme claimed that the Métis and Indians were able to live from hunting and fishing but not from agriculture or industry. They could not be transformed into whites and, hence, they were best left alone to exploit what nature had provided. He contended that with proper protection and assistance they would again be a happy people.[45]

The condition of the Métis in Alberta was desperate and served as an impetus to the creation of the Métis Association of Alberta in 1932 under the leadership of lay leaders such as Joseph Dion, Malcolm Norris and Jim Brady. The Association was a nonpartisan, nondenominational organization to promote the social and economic interests of Alberta Métis.[46] The question of a land base figured prominently in the minds of the Métis especially after the federal government transferred the control of Crown lands to provincial governments and the Association began to agitate for the setting aside of land for the exclusive use of the Métis.[47] At the insistence of the Association and its leaders the provincial government appointed a special commission in 1934, headed by Alfred Freeman Ewing, to study the matter in conjunction with the Métis and suggest solutions. Bishop Joseph Guy of Grouard appeared before the hearings of the Commission to present the claims of the Métis of northern Alberta.[48] The Commission's report resulted in the passage of the *Métis Population Betterment Act* on 21 December 1938 that set aside more than a million and a quarter acres of land in northern Alberta for the exclusive use of the Métis.

When Métis families began to establish themselves in colonies on these lands, Oblates were sent to erect churches and missions. At Fishing Lake, Irénée Gauthier arrived in 1939 and established a residence that was reminiscent of Oblate establishments nearly a century earlier. His chapel-residence consisted of two small rooms whose walls were papered with cardboard boxes. The furniture consisted of a table made from rough lumber, while butter cases served as chairs. Gauthier advised the Catholic Church Extension Society that 60 Métis families had settled in the colony and there were 80 children of school age. The residents did not have the means to build a church but were willing to do all the work and Gauthier asked the Society's assistance The Church Extension provided a gift of five hundred dollars and, with logs cut and provided by the Métis, a church and school were built.[49]

Roméo Levert who arrived in Fishing Lake in 1941 reported that, in terms of material goods, the colonies had not yet attained the success that some optimists had anticipated. He claimed that overnight one could not fashion model farmers out of peoples who had been hunters for centuries. He contended, furthermore, that very seldom did impressive government projects find the competent personnel necessary to implement them.[50] Levert was pleased with the spiritual and moral progress that had taken place in the colony. Grouped together in a colony the Métis were model Catholics on their own land. They had a church that they had built themselves and a priest who could preach to them in their own language. They could attend church services in their normal attire without fear of being ridiculed by white parishioners. According to Levert, even greater success could be obtained in the spiritual sphere if the school were under the direction of devoted nuns rather than lay teachers.[51]

Unfortunately, there were complaints that government officials sent to the colony to assist the Métis were not doing anything constructive. Gauthier charged that these individuals made the condition of the Métis worse because they forced them to work unassisted in the sawmill and abandon the trapping of muskrat that could have provided a decent living.[52] For his part, Levert encountered difficulties with officials when he went to teach catechism to the children in the last hour of the school day as permitted under the School Act. In 1942, a school inspector informed him that he could not teach catechism during regular school hours. When Levert protested, he was advised that the children were behind in their studies and, hence, the half hour of religious instruction had to be abandoned to allow them to catch up.[53] Levert protested this violation of the Alberta School Act but was informed by the deputy minister of Education that, insofar as Métis colony schools maintained by public funds were concerned, the government would not allow religious instruction in regular school hours. If provided, such instruction had to be given "at hours other than those authorized by law for the holding of school."[54]

The situation at Fishing Lake deteriorated and Henri Routhier, the Alberta-Saskatchewan provincial, authorized Gauthier to inquire into the state of affairs of Métis colonies with respect to the religious and spiritual welfare of the inhabitants. Routhier hoped to obtain a more just treatment for the Métis and the same rights as those given to Catholics in regularly organized districts.[55] In the meantime, the government had been pressed to provide more assistance to the Fishing Lake colony and the Oblates allegedly were advised by L. Maynard, minister of Municipal Affairs, that such collaboration would be forthcoming only if Gauthier were removed as resident missionary. Some time later, Gauthier advised the minister that while he had been absent for 18 months to prepare his survey, no noticeable improvement in government services had taken place. Gauthier claimed that the missionaries had assisted the government when requested because they were interested in the welfare of the Métis. He charged that the government's sole objective was to thwart the missionaries and cited the government's manipulation of the School Act and the selection of a supervisor on the colony who ridiculed the Oblates and the Catholic religion.[56]

As could be expected Gauthier's report on Fishing Lake was critical of government policy. He affirmed that, since the Oblates were denied access to the school during regular school hours and, hence, the Métis believed that the missionaries had abandoned them. He also accused the government of encouraging a "perfidious materialism" as a sign of progress to entice the Métis. Gauthier charged, furthermore, that the government wanted to displace the residents of Fishing Lake to give the land to the Tulliby Lake Cattlemen's Association. The local MLA was supporting the Cattlemen's Association, but the Métis refused to move and the authorities were punishing them by refusing all assistance.[57] At another Métis colony in Frog Lake, Alberta, where a church and school were being built, Gauthier encountered difficulties with Malcom Norris, a member of the Métis Association of Alberta. Norris, whose socialist views were well known, was described as "very fanatical" by Gauthier because he insisted on a policy that the missionary alleged would create many difficulties.[58]

In Saskatchewan, the government did not establish Métis colonies and the Oblates had to resort to more traditional means to assist the Métis. In Lebret, they organized a religious vacation school for Métis children in 1935. The religious vacation school lasted four days and had an average attendance of 58 children. Special classes were held for those who had not yet made their first communion. A picnic after the end of classes and prizes were awarded and the organizers judged the venture to have been a success.[59] The following year in 1936 another similar course was held but over a longer period of time. Ninety-five children registered and the average attendance was 80.[60]

These efforts on behalf of Métis children in Lebret were all that the Oblates could do for the destitute Métis population of the region who possessed neither land nor animals. In addition, the Métis lacked employment, food, adequate nourishment and lodging. The social assistance they received was insufficient to provide basic food and shelter. The Métis had asked the provincial government to set land aside for them and sought agricultural implements from the federal government. They asked to Oblates to assist them in their negotiations with the various levels of government.[61] When the federal government refused to provide assistance, Édouard Lamontagne, the Manitoba provincial, urged the Oblates at Lebret to enlist the assistance of the Archbishop of Regina to obtain immediate help for the Métis from the provincial authorities. Lamontagne supported the proposal put forth by the Lebret Oblates to establish a Métis colony but he indicated that the Oblates did not have the funds to finance the venture. He cautioned that while the proposed colony was a good idea, it would require much money and effort before it could be realized.[62]

In the meantime, the distress of the Métis continued and no practical solution appeared. For their part, the Métis desired land to cultivate in order to become self-sufficient and sought assistance from the government to obtain unoccupied Crown land. The Métis were willing to accept government supervision and an organizational structure resembling that of a reserve as long as the Oblates could continue to establish themselves in their midst.[63] In 1940, Emmanuel Duplain was designated by the Manitoba provincial to establish a Métis colony in the Qu'Appelle valley. Under the terms of a memorandum of agreement, the Province of Saskatchewan would contribute $5,000 to operate and equip the land owned by the Oblates as a farming unit. The Oblates would allow the Province to use the land for farming purposes and they would provide "continuous supervision, management and direction" for the venture.[64] Five families were established the first year and the results were so encouraging that in 1941 that the government decided to add one section of Crown land to the Métis farm and contributed an additional $2,000. The provincial interpreted these results as proof that:

> this kind of organization based on discipline, kindness and religious education is the proper system to inculcate the principles of civilization and protect them from subversive doctrines and bring them up to the standard of true and reliable citizens.[65]

As the manager of the farm's advisory board, Duplain reported in 1943 that nine suitable residences had been built in addition to a large granary, a pig pen and a chicken house. The land had been brought into a good state of cultivation and there were sufficient horses and machinery to properly operate the farm, which housed 25 head of cattle, 16 horses, 200 chickens and 50 pigs.[66] The government was obviously satisfied because it renewed the five-year agreement originally signed in 1940 and signed a 21-year lease of the Oblate property in 1943.[67] In leasing their land the Oblates were aware that they were alienating potential revenue from its exploitation but they decided to seek no additional compensation from the government because of the assistance the farm was providing to rehabilitate the Métis.[68]

The election of the Cooperative Commonwealth Federation in 1944 altered the good relations between the Oblates and the provincial government. The new minister of Social Welfare visited the farm in December of that year and the Oblates feared that he wanted to hear complaints from the Métis as a pretext for removing the Oblates and extending complete government control over the farm.[69] When the government indicated a desire to purchase the land, the Oblates refused because the offer was too low but, to avoid criticism and force the government to transport the nine residences built by the Métis, the Oblates offered to rent the land to the province.[70] For its part, the government gave assurances that its only interest in purchasing the land was to "benefit the Metis in the district tributary to Lebret."[71] In the end, the Oblates sold their farm to the government and expressed the hope that "that this property will always be operated in the interest of these people, and for their benefit."[72] In 1946, however, when the government decided to expand the Métis farm and inquired about purchasing adjacent land owned by the Oblates, it was advised that the property was needed for the residential school.[73]

The Alberta-Saskatchewan province received the visit of another canonical visitor in 1941 in the person of Anthime Desnoyers. He was pleased to note that the directives given by Labouré in 1936 had been implemented. Former residences and missions had been reoccupied and new ones had been built where possible. Although religious community life may have suffered, the ministry of the Oblates was much more effective as a result of this closer and more frequent contact. Desnoyers lamented the fact that it was impossible to place a resident Oblate missionary in each reserve and, hence, the missionaries were always required to travel. He contended that the dispersal of Native populations over vast areas was the most significant obstacle to the thorough Christianization of the Indians.[74]

With respect to Labouré's directive that Oblates master the Indian languages in order to become successful missionaries, Desnoyers noted that young missionaries had made a sincere effort. Unfortunately, the results were not sufficient because, while one could readily acquire a knowledge of grammar and vocabulary, years of study were needed to master the language and its nuances. Desnoyers urged that young missionaries be relieved of administrative duties as soon as recruitment permitted. He remarked also that Labouré's directives concerning the use of syllabic characters in the publication of prayer and hymn books was not yet fully implemented.[75]

Like Labouré, Desnoyers was concerned with the quality of spirituality among young Indians and he believed that Oblate personnel in residential schools would have to exercise a greater influence over their charges. Children were not to be inculcated with an exterior conformity that they would quickly abandon after leaving school but with an "interior discipline" that would remain forever. It was necessary to develop a spirituality and virtues that would be a source of strength and direction when they left school. The function of religious ceremonies had to be explained in order that children not regard them as mandatory obligations but as sources of grace that had to be tapped to assist them in living truly Christian lives.[76]

Desnoyers identified retreats and post-school activities as "extraordinary" means of spiritual regeneration and preservation. In addition to general retreats held at missions Desnoyers recommended that special closed retreats be held in schools prior to the beginning of holidays. Desnoyers was particularly concerned with what he identified as the critical period in the lives of young Indians, the time between their leaving school and their marriage. He noted that "painful defections" took place during these "perilous years." To prevent this from happening, he affirmed that school children would have to be closely supervised by missionaries and grouped into religious societies. It was crucial to maintain among former students a love for the institution that formed them. As means of accomplishing this Desnoyers suggested meetings and a banquet, the establishment of study groups, cooperatives, credit unions and workshops.[77]

At the end of his canonical visit Desnoyers drafted a series of recommendations to enhance the religiosity of Indians in the Alberta-Saskatchewan province. This document was sent to every Oblate involved in Indian or Métis missions in that jurisdiction for study and comment. Seventeen reports were prepared by missionaries and discussed during their annual retreat in July 1942. Afterwards, the provincial, Henri Routhier, prepared a report incorporating the recommendations and the substance of the discussions that had taken place. Routhier's report contained both old and new elements. With respect to the old, there were traditional theological references to the nature of humanity corrupted by sin and affirmation that Christian traditions were not to be found in the Indian and Métis temperament and environment. The new perspective was apparent in the identification and analysis of causal factors and this was a continuation of the challenge and innovative spirit generated by Labouré's visit and report.

Routhier's report freely admitted that after a century of evangelization the status of Christianity among Indians and Métis left much to be desired. There was apathy and indifference and, for many, Christianity was but a thin veneer. This state of affairs was attributed in part to human nature and sin. Temperament and environment were also deemed to be contributing factors because the passion of Indians for traveling, gambling and sun dances was not conducive to religious discipline.[78] The Oblates themselves were also to blame for this religious indifference. Routhier contended that there had been an insufficient number of missionaries and, furthermore, they had been changed too often. It was admitted that some Oblates lacked zeal, perseverance and an appropriate missiology. Principals of residential schools were reprimanded for abdicating their authority to nuns and allowing Indian children to be educated and formed in the same manner as whites. The government was also to blame because as a result of alleged Protestant and masonic influences, Oblates schools were not receiving adequate moral and financial support from the authorities. The government's neglect of students after they graduated was regarded as another major factor.[79]

Routhier's report proposed remedies for the problems it had identified. It reaffirmed that the missionary had to have faith in his Apostolate and the redemptive power of grace. Furthermore, the missionary had to love the Indian and not scorn him. Oblates had to become fluent in the Indian languages and it was suggested that young missionaries spend one year in the theoretical study of these languages. Afterwards, young missionaries would be apprenticed to another Oblate who was fluent in the language and the former could begin his ministry while studying the mentality of the Indians and perfecting his knowledge of their language. Frequent contact with Indians through visits in their homes was deemed necessary to overcome apathy and to provide the missionary with first hand knowledge of his flock. Routhier affirmed that it was the best Oblates who were required for service in the missions and not those who lacked intellect.[80]

With respect to specific proposals, Routhier's report affirmed that it was absolutely necessary that Oblates be responsible for boys in residential schools. Furthermore, the personnel in such institutions had to be trained and constantly upgraded. Oblates had to decide what it was their schools were to do for Indians and then formulate the methods appropriate to achieve that objective. The cumulative experience of the last century had to be documented, analyzed and synthesized and made available to new missionaries to facilitate their task. To produce good Christians it was necessary to have good catechisms and the catechism class had to be as enticing as the other classes. Catholic Action had to be adopted for young people to animate what had been learned in catechism classes and transform the child into a true Christian.[81]

While noting the importance of the school, Routhier's report declared that the school was but a preparation for life on the reserve. Hence, it was necessary to have a cordial and fraternal entente between the principal and the missionary on the reserve. Principals and missionaries worked in different areas but pursued the same goal. To ameliorate the economic status of Indians, Routhier recommended the establishment of model farms on reserves where Indians could find employment. It would be on this farm and not at the school that the shops would be located. Unfortunately, the Oblates possessed neither the resources nor the personnel to establish these model farms.[82]

Routhier's report also focused on a theme that was becoming popular in Oblate circles, the necessity of establishing some sort of continuing education for Indian youth between the time they left school and got married. Since nothing was done for young Indians at this critical time, moral corruption and degradation allegedly took place. At the Hobbema school a club had been established in 1941 to cure those who had been stricken by "social disease" and prevent "healthy" persons from being contaminated. The motto of the club was "Progress in every line" and to progress Indians had to be reminded of their duties toward God and country and provided with assistance to discharge those obligations. Re-education and re-inspiration were to come about through lectures and open discussions that made Indians aware of the corruption and deficiencies around them. Indians were made to realize that if they persevered they could be as successful as whites and be as good and useful citizens. The club organized different forms of entertainment such as picnics and sponsored a hockey team.[83]

In addition to a continuing education imbued with the principles of Catholic Action, Routhier's report suggested that pilgrimages presented a unique opportunity to make Indians reflect on the tenets of the Catholic faith. Three days of preaching and religious exercises were recommended as a preparation for the pilgrimage. The proceedings were to be policed to ensure that morality and order prevailed. Each mission was to have an annual retreat but the report noted that there were not enough Oblates to preach these retreats in the appropriate Indian languages. Routhier also recommended the printing of Albert Lacombe's collection of sermons in syllabic characters because Indians in distant posts rarely saw the missionary and suggested that this sermonary be published in Roman characters for children in residential schools.[84]

While both Desnoyers and Routhier had identified deficiencies in the Apostolate of the Oblates in the Alberta-Saskatchewan province, the assessment of one missionary in that jurisdiction was far more critical. According to Victor Le Calvez, Desnoyer's report hinted that not all of the 40 Oblates in the province were capable of relating to their Indian charges but did not state this explicitly. Le Calvez contended there were only three missionaries among the Blackfoot could speak that language, none among the Assiniboine and one among the Chipewyan. Four elderly Oblates could speak Cree fluently while nine others spoke enough to hear confessions and engage in simple conversation.[85]

Le Calvez claimed that at Hobbema, the largest Oblate mission, only a handful of Indians attended mass although the majority had been baptized. He suggested that the reason for this state of affairs was that there was no longer a sermon in Cree and, consequently, the Oblates had lost contact with the Indians. Furthermore, residents of the reserve had recently voted in favour of neutral day schools and he argued this never would have happened if the Oblates had been in close contact with the residents. He claimed that no Oblates had been present at a meeting among the Chipewyan at Le Goff convoked by the Indian Association of Alberta where the question of neutral schools was discussed again. Le Calvez asked the superior general to provide missionaries who were willing to learn the Indian languages and who were not ashamed to serve in the Indian missions. He recommended that these missionaries be placed under the direction of someone who knew the missions, could relate to Indians and provide directives. Only then would the Oblate Apostolate gain ground.[86]

The province of Manitoba also received a canonical visitor in 1941. Joseph Rousseau noted that students in residential schools displayed satisfactory outward manifestations of piety but, nevertheless, he entertained doubts as to the "interior dispositions" of students. He also observed that in some schools attendance at mass during the week was optional in order to avoid creating an aversion among students. As a result of their absence, however, children did not understand the priest's function at the altar and this was the real reason why they no longer assisted. The visitor concluded that if students were to assist at mass they would have to love the ceremony. Worldly attractions could not be utilized to achieve this goal because a love of the mass could only be achieved through comprehension and intimate participation in a "vital act" in which one replaced one's life by drawing from that of Christ.[87]

Twenty missionaries most of whom were young were actively working in the Indian missions of the Manitoba province and Rousseau regarded this "veritable renaissance" as very encouraging. He was pleased to witness the preparation of religious books in Indian languages as well as the publication of a missal in Saulteaux. He was also delighted that the residence of the Oblates at Fort Alexander had been altered in 1936 to establish a school for missionaries where they could be prepared for their future ministry as well as learn Saulteaux under Joseph Brachet, an experienced missionary and linguist.[88]

Rousseau also noted some deficiencies in the Indian missions of Manitoba. To begin with, there was an insufficient number of missionaries and their apostolic activities were handicapped because they resided in residential schools rather than on reserves and had obligations to fulfill in these schools. Rousseau asserted that missionaries had to be liberated to devote their energies exclusively to evangelization. More serious, however, was the virtual total absence of pastoral guidance for missionaries who had to rely on their individual initiatives. In the vicariate apostolics, the vicar apostolic was the organizer, initiator and promoter of missionary activity. The diocesan authority in the province of Manitoba was not involved in missionary work and, therefore, it was not able to provide the assistance that the Oblates required. According to Rousseau, the Oblate provincial administration had to assume complete authority for missions. To assist the provincial administration in providing this leadership function Rousseau suggested that missionary congresses be held and that they be organized like those of learned and scientific societies. He also recommended conventions for principals and personnel in residential schools as a means of unifying educational efforts and making them more effective.[89] These conventions would enhance the authority of the provincial administration by providing it with valuable data upon which to formulate decisions.

The canonical visits, discussions and reports created an atmosphere in which individual Oblates began to make a serious introspective evaluation of their apostolic and educational efforts. Siméon Perreault asked his provincial to relieve him of his duties at St. Philip Mission because there was too much work for one elderly person. Perreault claimed that the mission required the services of two zealous and dedicated young missionaries who spoke Saulteaux fluently. He alleged that provincials had never taken the number of Catholic Indians into account and, furthermore, had staffed the mission with persons who were devoid of zeal and could not speak the language. Consequently, the spiritual interests of Indians was neglected and they ceased to attend services and practice their faith. On the four neighboring reserves there were 705 Catholic Indians and 250 white Catholics in the region and he was responsible for ministering to them. Given the distance that separated these individuals, the apathy of the Indians and his advanced age Perreault asked to be sent elsewhere.[90]

Paul-Émile Tétrault, another Oblate sent to the mission in 1942, informed the provincial that an immense work of moral reconstruction was required. To accomplish this objective, he would require the assistance of young missionaries who possessed "courage, energy and enthusiasm." Individuals who had vegetated for years would not be capable of undertaking the work that was required. Tétrault claimed that Indians desired the priest and religious services. A chapel would have to be built because distances were too great to travel to the mission itself. He claimed that Indians could not remain good Christians if they were only visited by the missionary once a year. [91]

Other Oblates made suggestions to enhance the function and role of the residential school. While some of these proposals were related to administrative procedures such as the location of schools or the entrance age of pupils others raised far more fundamental issues.[92] There was a reaction on the part of some Oblates to the undue emphasis that had been placed on the school as an agent of conversion and Christianization. Henri Delmas, long time principal of St. Michel's Residential School in Duck Lake allegedly stated that with one school he could accomplish as much as five missionaries on reserves. According to Clément Chataigner, this dictum had resulted in missionaries being removed from reserves and placed in schools to serve as a "court" for principals. Chataigner believed that so much importance had been attached to schools and education by all levels of the Oblate hierarchy from principals to vicar apostolics and provincials that the missionary was lost sight of.[93]

These views were shared by Joseph-Amédée Angin, a former principal of residential schools at Delmas and St. Paul. He claimed that the school had crammed religion down the throats of students with the result that they were disgusted. He alleged that the school had attempted to make novices out of Indian students by insisting on a rigorous conformity that went against the dictates of common sense. Once they left school it was only natural that students rebelled against religion and abandoned religious practices. The "illogical methods" used by the Oblates were best suited to dechristianizing Indians. Angin suggested that students should have been made to observe the duties of a Christian in a progressive manner that suited their temperament rather than those of a religious novice. More freedom should have been permitted to Indians with respect to religious exercises that were not mandatory for Catholics such as attendance at daily mass and communion.[94]

For his part, Chataigner contended that the solution lay in Catholic Action whose goal was to transform an unfriendly environment into one where it was possible to think and live as Christians. According to Chataigner, Indians and Métis were underprivileged elements confronted by hunger and misery and they possessed neither education nor Christian traditions. Catholic Action implemented by a trained elite could alter this state of affairs. He proposed to make the church the centre of all activity, the soul of the parish. Thus, he advocated the creation of Indian parishes and the immediate establishment of perfect Christian institutions in their midst.[95]

The importance of being proficient in Indian languages was recognized by missionaries in the field. In 1938, for example, Marius Rossignol advised his superior, Martin Lajeunesse, Vicar Apostolic of Keewatin on

△ △ *Bishop Martin Lajeunesse's episcopal hat being used to filter gasoline after his boat capsized while on a pastoral visit, 1944.* (AD)

the most appropriate ways of directing the Métis in the vicariate. Rossignol recommended that Lajeunesse be accompanied by Patrick Beaudry, the second Métis Oblate, on his forthcoming pastoral visit. According to Rossignol, Beaudry would be more than the bishop's interpreter because the Métis would accept what he said.[96]

As the Oblates attempted to come to grips with the problems facing their ministry among the First Nations, they were confronted by the perennial problem of limited financial resources. The funding traditionally obtained from institutions such *l'Oeuvre de la Propagation de la Foi* had long proved insufficient and other avenues had to be exploited. Unlike parishes in settled areas, the Oblate missions could not expect the faithful to provide adequate financial support. While individual acts of charity towards Oblates by Indians were not unknown, the Sunday collection was not an ingrained tradition. Oblate attempts to inculcate in Indians notions of tithing and support for the clergy were seriously hampered by the recession that further reduced the meager income of the latter.

The economic recession forced the Oblates to seek other sources of revenue for their missions and institutions. The construction of churches and chapels was assisted by grants for the Catholic Church Extension Society.[97] From time to time, individual brothers and missionaries had returned to their native parishes or to areas where they were known and collected money for their missions. Others contacted their former seminary classmates and asked to make collections in their parishes. Mass intentions also provided a modest source of revenue for missions. Since priests were allowed to celebrate only one mass a day, they passed on excess masses to missionaries and paid them all or part of the honorarium that had been given.

For his part, Bishop Breynat had a detailed report on the teaching of French in the residential schools under his jurisdiction for Paul Suzor, the French Consul for western Canada. During his visit of western Canada Suzor had been impressed with the knowledge of French displayed by students at the residential school at Fort Chipewyan and others in Breynat's vicariate and he requested that the Ministry of Foreign Affairs provide an annual grant of 10,000 francs to Breynat. Suzor also wanted France to recognize the services of the older French Oblates by awarding them an honorific distinction.[98]

In addition to seeking new sources of funding, the Oblates also utilized new developments in technology to facilitate their apostolic ventures. In 1933, for example, Bishop Ovide Charlebois of Keewatin used radio station CKY in Winnipeg to transmit messages to his missionaries in the north. Messages sent to the station were broadcast on Wednesdays. The news of the death of Superior General Dontenwill was telegraphed to Le Pas at 10:00 A.M. and twelve hours later it was broadcast to the Oblates serving in the north.[99] The introduction of aircraft transformed the travel of missionaries. In 1936, Jean-Baptiste Ducharme flew from Beauval to his mission at Portage La Loche in one hour and fifteen minutes. This voyage normally took four days by dog team.[100] Three consecutive summers were normally required for a pastoral visit of the missions of the immense Vicariate of Keewatin. This time was reduced dramatically by using an airplane and the vicar apostolic was able to remain for a longer period in each mission.[101] In the Vicariate of Mackenzie, Breynat purchased an airplane, the *Sancta Maria,* and was able to visit all his missions in a three-week period. The flight from Edmonton to Aklavik took eleven hours by air as compared to two months by dog team.[102] In 1939, Breynat's famous *Sancta Maria* was used to transport the Apostolic Delegate during his visit of the missions. The plane was also used to transport students to residential schools in the northern vicariates of Mackenzie and Keewatin.[103]

With the introduction of modern technology in the form of the radio and the aircraft the curtain fell on the formative period of the Oblate Apostolate in the western provinces. This "classical" era had been characterized by a somewhat naive belief that the missionary's task was to announce the Gospel and prepare an environment that was conducive to the Gospel taking root and flowering. It was assumed that once Christianity matured it would be such a powerful force that a better society would emerge spontaneously within the Indian and Métis communities. In the 1930s and 1940s, however, the discrepancy between this ideal and reality was too great to be ignored and it had to be addressed directly by the Oblates.

Internal Oblate reports, and those of canonical visitors, were articles of faith in the very essence of the Oblate Apostolate. The concept of mission and the nature of the missionary edifice were never questioned, only the results of the Oblate enterprise were scrutinized and found wanting. As the products of a West European Christian society the Oblates assumed that which had contributed to the welfare of that society was *ipso facto* beneficial to other societies. Thus Oblate reports tended to comment on an idealized vision of the society of the First Nations rather than the true social and economic status of those peoples or the poverty and lack of opportunity on reserves. The Euro-Christian virtues of thrift, hard work and sobriety were likely to be recognized and rewarded in a society where there was a surplus of resources and where all citizens had equal access those resources.[104]

For their part, the First Nations were quick to realize the discrepancy between theory and reality and the designs of church and state lost whatever appeal they initially had. As time passed, Indians expressed greater dissatisfaction and discontent with concepts and institutions that were not relevant to their culture and traditions and that did not ameliorate their social status and poverty. In the period after World War II, the First Nations would no longer be satisfied with resisting, they would claim the right to fashion their own institutions and forge their own destiny.[105]

It was during this examination of means and objectives that the Oblates became aware of the importance of a suitable social and economic environment in nurturing the fragile seed of Christianity. Powerful though Christianity might be, it was recognized that it could not grow in the midst of the poverty and associated social ills that increasingly characterized life on Indian reserves and among the landless Métis. Thus, on both moral and practical grounds, it was imperative that the Oblates attempt to improve the social and economic well being of the Indian and Métis communities. Since the reserve would remain the basic institution in Indian life, the Oblates felt that the school would have to provide children with suitable skills to earn a livelihood on the reserve and become productive citizens in the process. The Oblates also identified the period immediately after leaving school and returning to the reservation as a critical time in the life of the young. Thus, proper post-school supervision and direction were necessary to prevent a return to traditional ways and the contamination of the young by an immoral milieu. Catholic Action was deemed to be an important instrument with which to transform an otherwise hostile environment.

Labouré's canonical visit and report had demonstrated the necessity of unity of action and collaboration of all elements involved in missionary activities. In the meantime, the Oblates became aware of the complex nature of missionary activities and the necessity of accessing knowledge from anthropology, history, linguistics, pedagogy and other disciplines to enhance their apostolic activities. The economic recession and WWII had imposed restraints on the Oblates and their limited resources and this is one of the reasons why no dramatic innovations are to be found in the period prior to 1945. In addition, the involvement of the Oblates in Indian residential education imposed restraints on the freedom of action of the missionaries because of the importance that was attached to these institutions as apostolic adjuncts and as sources of funding for the missions themselves.

The doctrinal rigidity within the Catholic Church in this era also imposed severe limitations on Oblate attempts to make Christianity a more relevant spirituality for the First Nations. While Oblates could relax discipline and reduce compulsion in schools with respect to attendance at religious services, there could be no deviation in the response to the Christian message or the structure of the church that they established. At this time, the universality of the Roman Catholic Church was identified and proclaimed through the conformity of its constituent parts to the parent institution in Rome. Indians and Métis who adhered to Catholicism had to accept the western values and traditions that were inherent in that faith, in other words, they became Latinized and westernized. Institutional conformity and rigidity would be breached only after the sessions of the Second Vatican Council, which met in 1962–65. The ecumenical spirit resulting from this assembly made it possible for a later generation of Oblates to begin to truly preach the gospel as had the early Apostles instead of presenting a Christian message clothed in western cultural accretions. In the meantime, those who were concerned with making Christianity a more meaningful spiritual expression had to content themselves with minor alterations to the manner in which the message was presented rather than encourage a unique response to the message based on the needs and traditions of those to whom the Gospel was being preached.

EPILOGUE

Redefining Church and Spirituality

The Oblate experience in the western provinces was a remarkable accomplishment if one considers the conditions under which the initial establishment took place, the resources available to the Oblates, the relatively few personnel involved and their lack of specialized preparation for the work that was undertaken. Within 40 years of their arrival in 1845, the Oblates had established a network of missions from the international boundary to the Arctic Circle and systems of transportation and supply had been put in place to sustain these missions and their personnel. After their initial establishment, most missions underwent a period of consolidation and their functions expanded.

Rudimentary schools, orphanages and hospitals evolved around missions because these institutions were absent on the frontier. In addition to need, these institutions especially the schools, were a reflection of the sophisticated nature and objectives of the apostolic process. Initially, Native populations were exposed to the fundamental tenets of Christianity and admitted to baptism when sufficiently instructed. Baptism and the other sacraments, however, were not ends in themselves but stations along a continuum of increasing spiritual maturity whose apogee was Christianization. Within this context, the school became an important adjunct to the Oblate missionaries as they attempted to fashion a suitable Christian environment for neophytes especially the young who were deemed to be the seed from which future Christian generations would evolve.

The Oblate Apostolate in the North West was the work of a disciplined religious, missionary congregation committed to preaching the Gospel to non-Christians. However, that congregation was made up of individuals each of whom possessed different personalities, aptitudes and aspirations. In the final analysis, not every Oblate was suited for missionary work among the First Nations. Not every Oblate was as talented a linguist as Valentin Végréville, Émile Grouard or Laurent Le Goff. Not every missionary was as successful as Albert Lacombe in adapting to and being accepted by Indian society. Henri Faraud displayed remarkable business acumen as an ecclesiastical administrator but left much to be desired in terms of personal relationships. Vital Grandin scored high on personal relationships but was accused of not adequately defending the material interests of his diocese.

The success or failure of Oblate institutions was in part a reflection of the different aptitudes and temperaments of those who were responsible for their governance. Jacqueline Gresko's research on the Qu'Appelle Industrial School demonstrates that under Joseph Hugonnard's direction the school "was part of community education and community history rather than a strict imposition on the Native population."[1] With respect to the Dunbow Industrial School, Brian Titley concludes that it was a failure from the day it opened its doors. This state of affairs was due in large part to Native opposition and a succession of Oblate principals who were far from possessing Hugonnard's ability to integrate the school into the community it was supposed to serve.[2] In contrast to the Qu'Appelle school, which was situated in proximity to six reserves in the Qu'Appelle valley, Dunbow was located at a great distance from reserves in southern Alberta and this alienated Indians and prevented an integration of school and community.

The spiritual achievements of the Oblates are far more difficult to quantify than the number of missions, schools and other institutions that were established or the number of sacraments that were administered. It is obvious that testimonials of missionaries concerning the remarkable conversion of Indians, statistics on baptisms, confessions, communions and other outward signs of religious conformity are not accurate barometers of true spirituality. Undoubtedly, many conversions were sincere but others may have been motivated by factors other than the need for redemption. Missions and their personnel were sources of supply for

△ △ *Celebration of mass during Lac Ste. Anne pilgrimage.* (PAA, OB 1086)

Indians and conversion facilitated access to the desired items. Disease and anxiety brought about by social change were other reasons for accepting Christianity. Be that as it may, Christianity made an impact on the Native community and this is evident in the continued participation of numerous members of the First Nations in Catholic services and in the annual July pilgrimage at Lac Ste. Anne, Alberta, a living testimonial to the faith implanted many years ago by the Oblates. However, the essence of this pilgrimage and the manner in which it manifests itself are both decidedly Indian and Métis in character. The syncretism evident at the famous pilgrimage suggests that it was appropriated by the First Nations "on terms consonant with native modes of thought and relevant to perceived needs."[3]

Consciously or unconsciously during the early phase of the Oblate Apostolate, white civilization became inextricably related to Christianization. The Oblates believed that this civilization would contribute to elevating the First Nations spiritually and materially. It would make them reflect more closely the Christian ideal of the individual created in the image of God. White civilization implied a sedentary lifestyle in which productive individuals ensured their own livelihood. It goes without saying that "civilization" facilitated and enhanced the process of evangelization. To begin with, sedentary communities were easier to instruct, gather for religious services and exercise social control to ensure that the desired standards of morality were maintained. In addition, the prosperity that would accrue as a result of the acquisition of "civilized" traits such as industriousness, thrift and sobriety would both reinforce and complement Christian values. The resistance of the First Nations to Christianity and its institutions such as schools was not so much against that spirituality as such but the loss of identity implied in "shucking" the old self. In reality, the acceptance of Christianity for the First Nations not only incorporated a spiritual regeneration but also a cultural metamorphosis.

With respect to the association between white civilization and Christianity the Oblates were not innovators but simply following in the mainstream of the western Christian tradition. Irrespective of denominational affiliation the Christian tradition professed to be universal in character but, nevertheless, demonstrated little sympathy for the cultural diversity of those whom it attempted to convert throughout the world. It was believed that those who were being evangelized were inferior because they were not Christians and possessed traditions and values that differed from those of the allegedly superior western European civilization and, hence, had to be regenerated spiritually and culturally.

In their attempts to elevate Natives and Métis to higher standards the Oblates were promoting a spiritual white man's burden, a *mission civilisatrice* in the literal sense of the term. In addition, the Christian tradition advocated by the Oblates also encompassed a model of the ideal Christian whose traits reflected western European norms and values. The insistence on conformity to this prototype accentuated cultural insensitivity because the rich cultural traditions of Natives were not incorporated in the implanted church. Nevertheless, the record indicates that the Oblates were cognizant of local customs and traditions and described and commented on them. The attention the Oblates placed on a knowledge of the indigenous languages was not only a reflection of a means to facilitate their ministry in western Canada but also of a desire to better understand the culture and customs of those whom they were evangelizing. The grammars and dictionaries prepared by the Oblate missionaries in the field contributed to the cultural survival of the groups who spoke those languages.[4]

Despite the altruistic motives of the Oblates, the contemporary generation has a generally negative view of work of Christian missionaries. This critical perspective is the product of a more thorough understanding of the intrinsic value of the culture and spiritual traditions of the First Nations. In addition, Canadians have come to realize that they had permitted and participated in attempts to assimilate the First Nations. The residential school stands out as the most forceful symbol of the attempts to transform Indians and alter their identity. A century later it is possible to excuse the unrealistic objectives of residential schools and their ill conceived and unrealistic curriculum. However, there are elements of the residential school experience that are difficult to pardon and impossible to forget. Recent court cases suggest that residential schools inflicted physical and sexual abuse on a captive audience that was far removed from the cares or concerns of the larger white community.

In the period prior to 1945, the objectives sought by the Oblates necessitated a social and cultural transformation on the part of those who were being evangelized. However, the preaching of missions and other forms of instruction was deemed to be too irregular and infrequent to bring about the changes and values that were deemed necessary. In addition, adults were too set in their ways and the local environment facilitated a return to ancestral traditions. Consequently, the Oblates became convinced that the school could provide a carefully controlled and suitable environment that facilitated conversion and, by implication, the adoption of white ways and values. Thus, residential schools became important adjuncts of mission. In orienting itself to the milieu it served, the residential school was, in fact, a missionary instrument to evangelize the reserves it served. The Christian youth it fashioned would facilitate the evangelization of parents and the older generations.

Given the centrality of the school within Oblate apostolic efforts and the association that evolved with the federal government, Oblate residential schools became institutionalized and did not exist for the benefit of their students. The school, like the Christianity that had been implanted, was another colonial institution that had been fashioned, established and administered by outsiders with little concern for the traditions or needs of those whom it served. Both within school and church Indians were marginalized and became a passive if not captive audience and this contributed to producing the thin veneer of Christianity and white civilization that became obvious as time passed.

As educators, the Oblates did not escape the consequences of institutionalization and circumstances would not permit them to withdraw from their venture into Indian residential education. Not only were these schools deemed crucial to the process of evangelization but, through careful management and the employment of religious personnel, they also generated funds that helped to maintain the entire missionary edifice. Principals became increasingly preoccupied with profane matters at the expense of spiritual considerations and schools became individual entities reflecting the strengths or weaknesses of those who directed them. Oblates also had to keep abreast of increasing professionalization within the teaching profession and found it difficult to remain "men of God" rather than administrators and business men.[5] In the final analysis, residential schools became the proverbial appendage that directed the Oblate Apostolate.

Thus, the Church and its institutions implanted by the Oblates and other Catholic missionaries among Aboriginal populations throughout the world was a foreign institution. It was to be an exact replica of the *Roman* Catholic Church of western Europe and not a local church reflecting indigenous traditions and aspirations. It mattered little whether the implantation was among the Salish of British Columbia, the Blackfoot of Alberta, the Kaffirs of Lesotho, the Veddas of Sri Lanka, or Mexicans in Texas, there was a remarkable similarity in process of evangelization, the institutions that were established, as well as the vocabulary used to describe indigenous populations.[6] Furthermore, the Oblate missionary experience throughout the world is unique only in the sense of variations in geography, climate and populations to be evangelized. In all other respects it operated in the mainstream of Catholic missionary activity and Oblate methods, objectives and results in western Canada were not significantly different, for example, than those of the Holy Ghost Fathers among the Masai of Tanzania.[7]

Nevertheless, the Oblate Apostolate in western Canada had one singular feature that distinguished it from the Catholic missionary experience among Aboriginal populations in other parts of the world: the virtual absence of an indigenous clergy. In Sri Lanka, the indigenous population constituted 12% in 1887 and 53% in 1926 of the clergy in the Diocese of Colombo and 7% and 52% in the same years in the Diocese of Jaffna.[8] Among the Oblates in Sri Lanka, Europeans worked under the indigenous clergy and in some instances were their vicars. A number of important missions were confided to the Sri Lankan clergy.[9] In Lesotho, the first Oblate bishop Joseph-Delphis Des Rosiers shared episcopal jurisdiction with two indigenous bishops by 1963. The sessions of the second Vatican Council (1960–65) were attended by 61 black African bishops who presented the needs and aspirations of their people in very forceful terms.[10]

△ △ *Corpus Christi procession at Cluny, Alberta, 1939.* (PAA, OB 10399)

△ △ *Pastorial visit of Bishop Émile Legal, Goodfish Lake, Alberta, 1920.*
(PAA, OB 855)

Despite the best intentions and efforts of the Oblates in western
Canada, however, a similar indigenous clergy and leadership did not
emerge from the midst of the Native and Métis populations and for that
matter in North America in general. In 1890, L.W. Reilly, editor of the
Catholic Columbian wrote to Valentin Végréville to ask why, despite the
desires of the Church to form an indigenous clergy, there were no native

△ △ *Seminarians enjoying a picnic near St. Albert, Alberta.* (PAA, OB 8539)

priests in America. He claimed that every other race was represented in the priesthood even Negroes but after being in the New World for 400 years not one native had been ordained. Reilly wondered whether the fault lay with the Native population and asked if missionaries had ever commented on this lack of vocations.[11]

This question of religious vocations among the Native and Métis populations of western Canada had preoccupied the missionaries since 1823 when Bishop Provencher began teaching two "quite talented" students, one of whom was Métis. Unfortunately, this venture was not successful and Bishop Taché, his successor, experienced the same frustrations in attempting to prepare Métis for the priesthood. Bishop Grandin adopted two young Indian boys and attempted to inculcate a religious vocation in them. They were sent to study in St. Boniface but left the college before completing their studies.[12] In 1877, Grandin established a minor seminary at St. Albert where Native and Métis children who desired to become priests could study Latin. Only one of the original four students persevered and was later ordained in 1890.[13] The Vicariate of Athabasca sent a promising young Métis from Lesser Slave Lake to Montreal to study for the priesthood but he left after a few years. Others had been sent to the Oblate juniorate in Edmonton but the results were not promising.[14]

The Oblates were keenly aware of the problems of recruiting an indigenous clergy. There were conflicting views on whether or not such a clergy should be trained apart from white seminarians or be trained with and in the same manner as the latter. In addition, there was a debate over

△ △ *Oblate cemetery at St. Albert, Alberta.* (PAA, OB 1809)

the meaning of the term indigenous. Some Oblates interpreted it to mean Native or Métis, whereas others contended that it meant a local clergy to minister to the population of a region. Hence, in the case of the multicultural population of western Canada, an indigenous clergy was not necessarily Native or Métis but representative of the population as a whole.[15] It was also argued that those of aboriginal ancestry who aspired to the priesthood would themselves object to the term "indigenous clergy" because these individuals regarded whites as superior and wished to be associated with them rather than with a class apart. Furthermore, religious life had to protect Indian and Métis priests and it would be inconceivable to separate white and aboriginal within an Oblate community. From a financial perspective, it was not possible to provide distinct training for Indian and Métis seminarians because of their small numbers. A majority of Oblates believed that a Native clergy that received a distinct formation would consider itself different and would be regarded as an inferior clergy by others.[16]

In neighboring British Columbia, George Forbes, principal of the residential school at Cranbrook informed his provincial in 1942 that he had tried "sincerely" to find a vocation among the Kootnay, Okanagan, Shuswap, Chilcotin and Carrier Indians but had failed. Forbes claimed that it would be difficult if not impossible to find "worthy priests" or members of religious congregations among British Columbia Indians unless the pope allowed Indian clergy to marry.[17] While many Oblates agreed that celibacy was a serious obstacle to the recruitment of a Native clergy Forbes argued that this was an assumption on their part that had never been verified by asking the First Nations whether they desired a celibate or married clergy.[18]

Forbes also identified another problem that confronted Indian clergy due to traditional customs and the mentality engendered by their status as a minority. Since there were eleven aboriginal languages in British Columbia, a Native priest had to remain among his own people in order to utilize his linguistic competence. However, Forbes claimed that it was unwise to send Native priests among their own people because they would not be accepted. He cited the experience of the provincial government in appointing Indian teachers and the reaction of Indians who felt insulted in not receiving a white teacher. There had been two Oblate vocations among the Indian population of British Columbia and Forbes claimed that after being ordained, one of them pretended that he could not speak his Native language. The other Native Oblate referred to by Forbes had to be transferred to the Alberta-Saskatchewan province because of the demands made on him by relatives.[19] Edward Cunningham, the first Métis Oblate in western Canada, also experienced similar problems. When Cunningham assumed responsibility for a mission, he was besieged by Indians who asked him to share the possessions of the mission with them.[20] Patrick Beaudry, the second Métis Oblate to be ordained in the western provinces, indicated a preference to minister to whites.[21]

While cultural and institutional factors had a significant influence on Native vocations, the degree to which Christianity had become a meaningful spirituality for Indians was also a determining factor. In commenting on the subject of an indigenous clergy the Oblates affirmed that the length of time a people had been Christianized was an important factor in the creation of an indigenous clergy and that many generations were necessary to produce sufficient vocations on a regular basis.[22] Be that as it may, one hundred years of Apostolate in western Canada had produced a half-dozen Métis priests and no Indian priests. Two Indian Oblates ordained in the 1960s later left the congregation. In 1981, there were only two Indian priests in all of Canada.[23]

Equally significant during this period is the absence of a strong lay leadership within the ranks of the First Nations who had embraced

Catholicism. This is another striking indication that Métis and Natives participated in a colonial church dominated by a white majority at all levels of organization. As could be expected, this colonial church impeded the emergence of mature indigenous Christian communities directed by their own leaders. The result was a "welfare Church" where Native people were looked after by "foreign" clergy and sisters and, hence, not expected to contribute to its upkeep or actively participate in its functioning.[24]

It should not be surprising that this church was artificial despite the best intentions of those who established it in the midst of the Native populations. The growth and maturity of this colonial church had nothing to do with events, aspirations and needs within the Native community but were determined by outsiders who were not familiar with local customs, traditions and languages. Commenting on this classical period of Oblate missionary activity Jacques Johnson, an Oblate well versed in post Vatican II thought and missiology, categorized the classical missionary establishment in these words:

> Instead of building on their spirituality and religious beliefs, instead of supporting their religious leaders and inviting them to assume responsibilities within the Church, we imposed a whole new system, foreign to them, oblivious that God had prepared their hearts for thousands of years, in a gradual way, much like He did for the Hebrew people, for the coming of His son, Jesus.[25]

With respect to the absence of a Native clergy, Johnson was not convinced that it was due to a lack of vocations and suggested that it resulted from: "the fact that we did not provide for them an environment and opportunities to bring to fruition, in an integrated way and without destroying them, that call from God to serve."[26]

The first century of Oblate missionary activity in the Canadian North West can be regarded as a classical era because it stressed total conformity to a preconceived spiritual, ecclesiological and prototype. The shortcomings of this effort were apparent to the Oblates before 1945 but they could attempt only to fine tune the mechanisms that were in place because circumstances and the prevailing mentality would not tolerate a radical restructuring of the missionary edifice. In the period after 1945, however, institutional conformity and rigidity were eroded by a combination of factors and the Oblates were able to fashion a radically different apostolic process that would make Christianity a more meaningful and dynamic expression of spirituality for Native populations.

With respect to Indian education, the post WWII era "was characterized by declining church influence, increased government control, and growing Indian involvement."[27] For its part, the federal government was having second thoughts about the cost of providing Indian education in association with religious denominations and, in 1951, it proposed to integrate Indian children into existing provincial public schools.[28] Changes in government policy and declining vocations made the Oblates aware that their traditional involvement in residential education would have to change. Nevertheless, they opposed the premature integration of Indian and white students in schools because the mentality and lifestyle of the former were significantly different from that of the larger community. The Oblates argued that, without adequate prior preparation, integration would not only result in failure but also create inequality between the two groups in school and engender a conviction on the part of Indian students that they had been rejected by whites. Furthermore, Indians had to be prepared and gradually initiated to modern Canadian society and the Oblates reiterated their conviction that, for the majority of Indians, the residential school remained the most efficient means of initiating them to contemporary society and preparing them to live in its midst as a respected and useful citizens who were proud of their Indian ancestry.[29]

In 1960, the Oblates rejected the integration policy proposed by the government and insisted that Natives should have "control over their own affairs."[30] The Indian community was no more in favour of integration than it had been of denominational residential education and it began to press for an autonomous system of Indian schools administered by Natives. In 1970, Blue Quills, the former Oblate residential school at St. Paul, Alberta, became the first school to be administered by an Indian band.[31]

As the Oblates gradually withdrew from an endeavour that had consumed so much of their energy and human resources, their institutional structures were altered accordingly. COOIE, which had been created to safeguard and enhance interests of Oblate missions and schools, was transformed into Oblate Services in August 1960 and became Indianescom in May 1962. Indianescom occupied itself with Indian residences as the role of the Oblates in residential schools became limited to that of administrator and chaplain. In 1968, Indianescom signed a two-year contract with the Department of Indian Affairs to provide two residences for Indian students in North Battleford.[32] In time, the social welfare and information services that Indianescom provided were gradually taken over by government and other agencies and by 1973, Indianescom exercised only two functions. It provided liaison with the government during the period when Catholic student residences were taken over by the Indians themselves, and it represented the views of the Church and scrutinized policy making.[33] By 1976, the residences had been taken over and Catholic interests were represented by a new institution, the Canadian Oblate Conference. Consequently, on 1 November 1976, Indianescom was dissolved and this action formally brought an end to nearly a century of Oblate association with Indian residential education.[34]

In addition to a decline in denominational involvement in Indian residential education, the period after WWII witnessed the end of colonial empires, a resurgence in liberal attitudes and increased sympathy for and sensitivity to minorities and their aspirations. With respect to Indians, it was obvious that they had not disappeared as a group nor were they likely to do so. Natives began to demand that their socio-economic status be improved and, furthermore, that they be allowed to determine their own destinies.[35] For its part, Vatican II presented "a number of interesting possibilities" and "emphasized the value of pluralistic cultures, the right to religious freedom, the meeting of churches and ecumenism."[36] The historic mission of the Church was also redefined by Vatican II and its decrees. In the tradition of the Apostles, the Gospel was to be proclaimed to all peoples not from a western European cultural perspective but from the historical context and cultural traditions of the peoples being evangelized.[37] This would simultaneously emphasize the universality of the Catholic Church and the equality of its constituent parts or "local churches."

Given their Native and Métis constituencies, the Oblates in western and northern Canada were in an ideal position to implement the structural changes advocated by Vatican II, especially after 1967 when a decree of the Holy See transformed existing apostolic vicariates into regular archdioceses and dioceses. Henceforth, there would no longer be missionary territories dependent on the Sacred Congregation of the Propaganda and the Oblates would carry out their missionary work under contract with the bishop of the diocese in which they worked.[38] The Oblate provincials in Canada met together as a group to study their new responsibilities and the Oblate Conference of Canada was created. In a report to the Canadian Conference of Catholic Bishops (CCCB) in 1971, the Oblate Conference of Canada urged the establishment of "an indigenous Church, authorized and encouraged to develop in accordance with its own particular vitality, as expressed in its customs, its social structures and its own special charisma."[39] For Native populations in Canada, this meant that the adoption of Christianity no longer entailed the loss of ancestral traditions.

At the same time, theologians such as Walbert Bühlmann spoke of the emergence of a "Third Church" to describe the changes that had taken place in Roman Catholicism as a result of Vatican II and the shift in church membership from Europe to the Third World. This "Third Church" consisting of African, Latin American and Asian segments was becoming indigenized and the influence of "foreign" missionaries was decreasing rapidly. This "Third Church" symbolized the new concept of mission because it was engaging in a dialogue and exchange with Christian communities in Europe and North America. It was believed that in their own unique way each of the constituent parts of the "Third Church" would contribute to the expansion of Christianity and the betterment of humanity.[40]

In Canada, Oblates such as Achiel Peelman contended that an Amerindian Church could be considered a fourth constituent part of Bühlmann's "Third Church" because Native peoples insisted on preserving their heritage and desired to experience a renaissance of the Christian faith within their own culture.[41] This Amerindian Church would not be an ethnic church for Indians, separate from the mainstream of Canadian Catholicism but a rebirth of Roman Catholicism among Native populations on their own terms and conforming to their cultural traditions.[42]

In 1982–83, Peelman conducted extensive research on the Church and Native populations in Canada and presented his conclusions to a meeting of the Canadian Conference of Catholic Bishops. As a result of unique cultural, political and economic factors in Canada Peelman believed that the Oblates were in a "privileged position" to implement the new concept of mission that emanated from Vatican II. He argued that:

> This strength and strategy should be directed toward forming and developing churches which are truly suited to the particular groups they serve and which represent the rich variety and special qualities of the peoples to whom the Gospel is brought. This need applies in a special manner to the dioceses of the North where the problems of close proximity with others and the resulting culture shock are felt on all levels of human existence.[43]

Peelman lamented the fact that the full thrust of the spirit of Vatican II and its decrees had not been implemented and that the Church, while it had identified a "great variety of mission situations," had "not yet found ways of functioning within this cultural and ecclesial pluralism."[44] Peelman's presentation to the CCCB provoked considerable discussion within Oblate ranks, especially among those who were still active in the mission field and who were disturbed that the work and contribution of predecessors had been dismissed because its alleged intent was "civilize to evangelize."[45]

The classical missionary period had been found wanting because it was predicted on acculturation and resulted in a one-way street leading from European Catholic Church to the people being evangelized. Within this context, dialogue and exchange were not possible and, in accepting Christianity, Aboriginal populations had to abandon their ancestral culture and traditions and accept those presented by the missionaries. The cultural insensitivity present in the classical period of Oblate missionary activity in western Canada was not the result of a deliberate attempt to eradicate the last vestige of Native culture but an unintentional consequence when the Oblates confused spirituality with their own manifestation of it and imposed their own culture at the expense of local culture. Furthermore, the pioneer Oblates lacked the intellectual preparation in the social sciences to comprehend social and cultural change and appreciate its significance. The Oblates were not the main instigators of social and cultural change in Native society although their missionary and educational activities contributed to the cumulative impact of those changes.[46]

In assessing the reasons for cultural conflict between missionaries and Native populations, a contemporary Oblate theologian has suggested that the main cause of "limited or distorted evangelization" was not the result of disdain for the people nor lack of respect for their culture but rather an inadequate theology of Church.[47] The Oblates were certainly well versed in Catholic theology as well as the fundamental differences between Catholicism and Protestantism but they lacked the same degree of understanding of Native religious traditions and often dismissed them as superstitions because they did not correspond to their preconceived notions of the ideal spirituality and its ecclesiological structures. Furthermore, in western Canada, the Oblates failed to comprehend the relationship between the Church and the life and traditions of local populations.[48] While the Oblates experienced no difficulty in admitting that Quebec had continued France's role as "eldest daughter of the Church" in North America, they never imagined that there could be an indigenous equivalent as a result of historical circumstances unique to the interior of this continent.

The post Vatican II era not only renounced acculturation in favour of a more universal Catholicism comprised of local churches but it also rejected conformity to the Latin prototype as a prerequisite for these constituent parts. In addition to the concept of the "Third Church," theologians began to speak of "inculturation" to reflect the second element of this new relationship. Inculturation has been defined as a unique "lived experience," because it is "the new response of a given culture to the initial proclamation of the Gospel and to the subsequent process of evangelization."[49] The missionary still has an important role to play in the process of inculturating the faith because he is responsible for the initial proclamation of the Gospel. As evangelizer, however, the missionary no longer establishes the Church he represents with all its cultural accretions, instead he invites individuals who hear him to find Christ within their daily lives. The process of inculturation itself is independent of the missionary and it occurs as the Word interacts with the recipient culture to produce a unique response. This encounter produces "a local Church, *the place of a culturally new response to the Gospel.*"[50]

The potential for development and dialogue inherent in the concepts of local church and inculturation made it possible for the Oblates to alter the traditional structures of their Apostolate in order to make Catholicism a more meaningful spirituality for Native and Métis populations in western Canada. In May 1977, for example, the Oblates held a regional conference in St. Norbert, Manitoba and adopted the training of religious leaders among the laity as the main priority for their missions. Lay ministry programmes were established and the Oblate Conference of Canada established a series of seminars for missionaries and Native leaders.[51] Subsequent discussions led to the establishment in 1980 of the Kisemanito Centre in Grouard, Alberta, to train Natives and Métis for the priesthood. In establishing the Kisemanito Centre the Oblates were able to benefit from the experience of other members of the congregation who had established a Native seminary in the Cameroun that was rooted in the experience of the people it served rather than the traditional European model that ignored African values and traditions.[52]

In 1985, at the plenary assembly of the Canadian Conference of Catholic Bishops, the eight Oblate bishops of Canada's northern dioceses discussed the status of their dioceses. They identified themselves as a Church "in the early stages of development" and declared that they "had hardly gone beyond the stage of pre-evangelization." The northern dioceses had to rely on clergy from the outside and were confronted by rapid socio-economic changes. As part of their goals the northern bishops committed themselves to: developing Christian communities directed by local leaders, establishing a dialogue with Native leaders, alleviating poverty and injustice and seeking out the alienated and abandoned.[53] In the more southern regions of Canada the Oblates had to contend with another phenomenon, the movement of Indians to urban areas and the particular problems that were associated with this migration.[54]

As the Oblates were attempting to initiate a dialogue with Natives to establish a "truly Amerindian Church" with an indigenous leadership that would have been inconceivable to their early predecessors, a vestige from the past surfaced to undermine their efforts. Beginning in the 1970s, and increasingly thereafter, members of the Native community began to accuse the Oblates of having engaged in a deliberate policy of cultural genocide through their participation in residential schools. A few years later, an even more serious allegation was levied against residential schools, that of the sexual and physical abuse of Native students by those responsible for the direction of those institutions.

Placed in a historical context, the residential school was but one of the many factors that affected the life and society of the First Nations.[55] Furthermore, not every reserve had a residential school and not every Indian child attended a residential school. Be that as it may, residential schools produced a traumatic experience among the ranks of those whom it touched directly or indirectly. The legacy of pain associated with that experience has impeded and will continue to impede a rapprochement between the First Nations and Canadians in general and missionaries in particular.

While some 30 per cent of Indian children attended residential schools and some of these for short periods of time, the pain and suffering associated with these institutions has become a collective phenomenon among the First Nations and a part of their cultural tradition.[56] What has made the residential school question such an important issue in the lives of the First Nations is that these institutions by their very nature and structure failed to meet their primary objective of adequately preparing the young to live in their society. To begin with, the purpose of Indian education was to prepare the young and impressionable for a new way of life predicated on Western European Christian values and traditions. Not only were Indian pupils to give up their traditional beliefs and culture, but these were depreciated and a white model extolled. The schools were not a product of the community they were to serve and parents had no voice in determining crucial issues such as curriculum and discipline. In the words of John Tootoosis, a former pupil, "the schools were oriented, not to prepare the children for their future role in life, but instead to divorce them from their past." In the process, students lost their pride, self-respect and self-confidence and became ashamed of being Indian.[57]

Worse than the unrealistic objectives and overall humiliating experience for pupils is the fact that in being partially successful in severing students from their past and culture, the schools produced a category of individuals whose place in society was ambiguous to say the least. Eleanor Brass, one of the first children born on the File Hills Colony in Saskatchewan attended a Presbyterian boarding school and stated that this encounter with white culture made it possible for her "to be an Indian and walk in two worlds."[58] The majority of Indian students, however, would have felt uncomfortable in either world. When they returned home, students experienced difficulty in speaking their own language and this complicated the adjustment to their traditional culture that was now foreign. As well, there was no place for them in white society because they lacked the necessary qualifications to compete equally and had to face the prejudices of the latter vis-à-vis Indians. John Tootoosis claimed that when he was discharged from Delmas as the age of 16, he returned to the Thunderchild Reserve "like a potato—'brown outside, white inside.' "[59]

Equally perplexing for many students was the fact that many learned very little of practical value in residential schools. John Tootoosis had only four years of schooling prior to reaching his sixteenth birthday and being discharged.[60] Others complained that too much attention was accorded to religious instruction and prayers, not to mention the countless hours spent in the shops and fields. The regimentation of daily life, the harsh discipline by Indian standards, the strange food and the general atmosphere of the institution all contributed to further alienate the students. The frustration, apathy and hostility of those who attended residential schools and, consequently, were caught between two worlds became the legacy of future generations.

In addition to the alienation produced by the foreign nature of residential schools, the pain suffered by those who were abused in these institutions produced a trauma that modern therapy will have great difficulty in healing. On the subject of physical abuse there is no doubt that the environment and discipline associated with residential schools were certainly radically different from that which Indian children were accustomed to. However, to qualify such conditions as physical abuse would be tenuous without undertaking a comprehensive study of life and discipline in all residential schools and comparing and contrasting the results with a similar study of contemporary white schools both public and private. Only then could one begin to make conclusions that would be based on fact and the nature and function of discipline as it was understood by society and the educators it fashioned and employed. The Oblates became cognizant of the unique nature of Indian children and the fact that excessive discipline and regimentation failed to ensure the achievement of the schools' objectives. White schools operated by Catholic religious communities could have derived an important lesson from the policies implemented at the Qu'Appelle Residential School in the 1940s to produce a genuine Christian spirituality as opposed to a sterile outward conformity.

With respect to the allegations of sexual abuse, the research conducted to prepare this study has failed to reveal any conclusive evidence for the period prior to 1945. The absence of documentary evidence should not be interpreted to mean that sexual abuse did not take place in this early period. To begin with, human nature is relatively constant through time and sexual preferences that appear to be widespread in recent decades also must have been present in the period prior to 1945. The allegations of Jean L'Heureux's homosexual activities with Blackfoot boys suggest that this tendency existed. It should be remembered, however, that no investigation was conducted by the authorities to ascertain the veracity of these allegations and L'Heureux was summarily dismissed. As in the present, the evidence was lacking but convictions were strong.

It should also be remembered that the generation prior to 1945 was not as liberated emotionally and mentally as the contemporary one and abuse, regardless of degree or kind, was endured in silence to avoid being embarrassed and/or shamed by one's friends and family in particular and by society in general. The mortification and humiliation of victims was compounded by the comments of contemporaries who reflected the prevailing tendency of cloaking abuse in a veil of silence. When comment was deemed necessary it took the form of ambiguous and oblique references. The Reverend Tims was certainly an exception with his unequivocal denunciation of L'Heureux's homosexual acts. The more common method was to suggest that someone "had a problem" but this results in creating a situation of double jeopardy because the unknown is explained by the more unknown.

The allegations of sexual abuse in residential schools are indicative of a possible human failing. In the case of an ordinary individual, sexual abuse is reprehensible but it is even more so when the allegation is directed against the Oblates and other clergy. To begin with, the clergy were in a privileged position of trust in society and, as students in residential schools, Indian children were a defenceless captive audience. As wards of the state their parents were a powerless group who had no one to turn to for support or assistance. In the past decade, allegations of sexual abuse have resulted in investigations and prosecutions. These events were widely publicized in the press and the larger white community became increasingly dismayed when investigations of sexual abuse began to shift to institutions within its midst. From Newfoundland to British Columbia there were investigations of improprieties that had taken place in parishes, schools and orphanages and other institutions. The subject of sexual abuse in residential schools will have to be studied in the context of abuse in the larger society.

In the meantime, the Oblates had to come to grips with the highly charged and emotional residential school question. On 24 July 1991, Douglas Crosby, president of the Oblate Conference of Canada, presented an homily and the apology of the Oblate missionaries to the First Nations of Canada during the annual pilgrimage at Lac Ste. Anne, Alberta. After apologizing for "certain aspects" of the Oblate ministry that had contributed to a cultural and spiritual imperialism and a depreciation of Native culture and traditions, Crosby, on behalf of the 1200 Oblates in Canada, concluded by stating:

> Despite past mistakes and many present tensions, the Oblates have felt all along as if the Native peoples and we belonged to the same family. As members of the same family, it is imperative that we come again to that deep trust and solidarity that constitutes family. We recognize that the road beyond past hurt may be long and steep but we pledge ourselves anew to journey with Native peoples on that road.[61]

At this point in time, it is too early to tell whether the desired rapprochement will come about or to describe the future relationship between the Oblates and the Native community. What is certain, however, is that the First Nations must have the deciding voice in determining the nature of that relationship. Attractive as the concepts of the "Amerindian Church" and inculturation might be to the current generation of missionaries, these ideas cannot be imposed on the First Nations as the only legitimate expression of spirituality. To do so would be to invite a far greater frustration and disenchantment than that brought about by the classical period of missionary activity. The First Nations themselves must decide if they are willing to accept Christianity and on what terms. Then and only then, can the unique and creative response to the Gospel take place and a truly "Amerindian Church" emerge.

△ △ △ △ △ △ △ △ △ △ △ △ △ △ △ △ △ △ △ △

APPENDIX I

Religious Jurisdictions in the Canadian North West

VICARIATES OF MISSIONS

1851   Vicariate of Missions of Red River

1864   Vicariate of Missions of Athabasca-Mackenzie

    1901   Vicariate of Missions of Mackenzie

    1901   Vicariate of Missions of Athabasca

        1927   Vicariate of Missions of Grouard

1868   Vicariate of Missions of Saskatchewan

    1871   Vicariate of Missions of St. Albert and Saskatchewan

1911   Vicariate of Missions of Keewatin

PROVINCES

1904   Manitoba

1921   Alberta-Saskatchewan

△ △ △ △ △ △ △ △ △ △ △ △ △ △ △ △ △ △ △ △

APPENDIX II

Vicars of Missions

MISSION OF RED RIVER

Pierre Aubert (Superior)   1845–1851

ST. BONIFACE

Alexandre-Antonin Taché	1851–1887
Charles-Joseph Camper	1887–1893
Louis-Philippe-Adélard Langevin	1893–1900
Charles-Jospeh Camper	1900–1901
Prisque Magnan	1901–1904

ATHABASCA-MACKENZIE

Vital-Justin Grandin	1864–1865
Henri Faraud	1865–1890
Émile Grouard	1890–1901

ATHABASCA

Émile Grouard   1901–1927

GROUARD

Émile Grouard	1927–1930
Jules Calais	1930–1932

Joseph Guy	1932–1938
Ubald Langlois	1938–1944
Henri Routhier	1944–1950

ST. ALBERT AND SASKATCHEWAN

Vital-Justin Grandin	1868–1897
Émile Legal	1897–1906
Henri Grandin	1906–1921

KEEWATIN

Ovide Charlebois	1911–1933
Martin Lajeunesse	1933–1954

Provincials

MANITOBA

Prisque Magnan	1904–1911
Charles-Arthur Cahill	1911–1917
Jean-Baptiste Beys	1918–1926
Josaphat Magnan	1926–1936
Edouard Lamontagne	1936–1942
Majorique Lavigne	1942–1948

ALBERTA-SASKATCHEWAN

Henri Grandin	1921–1923
François Blanchin	1923–1926
Jean-Baptiste Beys	1926–1929
Ubald Langlois	1929–1938
Henri Routhier	1938–1944
Armand Boucher	1944–1950

△ △ △ △ △ △ △ △ △ △ △ △ △ △ △ △ △ △ △ △

APPENDIX III

Ecclesiastical Jurisdictions in the Canadian North West

1820   District of the North West

1844   Vicariate Apostolic of Hudson's Bay and James Bay

1847   Diocese of the North West

1851   Diocese of St. Boniface

1871   Archdiocese of St. Boniface

1862   Vicariate Apostolic of Athabasca-Mackenzie
        1901   Vicariate Apostolic of Mackenzie
        1901   Vicariate Apostolic of Athabasca
                1927   Vicariate Apostolic of Grouard

1862   Diocese of St. Albert
        1912   Archdiocese of Edmonton

1910   Vicariate Apostolic of Keewatin

1930   Diocese of Gravelbourg

△ △ △

The following jurisdictions in the prairie provinces were created from within the boundaries of the old Ecclesisastical Province of St. Boniface but never had Oblates as bishops when they were established:

1910 Diocese of Regina
    1915 Archdiocese of Regina

1912 Diocese of Calgary

1915 Archdiocese of Winnipeg

1933 Diocese of Saskatoon

1948 Diocese of St. Paul

△ △

APPENDIX IV

Oblate Bishops

RED RIVER / ST. BONIFACE

JOSEPH-NORBERT PROVENCHER
Titular Bishop of Juliopolis for the District of the North West (1820); Vicar
Apostolic of Hudson's Bay and James Bay (1844); Bishop of the North West
(1844); Bishop of St. Boniface (1851); died 1853.

ALEXANDRE-ANTONIN TACHÉ, OMI
Titular Bishop of Arad and Coadjutor to the Bishop of the North West
(1850); Bishop of St. Boniface (1853); first Archbishop of
St. Boniface (1871); died 1894.

LOUIS-PHILIPPE-ADÉLARD LANGEVIN, OMI
Archbishop of St. Boniface (1895); died 1915.

Subsequent archbishops were not Oblates

ATHABASCA-MACKENZIE

HENRI FARAUD, OMI
Titular Bishop of Anemurium and Vicar Apostolic of Athabasca-Mackenzie
(1862); died 1890.

ISIDORE CLUT, OMI
Titular Bishop of Arindela and Auxiliary to the Vicar Apostolic of
Athabasca-Mackenzie (1865); died 1903.

ÉMILE GROUARD, OMI
Titular Bishop of Ibora and Vicar Apostolic of Athabasca-
Mackenzie (1890).

ATHABASCA / GROUARD

ÉMILE GROUARD, OMI
Titular Bishop of Ibora and Vicar Apostolic of Athabasca-Mackenzie (1890);
first Vicar Apostolic of Athabasca (1901); first Vicar Apostolic of Grouard
(1927); resigned 1929; Titular Archbishop of Aegina (1930); died 1931.

CÉLESTIN JOUSSARD, OMI
Titular Bishop of Arcadiopolis and Coadjutor to the Vicar Apostolic of
Athabasca (1909); resigned 1929; died 1932.

JOSEPH GUY, OMI
Titular Bishop of Zerta and Vicar Apostolic of Grouard (1930); Bishop of
Gravelbourg (1937); resigned 1942; died 1951.

UBALD LANGLOIS, OMI
Titular Bishop of Risinium and Vicar Apostolic of Grouard (1938); died 1953.

HENRI ROUTHIER, OMI
Titular Bishop of Naissus and Coadjutor to the Vicar Apostolic of Grouard
(1951); first Archbishop of Grouard-McLennan (1967), resigned 1972;
died 1989.

ST. ALBERT / EDMONTON

VITAL-JUSTIN GRANDIN, OMI
Titular Bishop of Satala and Coadjutor to the Bishop of St. Boniface (1857);
first Bishop of St. Albert (1871); died 1902.

ÉMILE LEGAL, OMI
Titular Bishop of Pogla and Coadjutor to the Bishop of St. Albert (1897);
Bishop of St. Albert (1902); first Archbishop of Edmonton (1912), died 1920.

Subsequent bishops were not Oblates

OVIDE CHARLEBOIS, OMI
Titular Bishop of Berenice and Vicar Apostolic of Keewatin (1910); died 1933.

MARTIN LAJEUNESSE, OMI
Titular Bishop of Bonusta and Coadjutor to the Vicar Apostolic of Keewatin (1933); Vicar Apostolic of Keewatin (1933); resigned 1954; died 1961.

PAUL DUMOUCHEL, OMI
Titular Bishop of Sufes and Vicar Apostolic of Keewatin (1955); first Archbishop of Keewatin-Le Pas (1967).

GRAVELBOURG

JOSEPH-M.-R. VILLENEUVE, OMI
Bishop of Gravelbourg (1930); Archbishop of Quebec (1931); Cardinal (1933); died 1947.

JOSEPH GUY, OMI
Titular Bishop of Zerta and Vicar Apostolic of Grouard (1930), Bishop of Gravelbourg (1937); resigned 1942, Titular Bishop of Photice (1942), died 1951.

Subsequent bishops were not Oblates

△ △

NOTES

PREFACE

1. James Axtell, *The Invasion Within: The Contest of Cultures in Colonial North America* (New York: Oxford University Press, 1985).

2. Bruce G. Trigger, *Natives and Newcomers: Canada's "Heroic Age" Reconsidered* (Montreal: McGill-Queen's University Press, 1986).

3. James Axtell, "Some Thoughts on the Ethnohistory of Mission," *Ethnohistory* 29 (1982): p. 36.

4. Ibid., pp. 36–38.

5. Trigger, *Natives and Newcomers*, p. 49.

INTRODUCTION

1. Henri Bourassa, *La langue gardienne de la foi* (Montréal: Bibliothèque de l'Action française, n.d.).

2. Axtell, *The Invasion Within*, p. 329.

3. Philip M. Hanley, "The Catholic Ladder, and Missionary Activity in the Pacific Northwest" (M.A. thesis, University of Ottawa, 1965), p. 2. It has since been edited and published: P.M. Hanley, *History of the Catholic Ladder*, ed. by Edward J. Kowrach (Fairfield, WA: Ye Galleon Press, 1994). Subsequent references are to the thesis.

4. A.-A. Taché, o.m.i., "Vingt années de missions dans le Nord-Ouest de l'Amérique, 18 sept. 1865," *Missions de la Congrégation des Missionnaires*

Oblats de Marie Immaculée [hereafter *Missions*] 5 (1866): pp. 73–108, 145–215, 352–75, 532–68.

5. Alexandre-Antonin Taché, o.m.i. *Vingt années de missions dans le Nord-Ouest de L'Amérique* (Montréal: Eusèbe Senécal, 1866), p. 17. A second edition was published in 1888 by Librairie Saint-Joseph, Montréal. In 1885, Taché began to prepare a sequel entitled "Après quarante ans de mission," but it was never completed, Archives Deschâtelets [hereafter AD], L 301 M27R 21.

6. Émile Grouard, *Souvenirs de mes soixante ans d'apostolat dans L'Athabasca-Mackenzie* (Lyon: Oeuvre Apostolique de Marie Immaculée, [1922]).

7. Gabriel Breynat, *Cinquante ans au pays des neiges* (Montréal: Fides, 3 vols., 1945–48).

8. Gabriel Breynat, OMI. *Bishop of the Winds: Fifty Years in the Arctic Region* (New York: P.J. Kennedy, [ca. 1955]). The French edition had been published two years earlier: *Évêque volant: Cinquante ans au Grand Nord* (Paris: Amiot-Dumont, 1953).

9. Other translated works include: Pierre Duchaussois, OMI, *Hidden Apostles: Our Lay Brother Missionaries* (Buffalo, N.Y.: Missionary Oblates of Mary Immaculate, 1937), *Mid Snow and Ice: The Apostles of the North-West* (London: Burns, Oates and Washbourne, 1923); Paul-Émile Breton, OMI, *The Big Chief of the Prairies: The Life of Father Lacombe* ([Edmonton?], Palm Publishers, [1955]), *Blacksmith of God* (Edmonton: Éditions de l'Ermitage, 1960). For a genuine English account, consult W. Leising, OMI, *Arctic Wings* cited in note 12. Two English language books have appeared on the Oblate experience in British Columbia. Kay Cronin's *Cross in the Wilderness* (Toronto: Mission Press, 1976) is a well written but general survey. Margaret Whitehead's *The Caribou Mission: A History of the Oblates* (Victoria: Sono Nis Press, 1981) is a more scholarly regional history.

10. Frank Dolphin, *Indian Bishop of the West: The Story of Vital Justin Grandin, 1829–1902* (Ottawa: Novalis, 1986).

11. Brian Owens and Claude Roberto, eds., *The Diaries of Bishop Vital Grandin, 1875–1877*, vol. 1, trans. Alan D. Ridge (Edmonton: The Historical Society of Alberta, Amisk Waskahegan Chapter, 1989).

12. Adrien-Gabriel Morice, o.m.i., *Souvenirs d'un missionnaire en Colombie britannique* (Winnipeg: Chez l'auteur, 1933); D.L.S. [A.-G. Morice], *Fifty Years in Western Canada: Being the Abridged Memoirs of A.G. Morice, O.M.I.* (Toronto: Ryerson Press, 1930); Lucien Delalande, o.m.i., *Sous le soleil de minuit* (Montréal: Rayonnement, 1958); William Leising, OMI, *Arctic Wings* (Garden City, NY: Echo Books (Doubleday), 1965).

13. Gaston Carrière, o.m.i., *L'Apôtre des Prairies: Joseph Hugonnard, o.m.i., 1848–1917* (Montréal: Rayonnement, 1967); *Le père du Keewatin: Mgr Ovide Charlebois, o.m.i., 1862–1933* (Montréal: Rayonnement, 1962).

14. Paul-Émile Breton, o.m.i., *Vital Grandin: La merveilleuse aventure de l'évêque des Prairies et du Grand Nord*, Bibliothèque Ecclesia 58 (Paris: Librairie Arthème Fayard, 1960); *Le grand chef des prairies: Le père Albert Lacombe, o.m.i., 1827–1916* (Edmonton: Éditions de l'Ermitage, 1954).

15. Gaston Carrière, o.m.i., "Fondation et développement des missions catholiques dans la Terre de Rupert et les Territoires du Nord-Ouest," *Revue de l'Université d'Ottawa* 41 (1971): pp. 253–81, 397–427; "L'Honorable Compagnie de la Baie d'Hudson et les missions dans l'Ouest canadien," ibid., 36 (1966): pp. 15–39, 232–57; "Le père Albert Lacombe, o.m.i., et le Pacifique canadien," ibid., 37 (1967): pp. 287–321, 510–39, 611–38; 38 (1968): pp. 97–131, 316–50; "Une mission de paix: le père André et les Sioux, 1863–1865," *Études Oblates* 27 (1968): pp. 189–224, 299–340.

16. *Dictionnaire biographique des Oblats de Marie Immaculée au Canada* (Éditions de l'Université d'Ottawa, 3 vols., 1976–79). A fourth volume was prepared by Maurice Gilbert, o.m.i., and Normand Martel, o.m.i., (Montréal: Maison provinciale, 1989). These four volumes contain 2142 entries of Oblates who died prior to 31 December 1987.

17. Joseph-Étienne Champagne, *Les missions catholiques dans l'Ouest canadien (1818–1875)* (Ottawa: Éditions des *Études Oblates*, 1949).

18. Claude Champagne, *Les débuts de la mission dans le Nord-Ouest canadien: Mission et Église chez Mgr Vital Grandin, o.m.i., 1829–1902* (Ottawa: Éditions de l'Université d'Ottawa, 1983).

19. Hanley, "The Catholic Ladder"; R. Nowakowski, OMI, "Indian Residential Schools in Saskatchewan Conducted by the Oblate Fathers" (M.A. thesis, University of Ottawa (Institute of Missiology), 1962).

20. Jacqueline Kennedy, "Qu'Appelle Industrial School: White Rites for the Indians of the Old Northwest" (M.A. thesis, Canadian Studies, Carleton University, 1970).

21. Martha McCarthy, "The Missions of the Oblates of Mary Immaculate to the Athapascans, 1846–1870: Theory, Structure and Method" (Ph.D. thesis, University of Manitoba, 1981). This study has been revised and has been published: Martha McCarthy, *From the Great River to the Ends of the Earth: Oblate Missions to the Dene, 1847–1921* (Edmonton: University of Alberta Press, 1995).

22. Antonio Gualtieri, *Christianity and Native Traditions: Indigenization and Syncretism Among the Inuit and Dene of the Western Arctic*, vol. 2, *The Church and the World* (Notre Dame, Indiana: Cross Road Books, 1984).

23. John Webster Grant, *Moon of Wintertime: Missionaries and the Indians of Canada in Encounter Since 1534* (Toronto: University of Toronto Press, 1984).

24. David Mulhall, *Will to Power: The Missionary Career of Father Morice* (Vancouver: University of British Columbia Press, 1986).

25. Raymond Huel, "L'Association Catholique Franco-Canadienne de la Saskatchewan: A Response to Cultural Assimilation 1912–1934" (M.A. thesis, University of Regina, 1969).

26. Raymond Huel, "The French Language Press in Western Canada: *Le Patriote de l'Ouest, 1910–41*," *Revue de l'Université d'Ottawa* 46 (1976): pp. 476–99.

27. George F.G. Stanley, *Louis Riel* (Toronto: Ryerson Press, 1963); Thomas Flanagan, *Louis "David" Riel: Prophet of the New World* (Toronto: University of Toronto Press, 1979).

28. Paul Crunican, *Priests and Politicians: Manitoba Schools and the Election of 1896* (Toronto: University of Toronto Press, 1974); P. Crunican, "Father Lacombe's Strange Mission: The Lacombe-Langevin Correspondence on the Manitoba School Question," Canadian Catholic Historical Association, *Report* 26 (1959).

29. Diane Payment, *Batoche (1870–1910)* (Saint-Boniface: Les Éditions du Blé, 1983); La Société Historique de Saint-Boniface, *Histoire de Saint-Boniface*, tome 1, *À l'ombre des cathédrales: Des origines de la colonie jusqu'en 1870* (Saint-Boniface: Les Éditions du Blé, 1991).

30. M.B. Venini Byrne, *From the Buffalo to the Cross: A History of the Diocese of Calgary* (Calgary: Calgary Archives and Historical Publishers, ca. 1973).

31. Une Soeur de la Providence, *Le Père Lacombe «L'Homme au bon coeur» d'après ses mémoires et souvenirs* (Montréal: au *Devoir*, 1916); Patricia Meyer, ed., *Honoré-Timothée Lempfrit, O.M.I.: His Oregon Trail Journal and Letters from the Pacific Northwest, 1848–1853* (Fairfield, Washington: Ye Galleon Press, 1985); Margaret Whitehead, ed., *They Call Me Father: The Memoirs of Father Nicolas Cocolla* (Vancouver: University of British Columbia Press, 1988).

1   THE FRENCH ANTECEDENTS

1. This title was bestowed upon the Oblates by Pius XI, see Gaston Carrière, o.m.i., "Méthodes et réalisations missionnaires des Oblats dans l'Est du Canada (1841–1861)," *Études Oblates* 16 (1957): p. 37. For the precise wording of the Pope's declaration, consult Josef Pielorz, o.m.i., "L'affirmation:

«Les Oblats sont les spécialistes des missions difficiles» est-elle de Pie XI?"
Vie Oblate Life 51 (1992): pp. 99–101.

2. In Canada, these popular missions were known as parish retreats in which residents of town and country were gathered together for an intense period of spiritual regeneration through the intermediary of instruction, preaching, confession and communion: "Lectures du Centennaire," *Missions* 60 (1926): p. 275.

3. Donat Levasseur, o.m.i., *Histoire des Missionnaires Oblats de Marie Immaculée: Essaie de synthèse*, vol. 1, 1815–1898 (Montréal: Maison Provinciale O.M.I., 1983), pp. 28–29.

4. Ibid., p. 37, p. 62. The term "oblate" identifies a person who has dedicated himself/herself to the service of God through religious life. For the Oblates of Mary Immaculate this was done in a formal ceremony, the perpetual oblation or vows, that took place prior to ordination.

5. Claude Champagne, o.m.i., *Les débuts de la mission* (Ottawa: Éditions de l'Université d'Ottawa, 1983), pp. 20–21, 30.

6. Claude Champagne, o.m.i., "La formation des Oblats, missionnaires dans le Nord-Ouest canadien," Société canadienne d'histoire de l'Église catholique, *Sessions d'Étude* 56 (1989): pp. 23–24; Martin Quéré, o.m.i., "Monseigneur de Mazenod et le missionnaire Oblat," *Études Oblates* 20 (1961): p. 249.

7. Quéré, "Mgr de Mazenod," pp. 246–47.

8. Among the manuals in use one finds *Somme théologique de saint Thomas d'Aquin*, Jean-Baptiste Bouvier's *Institutiones theologicae ad usum seminariorum*, and two anonymous texts attributed to Joseph Fabre, the second Superior General of the Oblates: *Tractatus de Religione revelata maxime christiana* and *Tractatus de Vera Christi Ecclesia*, C. Champagne, "La formation des Oblats," pp. 25–26.

9. C. Champagne, "La formation des Oblats," pp. 27–30. A more detailed analysis is to be found in the same author's *Les débuts de la mission*, pp. 36–40: "Analyse de quelques thèmes des manuels de théologie."

10. Matt. 28, 18–19.

11. Joseph-Étienne Champagne, o.m.i., *Manuel d'action missionnaire* (Ottawa: Éditions de l'Université d'Ottawa, 1947), p. 27.

12. E. Champagne, p.b., "Le missionnaire, ses qualités, sa préparation," *Semaines d'études missionnaires* (Ottawa: Le Secrétariat, Université d'Ottawa, 1934), p. 172.

13. Alexandre Audruger, o.m.i., *Directoire pour les missions à l'usage des Missionnaires Oblats de Marie Immaculée* (Tours: A. Mame et Fils, 1881),

p. 2. Similar directives for missionary activity were compiled at the regional level, for example, AD, L 31 M27R, R.P. Bermond, Visiteur, "Directoire des Missions, Saint Joseph d'Olympia [Oregon], 17 sept. 1858," Mgr Martin Lajeunesse, o.m.i., *Directives missionnaires* (le Pas: Évêché, 1942).

14. Audruger, *Directoire pour les missions*, p. 10.
15. Ibid., p. 16. "Be ye followers of me, as I also am of Christ," 1 Cor. 11: 1.
16. Ibid., p. 2.
17. Émilien Lamirande, o.m.i., "L'Annonce de la parole de Dieu selon Mgr de Mazenod. Le ministère évangélique de la Congrégation," *Études Oblates* 18 (1959): pp. 111, 123–25.
18. C. Champagne, *Les débuts de la mission*, p. 6.
19. Bx de Mazenod, *Lettres aux correspondants d'Amérique, 1851–1860*, Écrits Oblats II (Rome: Postulation générale O.M.I., 1977), p. 242, Mazenod to [Végréville], 17 avril 1860.
20. Ibid., Mazenod to [Ricard], 6 déc. 1851, p. 31.
21. Levasseur, *Histoire*, Vol. I, pp. 166–67.
22. J.-C. Beaumont, J. Gadille, Xavier de Montclos, "L'Exportation des modèles de christianisme français à l'époque contemporaine. Pour une nouvelle problématique de l'histoire missionnaire," *Revue d'Histoire de l'Église de France* 63 (1977): p. 15.
23. Its original title was "Appendix De Exteris Missionibus. Instructio Illustrissimi Ac Reverendissimi D.D. Caroli-Joseph-Eugenii de Mazenod . . ." *Constitutiones Et Regulæ Congregationis Missionariorum Oblatorum Sanctissimæ Et Immaculatæ Virginis Mariae* (Parisiis: E Typis priv. O.M.I., 1887), pp. 167–82. The references are to a later French language version: *Instruction de notre Vénéré Fondateur relative aux missions étrangères* [hereafter *Instruction*] (Rome: Maison générale, 1936), p. 4, p. 7.
24. *Instruction*, p. 5, p. 7.
25. Ibid., pp. 12–14. Mazenod used the French term *sauvage* to designate Aboriginal populations. In his overview of the North West published in 1869 Bishop Taché used the same term to designate the Aboriginal inhabitants of the region. According to Taché, the term *sauvage* was used not because these individuals *"soient d'un caractère barbare, féroce ou sauvage, mais bien parce qu'il y a quelque chose de sauvage dans leur genre de vie, ou par opposition au titre de civilisés, donné aux nations qui pratiquent une religion, vivent sous une forme de gouvernement, obéissent à des lois et se livrent aux arts ou à l'industrie."* Alexandre-Antonin Taché,

o.m.i., *Esquisse sur le Nord-Ouest de l'Amérique*, 2e éd. (Montréal: Beauchemin et Fils, 1901), p. 85.

26. Ibid., p. 12.

27. Ibid., pp. 14–15.

28. In the Canadian North West, the Vicar of Missions was also the bishop or vicar apostolic who, *ipso facto*, exercised both religious and ecclesiastical authority. The vicar apostolic is a titular bishop appointed by the Sacred Congregation for the Propagation of the Faith to administer the affairs of the Church in a missionary territory that lacks regular ecclesiastical organization and the establishment of the hierarchy. As titular bishop, the vicar apostolic is endowed with the authority and dignity of a regular resident bishop but is subject directly to the pope. Consult *New Catholic Encyclopedia*, "Vicar Apostolic," vol. 14, pp. 638–39.

29. *Instruction*, p. 8.

30. Ibid., p. 12.

31. Ibid., p. 9.

32. Donat Levasseur, o.m.i., *Les Oblats de Marie Immaculée dans l'Ouest et le Nord du Canada, 1845–1967* (Edmonton: University of Alberta Press, 1995), pp. 111–12. The publication of *Missions* was suspended temporarily in 1871 during the occupation of Paris, during WWI (1915–1918) and WWII (1940–1946).

33. Provincial Archives of Alberta [hereafter PAA], Oblates of Mary Immaculate, Fonds Alberta-Saskatchewan [hereafter OMI], Administration [hereafter Adm.], Correspondance de J. Fabre 1861–63, Fabre to Mgr et bien bon père [Taché], 13 mars 1863. Italics in original.

34. Levasseur, *Histoire*, vol. 1, p. 42.

35. Donat Levasseur, o.m.i., *Les Constitutions et Règles des Missionnaires Oblats de Marie Immaculée à la lumière de Vatican II* (Bibliothèque Oblate XV) (Ottawa: Éditions des Études Oblates, 1967), ch. 2, "Un état de vie apostolique," pp. 15–26.

36. See infra, pp. 69–70.

37. The following are a sample of numerous Oblate references to the disappearance of the buffalo: "Lettre du R.P. Leduc au T.R.P. Supérieur Général," 22 déc. 1870, *Missions* 11 (1873): pp. 204–5; PAA, OMI, Dossiers du Personnel [hereafter DP], J. Tissot 1856–73, Tissot to Mon bien cher père, 18 nov. 1873; "Lettre du R.P. Lacombe au Bien-aimé et T.R.P. Général," 24 déc. 1877, *Missions* 16 (1878): p. 174; PAA, OMI, Macleod 6, *Codex historicus*, 1879, p. 18.

38. "He sent me to evangelize the poor." Isa. 61, 1.

1. Joseph-Étienne Champagne, o.m.i., "Aux origines de la mission de la rivière Rouge (1818–1845)," *Études Oblates* 4 (1945): p. 50. In 1820, Plessis was
   able to divide his diocese into five districts including Quebec and confide
   their respective administration to coadjutors. The other four districts later
   became dioceses in their own right: Charlottetown (1829), Montreal
   (1836), Kingston (1826), the Hudson's Bay territory or North West (1847).
   The district of the North West was erected as the Vicariate Apostolic of
   Hudson's Bay and James Bay in 1844; it became the Diocese of the
   North-West three years later in 1847. At Taché's request, the title was
   altered to Diocese of St. Boniface in 1851. The final change in status took
   place in 1871 with the creation of the Ecclesiastical Province of St.
   Boniface. Changes in ecclesiastical and religious jurisdictions and person-
   nel are identified in the appendices.

2. Selkirk had sent out a priest with the first contingent but this individual
   had not gone beyond York Factory before returning to Europe; Martha
   McCarthy, *To Evangelize the Nations: Roman Catholic Missions in
   Manitoba, 1818–1870*, Papers in Manitoba History, Report No. 2
   (Winnipeg: Manitoba Culture, Heritage and Recreation Historic
   Resources, 1990), pp. 3–4; J.-E. Champagne, "Aux origines," pp. 42–43.

3. Grace L. Nute, ed., *Documents Relating to the Northwest Mission,
   1815–1827* (St. Paul: Minnesota Historical Society, 1942), pp. 4–5. There
   were other influential factors that determined Plessis's selection of Red
   River as the site of a Catholic mission. To begin with, Selkirk had made a
   grant of land contingent on a Catholic establishment at Red River and
   the Governor of Lower Canada, J.C. Sherbrooke, supported this proposal; see McCarthy, *To Evangelize the Nations*, pp. 4–5.

4. Nute, *Northwest Mission*, pp. 58–61; McCarthy, *To Evangelize the Nations*,
   p. 6.

5. McCarthy, *To Evangelize the Nations*, pp. 8–9.

6. Brenda Gainer, "The Catholic Missionaries as Agents of Social Change"
   (M.A. thesis, Carleton University, 1978), p. 22.

7. Ibid., p. 10; McCarthy, *To Evangelize the Nations*, p. 21.

8. McCarthy, *To Evangelize the Nations*, pp. 13–14.

9. Provencher often complained about the lack of training of priests who
   came to Red River and suggested that they asked to return to Quebec
   when they had acquired experience or a knowledge of Indian languages
   and, consequently, they were never able to render useful service in the
   mission field; D. Roy, "Monseigneur Provencher et son clergé séculier,"

Société canadienne d'histoire de l'Église catholique, *Sessions d'Études* 37 (1970): p. 8.

10. In French, members of the secular clergy are addressed as *abbé* whereas members of the regular clergy, such as Oblates and Jesuits, are identified as *père*.

11. Frits Pannekoek, *A Snug Little Flock: The Social Origins of the Riel Resistance, 1869–70* (Winnipeg: Watson and Dwyer Publishing, 1991), p. 94. The conflict between Provencher and Belcourt had another important dimension. Provencher tended to support the HBC whereas Belcourt actively sympathized with and assisted the Métis in the dispute over free trade in Red River, ibid., p. 80; see also D. Frémont, *Monseigneur Provencher et son temps* (Winnipeg: Éditions de *La Liberté*, 1935), p. 249.

12. McCarthy, *To Evangelize the Nations*, pp. 18–20.

13. Taché, *Vingt années de missions*, p. 20; J.-E. Champagne, "Aux origines," p. 59.

14. Léon Pouliot, s.j., "Mgr Ignace Bourget et la mission de la Rivière Rouge," Société canadienne d'histoire de l'Église catholique, *Sessions d'Étude* 37 (1970): p. 19.

15. Taché, *Vingt années*, p. 21. The Holy See also erected the Oregon Territory into another autonomous vicariate apostolic with Norbert Blanchet as Bishop. Blanchet and Modeste Demers had been the two first missionaries sent to the Pacific slope by Provencher in 1838.

16. Pannekoek, *A Snug Little Flock*, pp. 111–12.

17. McCarthy, *To Evangelize the Nations*, pp. 34–35.

18. Ibid., pp. 25–26.

19. Ibid., p. 41, p. 21.

20. Carrière, "Fondation et développement," p. 254. Simpson's reply is cited in fn. 11. Simpson's opposition was motivated by his fear of American influences in the North West and the difficulty of maintaining the HBC's authority and monopoly in that area; McCarthy, *To Evangelize the Nations*, p. 23.

21. Gaston Carrière, o.m.i., *Histoire documentaire de la Congrégation des Missionnaires Oblats de Marie-Immaculée dans l'Est du Canada*, vol. 3 (Ottawa: Les Éditions de l'Université d'Ottawa, 1961), p. 166. The letter is cited in Carrière, "Fondation et développement," p. 255.

22. McCarthy, *To Evangelize the Nations*, p. 24; AD, HPK 2001 N32R 38, Provencher to Signay, 22 avril 1844.

23. Carrière, *Histoire documentaire*, III, p. 164; Gaston Carrière, o.m.i., "Mgr

Ignace Bourget et les Oblats," *Revue de l'Université d'Ottawa* 30 (1960): pp. 403–7.

24. The text of Bourget's letter is reproduced in Carrière, *Histoire documentaire*, tome 3, p. 165. Bourget also reiterated Provencher's desire that some of the first Oblates should be Canadian to circumvent the opposition of the HBC; Bx de Mazenod, *Lettres aux correspondants d'Amérique, 1841–1850*, Écrits Oblats I (Rome: Postulation générale O.M.I., 1977), Mazenod to [Guigues], 5 déc. 1844, p. 116.

25. Mazenod, *Lettres 1841–1850*, Mazenod to Mgr l'Évêque de Montréal, 6 fév. 1845, p. 120; Mazenod to [Guigues] 24 mai 1845, pp. 124–25.

26. Ibid., Mazenod to [Bourget], 9 juillet 1845, p. 128.

27. Ibid., Mazenod to Mgr l'Évêque de Québec, 8 juin 1844, p. 93.

28. Ibid., Mazenod to [Guigues], 6 juillet 1845, p. 127.

29. Ibid., Mazenod to Aubert, 21 fév. 1846, p. 133.

30. Dom Benoît, c.r.i.c. [Joseph-Paul Augustin], *Vie de Mgr Taché, Archevêque de St-Boniface*, vol. 1 (Montréal: Librairie Beauchemin, 1904), p. 87. When he embarked on the voyage to Red River, Taché was still 21 years of age and hence could not be ordained according to the requirements of Canon Law in force at that time. During the trip, however, he attained his 22nd birthday (July 23) and could be ordained anytime thereafter. In a letter to Archbishop Signay Provencher stated: *"Deo Gratias voilà au moins de la graine de religieux. C'est sur cette espèce d'hommes que je compte depuis longtemps pour travailler efficacement aux missions sauvages,"* AD, HPK 2001 N82 R 40, Provencher to Signay, 29 août 1845.

31. Mazenod, *Lettres 1841–1850*, Mazenod to Aubert, 21 fév. 1846, p. 133. Taché's vows were the first to be pronounced by a Catholic clergyman in the North West but even more fitting was the fact that he was a grand nephew of Varrennes de la Vérendry who had discovered and explored the Red River and Lake Winnipeg basins; Taché, *Vingt années*, pp. 27–28.

32. Taché, *Vingt années*, pp. 28–29. The Chipewyan bore no resemblance to the Montagnais, a tribe that inhabited the Laurentian mountains on the north shore of the St. Lawrence River. Furthermore, there were no mountains in the lands of the Chipewyan. Taché, who made an analysis of the etymology of the term "Chipewyan," was aware of this and postulated that the name *"Montagnais"* erroneously had been applied by French Canadian voyageurs; G. Carrière, o.m.i., "Letter from Bishop Alexandre Taché to his Mother Concerning his Life with the Chipewyan Nation [4 Jan. 1851]," *Prairie Forum* 3 (1978): p. 133.

33. Mazenod, *Lettres 1841–1850*, Mazenod to Guigues, 14 et 16 mai 1846,

p. 136; Taché, *Vingt années*, pp. 29–30; Aristide Philippot, o.m.i., "Mgr H.-J. Faraud, o.m.i., 1823–1890," *L'Ami du foyer*, sept. 1959, p. 10.

34. McCarthy, *To Evangelize the Nations* (p. 110), states that Bermond worked among the Saulteaux in the spring of 1846 whereas Taché's *Vingt années* (p. 29) affirms that he arrived in St. Boniface on 5 September 1846.

35. McCarthy, *To Evangelize the Nations*, pp. 81–82.

36. Ibid., p. 119.

37. Carrière, "Fondation et développement," p. 258. In footnote 34, Carrière cites from Provencher's letter to Mgr P.-F. Turgeon, Coadjutor Bishop of Quebec, 4 Dec. 1847, in which the former states that the mission has been closed because "*les sauvages n'ont pas voulu entendre parler de religion.*"

38. Taché to [S.J.] Dawson, 7 fév. 1859, *Missions* 2 (1863): pp. 166–67.

39. McCarthy, *To Evangelize the Nations*, pp. 9–10.

40. Axtell, "Some Thoughts on the Ethnohistory of Mission," p. 40.

41. Levasseur, *Les Oblats de Marie Immaculée*, p. 39. Aubert subsequently rendered sterling service as *curé* of the cathedral in St. Boniface and as the bishop's Grand Vicar.

42. Ibid., p. 119.

43. Taché wrote this lengthy insightful letter to his mother while he was at Île-à-la-Crosse, 4 Jan. 1851. Although it was not written for the public, it was published numerous times beginning in January 1852 in *Rapport de l'association de la Propagation de la Foi pour le district de Montréal*, pp. 67–93. It was translated into English and annotated by the Oblate historian G. Carrière: "Letter from Bishop Taché," pp. 131–56. The Carrière text will be used because it is in English and more readily available. Taché is referring (p. 132) to Atala, a detached episode in Chateaubriand's *Le génie du Christianisme* (1802). Atala was a young Indian whose mother had promised her to the God of Christians. However, Atala fell in love with the warrior Chactas and rather than going against her mother's wishes, she poisoned herself.

44. É. Lamirande, "Le père Honoré-Timothée Lempfrit: son ministère auprès des autochtones de l'île de Vancouver (1849–1852)," in *Western Oblate Studies 1 / Études Oblates de l'Ouest 1*, ed. by R. Huel (Edmonton: Western Canadian Publishers and Institut de recherche de la Faculté Saint-Jean, 1990): pp. 67–68.

45. AD, HE 2224 T12R 1, Taché to Ma bonne mère, 3 jan. 1850.

46. Grant, *Moon of Wintertime*, p. 239, 245.

47. McCarthy, *From the Great River*, ms., p. 178.

48. Carrière, "Fondation et développement," p. 268–70.

49. Carrière, "Letter from Bishop Taché," pp. 135–36.

50. Ibid., pp. 137–43.

51. Ibid., p. 141, 153–54.

52. Taché, *Vingt années*, pp. 32–48. The lay brother (*frère convers*) was a non-clerical, lay member of the congregation. He is a consecrated layman who dedicates his life to the service of the order. The lay brother takes the same vows and forms part of the same community as the ordained Oblates by sharing the same dining room and spiritual exercises. The function of the lay brother was enhanced when the Oblates accepted foreign missions. Lay brothers became missionaries, builders of churches and schools and assumed apostolic responsibilities as catechists and teachers in schools. The *Constitutions and Rules* of the congregation were subsequently amended to account for these changes in status culminating in 1980 with the formal recognitions that Oblate lay brothers shared in the one priesthood of Christ. Consult W.H. Woestman, OMI, "Juridical History of the Oblate Brothers," *Vie Oblate Life* 44 (1985): pp. 219–62.

53. Mazenod, *Lettres 1841–1850*, Mazenod to [Guigues], 30 juillet 1846, p. 141. Two years earlier Mazenod had given instructions to the Oblates in the missions of Quebec that they should imitate the Jesuits and always work in pairs: ibid., Mazenod to [Honorat], 1 mars 1844, p. 83.

54. Mazenod, *Lettres 1851–1860*, Mazenod to [Taché], 29 nov. 1854, p. 88.

55. Ibid., Mazenod to Faraud, 6 mars 1857, p. 146. In 1856 Faraud founded St. Joseph's Mission, at Fort Resolution.

56. Ibid., Mazenod to Faraud, 1 mai 1852.

57. Ibid., *Lettres 1841–1850*, Mazenod to [Aubert], 3 fév. 1847, p. 170. He informed bishop Guigues of Bytown that he cheerfully paid the postage on letters that were completely filled "*mais je ne paye pas volontiers du papier blanc au prix de l'or*," ibid., 10 mai 1849, p. 230. The letter Mazenod anticipated receiving was "*non pas quelques lignes, mais une bonne lettre bien remplie sur les quatre faces du papier*," ibid., *Lettres 1851–1860*, Mazenod to [Végréville], 25 mars 1857, p. 151.

58. McCarthy, *To Evangelize the Nations*, p. 31; Bx de Mazenod, *Lettres à la Sacrée Congrégation et à l'Oeuvre de la Propagation de la Foi, 1832–1861*, Écrits Oblats V (Rome: Postulation générale O.M.I., 1981), Mazenod to Messieurs les Membres du Conseil central du Midi pour l'Oeuvre de la Propagation de la Foi, 18 mars 1845, p. 178.

59. Mazenod, *Lettres à la Sacrée Congrégation*, Mazenod to Messieurs les Membres du Conseil central du Midi, pour l'Oeuvre de la Propagation de la Foi à Lyon, 15 mai 1846, p. 192.

60. Ibid., Mazenod to Messieurs du Conseil central du Midi de l'Oeuvre de la Propagation de la Foi à Lyon, 14 oct. 1847, p. 203.

61. Ibid., Mazenod to Messieurs du Conseil central du Midi pour l'Oeuvre de la Propagation de la Foi, Lyon, 30 août 1847, p. 201.

62. Mazenod, *Lettres 1841–1850*, Mazenod to [Bourget], 16 avril 1850, p. 249; ibid., *Lettres 1851– 1860*, Mazenod to [Guigues] 8 oct. 1852, p. 45.

63. Paul-Émile Breton, o.m.i., "Le Fondateur des Oblats d'après les écrits de Mgr Grandin," *Études Oblates* 18 (1959): p. 343.

64. Taché, *Vingt années*, p. 48. Laflèche returned to Quebec in 1856 and in 1870 was named Bishop of Trois-Rivières.

65. Carrière, "Mgr Ignace Bourget et les Oblats," p. 417.

66. Levasseur, *Les Oblats de Marie Immaculée*, p. 42.

67. Mazenod, *Lettres 1841–1850*, Mazenod to [Bourget], 16 avril 1850, p. 249.

68. Ibid., Mazenod to [Bermond], 26 mai 1854, p. 78. However, not everyone regarded Taché's nomination as providential. Some of his older French colleagues in Red River felt slighted that a younger person and worse, a Canadian, had been selected instead. Bishop Grandin recalled later that when Taché returned to Île-à-la-Crosse, "*Il se passa des choses bien regrettables, à peine croyables.*" Vital Grandin to Dom Benoit, "Quelques notes sur Mgr Taché," Écrits de Mgr Grandin [hereafter Grandin, Écrits], vol. 5, pp. 278–81.

69. Levasseur, *Les Oblats de Marie Immaculée*, p.43.

70. Mazenod, *Lettres 1851–1860*, Mazenod to [Faraud], 24 nov. 1851, p. 28.

3   THE MISSIONARY FRONTIER AND THE OBLATES:
      ADAPTATION AND INNOVATION

1. Quéré, "Mgr de Mazenod," p. 245.

2. Mazenod, *Lettres 1841–1850*, Mazenod to [Aubert], 4 mars 1849, p. 221.

3. PAA, OMI, Papiers Personnels [hereafter PP], L. Doucet, Journal 1868–90, 9 oct. 1870, p. 14. Doucet remarked that his was the first and the last ordination to take place in the "shack" that served as the cathedral in St. Albert.

4. PAA, OMI, DP, J. Le Treste 1883–85, Le Treste to Bien chère tante, 11 déc. 1885.

5. Mazenod, *Lettres 1851–1860*, Mazenod to [Taché], 29 nov. 1854, p. 88. Of the 94 Oblates sent to the North West and British Columbia in the period 1845–71, only three left the congregation: one entered a contemplative order in France, another joined the Anglican clergy and a lay brother was exempted from his vows. Three other members of this original con-

tingent left the order after 1871, consult Levasseur, *Les Oblats de Marie Immaculée*, p. 118.

6. Ibid., Mazenod to [Bermond], 26 mai 1854, p. 78; Mazenod to [Taché], 28 mai 1854, p. 81.

7. Ibid., Mazenod to [Guigues], 16 oct. 1857, p. 170; Mazenod to [Maisonneuve and Tissot], 24 nov. 1858, p. 212. Lacombe had already served in Pembina, North Dakota in 1849–51 and then returned to Quebec for a year prior to returning to the West in 1852. In addition to Lacombe, seven other members of the secular clergy who served the North West and British Columbia in the period 1845–1871 joined the ranks of the Congregation. Among their ranks was Émile Grouard who became Bishop of Ibora and Vicar Apostolic of Athabasca-Mackenzie, consult Levasseur, *Les Oblats de Marie Immaculée*, p. 117, fn. 33.

8. Ibid., Mazenod to [Taché], 22 mai 1857, p. 154.

9. Mazenod, *Lettres 1851–1860*, Mazenod to [Taché], 15 nov. 1858, p. 208.

10. Ibid., Mazenod to [Taché], 17 avril 1860, p. 239.

11. Ibid., Mazenod to [Taché], 16 juillet 1860, p. 247.

12. Quéré, "Mgr de Mazenod," pp. 247–48.

13. AD, HE 2224 T12R 1, Taché to P. Boucher de Labruière, 24 juin 1846. He also claimed that it was difficult to live with individuals who had few notions of cleanliness.

14. G. Carrière, o.m.i., "Contribution des missionnaires à la sauvegarde de la culture indienne," *Études Oblates* 31 (1972): p. 176. In this detailed examination of the linguistic contribution of the Oblate missionaries in the western and northern regions of Canada including Oregon, Carrière lists 181 dictionaries and 76 grammars in manuscript form and 11 dictionaries and 12 grammars published. These manuscripts and publications encompass 26 languages. To this should be added 30 manuscripts and three published works involving four languages in eastern Canada, p. 203.

15. Ibid., p. 179.

16. PAA, OMI, DP, J. Moulin 1860–67, Moulin to Mgr et bien aimé Père, 16 9bre 1862.

17. Lacombe to Très Rév. Père Supérieur Général, 6 jan. 1866 [sic], *Missions* 7 (1868): pp. 258–62.

18. PAA, OMI, PP, A. Lacombe, 1856–70, Lacombe to Végréville, 11 juin 1856.

19. Fernand-Michel [François Fortuné], *Dix-huit ans chez les sauvages: voyages et missions dans l'Extrême Nord de l'Amérique britannique* (Paris: Régis Ruffert et Cie, 1870), p. 29, 66. The author was Bishop Faraud's cousin. Bishop Grandin thought that the author, despite his excellent intentions,

had rendered Faraud a disservice because the contents were too exaggerated. Consequently, Grandin kept the book hidden from his own clergy; Archives oblates de Montréal [hereafter AOM], Personnes: V. Grandin, Grandin to Taché, 25 sept. 1866. Another contemporary of Faraud's described the book as "*le volume couleur de rose.*" AD, HE 2221 T12Z 177, Mestre to Mgr [Taché], 22 10bre 1864 [sic]. The description of Faraud in almost heroic proportions earned him the reputation in the congregation of not being a true Oblate.

20. AD, H 5102 G75M 1, Grandin to Maisonneuve, 14 xbre [Dec.] 1856.

21. C. Champagne, *Les débuts de la mission*, p. 104.

22. PAA, OMI, Adm., Vicariat Mackenzie: Correspondance 1858–60, Clut to Mon Rév. et bien cher père [Végréville], 23 déc. 1858.

23. AD, HE 2221 T12Z 21, Clut to Monseigneur [Taché], 27 déc. 1860.

24. Le Doussal to Directeur des Annales, 20 sept. 1892, *Missions* 31 (1893): p. 46.

25. D, HE 2221 T12Z 32, Clut to Mgr et bien cher père [Taché], 15 avril 1863.

26. AD, HE 1861 G87C 61, Grouard to Mes bien chères soeurs, 13 juin 1884.

27. AD, HE 1861 G87C 78, Grouard to Ma bien chère enfant, 25 août 1890.

28. Grandin, Écrits, 5, p. 298.

29. C. Champagne, *Les débuts de la mission*, p. 106, see also PAA, OMI, St. Albert 7, *Codex historicus*, 17 mars 1879, p. 120 and *Acte de visite du R.P. Soullier, premier assistant général pour le vicariat de Saint-Albert. Octobre 1883* (Saint-Albert: Typographie privée O.M.I. [1885]), p. 23, p. 25.

30. PAA, OMI PP, Z. Lizée: Journal 1887–88, especially the introspective entries of 14 août 1886, 23 jan. 1887, 24 jan. 1887 and 25 oct. 1887 that refer to his difficulties with the Cree language. The entries of 29 Sept. and 25 Oct. 1887 relative to the English language are also revealing.

31. PAA, OMI, DP, L. Le Goff 1885–1922, H. Grandin to Mon cher père Le Goff, n.d.; Ibid., A. Gasté 1863–64, Gasté to Mgr et bien cher père [Taché], 6 avril 1863.

32. PAA, OMI, PP, L. Doucet: Journal 1868–90, p. 7.

33. PAA, OMI, PP, L. Lizée: Journal 1887–88, 25 oct. 1887.

34. PAA, OMI, PP, L. Doucet: Journal 1868–90, p. 91.

35. AD, HE 1861 G87C 61, Grouard to Mes biens chères soeurs, 13 juin 1884. Fernand-Michel, *Dix-huit ans*, p. 121.

36. AD, LC 3 M14R 16, Grouard to Taché, 30 déc. 1862. When Taché visited Lake Athabasca in 1847 he was only 24 years old and the Indians would not take him seriously because they felt he was too young. *Abbé* Thibault, the first missionary to visit the region, had a few white hairs and hence was acceptable to the Indians who equated wisdom with

age and experience, C. Champagne, *Les débuts de la mission*, p. 12.

37. Raymond Huel, "La mission Notre-Dame des Victoires du lac la Biche et l'approvisionnement des missions du nord: le conflit entre Mgr V. Grandin et Mgr H. Faraud," in *Western Oblate Studies 1 / Études Oblates de l'Ouest 1*, ed. by R. Huel (Edmonton: Western Canadian Publishers and Institut de recherche de la Faculté Saint-Jean, 1990): pp. 17–36.

38. AD, HE 2221 T12Z 122, Lacombe to [Taché], 30 août 1862. C. Champagne, *Les débuts de la mission*, pp. 96–97.

39. Gaston Carrière, o.m.i., "L'Honorable Compagnie de la Baie-d'Hudson et les mission dans l'Ouest canadien," Société canadienne d'histoire de l'Église catholique, *Sessions d'Études* 32 (1965): p. 72. The quotation is from a letter of Eden Colville, Governor of Rupert's Land to Sir George Simpson, Governor in Chief of Rupert's Land, 14 July 1851. The second comment was made by Simpson in his report to the Governor and Committee, 20 June 1853.

40. Taché to [S.J.] Dawson, 7 fév. 1859, *Missions* 2 (1863): pp. 180–81.

41. AD, HE 1864 G87L 48, Grouard to MacFarlane, 29 June 1884.

42. PAA, OMI, DP, A. Gasté 1861–64, Gasté to Mgr et bien aimé père [Taché], 7 mai 1864.

43. AD, HE 1821 F26K 57, Faraud to McFerlane [sic], 25 nov. 1883.

44. AD, HE 1864 G87L 48, Grouard to MacFarlane, 29 June 1884.

45. AD, HE 2221 T12L 25, Taché to Bien chère maman, [5 jan. 1853].

46. AD, HPK 2001 N82R 25, "Les méthodes missionnaires des Oblats dans l'Ouest canadien 1845–75," unpaginated manuscript, cf., J.-E. Champagne, o.m.i., "Les méthodes missionnaires dans l'Ouest canadien 1845–75," *Études Oblates* 5 (1946): pp. 143–60.

47. David Leonard, "Anglican and Oblate: The Quest for Souls in the Peace River Country 1867–1900," in *Western Oblate Studies 3 / Études Oblates de l'Ouest 3*, ed. by R. Huel (Edmonton: Western Canadian Publishers, 1994): p. 127.

48. Dan Kennedy (Ochankugahe), *Recollections of an Assiniboine Chief* (Toronto: McClelland and Stewart, 1972), p. 55.

49. "Lettre du R.P. Bonnald au R.P. Soullier," 29 août 1892, *Missions* 31 (1893): pp. 42–43.

50. Robert Choquette, "Les rapports entre catholiques et protestants dans le Nord-Ouest du Canada avant 1840," in *Western Oblate Studies 1 / Études Oblates de l'Ouest 1*, ed. by R. Huel (Edmonton: Western Canadian

Publishers and Institut de recherche de la Faculté Saint-Jean): pp. 138–40.

51. These comments appear frequently in the letters of Étienne Bonnald who served for many years in northern Manitoba. His annual reports were published in *Missions*.

52. Walter Vanast, MD, "Compassion, Cost and Competition: Factors in the Evolution of Oblate Medical Activities in the Canadian North," in *Western Oblate Studies 2 / Études Oblates de l'Ouest 2*, Centre for the Study of North American Religion Series #1, ed. by R. Huel (Lewiston: Edwin Mellen Press, 1992): p. 188.

53. I. Tourigny, "Le père Joseph Hugonard, o.m.i. Son oeuvre apostolique," Société canadienne d'histoire de l'Église catholique, *Sessions d'Études* 15 (1948): p. 25.

54. Quéré, "Mgr de Mazenod," p. 251.

55. AD, HE 2221 T12Z 34, Clut to Mgr et Révme P [Taché], 15 juillet [1863].

56. AD, HE 2221 T12Z 38, Clut to Mgr [Taché], 15 déc. 1864.

57. Carrière, *DBOC*, I, "Charlebois, Ovide," p. 186; AOM, Personnes: O. Charlebois, Charlebois to Rév. et bien cher Père Maître [des Novices], 25 avril 1891. Ironically during his years at the noviciate and scholasticate Charlebois indicated that while he would like to be sent to a mission he would not want to be left alone.

58. PAA, OMI, DP, A. Gasté 1861–64, Gasté to Mgr et bien cher Père [Taché], 6 avril 1863. For a detailed study of early mission life and furnishings consult Joan MacKinnon, "Oblate House Chapels in the Vicariate of Athabasca-Mackenzie," in *Western Oblate Studies 2 / Études Oblates de l'Ouest 2*, ed. by R. Huel (Lewiston: Edwin Mellen Press, 1992): pp. 219–30.

59. PAA, OMI, Adm., Vicariat MacKenzie: Correspondance 1876–84, Faraud, to Bien Cher Père Lacombe, 10 juillet 1882.

60. PAA, OMI, Adm. Saint Boniface: Correspondance de Mgr Taché 1854–59, Taché to Mon bien cher Père [Végréville], 4 déc. 1858.

61. PAA, OMI, DP, A. Gasté 1861–64, Gasté to Mgr et bien aimé père [Taché], 10 avril 1864.

62. PAA, OMI, DP, A. André 1865–85, André to Rsme et bien aimé père [Supérieur général], 4 jan. 1867.

63. PAA, OMI, Adm., Vicariat Mackenzie: Correspondance 1858–60, Faraud to Mon Cher Père [Végréville], 30 juin 1859.

64. PAA, OMI, PP, L. Doucet: Voyage au lac Vert, oct. 1873.

65. AD, H 5102 G75M 1, Grandin to Maisonneuve, 20 mars 1856.

1. Barbara Benoit, "The Mission at Île-à-la-Crosse," *The Beaver*, Winter (1980): p. 41.
2. Carrière, "Fondation et développement," p. 260, p. 268.
3. Ibid., p. 270.
4. Ibid., p. 273; AD, HE 2221 T12L 25, Taché to Bien chère maman, [5 jan. 1853].
5. Carrière, "Fondation et développement," p. 398; Martha McCarthy, "The Founding of Providence Mission," in *Western Oblate Studies 1 / Études Oblates de l'Ouest 1*, ed. by R. Huel (Edmonton: Western Canadian Publishers and Institut de recherche de la Faculté Saint-Jean, 1990): p. 46.
6. "Rapport de Mgr Faraud 1866–68," *Missions* 9 (1870): p. 24; "Rapport sur le Vicariat d'Athabasca-Mackenzie," ibid., 11 (1873): p. 362; AD, HE 2223 T12Z 3, Husson to Mgr [Grandin], 1 avril 1877.
7. "Les missions catholiques chez les Pieds-Noirs," *Missons* 29 (1891): p. 49; Carrière, "Fondation et développement," p. 264; PAA, OMI, PP, L. Doucet: Journal 1868–90, pp. 76–77.
8. D.W. Moodie, "The St. Albert Settlement: A Study in Historical Geography" (M.A. thesis, University of Alberta, 1965), p. 163.
9. Carrière, "Fondation et développement," p. 266; Taché, *Vingt années*, p. 80.
10. "Les missions catholiques chez les Pieds-Noirs," *Missions* 29 (1891): p. 49.
11. Lestanc to Aubert, 30 juillet 1879, *Missions* 18 (1880): p. 167.
12. Lacombe to Très Rév. Père Supérieur Général, 6 jan. 1866 [sic] (1865), pp. 225–33.
13. AD, L 2003 A33R 1, "Renseignements demandés," Saint-Paul des Cris, 20 oct. 1868, août 1869; Lestanc to Aubert, 30 juillet 1879, *Missions* 18 (1880): p. 168.
14. Ibid., déc. 1870.
15. "Journal de Mgr Grandin (1869)," *Missions* 9 (1870): p. 247.
16. "Rapport sur le Vicariat de Saint-Albert," *Missions* 17 (1879): pp. 449–50; AD, L 2641 A33R 3, Histoire de la mission du lac d'Oignon.
17. PAA, OMI, PP, L. Doucet: Journal 1868–90, p. 25, pp. 76–77.
18. Lacombe to Très Rév. Père Supérieur Général, 12 mai 1870, *Missions* 9 (1870): pp. 257–60.
19. Ibid.
20. McCarthy, *To Evangelize the Nations*, pp. 121–24.

21. "Feu le R.P. Joachim Allard, o.m.i.," *Les Cloches de Saint-Boniface* 16 (1917): p. 52; McCarthy, *To Evangelize the Nations*, pp. 219–28.

22. Levasseur, *Les Oblats de Marie Immaculée*, pp. 193–94.

23. Taché, *Vingt années*, p. 34, p. 40. Louis Dubé was also the first French Canadian Oblate lay brother to serve in the missions of the North-West, see Carrière, *DBOC*, 1, "Dubé, Louis," p. 302.

24. Taché, *Vingt années*, p. 108. Secular clergy attached to the Diocese of Saint Boniface continued to accompany the hunters. *L'abbé* Laflèche was present at the famous battle of Grand Coteau in 1851 when the Métis defeated a larger number of Sioux warriors. This significant event in plains history has been studied by W.L. Morton, "The Battle at the Grand Coteau, July 13 and 14, 1851," *Papers Read Before the Historical and Scientific Society of Manitoba*, Series III, 16 (1961), pp. 37–49.

25. AD, L301 M27R 18, Hivernements à la Montagne de Bois; ibid., L 301 M27R 19, Hivernements de la famille Grant.

26. G. Carrière, o.m.i., "Une mission de paix," pp. 189–224, 299–340; Jean-Guy Quenneville, "Le R.P. Alexis André, o.m.i., et quelques autres plénipotentiaires auprès des Sioux," in *Western Oblate Studies 2 / Études Oblates de l'Ouest 2*, ed. by R. Huel (Lewiston: Edwin Mellen Press, 1992): pp. 51–70; AD, HPK 2001 N82H 1, Résumés des lettres du père L. Genin, 10 avril 1867.

27. PAA, OMI, PP, J.-M. Lestanc: Souvenirs 1860–80, 1870, pp. 15–16.

28. René Rémas, "Mission à la prairie entre Calgary et Edmonton 1860," *Missions* 64 (1930): pp. 522–23.

29. Lestanc to Aubert, 30 juillet 1879, *Missions* 18 (1880): pp. 186–88.

30. J.E. Foster, "*Le missionnaire* and *le chef Métis*," in *Western Oblate Studies 1 / Études Oblates de l'Ouest 1*, ed. by R. Huel (Edmonton: Western Canadian Publishers and Institut de recherche de la Faculté Saint-Jean, 1990): pp. 121–22.

31. AD, LC 7001 K26R 1, A. Gasté, "Relations des travaux de mission et *Codex historicus*," Lac Caribou 1885–87 [hereafter "Relations, Lac Caribou"], 28 juin, 15 juillet, 6 août 1886.

32. "Rapport sur le Vicariat d'Athabasca et Mackenzie," *Missions* 17 (1879): p. 461.

33. AD, LC 6301 K36R 7, Allocation demandée pour la mission de l'Île-à-la-Crosse, juin 1876.

34. AD, HEC 2642 J43C 11, Lestanc to Maisonneuve, 15 mai 1875.

35. PAA, OMI, DP, P. Légéard 1868–79, Légéard to Lacombe, 8 jan. 1876.

36. PAA, OMI, PP, H. Leduc 1866–88, Leduc to Guillet, l'Ascension [9 mai] 1887.

37. PAA, DP, A. Laity 1870–73, Laity to Mon rév. et cher père, 9 juillet 1873. Italics in original; ibid., Laity to Mon rév. et bien cher père, 28 jan. 1872.
38. Grandin, Écrits, 5, Grandin to Benoit, p. 295.
39. C. Champagne, *Les débuts de la mission*, pp. 95–96; see supra, pp. 36–37.
40. *Acte général des visites canoniques faites dans le vicariat de Saint-Albert* (Paris: Typographie privée O.M.I., 1885), p. 29.
41. *Acte de visite du vicariat d'Athabasca 1912, R.P. W.J. Murphy, o.m.i., Visiteur* (Bordeaux: Imprimerie Victor Cambette, 1913), p. 13.
42. É. Bonnald to Directeur des *Annales*, 7 nov. 1900, *Missions* 38 (1900): p. 24.
43. PAA, OMI, Saddle Lake 2, *Codex historicus*, pp. 198–201.
44. PAA, OMI, PP, H. Leduc, 1866–88, Leduc to Végréville, 16 7bre [sic] 1878.
45. PAA, OMI, Adm. St. Boniface, Correspondance de Mgr Taché 1854–59, Taché to Mon bien cher père [Végréville], 21 nov. 1854.
46. For a more detailed study of the function of the Lac La Biche mission consult R. Huel, "La mission Notre-Dame des Victoires du lac la Biche," pp. 17–36.
47. Ibid., p. 35.
48. AD, HE 1821 F26K 6, Faraud to Maisonneuve, 23 avril 1870.
49. AD, HEB 2142 A33L 24, Lacombe to Ritchot, 23 avril 1870.
50. AD, HE 1821 F26K 1, Faraud to Kew, 4 mai 1870.
51. AD, HEC 2142 A33L 42, Lacombe to Maisonneuve, 16 mai 1870.
52. PAA, OMI, St. Albert 7, *Codex historicus*, 8 mai 1877, p. 56, 26 juillet 1877, p. 63; ibid., PP, L. Doucet Journal 1868–90, mai 1877, p. 99.
53. "Rapport sur le Vicariat Athabasca-Mackenzie," *Missions* 31 (1893): p. 383.
54. AD, HE 1861 G87C 31, Grouard to Ma chère Marie, 10 nov. 1903.
55. "Rapport du Vicariat d'Athabasca-Mackenzie," *Missions* 36 (1898): pp. 182–83.
56. PAA, OMI, DP, J. Tissot, 1856–73, Tissot to Mon cher père, 13 juin 1856. Tissot was referring to conditions at Lac La Biche.
57. AD, HE 2221 T12Z 28, Clut to Mgr [Taché], 14 sept. 1862.
58. AD, HE 2221 T12Z 189, Moulin to Mgr et bien aimé père [Taché], 8 mai 1862.
59. PAA, OMI, DP, A. Maisonneuve 1860–64, Maisonneuve to Mgr [Taché], 15 xbre [sic] 1862.
60. PAA, OMI, DP, J.-E. Teston 1878–1929, Teston to Boisramé, 8 mai 1887.
61. AD, HPK 2001 N82H 1, Résumés des lettres au R.P. Supérieur Général par les pères des vicariats de la Rivière Rouge, de Mackenzie et de la Saskatchewan [hereafter Résumés des lettres], V. Grandin, 12 août 1868.

62. AD, HE 2221 T12Z 28, Clut to Mgr [Taché], 14 sept. 1862.

63. AD, HE 2221 T12Z 244, Tissot to Mgr [Taché], 16 avril 1864.

64. AD, LC 6461 K26R 2, Bonnald, *Us et coutumes de la mission Ste. Gertrude, Pelican Narrows* [hereafter *Us et coutumes*]. The amount paid by Bonnald was between ten and fifteen dollars a month.

65. PAA, OMI, Adm., Saint-Boniface Correspondance de Mgr Taché 1861–64, Engagement de George Bourque, 17 juin 1862.

66. Ibid., Engagement de Jos Cyr, 18 juin 1862.

67. PAA, OMI, PP, A. Lacombe 1856–70, Lacombe to Mon rév. et bien cher père, 22 nov. 1869.

68. Émile Jonquet, o.m.i., *Mgr Grandin, o.m.i., premier évêque de Saint-Albert* (Montréal: 20 rue Saint-Vincent, 1903), p. 270.

69. Ibid., pp. 270–71.

70. AD, HPK 2001 N82H 1, Résumé des lettres, Grandin, 12 août 1868.

71. AD, HE 2224 T12R 1, A. Philippot, o.m.i., "Celles qui précédèrent les Oblats dans les Pays d'en Haut," ms., pp. 32–33.

72. PAA, OMI, Lac Sainte Anne 25, Emery to Très honorée mère [Deschamps], 4 déc. 1859.

73. AOM, Athabasca-Mackenzie 1867–80, Faraud to Vénéré père [Guigues], 24 sept. 1867.

74. PAA, OMI, Lac Ste Anne 25, Lamay to Très honorée et bonne mère [Deschamps], 4 déc. 1859.

75. Paul-Émile Breton, o.m.i., "Le Fondateur des Oblats," p. 357.

76. AD, HBK 2001 N82F 1, Fabre to Taché, 11 mars 1864.

77. *Acte général des visites canoniques faites dans le vicariat de Saint-Albert*, pp. 35–36.

78. Ibid., pp. 36–37.

79. AD, HE 2221 T12Z 185, Moulin to Mgr et bien cher père [Taché], 8 avril 1863.

80. PAA, OMI, DP, J.-M.T. Caër 1861–64, Caër to Mon révérendissime seigneur et père, 1 mai 1863.

81. AD, HPK 2001 N82H 1, Résumés des lettres, J. Moulin, 10 jan. 1868; J. Pérréard, 6 juin 1868.

82. AD, HE 2221 T12Z 58, Faraud to Mgr et bien cher ami [Taché], 19 mai 1862.

83. AD, HE 2221 T12Z 60, Faraud to Mgr [Taché], 16 9bre [sept.] 1862.

84. AD, LC 3 M14R 16, Faraud to Taché, 7 juin 1869.

85. AD, H 5102 G75M 1, Grandin to Tissot, [1866].

86. AD, HE 1864 G87L 2, Grouard to MacFarlane, 30 Nov. 1872.

87. AD HE 1864 G87L 19, Grouard to Mon rév. et bien cher père, 1 mai 1879.

88. AD, HE 1864 G87L 23, Grouard to Mon Rév. et bien cher père, 18 août 1879.

89. AD, HE 1821 F26K 36, Faraud to Maisonneuve, 27 juin 1878.

90. AD, HE 1821 F26K 75, Faraud to Maisonneuve, 3 juillet 1887.

91. AD, HE 1821 F26C 13, Deschamps to Faraud, 20 déc. 1883.

92. AD, HEC 2516 L38C 4, Le Goff to Mon rév. et bien cher père, 1 oct, 1880.

93. J.-E. Champagne, *Manuel d'action missionnaire*, pp. 445–47, 460–61.

94. Bx de Mazenod, *Lettres à la Sacrée Congrégation*, Mazenod to Messieurs du Conseil central de l'Oeuvre de la Propagation de la Foi à Lyons, 12 déc. 1845, pp. 187–88; ibid., Mazenod to Messieurs du Conseil central du Midi de l'Oeuvre de la Prop. de la Foi à Lyon, 14 oct. 1847, p. 203.

95. AD, HPK 2001 N82 F 1, Fabre to Taché, 11 mars 1864. Taché's classic *Vingt années de missions dans le nord-ouest de l'Amérique* had been prepared at the request of Superior General Fabre.

96. AD, L2381 A33C 2, Faraud to Mons. le Président [Desglajeux], 11 juin 1865.

97. AD, HE 2221 T12L 91, Taché to Sardou, 14 juillet 1882; ibid., H 5102 G 75L 9, Grandin to Mgr, 9 déc. 1882.

98. National Archives of Canada [hereafter NAC], MG 20 / HBC, D5/25 folio 312–13, Provencher to Simpson, 27 juin 1849.

99. AOM, Personnel H. Leduc, Leduc to Mon très rév. cher père, 21 xbre [sic] 1870.

100. "NB de la rédaction," *Missions* 11 (1873): p. 207.

101. AD, L74 M27E 7, Rapport à la Propagation de la Foi, oct. 1885; ibid., L 74 M27E 8, État des recettes et dépenses, observations 1892.

102. AD, L 74 M27E 1, État de l'Oeuvre c1860.

103. AD, HE 2221 T12L 92, Girardin to Mgr [Taché], 30 mai 1862; ibid., HE 2221 T12l 68, Taché to Mon bien cher monsieur, 7 jan. 1863.

104. AD, HE 2221 T12L 74, Rapport de Mgr Taché à l'Oeuvre de la Sainte Enfance, 1864.

105. AD, L74 M27E 18, Oeuvre de la Sainte Enfance. Rapport pour 1897; "Rapport sur l'école industrielle Saint-Joseph à Dunbow," *Missions* 64 (1910): p. 30.

106. AD, L72 M27P 66, Allocation de la Propagation de la Foi pour Manitoba 1924; ($4,558.18) ibid., L72 M27P 67, Allocation de la Sainte-Enfance ($443.70). The deficit for the Oblate Province of Manitoba for the year 1907 was 78,000 francs, ibid., L 72 M27P 2; for 1908, 81,300 francs, ibid., L 72 M27P 3; for 1921, 150,725 francs, ibid., L 72 M27P 36.

107. Bonnald, Us et coutumes.

108. AD, L 581 M27L 48, É. Bonnald, Notes. Nov. [1921].

109. PAA, OMI, Saddle Lake 2a, *Codex historicus,* 25 déc. 1906, p. 131. The collection netted $9.40 and some individuals provided candles.

110. AD, L 74 M27E 23, Langevin to Mme la Présidente de l'Oeuvre Apostolique de Paris, 4 nov. 1897.

111. Jules Le Chevalier, o.m.i., *Saint-Michel de Duck Lake: Épreuves et progrès d'une école indienne durant un demi-siècle, 1894–1944* (Edmonton: Imprimerie de *La Survivance,* 1944), p. 16.

112. PAA, OMI, PP, A. Lacombe, jan.-juin 1901, Van Horne to Lacombe, 19 may 1901. As early as 1864, Lacombe had been called "*le plus fin quêteur de la contrée,*" AD, HE 2221 T12Z 244, Tissot to Mgr [Taché], 16 avril 1864.

113. Axtell, "Some Thoughts on the Ethnohistory of Missions," p. 40. Italics in original.

5   INITIATION TO CHRISTIANITY

1. Howard L. Harrod, *Mission Among the Blackfeet,* The Civilization of the American Indian Series, vol. 122 (Norman, OK: University of Oklahoma Press, [1971]), p. 52.

2. C. Champagne, *Les débuts de la mission,* p. 138, 156; Pénard to Très Rév. Père Général, 10 avril 1900, *Missions* 38 (1900): pp. 246–47.

3. C. Champagne, *Les débuts de la mission,* p. 138.

4. Axtell, *Conflict of Cultures,* p. 329.

5. PAA, OMI, PP, A. Lacombe: Documents *re* Pieds-Noirs, Lacombe to Editor, Lethbridge *News,* 1 Nov. 1889.

6. Axtell, *Conflict of Cultures,* p. 330.

7. Grant, *Moon of Wintertime,* p. 25.

8. Ibid., p. vii, ch. XI.

9. Axtell, "Some Thoughts on the Ethnohistory of Missions," pp. 36–37.

10. In the Pacific North-West the Oblates also insisted that the First Nations transport them free of charge from one destination to another. Consult Gabriel Dionne, "Histoire des méthodes missionnaires utilisées par les Oblats de Marie Immaculée dans l'évangélisation des Indiens du «versant pacifique», au dix-neuvième siècle" (M.A. thesis, University of Ottawa, 1947), pp. 80–81, p. 79; Rapet to Très Rév. Père Général, 19 jan. 1900, *Missions* 38 (1900): p. 271.

11. C. Champagne, *Les débuts de la mission,* p. 109.

12. PAA, OMI, PP, L. Doucet: Journal 1868–70, 1872, Île-à-la-Crosse, p. 41.

13. Lacombe to Très Rév. Père Sup. Gén., 6 jan. 1865 [sic], *Missions* 7 (1868): pp. 230–31.

14. "Journal de Mgr Grandin, (1869)," *Missions* 9 (1870): p. 247.

15. Légéard to Mon rév. et bien-aimé père, 17 jan. 1875, *Missions* 13 (1875): p. 488.

16. Charlebois to Très Rév. Père Général, [1900], *Missions* 38 (1900): p. 31.

17. Légéard to Rév. père Martinet, n.d., *Missions* 15 (1877): p. 315.

18. Ibid.

19. "René Rémas: mission à Saint Bernard 1866," *Missions* 64 (1930): p. 517.

20. PAA, OMI, V. Végréville: Notes 1867. Végréville's claims concerning the number of converts he had made were dismissed by Bishop Taché, ibid., Adm., Saint-Boniface Correspondance de Mgr Taché 1860–69, Taché to Végréville, 30 nov. 1866.

21. PAA, OMI, PP, V. Végréville, 1866–96, Végréville to Très Rév. Père Sup. Gén., 16 mars 1866.

22. Ibid., some years later when Végréville was sent to Winterburn (Alberta), he attributed the population's lack of religious fervour to the fact that previous missionaries had an imperfect knowledge of the language. He also claimed that he had been sent three times to Lac Ste. Anne (Alberta) to revivify the population's spirituality and morality and, as a result, the mission *"promet maintenant beaucoup."* PAA, OMI, Winterburn 4, *Codex historicus*, 13 oct. 1899, p. 11.

23. AD, H 5102 G75Z 1, G. Chapellière, lac Poule d'Eau, 6 jan. 1879, p. 520, p. 534.

24. Ibid., p. 534.

25. AD LC 6461 K26R 2, É. Bonnald, Us et coutumes.

26. Bonnald au Directeur des *Annales*, 1 nov. 1898, *Missions* 37 (1899): p. 162.

27. Decorby to Martinet, 12 avril 1893, *Missions* 31 (1893): p. 178.

28. AD, LC 6461 K26R 2, Bonnald, Us et coutumes.

29. PAA, OMI, DP, F. Hert, Hert to RRPP Le Jeune et Chirouse, 18 déc. 1879.

30. PAA, OMI, DP, J. Moulin 1862–94, Moulin to Supérieur Général, 22 juillet 1862.

31. C. Champagne, *Les débuts de la mission*, p. 151.

32. "Journal de Mgr Grandin, 1881," *Missions* 20 (1882): p. 317.

33. AD, HEC 2642 J43C 16, Lestanc to Rév. et bien cher Père Camper, 9 nov. 1882.

34. AOM, Personnes: L. Van Tighem, Van Tighem to Boisramé, 6 juin 1879.

35. AD, HE 1821 F26C 5, Faraud to Rév. Père F. Durocher, 16 9bre [sept.] 1869.

36. PAA, OMI, Cardston 37, Lacombe to the Editor, Macleod *Gazette*, n.d.

37. Grant, *Moon of Wintertime*, ch. 11, "A Yes That Means No?" p. 250.

38. C. Champagne, *Les débuts de la mission*, p. 133; Dionne, "Histoire des méthodes missionnaires," p. 55.

39. Dionne, "Histoire des méthodes missionnaires," p. 57; C. Champagne, *Les débuts de la mission*, pp. 109–10, p. 133.

40. AD, OMI, HE 2221 T12L 34, Taché to Ma bonne mère, 2 mai 1855.

41. Dionne, "Histoire des méthodes missionnaires," p. 54, p. 56.

42. C. Champagne, *Les débuts de la mission*, pp. 132–33.

43. Ibid., p. 149.

44. Carrière, "Fondation et développement," p. 400, p. 403.

45. PAA, OMI, Adm., Vicariat Mackenzie: Correspondance à Mgr Taché, Clut to Taché, 30 juin 1860.

46. PAA, OMI, DP, É. Bonnald 1876–1885, Bonnald to Guillet, 2 juillet 1883.

47. Ibid., Bonnald to Mgr et bien aimé père, 27 août 1885.

48. Bonnald to R.P. Soullier, 10 nov. 1891, *Missions* 30 (1892): p. 197. Pope Pius IX had approved of this practice.

49. PAA, OMI, DP, L. Doucet 1872–1942, Doucet to Mon Rév. et bien cher père [Lacombe], 13 fév. 1883.

50. C. Champagne, *Les débuts de la mission*, pp. 141–42.

51. Ibid., p. 145. In seventeenth century France the Jansenists were a group of austere Catholics who emphasized the teachings of St. Augustine on the depravity of man and the need for divine grace.

52. Ibid., p. 148.

53. Ibid., p. 150.

54. Ibid., p. 149.

55. Ibid., p. 143.

56. Grandin, Écrits, 5, "À Dom Benoît," p. 297.

57. Ibid.

58. *Acte général des visites canoniques, faites dans le vicariat de Saint-Albert*, pp. 27–28.

59. C. Champagne, *Les débuts de la mission*, p. 147.

60. Ibid., p. 148.

61. Ibid., p. 122.

62. AD, HE 2223 T12Z 3, Grandin to Taché and Lacombe, 6 fév. 1876.

63. C. Champagne, *Les débuts de la mission*, p. 122, p. 133, p. 150. The Oblates used the term *"vivre dans le désordre"* to denote marriages that had not been regularized by the Church.

64. A. Turquetil, o.m.i., "Le mariage chez les Esquimaux en regard des facultés de dispense accordées aux missionnaires," *Revue de l'Université d'Ottawa* 5 (1935): pp. 125–26.

65. Ibid.

66. Ibid.

67. C. Champagne, *Les débuts de la mission*, p. 122.

68. Ibid.

69. Ibid., p. 123.

70. Fernand-Michel, *Dix-huit ans*, pp. 122–23.

71. Leduc to Rév. Père Martinet, 29 déc. 1872, *Missions* 10 (1872): p. 516. According to Leduc, no one contested the clergy's right to use force to separate couples living in sin.

72. Grandin to Très Rév. Père Supérieur Général, 15 août 1870, *Missions* 9 (1870): pp 188–89.

73. AD, HE 2223 T12Z 3, Grandin to Mgr et bien cher père [Taché], 5 jan. 1866.

74. AD, HE 2221 T12Z 22, Clut to Monseigneur [Taché], 10 mars 1861.

75. PAA, OMI, Adm., Vicariat Mackenzie: Correspondance 1861–63, Clut to Mon Rév. et Bien Cher Père [Végréville], 17 juin 1862.

76. PAA, OMI, L.-J. Doucet, Catéchisme cris, pp. 95–96, p. 101, p. 104.

77. Ibid., 6e commandement, pp. 62–66.

78. Ibid., supplément au 6e commandement, pp. 105–118.

79. PAA, OMI, DP, P.-E. Lecoq 1883, 1924, Le Coq to Guillet, 21 août 1883.

80. PAA, OMI, Winterburn 4, *Codex historicus*, 13 nov. 1899, p. 15.

81. PAA, OMI, Adm., Cluny IRS: Correspondance, 1908, 1911–12, Legal to Rév. père Le Vern, 23 déc. 1901.

82. PAA, OMI, Adm., Cluny IRS: Correspondance, 1902–03, Markle to Riou, 11 Aug. 1903.

83. PAA, OMI, Adm., Cluny IRS: Correspondance, 1908, 1911–12, Legal to Riou, 14 fév. 1914.

84. AOM, Alberta-Saskatchewan, Grandin to Hon. E. Dewdney, 5 April 1892.

85. Ibid.

86. PAA, OMI, PP, L. Doucet 1872–1942, Doucet to Mon rév. et bien cher père [Lacombe], 13 fév. 1883.

87. Bonnald to Augier, 6 nov. 1895, *Missions* 34 (1896): pp. 7–8.

88. Hanley, "The Catholic Ladder," p. 3, p. 5, p. 235.

89. Ibid., pp. 223–26.

90. C. Champagne, *Les débuts de la mission*, pp. 113–16. An 1896 version of Lacombe's ladder was published in English and French. A detailed explanation of Lacombe's ladder is found in Philip M. Hanley, "Father Lacombe's Ladder," *Études Oblates* 32 (1973): pp. 82–99.

91. Ibid. The value of the Catholic ladder as a pedagogical instrument is confirmed by the appearance of Protestant versions. Consult Hanley, "The Catholic Ladder," pp. 170–72, p. 206, p. 219. There is a similarity between Lacombe's Catholic ladder and the climbing pole by which the

shaman ascends into heaven and returns to earth. Whether or not Lacombe was aware of this is uncertain but this parallel may have contributed to the success of the ladder as a teaching aid. The use of the climbing pole is described in Mircea Eliade, *Shamanism Archaic Techniques of Ecstasy.* Translated from the French by William R. Trask (NY: Bollingen Foundation, 1964).

92. Albert Lacombe, o.m.i., *Le catéchisme en images pour l'instruction des sauvages* (Montréal: Imprimerie de l'Asile de la Providence, 1874), préface.

93. C. Champagne, *Les débuts de la mission*, p. 116. In using European art forms and models the western Oblates were following a tradition initiated by the Jesuits in seventeenth century New France. Consult François-Marc Gagnon, *La conversion par l'image: Un aspect de la mission des Jésuites auprès des Indiens du Canada au XVII siècle* (Montréal: Éditions Bellarmin, 1975).

94. Cornelius Jaenen, "Missionary Approaches to Native Peoples," in *Approaches to Native History*, ed. by D.A. Muise (Ottawa: National Museums of Man, Mercury Series, History Division Paper No. 25, 1977), pp. 5–6.

6   EDUCATION: AN EXTENSION AND ENHANCEMENT OF MISSION

1. C. Champagne, *Les débuts de la mission*, p. 137.

2. G. Carrière, o.m.i., "La réponse des Oblats de l'Ouest canadien à la perception de la «mission» chez Mgr de Mazenod," *Vie Oblate Life* 42 (1983): p. 210.

3. "Rapport sur le vicariat de Saint-Albert," *Missions* 31 (1893): p. 358.

4. AD, H 5101 G75C 25, Grandin Aux RRds PP Oblats de M. I., Supérieurs et autres chargés du Séminaire de Saint-Albert et à nos jeunes séminaristes, 5 mars 1900.

5. PAA, OMI, DP, R. Rémas 1861–64, Rémas to Mgr et bien aimé père, 3 mai 1861.

6. AD, HE 2221 T12Z 228, Simonet to Mgr [Taché], [1 nov] 1863.

7. "Extrait d'une lettre du père Fourmond, 14 déc. 1881," *Missions* 20 (1882): p. 323.

8. PAA, OMI, Fort Macleod 6, *Codex historicus* 1883, p. 36.

9. PAA, OMI, PP, C. Guillet: Journal 1868–69, 20 juin 1870, p. 20.

10. Ibid., 27 juin 1870, p. 21.

11. AOM, Personnes: O. Charlebois, Charlebois to Rév. et Bien cher père maître [des novices], 25 avril 1891.

12. AD, HE 2221 T12Z 253, Végréville to Mgr et rév. père [Taché], 12 juin 1861.

13. AD, HEC 2500 P96C 4, Légéard to Maisonneuve, 9 avril 1871.
14. "Le Lac La Biche," *Missions* 14 (1876): p. 428.
15. Légéard to Martinet, 10 nov. 1873, *Missions* 12 (1874): p. 532.
16. Légéard to Martinet, 7 juin 1872, *Missions* 12 (1874): pp. 50–51.
17. PAA, OMI, DP, R. Rémas 1861–64, Rémas to Mgr et bien aimé père, 3 mai 1861.
18. PAA, OMI, PP, L. Doucet: Journal 1868–90, Nov. 1883, p. 169.
19. AD, HE 2221 T12Z 253, Végréville to Mgr et rév. père, 12 juin 1861.
20. PAA, OMI, PP, C. Scollen 1862–72, Scollen to [?], (extract), 3 jan. 1866. This difference of opinion concerning the value of French or English can be explained by the fact that Végréville originated from France whereas Scollen had been born in Ireland. Bernice Venini (Venini Byrne) states that in 1860 Taché and Grandin decided that lay brothers would be needed for the western missions and that these individuals should be English-speaking because the missions were near HBC posts: "Father Constantine Scollen, Founder of the Calgary Mission," Canadian Catholic Historical Association, *Study Sessions* 9 (1942): p. 76.
21. McCarthy, *To Evangelize the Nations*, pp. 29–30. The schools outside Manitoba's 1870 territorial limits were located at Reindeer Lake, Fort Alexander and Duck Bay.
22. C. Champagne, *Les débuts de la mission*, p. 190.
23. Grandin, "Les missions sauvages du Nord-Ouest," *Missions* 21 (1883): p. 129.
24. C. Champagne, *Les débuts de la mission*, pp. 173–74, p. 190.
25. Ibid., pp. 188–90.
26. "Rapport sur le vicariat du diocèse de Saint-Albert," *Missions* 11 (1873): p. 350.
27. C. Champagne, *Les débuts de la mission*, p. 175.
28. Department of Indian Affairs, *Report*, 1882, p. xi, cited in Morris Zaslow, *The Opening of the Canadian North, 1870–1914*, The Canadian Centenary Series, vol. 16 (Toronto: McClelland and Stewart, 1971), p. 19.
29. Ibid.
30. *Acte général de visites canoniques faites dans le vicariat de Saint-Albert*, pp. 64–65.
31. C. Champagne, *Les débuts de la mission*, p. 189.
32. Grandin to McLeod [sic], 3 jan. 1876, cited in C. Champagne, *Les débuts de la mission*, p. 186.
33. NAC, RG 10, Vol. 3708, f. 19502, Pt. 1, [Grandin] to Langevin, [ca. sept. 1879], cf, ibid., Grandin to Schultz, 13 jan 1880.

34. Ibid. See also Grandin to Laird, 2 avril 1880, cited in C. Champagne, *Les débuts de la mission*, p. 187.

35. NAC, RG 10, Vol. 3708, f. 19502, Pt. 1, [Grandin] to Langevin [ca. Sept. 1879].

36. Ibid., Grandin to Macdonald, 27 sept. 1880. A variant of this proposal is to be found in ibid., [Grandin] to Langevin [ca. sept. 1879].

37. Ibid., [Grandin] to Langevin, [ca. sept. 1879]; ibid., Grandin to Macdonald, 27 sept. 1880.

38. Ibid., Grandin to Macdonald, 27 sept. 1880.

39. Ibid.

40. NAC, RG 10, Vol. 3788, f. 43943, Grandin, Petition to Rt. Hon. Sir John A. Macdonald [1883].

41. NAC, RG 10, Vol. 3673, f. 11422, Pétition de l'Archevêque et des Évêques du Québec, fév. 1883.

42. NAC, RG 10, Vol. 3649, f. 8185, Faraud to Meredith, 12 March 1877.

43. Ibid., Vankoughnet: Memo to Superintendent General of Indian Affairs, 6 June 1877.

44. NAC, RG 10, Vol. 3649, f. 8185, Meredith to Rt. Rev. Sir, 11 June 1877.

45. Ibid., Faraud to Marquis of Lorne, 10 oct. 1880.

46. Ibid., Charlebois to Macdonald, [Feb. 1882].

47. Ibid., Draft reply to Sister Charlebois, 6 Nov. 1882, marginal note, 7 Nov. 1882.

48. NAC, RG 10, Vol. 3578, f. 508, Vankoughnet: Memo for J.A. Macdonald, 20 Feb. 1885.

49. Ibid.

50. AOM, Personnes: A. Lacombe, Lacombe to Mon bien cher père et ami, 20 oct. 1871.

51. AD, HE 2223 T12Z 3, Grandin to Mgr et bien cher père [Taché], 2 mai 1872.

52. Ibid.

53. AD, H 5102 G75 M 1, Grandin to Mon rév. et bien cher père [Maisonneuve], 12 nov. 1878.

54. AD, H 5102 G75L 16, Grandin to Laflèche, 18 juillet 1887; see also HE 2223 T12Z 3, Grandin to Taché, 28 juin 1887.

55. AD, H 5102 G75L 16, Grandin to Laflèche, 18 juillet 1887; ibid., HE 2223 T12Z 3, Grandin to Taché, 28 juin 1887.

56. AD, H 5102 G75L 60, Grandin to RRimes Archevêque et Évêques de la Province d'Ontario, 26 avril 1901.

57. Grandin, *Écrits*, 8, Grandin to Bourget, 25 avril 1876, p. 183.

58. Ibid., 15, Grandin to Lacombe, 28 juillet 1875, p. 345.

59. Ibid.

60. AD, H 5102 G75L 68, Grandin to Mons. le Président, l'Oeuvre de la Propagation de la Foi, 7 juin 1878.

61. Ibid.

62. AD, H 5102 G75L 68, Grandin, "Oeuvre des écoles du Nord-Ouest," [1878].

63. NAC, Macdonald Papers, 35424, Grandin to Madame, 17 jan. 1878.

64. AD, HE 5102 G75L, Grandin, "Oeuvre des écoles du Nord-Ouest," [1878].

65. AD, H 5102 G75L 69, Mainet to Mons. le Président [Oeuvre de la Propagation de la Foi], 28 juin 1878.

66. AD, HE 2223 T12Z 3, Grandin to Mgr de Québec and Mgr de Toronto, 12 avril 1879.

67. Ibid., Grandin to Mgr et bien cher père [Taché], 30 jan. 1883.

68. Lettre pastorale des Évêques de la Province Ecclésisastique de Québec, 3 avril 1883, *Missions* 21 (1883): pp. 206–7.

69. NAC, RG 10, Vol. 3622, f. 4593, Mills: Memorandum, 7 Dec. 1876.

70. Ibid., Laird to My Lord [Grandin], 31 July 1875.

71. Ibid., Grandin to Meredith, 7 jan. 1876.

72. Ibid., Mills: Memorandum, 7 Dec. 1876; ibid., Vol. 3643, F. 7780 Pt. 2, [?] to Grandin, 21 juin 1877.

73. Grandin to Laird, 2 avril 1880, cited in C. Champagne, *Les débuts de la mission*, p. 187.

74. Ibid., p. 188.

75. Grandin, Écrits, 16, Grandin to Lestanc, 3 avril 1880, pp. 381–82.

76. Ibid., 8, Grandin to Bourget, 25 avril 1876, p. 183.

77. NAC, Macdonald Papers, 35422, Grandin to Madame, 17 jan. 1878.

78. Grandin, Écrits, 1, Visite au pénitencier de Citeaux, France, 12 avril 1878, p. 132.

79. Grandin, "Les missions sauvages du Nord-Ouest," *Missions* 21 (1883): p. 129.

80. NAC, Macdonald Papers, 35423, Grandin to Madame, 17 jan. 1878.

81. Brian Titley, *A Narrow Vision: Duncan Campbell Scott and the Administration of Indian Affairs in Canada* (Vancouver: UBC Press, 1986), p. 18.

7   INDIAN INDUSTRIAL SCHOOLS: A PROMISING OBLATE VENTURE

1. Nowakowski, "Indian Residential Schools," p. 24.

2. NAC, Macdonald Papers, 61386–389, Vankoughnet: Memo, 14 March 1885. Statistics in this memo indicate that there were 10 Anglican, 10

Roman Catholic, 2 Presbyterian and 8 Methodist day schools on reserves in Treaty 1, 3, 4, 5, 6, and 7 in 1885.

3. Nowakoski, "Indian Residential Schools," pp. 19–23; NAC, RG 10, Vol. 3577 File 468, Copy of a Report of a Committee of the Hon. Privy Council approved by His Excellency the Governor-General in Council on 11 April 1882.

4. NAC, RG 10, Vol. 3673, File 11422, N.F. Davin: Report on Industrial Schools for Indians and Half-Breeds, 14 March 1879, (Confidential), p. 1.

5. Cited in Marion Joan Boswell, "Civilizing the Indian: Government Administration of Indians" (Ph.D. thesis, University of Ottawa, 1977).

6. Nowakowski, "Indian Residential Schools," p. 38.

7. "Missions du Natal," *Missions* 3 (1864): p. 12; "Lettre de Mgr D'Herbomez au T.R.P. Supérieur général, 28 nov. 1868," ibid., 9 (1870): p. 90.

8. Nowakowski, "Indian Residential Schools," p. 34.

9. NAC, Macdonald Papers, 188068, Grandin to Macdonald, 22 May 1883.

10. NAC, RG 10, Vol. 3788, File 43943, Grandin to Macdonald, n.d.

11. AD, HE 2223 T12Z 3, Grandin to Mgr et bien cher père [Taché], 2[7?] sept. 1883.

12. NAC, RG 10, Vol. 3788, File 43943, Grandin to Langevin, 15 Sept. 1883.

13. Ibid., Grandin to Langevin, 27 Sept. 1883, (Private), [translation].

14. See infra, chapter 9.

15. NAC, RG 10, Vol. 3788, File 43943, Grandin to Langevin, 27 Sept. 1883, (Private), [translation].

16. *Acte général de visites canoniques faites dans le vicariat de Saint-Albert*, p. 63.

17. AD, L 2221 A33R 3, Leduc to l'Hermite, 31 déc. 1887.

18. NAC, Macdonald Papers, 192606, Taché to Macdonald, 30 Jan. 1884; 193101, Taché to Macdonald, 22 Feb. 1884.

19. Ibid., 198230, Lacombe to Macdonald, 6 Jan. 1885.

20. PAA, OMI, Dunbow 24, Record of St. Joseph's Industrial School, 5, 20 Nov. 1884, 27 Dec. 1884. L'Heureux was an enigmatic and controversial character who was associated with some of the leading figures in western Canadian history such as Lacombe, Crowfoot and Louis Riel. Consult R. Huel, "Jean L'Heureux canadien errant et prétendu missionnaire auprès des Pieds-noirs," in *Après Dix Ans . . . Bilan et Prospective*, Les actes du onzième colloque du Centre d'études franco-canadiennes de l'Ouest, ed. by Gratien Allaire et al. (Edmonton: Institut de recherche de la Faculté Saint-Jean, 1992), pp. 207–22.

21. PAA, OMI, Dunbow 24, Record of St. Joseph's Industrial School, 15, 16 Nov. 1884, 1 Dec. 1884.

22. Ibid., 8 March 1885.
23. PAA, OMI, Cardston 16, *Codex historicus*, Mission Saint-François-Xavier, pp. 9–10.
24. PAA, OMI, Dunbow 1, Lacombe to Hon. Indian Commissioner [Dewdney], 24 March 1885.
25. PAA, OMI, PP, A. Lacombe 1885–89, Dewdney to Lacombe, 17 Dec. 1889.
26. PAA, OMI, Dunbow 24, Record of St. Joseph's Industrial School, 31 Dec. 1884, 14 Jan. 1885.
27. "Rapport sur l'École industrielle Saint-Joseph à Dunbow," *Missions* 48 (1910): p. 27.
28. PAA, OMI, Dunbow 1, Lacombe to Hon. Indian Commissioner Dewdney, 12 June 1885.
29. PAA, OMI, Dunbow 2, Reed to Lacombe, 10 Nov. 1885.
30. PAA, OMI, DP, L. Doucet 1872–1942, Doucet to l'Hermite, 13 nov. 1885; "Rapport sur l'École industrielle Saint-Joseph à Dunbow," *Missions* 48 (1910): p. 29.
31. PAA, OMI, DP, L. Doucet 1872–1942, Doucet to L'Hermite, 28 avril 1886.
32. PAA, OMI, PP, H. Leduc 1866–88, Leduc to Lestanc, 18 juin 1886; The government had sent Joseph Hugonnard of the Qu'Appelle Industrial School to inspect Dunbow and he admitted that the books were poorly kept and that the institution was poorly administered; ibid., Leduc to Lestanc, 9 juin 1886.
33. Ibid., pp. 30–31.
34. NAC, Hayter Reed Papers, MG 29 E 106, Vol. 18, Personnel H-L, Tims to Indian Commissioner, 4 Oct. 1891 (I am grateful to Brian Titley for this reference); PAA, OMI, PP, L. Doucet: Journal 1891–1920, 18 nov. 1891, pp. 16–17. The allegation of homosexuality also had been made by the Jesuits in Montana in the 1850s–60s, consult Huel, "Jean L'Heureux canadien errant," p. 208.
35. PAA, OMI, Pincer Creek 7, *Codex historicus*, mission Saint François-Xavier, 17 nov. 1903.
36. PAA, OMI, Brocket 6a, *Codex historicus*, mission Saint-Paul des Piéganes, p. 21.
37. PAA, OMI, *Codex historicus*, mission Saint-François-Xavier, 17 nov. 1903.
38. "Rapport du R.P. Lépine au Très Rév. Père Supérieur Général," n.d., p. 177.
39. "Rapport sur le vicariat de Saint-Albert," *Mission* 31 (1893): p. 362. By the same token the Oblates admitted that "salaried foreigners" would have to be replaced by Oblate administrators, lay brothers would have to assume responsibility for workshops and Grey Nuns would instruct the girls. This

would result in a true religious community as well as guarantee adequate resources.

40. B. Titley, "Dunbow Indian Industrial School: An Oblate Experiment in Education," in *Western Oblate Studies 2 / Études Oblates de l'Ouest 2*, ed. by R. Huel (Lewiston: Edwin Mellen Press, 1992): p. 100–101.

41. PAA, OMI, Adm., Cluny IRS, Correspondance 1901, Laird to Principal, Roman Catholic Crowfoot Boarding School, 18 June 1901.

42. PAA, OMI, Dunbow 18, Grandin to Scott, 13 June 1917.

43. Ibid., MacLean to Grandin, 13 Aug. 1917.

44. Titley, "Dunbow Indian Industrial School," pp. 105–6.

45. PAA, OMI, Adm., Calgary Dunbow 1913–19, Scott to McNally, 9 Jan. 1919.

46. PAA, OMI, Dunbow 19, Scott to Right Rev. Sir [McNally], 27 Feb. 1919.

47. Ibid., McNally to Dotenwill, 6 July 1919.

48. Ibid., [Grandin] to Demers, 16 sept. 1919.

49. AA, OMI, Dunbow 20, [Grandin] to McNally, 7 avril 1920.

50. PAA, OMI, Dunbow 21, Guy to Scott, 7 June 1921.

51. Ibid., [Grandin] to Guy, 28 avril 1922.

52. Ibid., Guy to Scott, 16 May 1922.

53. Ibid., Guy to Grandin, 29 mai 1922; ibid., McLean to Grandin, 12 Oct. 1922.

54. AD, 281 M27R 69, Hugonnard to Mgr. [Taché], 17 fév. 1887; Nowakowski, "Indian Residential Schools," p. 82.

55. AD, L 281 M27R 2, Langevin, l'École industrielle de Qu'Appelle, [1894].

56. NAC, RG 10, Vol. 3723, File 27098, Hugonnard to Dewdney, 16 Feb. 1886.

57. AD, HEB 7896 J83C 18, Hugonnard Rapport (ms.), 22 fév. 1908.

58. Nowakowski, "Indian Residential Schools," p. 83.

59. J.R. Miller, "Indian-White Relations in Canada: The Case of Residential Schooling," paper presented at the Association for Canadian Studies in Australia and New Zealand, Griffith University, Nathan, Qld., May 14–16, 1986, p. 15.

60. AD, L 281 M27R 69, Hugonnard to Mgr [Taché], 17 fév. 1887; Nowakowski, "Indian Residential Schools," p. 84.

61. AD, L 281 M27R 69, Hugonnard to Mgr [Taché], 17 fév. 1887.

62. Nowakowski, "Indian Residential Schools," p. 82.

63. Tourigny, "Le père Joseph Hugonard [sic]," pp. 34–35; Magnan to Soullier, 10 fév. 1893, *Missions* 31 (1893): p. 77.

64. AD, L 281 M27R 69, Hugonnard to [Taché], 17 fév. 1887. According to Hugonnard, once the gathering had disbanded three persons individually approached him and provided him with one child each.

65. Tourigny, "Le père Joseph Hugonard [sic]," p. 33; Nowakowski, "Indian Residential Schools," p. 102.

66. AD, L 281 M27R 69, Hugonnard to Mgr [Taché], 17 fév. 1887.
67. Dom Benôit, c.r.i.c. [Joseph-Paul Augustin], *Vie de Mgr Taché, Archevêque de Saint Boniface*, vol. 2, (Montréal: Librairie Beauchemin, 1904), p. 708.
68. L.-P.-A. Langevin, "Rapport du Vicariat de Saint-Boniface," *Missions* 36 (1898): p. 272.
69. AD, L 1341 M27R 6, Reid to Comeau, 28 April 1896; ibid., L 1341 M27R 7, Comeau to Langevin, 28 avril 1896.
70. AD, L 1341 M27R 4, McLean to Indian Commissioner, 5 Feb. 1902.
71. AD, L 1341 M27R, 11, Dorais to Rév. Père Vicaire, 11 mars 1903.
72. AD, L 1341 M27R 15, Langevin to Sifton, 12 March 1903.
73. P. Magnan, "Rapport 1905," *Missions* 42 (1904): p. 134. The St. Boniface Industrial School became the Juniorat de la Sainte-Famille.
74. Nowakowski, "Indian Residential Schools," p. 85. School attendance became compulsory in 1908.
75. Miller, "Indian-White Relations in Canada," p. 9.
76. Nowaskowski, "Indian Residential Schools," p. 79.
77. Jacqueline Gresko, "Creating Little Dominions Within the Dominion: Early Catholic Schools in Saskatchewan and British Columbia," in *Indian Education in Canada*, vol. 1, *The Legacy*, ed. by Jean Barman et al (Vancouver: University of British Columbia Press, 1986), p. 93.
78. "Rapport du vicariat de Saint-Boniface," *Missions* 36 (1898): p. 287.
79. Nowakowski, "Indian Residential Schools," p. 80.
80. Jacqueline Gresko, "White 'Rites' and Indian 'Rites': Indian Education and Native Responses in the West, 1870–1919," in *Western Canada Past and Present*, ed. by A.W. Rasporich (Calgary: McClelland and Stewart West, 1975), p. 170.
81. Nowakowski, "Indian Residential Education," pp. 59–60, 68–69. The initial curriculum in industrial school was divided into six standards or grades with the higher standards being more difficult. The acquisition of English language skills was stressed by the Department of Indian Affairs. The subjects of study included English, General Knowledge, Writing, Arithmetic, Geography, Ethics, Reading, Recitation, History, Vocal Music, Calisthenics and Religious Instruction, ibid., pp. 60–61.
82. Gresko, "Creating Little Dominions," p. 93.
83. As a Catholic born in France, however, Hugonnard was aware of the association of the French as a covenant people popularized by the idiom *Gestae Dei Per Francos* (the deeds of God through the actions of the French). In Canada, the most eloquent thesis describing the unity of the French language and Catholicism was Henri Bourassa's *La langue gardienne de la foi*.

84. V. McNally, "A Lost Opportunity? A Study of Relations Between the Native People and the Diocese of Victoria," in *Western Oblate Studies 2 / Études Oblates de l'Ouest 2*, ed. by R. Huel (Lewiston: Edwin Mellen Press, 1992): p. 175.

85. Gresko, "Creating Little Dominions," p. 93. This was in keeping with the French meaning of the term "parent."

86. Ibid., p. 92.

87. AD, L 281 M27R2, "École industrielle de Qu'Appelle," [1894].

88. Nowakowski, "Indian Residential Schools," p. 76.

89. Tourigny, "Le père Joseph Hugonard [sic]," p. 37.

90. Nowakowski, "Indian Residential Schools," p. 90.

91. The description is from Titley, *A Narrow Vision*, p. 18; Elizabeth Brass, "The File Hills Ex-Pupil Colony," *Saskatchewan History* 6 (1953): pp. 67–68. Sarah Carter argues that the government used the File Hills Colony to demonstrate to the public that graduates of Indian schools could become cultural replicas of Euro-Canadians; "Demonstrating Success: The File Hills Farm Colony," *Prairie Forum* 16 (1991): p. 157.

92. Gresko, "White 'Rites' and Indian 'Rites,'" p. 164.

93. R.F. Berkhofer, Jr., *Salvation and the Savage: An Analysis of Protestant Missions and American Indian Responses, 1787–1862* (Lexington: University of Kentucky Press, 1965), pp. 16–17. This study identifies the similarity of Catholic and Protestant views and goals in Canada and the United States.

94. James T.M. Anderson, *The Education of the New Canadian: A Treatise on Canada's Greatest Educational Problem* (Toronto: J.M. Dent & Sons, 1918), p. 114.

95. Axtell, "Some Thoughts on the Ethnohistory of Missions," p. 40.

96. Norma Sluman, *John Tootoosis as told by Jean Goodwill and Norma Sluman* (Winnipeg: Pemmican Publications, 1984), p. 94.

97. Miller, "Indian-White Relations in Canada," p. 6.

98. Gresko, "White 'Rites' and Indian 'Rites,'" pp. 174–75.

99. Kennedy, *Recollections of an Assiniboine Chief*, pp. 54–55.

8   INDIAN RESIDENTIAL SCHOOLS:
    A FRUSTRATING OBLATE EXPERIENCE

1. AD, L III M27C 11, Raison d'être et utilité de l'école-pensionnat, p. 9; ibid., L 72 M27P 104, Exposé, province du Manitoba, 1931; "Rapport du R.P. Provincial du Manitoba," *Missions* 54 (1920): p. 279.

2. Sarah Carter, *Lost Harvests: Prairie Indian Reserve Farmers and Government*

Policy (Montreal & Kingston: McGill-Queens University Press, 1990), p. 18.

3. Ibid., pp. 16–18.

4. Brian Titley, "Hayter Reed and Indian Administration in the West," in *Swords and Ploughshares: War and Agriculture in Western Canada*, ed. by R.C. Macleod (Edmonton: University of Alberta Press, 1993), p. 139.

5. Titley, *A Narrow Vision*, cited on inside front cover.

6. Brian Titley, "Dunbow Indian Industrial School," p. 102.

7. Nowakowski, "Indian Residential Schools," pp. 40–41.

8. J.R. Miller, "The Irony of Residential Education," *Canadian Journal of Native Education* 14 (1987): pp. 5–9.

9. Miller, "Indian-White Relations in Canada," pp. 17–19.

10. Nowakowski, "Indian Residential Schools," p. 83.

11. Miller, "Indian-White Relations," p. 22.

12. Gaston Carrière, o.m.i., "Le martyr du devoir Mgr Ovide Charlebois, o.m.i., 1862–1933," vol. 1, "Le missionnaire," ms., p. 454.

13. Ibid., pp. 448–49; Nowakowski, "Indian Residential Schools," p. 80.

14. Carrière, "Le martyr du devoir," p. 455.

15. PAA, OMI, Saddle Lake 2, *Codex historicus*, 6 août 1903, pp. 125–26.

16. PAA, OMI, Winterburn 4, *Codex historicus*, 16 juin 1899, p. 6.

17. AD, HEB 7896 J83C 17, M. Kalmès, Quelques notes sur les dernières années de la vie du R.P. Hugonnard, 19 mars 1922, pp. 3–4.

18. PAA, OMI, Onion Lake 1, Contrat de Alexis Olaksy, 27 oct. 1893.

19. AD, LC 6484 K26R 31, Thomas to Mon rév. et bien cher père, 4 jan. 1910.

20. AD, HE 6484 K26R 35, Lecoq to Mon rév. et bien cher père, 28 mai 1910.

21. Titley, *A Narrow Vision*, pp. 90–91.

22. Nowakowski, "Indian Residential Schools," p. 82.

23. AD, L 285 M27L 40, Léonard to R.P. provincial [Beys], 20 nov. 1919.

24. PAA, OMI, Delmas IRS, Correspondance 1935, Allard to Rév. et bien cher père provincial, 21 fév. 1935.

25. AD, HEC 2161 D72C 12, Laferrière to Desjardins, 27 déc. 1937.

26. PAA, OMI, St-Paul Blue Quills 49, Laird to Principal Blue Quill Boarding School, 17 Nov. 1903.

27. PAA, OMI, Saddle Lake 2, *Codex historicus*, 5 nov. 1904.

28. AD, L 811 M27C 10, Lecoq to Magnan, 2 fév. 1910.

29. AD, L 811 M27C 12, Magnan to Lecoq, 8 mars 1910.

30. PAA, OMI, Brocket 6a, *Codex historicus*, mission Saint-Paul des Piéganes, 1916, p. 31.

31. Ibid., juillet 1917, p. 32.

32. AD, L 535 M27L 133, Émard to Beys, 5 déc. 1922.
33. AD, L 535 M27L 136, Geelen to Rév. père provincial, [Dec. 1922].
34. AD, L 535 M27L 134, Beys to Scott, 17 Dec. 1922.
35. AD, L 541 M27L 69, Brachet to Rév. père provincial [Beys], n.d.
36. AD, L 235 M27L 32, Bousquet to R.P. provincial [Beys], 24 nov. 1919.
37. AD, L 235 M27L 37, Bousquet to Beys, 9 mars 1921.
38. Carrière, *DBOC*, I, "Bousquet, Paul," pp. 126–27.
39. AD, L 235 M27L 105, Bousquet to Magnan, 12 mars 1927.
40. Ibid.
41. AD, L 541 M27L 266, Brachet to Rév. père provincial [Magnan], 20 oct. 1928.
42. AD, L 235 M27L 115, Geelen to Rév. père, 9 août 1928.
43. AD, L 281 M27C 4, *Codex historicus*, École industrielle des Saints-Anges.
44. Ibid.
45. AD, L 235 M27L 116, Kalmès to Rév. père, 12 oct. 1928.
46. AD, L 235 M27L 117, Kalmès to Magnan, 7 nov. 1928.
47. PAA, OMI, Paroises noninventoriées: Brocket Correspondance 1930–1951, Phelan to Levern, 28 June 1934; ibid., Hobbema 84, Phelan to Lewis, [1938].
48. PAA, OMI, Hobbema 88, [Pratt] to Lewis, 27 June 1938.
49. PAA, OMI, Hobbema 83, [Moulin] to Dear Sir, 8 Jan. 1933.
50. PAA, OMI, DP, E. Pratt 1912–36, Pratt to Balter, 15 sept. 1936.
51. Nowakowski, "Indian Residential Schools," p. 84.
52. PAA, OMI, Adm., Cluny IRS, Correspondance 1902–3, Riou to Legal, 18 jan. 1902.
53. "Rapport sur l'École industrielle Saint-Joseph à Dunbow," *Missions* 48 (1910): p. 28.
54. PAA, OMI Saddle Lake 2, *Codex historicus*, p. 130.
55. PAA, OMI, DP, L.-J. Dauphin 1885–1930, Dauphin to Leduc, 1[?] nov. 1914.
56. PAA, OMI, Saddle Lake 2, *Codex historicus*, 12 nov. 1901, pp. 185–86.
57. Ibid., 1903, p. 131.
58. Ibid., p. 172.
59. AD, L 285 M27L 54, Léonard to Beys, 22 déc. 1921.
60. PAA, OMI, Duck Lake 58, Guy to Mon révérend père, 18 oct. 1922; ibid., Hobbema 140, Guy to Moulin, 23 juin 1925. The king alluded to was Indian Commissioner W.M. Graham.
61. PAA, OMI, Saddle Lake 2, *Codex historicus*, p. 130.
62. PAA, OMI, DP, L.-J. Dauphin 1885–1930, Dauphin to Leduc, 1[?] nov. 1914.
63. AD, L 1021 M27L 1, Campeau to Langevin, 25 jan. 1899.

64. PAA, OMI, Cardston 38, Riou to Superintendent General of Indian Affairs, 2 Sept. 1899.

65. PAA, OMI, Adm., Correspondance avec le gouvernement 1910–19, Scott to Grondin [sic], 17 Nov. 1913.

66. Ibid., [Grandin] to Deputy Superintendent General, 24 Nov. [1913].

67. AD, HEB 2132 C47C 3, Cahill to Magnan, 24 juin 1913.

68. AD, L 286 M27L 18, Pedley to Cahill, 29 July 1913.

69. AD, L286 M27 19, Cahill to Roche, 1 Aug. 1914.

70. AD, L 286 M27L 22, McLean to Hugonnard, 9 Oct. 1914.

71. AD, L 286 M27L 21, Scott to Cahill, 16 August 1915.

72. PAA, OMI, Hobbema 69, Moulin to Hon. Sir, 4 March 1918.

73. AD, L 1027 M27L, Guy to Carrière, 8 fév. 1922.

74. PAA, OMI, Paroisses noninventoriées: Brocket Correspondance 1922–29, Le Vern to Scott, 12 Sept. 1927.

75. Ibid., Scott to Le Vern, 30 Sept 1927.

76. Ibid., Christianson to Le Vern, 28 Aug. 1934.

77. PAA, OMI, Saddle Lake 2a, *Codex historicus*, 31 déc. 1905, pp. 115–16.

78. PAA, OMI, Hobbema 75, Ferrier to Church Authorities, Principals and Departmental Representatives, 20 May 1925.

79. PAA, OMI, Hobbema 87, Hoey to Church Authorities, Principals and Departmental Representatives, 30 March 1937.

80. PAA, OMI, Cardston 32 a, [Le Vern] to Plourde, 13 fév. 1938.

81. AD, L 1021 M27L 38, Fafard to Beys, 1 sept. 1918.

82. PAA, OMI, PP, A. Lacombe 1893–95, Reed to Lacombe, 1 April 1893, (Private).

83. PAA, OMI, Adm., Delmas Indian Residential School, Correspondance 1926–27, Macdonald to Angin, 28 Nov. 1927.

84. AD, L 509 M27L 10, Gendreau to Rév. père provincial [Magnan], 26 oct. 1901.

85. PAA, OMI, Adm., Saint-Paul IRS Blue Quills, Correspondance 1937–42, [Langlois] to Balter, 30 mai 1937.

86. AD, L 235 M27L 31, Bousquet to Rév. père provincial [Beys], 22 oct. 1922.

87. *Acte général de visite des missions indiennes du Nord-Ouest canadien*, pp. 73.

88. Claude Roberto, "Relations entre les Oblats et les autres communautés religieuses dans le fond oblat de l'Alberta-Saskatchewan," in *Western Oblate Studies 3 / Études Oblates de l'Ouest 3*, ed. by R. Huel (Edmonton: Western Canadian Publishers, 1994): p. 69.

89. PAA, OMI, Hobbema 157, Entente entre les RR. PP. Oblats qui désignent le principal de l'école de Delmas, Saskatchewan et les RR. Soeurs qui ont l'administration de l'école, 14 nov. 1924.

90. Roberto, "Relations entre les Oblats et les autres communautés religieuses dans le fonds oblat de l'Alberta-Saskatchewan," p. 65.

91. Ibid., Grandin to Très Rde Mère Jean l'Évangeliste, 25 avril 1919.

92. Roberto, "Relations entre les Oblats et les autres communautés religieuses dans le fonds oblat de l'Alberta-Saskatchewan," pp. 67–69.

93. Margaret McGovern, SP, "Perspective on the Oblates: The Experience of the Sisters of Providence," in *Western Oblate Studies 3 / Études Oblates de l'Ouest 3*, ed. by R. Huel (Edmonton: Western Canadian Publishers, 1994): pp. 92–94.

94. Ibid., p. 106.

95. AD, L 1021 M27L 8, Langevin to Campeau, 5 mars 1900.

96. PAA, OMI, Adm., Saint-Boniface, Correspondance de Mgr Langevin, 1900–12, Langevin to [Lacombe], 25 avril 1900.

97. PAA, OMI, Saddle Lake 2, *Codex historicus*, 1903, p. 134.

98. PAA, OMI, Saddle Lake 2a, *Codex historicus*, 1908, p. 171.

99. PAA, OMI, Hobbema IRS, Correspondance 1911–25, Grandin to Moulin, 28 fév. 1916.

100. Ibid., [Grandin] to Moulin, 3 nov. 1916.

101. AD, L 535 M27L 80, Dugas to Cahill, 13 jan. 1917.

102. Ibid.

103. AD, L 1052 M27 K 6, Decorby to Rév. et bien cher père, n.d., [1902].

104. PAA, OMI, PP, J.- J.-M. Lestanc, Journal 1901, 25 avril, 27 avril, 30 août.

105. PAA, OMI, Brocket 6a, *Codex historicus*, mission Saint-Paul des Piéganes, p. 20, p. 22.

106. PAA, OMI, Paroisses noninventoriées: Brocket, *Codex historicus*, mission Saint-Paul des Piéganes, 21 sept. 1922, p. 53.

107. PAA, OMI, Adm., Brocket IRS, Correspondance 1922–24, Le Vern to Rév. et Bien cher père provincial [Beys], 29 déc. 1924.

108. PAA, OMI, Paroisses noninventoriées: Brocket, *Codex historicus*, mission Saint-Paul des Piéganes, 25 nov. 1933.

109. AD, L 541 M27L 4, Langevin to Bousquet, 24 jan. 1902.

110. AD, L 541 M27L 6, Bousquet to Révde Mère Supérieure Générale, 10 fev. 1902.

111. AD, L 541 M27L 12, Camper to Très rév. père provincial, 11 oct. 1905.

112. AD, L 541 M27L 14, Camper to Rév. et bien cher père provincial, 8 nov. 1905.

113. AD, L 535, M27L 150, Geelen to Rév. et bien aimé père [Guy], 4 oct. 1933.

114. AD, L 541 M27L 238, Brachet to Magnan, 25 oct. 1927.

115. PAA, OMI, Adm., Cluny IRS, Correspondance 1924–25, Riou to McNally, 8 April 1924.

116. AOM, Personnes: O. Charlebois, Charlebois to Rév. et bien cher père maître, [des novices], 25 avril 1891.

117. PAA, OMI, DP, L.-J. Dauphin 1885–1930, Dauphin to Leduc, 1[?] nov. 1914.

118. Jean Ducharme, "La mission du Portage la Loche," *Missions* 56 (1922): p. 65.

119. PAA, OMI, DP, D. Foisy 1877–97, Foisy to Fabre, 25 avril 1889.

120. PAA, OMI, Rivière Qui Barre 2, *Codex historicus*, mission Saint-Alexandre, 1 mai 1887.

121. Ibid., 22 mai 1887, pp. 9–10; 5 mars 1888, p. 31.

122. PAA, OMI, Cluny 13a, *Codex historicus*, mission de la Sainte-Trinité des Pieds-Noirs, 1894, p. 50.

123. The themes of cultural replacement, cultural synthesis and cultural continuity are discussed in David A. Nock, *A Victorian Missionary and Canadian Indian Policy: Cultural Synthesis vs. Cultural Replacement*, Editions SR/9 (Waterloo: Wilfrid Laurier Press, 1988).

124. "Province du Manitoba," *Missions* 57 (1923): p. 22.

125. AD, L541 M27L 367, [Magnan] to Scott, 27 Oct. 1930.

126. "L'incendie de Cross Lake," *Missions* 64 (1930): pp. 59–60.

127. Ibid.

9   THE OBLATES AND THE FEDERAL GOVERNMENT: A TENUOUS RELATIONSHIP

1. AD, HE 2221 T126 94, Taché to Baby, 31 oct. 1879.

2. C. Champagne, *Les débuts de la mission*, p. 101.

3. NAC, RG 10, v. 3817, f. 57562, Grandin to Reed, 28 July 1889.

4. Archives of the Diocese of Prince Albert [hereafter ADPA], Mémoire de l'Évêque de Saint-Albert sur ses difficultés avec le Département indien [hereafter Mémoire], p. 1.

5. Ibid., pp. 2–3.

6. Ibid., pp. 4–5. Treaty Six was signed at Fort Carlton on 23 August 1876 and at Fort Pitt on 9 Sept. 1876.

7. NAC, Macdonald Papers, 187212, Leduc to Macdonald, 4 avril 1883.

8. Ibid., 188068, Grandin to Macdonald, 22 May 1883.

9. Ibid., 188070, Grandin to Macdonald, 26 mai 1883; ibid., 204290, Tabaret to Macdonald, 3 Nov. 1885.

10. Ibid., 209326, Leduc to Macdonald, 21 July 1886.

11. AD, HE 2223 T12Z 3, Grandin to Mgr et bien cher père [Taché], 5 oct. 1886.

12. NAC, RG10, v. 3708, f. 19502 pt. 1, Macdonald to Rt. Rev Bishop of St. Albert, 9 Dec. 1886.

13. AD, HE 2223 T12Z 3, Grandin to Mgr et bien cher père [Taché], 8 nov. 1887.

14. Ibid., Grandin to Mgr et bien cher père [Taché], 16 nov. 1887.

15. AD, H 5102 G75L 16, Grandin to Laflèche, 18 juillet 1887.

16. AD, H 5102 G75L 19, Grandin to Laflèche, 8 août 1888.

17. Brian Titley, "Hayter Reed and Indian Administration in the West," p. 119.

18. AD, HE 2223 T12Z 3, Grandin to Mgr et bien cher père [Taché], 15 oct. 1889.

19. Ibid., Grandin to Dewdney, 18 déc. 1889.

20. NAC, RG 10, v. 3841, f. 71345, L. Vankoughnet: Memorandum on the various points of contention in His Lordship Bishop Grandin's protocol, enclosed in the Bishop's letter of 9th ultimo to the Superintendent-General of Indian Affairs, 5 Sept. 1890.

21. NAC, Reed Papers, vol. 16, Church-Agency Relations 1888–92, Reed to Pinkham, 8 Jan. 1889. This file contains numerous letters of complaint from Protestant clergymen.

22. NAC, RG 10, v. 3817, f. 57562, MacDonald to Reed, 16 Dec. 1890.

22. Ibid., Mackay to Indian Commissioner, 17 Feb. 1891.

24. Titley, "Hayter Reed and Indian Administration in the West," p. 131. Titley concludes that Reed was "generally successful" as a diplomat.

25. NAC, RG 10, v. 3817, f. 57562, Memorandum for Department, [12 Aug.], [1889].

26. ADPA, Grandin, Mémoire, pp. 24–26.

27. Ibid., v. 3708 f. 19502 pt. 1, Grandin to Dewdney, 9 Aug. 1890.

28. NAC, Macdonald Papers, 151340–343, Memoir of Bishop of St. Albert to Hon. E. Dewdney, 9 Aug. 1890.

29. Ibid., 151334, Grandin to Macdonald, 9 Aug. 1890.

30. Ibid., 209764, Taché to Macdonald, 26 Aug. 1886 (Private).

31. Ibid., 211620–623, Taché to Macdonald, 3 Nov. 1886.

32. Ibid., 149150–155, Taché to His Exc. the Gov.-Gen. in Council (Confidential), [28 July 1889].

33. PAA, OMI, PP, A. Lacombe 1890–92, Reed to Sir, 31 Oct. 1890.

34. NAC, RG10 v. 3844, f. 73070, Reed to Taché, 31 Oct. 1890.

35. AD, H 5101 675C 54, Dewdney to My Dear Lord Bishop [Grandin], 5 Sept. 1890.

36. P.-T. Campeau to Très Révérend Père Supérieur Général, jan. 1895, *Missions* 33 (1895): p. 280.

37. PAA, OMI, PP, J.-J.-M. Lestanc 1892, 1896, Forget to Lestanc, 22 July 1896.

38. NAC, Macdonald Papers, 1478900, Taché et al. to Macdonald, 4 June 1888.

39. PAA, OMI, Rivière Qui Barre, *Codex historicus*, mission Saint-Alexandre, Gendreau to Blanchet, 27 oct 1888, p. 102; ibid., 10 fév. 1890, 6 mars 1890, p. 28.

40. AD, HE 2223 T12Z 3, Grandin to Mgr et bien cher père [Taché], 19 nov. 1887.

41. ADPA, Mémoire, p. 28.

42. AD, HE 2223 T12Z 3, Grandin to Mgr et bien cher père, 26 avril 1888.

43. AD, HEC 2142 A33L 43, Lacombe to ?, n.d. [1888].

44. AD, HE 2223 T12Z 3, Grandin to Mgr et bien cher père [Taché], 28 jan. 1888.

45. PAA, OMI, Rivière Qui Barre 2, *Codex historicus*, mission Saint-Alexandre, Macdonald to Gendreau, 8 May 1888.

46. Ibid., Gendreau to Blanchet, 9 mai 1888.

47. PAA, OMI, PP, L. Doucet: Journal 1868–90, 4 juillet 1888, p. 221.

48. Rapport sur le vicariat de Saint-Albert," *Missions* 31 (1893): p. 257.

49. PAA, OMI, PP, A. Lacombe 1867–1901, Lacombe to Antoine, 9 oct. 1889.

50. NAC, RG 10, v. 3708, f. 19502 pt. 1, J.H. Pope, Memorandum of a conversation between Arch. Taché, Sir John A. Macdonald, Father Gendreau at the Ottawa College, 18 Jan. 1889.

51. PAA, OMI, Rivière Qui Barre 2, *Codex historicus*, mission Saint-Alexandre, Gendreau to Blanchet, 23 fév. 1889.

52. AOM, Alberta-Saskatchewan, Pascal to Gendreau, 1 oct. 1891; NAC, RG 10, v. 3858, f. 82112, Grandin to Gendreau, 4 août 1891.

53. AOM, Alberta-Saskatchewan, Lacombe to Gendreau, 17 juillet 1891.

54. Ibid., Grandin to Gendreau, 21 xbre [sic] 1891.

55. Ibid., Lacombe to Gendreau, 17 oct. 1891.

56. Ibid., Grandin to Gendreau, 14 sept. 1894.

57. Carrière, *DBOC*, II, "Gendreau, Edmond," pp. 76–78.

58. Maurice Lewis, "The Anglican Church and its Mission Schools Dispute," *Alberta Historical Review* 14 (1966): pp. 10–12.

59. Grant, *Moon of Wintertime*, p. 195.

60. PAA, OMI, Adm., Correspondance avec J. Guy 1921–22, [Grandin] to Guy, 28 mai 1921.

61. Ibid., Guy to Grandin, 10 juin 1921.

62. AD, HR 6651 C73R 4, Riou to Guy, 22 mai 1922.

63. PAA, OMI, Duck Lake 58, Guy to Mon révérend père, 18 oct. 1922.

64. PAA, OMI, Adm., Correspondance avec le gouvernement 1926–30, [Guy] to Mon révérend père, 18 oct. 1922.

65. PAA, OMI, Duck Lake 58, Guy to Mon rév. père, 18 oct. 1922.

66. Ibid., Duck Lake 59, Guy to Beys, 12 sept. 1924.

67. Ibid., Duck Lake 60, Delmas to Bien cher père, 11 fév. 1925.

68. AD, L 235 M27L 87, Guy to Bousquet, 22 juin 1925.

69. PAA, OMI, Hobbema 140, Guy to Moulin, 2 déc. 1925.

70. AD, L 235 M27L 104, Guy to Bousquet, 31 jan. 1927.

71. AOM, Personnes: J. Guy, Villeneuve to Guy, 12 juin 1925.

72. Ibid., Lefebvre to Villeneuve, 6 mai 1926.

73. AD, L 281 M27R 42, Memorandum de la convention des principaux des écoles indiennes à Lebret, 28–29 août 1924.

74. AD, L 1027 M27L 124, Scott to Guy, 17 April 1926.

75. Ibid., Guy to Mon Rév. et Bien cher père (circular letter), 22 juin 1926.

76. PAA, OMI, Duck Lake 61, Le Chevallier to Guy, 31 mars 1926.

77. "Rapport de la convention des principaux des écoles indiennes de la Province d'Alberta-Saskatchewan," *Missions* 68 (1934): pp. 21–22.

78. Ibid., p. 23.

79. Ibid., p. 23.

80. PAA, OMI, Duck Lake 65, Résolutions, convention de Saint-Boniface, 25–26 fév. 1942.

81. AD, HR 6615 C73R 17, Reed to Agents, Inspectors and Principals of Industrial and Boarding Schools, 31 Oct. 1890.

82. NAC, RG 10, v.3858, f. 81812, C. Sifton: Memorandum du Superintendent General, 15 Dec. 1897.

83. PAA, OMI, Hobbema 14, Résumé du ministère du R.P. Moulin, 1904, p. 1.

84. AD, L 535 M27L 5, Dennely to Magnan, 10 juillet 1895.

85. PAA, OMI, Hobbema 14, Résumé du ministère du père Moulin, 1904, p. 1.

86. PAA, OMI, Duck Lake 58, Scott to Guy, 24 Dec. 1921.

87. Ibid., Guy to Scott, 15 Feb. 1921.

88. Ibid., Scott to Guy, 6 April 1922.

89. AD, L 1027 M27L 70, Guy to Carrière, 9 mai 1922; PAA, OMI, Duck Lake 58, Guy to Mon rév. père, 18 oct. 1922.

90. PAA, OMI, Hobbema 140, Guy to Moulin, 13 nov. 1923.

91. Ibid., Guy to Moulin, 8 nov. 1926.

92. AD, L 1034 M27L 103, Ferrier to Magnan, 4 Feb. 1927.

93. PAA, OMI, Hobbema 81, [Moulin] to Knott, 8 April 1931.

94. AD, L 235 M27L 113, Kalmès to Guy, 27 avril 1928.

95. Vanast, "Compassion, Cost and Competition," pp. 187–95.

96. AD, HR 8001 C73R 5, "Indian and Eskimo Commission Observes Silver Jubilee," Agence romaine des Oblats de Marie Immaculée, Nov. 1961.

10   THE OBLATES AS "FATHERS, GUIDES AND PROTECTORS" OF
     ABORIGINAL COMMUNITIES

1. AD, LC 7001 K26R 1, Gasté, Relations, 8 avril 1885.
2. Ibid., 1 jan. 1894.
3. AD, HEB 6255 A45C 19, Gasté to MacFarlane, 19 nov. 1896.
4. Étienne Bonnald to Rédacteur des *Annales*, 7 nov. 1899, *Missions* 38 (1900): pp. 23–24.
5. Arsène Turquetil, o.m.i., "Chronique historique de la mission Saint-Pierre du lac Caribou depuis 1846 jusqu'à nos jours, 1912," *Missions* 50 (1912): pp. 286–87.
6. PAA, OMI, PP, J. Letreste, Mes Souvenirs, p. 101.
7. Ibid.
8. Ibid. p. 118.
9. Jean-Marie Pénard to Très Rév. Père Supérieur Général, 10 avril 1900, *Missions* 38 (1900): pp. 259–60.
10. "Vicariat Apostolic d'Athabasca. Rapport de Mgr Grouard," *Missions* 40 (1902): pp. 266–67.
11. AD, HE 2221 T12Z 132, Lacombe to Mgr [Taché], 28 mars 1864.
12. A. Lacombe au Très Rév. Père Supérieur Général, 12 mai 1870, *Missions* 9 (1870): p. 263.
13. AD, HE 1864 G87L 44, Grouard to MacFarlane, 10 Dec. 1882.
14. AD, HE 1864 G87L 46, Grouard to MacFarlane, 11 Sept. 1883.
15. AD, HE 1861 G87C 51, Grouard to Ma chère Marie, 6 juin 1911.
16. AD, HE 2221 T12Z 37, Clut to Mgr [Taché], 1 juillet 1864.
17. AD, HE 1821 F26C 5, Faraud to Durocher, 16 9bre [sept.] 1869.
18. V. Fourmond to Très Rév. Père Supérieur Général, 26 déc. 1870, *Missions* 10 (1872): p. 484.
19. AD, L 2003 A33R 1, Renseignements demandés par Mgr Taché sur les missions et les missionnaires de Mgr Grandin depuis l'érection du vicariat religieux de St. Albert 1868 jusqu'en 1872, p. 1.
20. AD, LC 7001 K26R 1, Relations, 4 août, 28 août, 18 sept. 1885.
21. "Vicariat de la Saskatchewan, lettres du R.P. O. Charlebois, 12 sept. [1887]," *Missions* 34 (1896): p. 121.
22. PAA, OMI, PP, L. Le Goff, Mémoires 1930, p. 24.
23. PAA, Fort Macleod, *Codex historicus*, 1878, p. 17.

24. PAC, RG 10, v. 3695, f. 14942, Scollen to Irvine, 13 April 1879.

25. Ibid.

26. See supra, pp. 111.

27. NAC, RG 10, v. 3727, f. 25276, Taché to Vankoughnet, 6 Dec. 1880.

28. *Acte général des visites canoniques faites dans le vicariat de Saint-Albert*, p. 24.

29. PAA, OMI, PP, A. Lacombe 1886, Lacombe to Grandin, 25 juin 1886.

30. PAA, OMI, Rivière qui Barre 2, *Codex historicus*, mission Saint-Alexandre, 27 fév. 1888, pp. 27–28.

31. Ibid., 23 avril 1888, p. 67.

32. Ibid., 3 fév. 1887, pp. 6–8.

33. PAA, OMI, Saint-Paul Blue Quills 42, Forget to Grandin, 4 Aug. 1896.

34. "Rapports au Chapitre général de 1908: Alberta-Saskatchewan," *Missions* 47 (1909): p. 140.

35. PAA, OMI, PP, A. Lacombe 1885–89, Lacombe to Dewdney, 17 Dec. 1889.

36. NAC, RG 10, v. 3897 f. 98330, Grandin to Minister of the Interior [Daly], 8 Nov. 1892.

37. Ibid., Reed to Daly, 10 Jan. 1893.

38. PAA, OMI, Cardston 37, Grandin to Superintendent General of Indian Affairs, 7 July 1894.

39. PAA, OMI, PP noninventoriés: E. Legal, Correspondance 1902, Legal to Sibbald, 20 Aug. 1902.

40. PAA, OMI, DP, G. Simonin 1903–42, Simonin to Mon Rév. et Bien Cher Père, 8 fév. 1908.

41. PAA, OMI, Adm., Correspondance avec le gouvernement 1909–19, [Grandin] to Scott, 3 Aug. [1917].

42. AD, HE 2223 T12Z 3, Grandin to Mgr et bien cher Père [Taché], 25 avril 1892.

43. PAA, OMI, Saint-Paul Blue Quills 44, Forget to Grandin, 18 April 1898.

44. PAA, OMI, Rivière qui Barre 2, *Codex historicus*, mission St-Alexandre, 16 avril 1886, p. 3.

45. PAA, OMI, Adm., Cluny, Crowfoot IRS, Correspondance 1900, Danis to Laird, 10 Oct. 1900.

46. PAA, OMI, Hobbema 66, Moulin to Dear Sir, 7 Oct. 1914.

47. PAA, OMI, Hobbema 81, [Moulin] to Ferrier, 15 Aug. 1931.

48. Ibid., Mackenzie to Moulin, 22 Aug. 1931.

49. PAA, OMI, Cluny 13a, *Codex historicus*, mission de la Sainte-Trinité des Pieds-Noirs, pp. 20–22.

50. Ibid., p. 277.

51. PAA, OMI, St. Albert 8, *Codex historicus*, 20 avril 1885, Scollen to Rev. and Dear Father, 14 April 1885.

52. PAA, OMI, Cluny 13a, *Codex historicus*, mission de la Sainte-Trinité des Pieds-Noirs, p. 108.

53. PAA, OMI, Adm., Brocket Indian Residential School, Correspondance 1922–24, Le Vern to Rév. et bien cher père provincial [Beys], 1[?] juin 1924.

54. Grandin, Écrits, 16, pp. 37–38.

55. AD, HE 2223 T12Z 3, Grandin to Mgr et bien cher père [Taché], 29 août 1872. The dispersal of the Manitoba Métis is discussed in D.N. Sprague, *Canada and the Métis, 1869–1885* (Waterloo: Wilfrid Laurier Press, 1988), especially chapters 6–8.

56. T. Flanagan, *Riel and the Rebellion: 1885 Reconsidered* (Saskatoon: Western Producer Prairie Books, 1983), chapters 2–3, cf Sprague, *Canada and the Métis*.

57. Grandin, Écrits, 4, p. 315.

58. Ibid., p. 281.

59. PAA, OMI, Saint Albert 8, *Codex historicus*, 15 avril 1885.

60. PAA, OMI, PP, A. Lacombe 1885, Lacombe to Legal and Van Tighem, 26 mars 1885.

61. "Vicariat de St-Albert. Rapport de Mgr Grandin au T.R.P. Supérieur Général," *Missions* 24 (1886): p.17.

62. PAA, OMI, Saint-Albert 8, *Codex historicus*, 25 juillet 1885, Grandin et al. to Campbell, 10 July 1885.

63. AD, HE 2223 T12Z 3, Grandin to Mgr et bien cher Père [Taché], 27 nov. 1885; ibid., Grandin to Taché, 7 mars 1886.

64. Ibid., Grandin to Mgr et bien cher père [Taché], 14 juillet 1885; PAA, OMI, DP, L.-J. Dauphin 1885–1930, Dauphin to Mgr et bien aimé père [Grandin], 22 mars 1886.

65. Grandin, Écrits, 4, 1 mai 1898, p. 224.

66. Ibid., 2, 1 mai 1898, p. 331.

67. C. Champagne, *Les débuts de la mission*, p. 184.

68. PAA, OMI, Adm., Saint-Boniface Correspondance de Mgr Taché 1885–89, Taché to Lebret, 6 avril 1885.

69. PAA, OMI, Saint-Albert 8, *Codex historicus*, 7 juin, 11 juin, 30 juin 1885.

70. "Vicariat de la Saskatchewan," Charlebois, to Très Rév. Père Général, n.d., *Missions* 39 (1901): p. 32.

71. AD, LC 6461 K26R 1, Journal, 12 avril, 17 avril, 31 mai 1909.

72. PAA, OMI, Saint-Laurent 5, Petite Chronique, vol. 2, 1890, pp. 45–47.

73. PAA, OMI, PP, A. Lacombe, Saint-Paul 1893–96, Annex "B" to P. C. 3723, 28 December 1896.

74. Ibid., Annex "A," Burgess to Sir, 28 Dec. 1895.

75. AD, L 2521 A33R 4, Lacombe, to À Mes chers enfants et amis, les Métis du Manitoba et du Nord-Ouest, n.d.

76. Grandin, Écrits, 12, p. 554.

77. PAA, OMI, PP, noninventoriés: É. Legal Correspondance re Saint-Paul des Métis 1989–1902, Thérien to Legal, 18 mars 1898.

78. Ibid., Thérien to Legal, 2 avril 1898.

79. Ibid.

80. Grandin, Écrits, 17, "Documents collectifs," 7 mars 1899.

81. PAA, OMI, PP, H. Leduc 1901–02, Leduc to Lacombe, 25 nov. 1901, 18 fév. 1903.

82. PAA, OMI, Saint-Paul 3, Codex historicus, p. 4.

83. AD, L 2501 A33R 6, Paroissiens de Saint-Laurent de Grandin au Supérieur Générale des Oblats de Marie Immaculée, 8 mai 1896.

84. "Rapports au chapitre général de 1908, Alberta-Saskatchewan," Missions 47 (1909): p. 140.

85. PAA, OMI DP, J. Angin 1916–38, [Grandin] to Angin, 11 nov. 1921.

86. PAA, OMI, DP, A. Thérien 1916–24, Thérien to Rév. père prov., 16 juin 1924.

87. Ibid.

88. "Statistiques Missions Indiennes du Canada," Missions 65 (1931): p. 631.

89. "Rapport Alberta Saskatchewan," Missions 66 (1932): p. 361.

90. Raymond Huel, "Louis Schmidt Patriarch of St. Louis," Saskatchewan History 40 (1987): pp. 9–10.

91. Auguste-Henri de Trémaudan, Hold High Your Heads (History of the Métis Nation in Western Canada), trans. by E. Maguet (Winnipeg: Pemmican Publications, 1982), pp. xii–xiii.

92. AD, HF 245 A24Z 8, Nault to Morice, 10 fév. 1925.

93. La Liberté, 5 août 1925.

94. Ibid., 19 août; 9, 19, 23 sept. 1925.

95. Auguste-Henri de Trémaudan, Histoire de la nation Métisse dans l'Ouest Canadien (Montréal: Éditions Albert Lévesque, 1936), p. 22, Appendice, pp. 403–48.

96. Adrien-Gabriel Morice, o.m.i., La race métisse: Étude critique en marge d'un livre récent (Winnipeg: Chez l'auteur, 1938). This critique was also published serially in La Revue de l'Université d'Ottawa 7 (1937): pp. 160–83, 364–79, 475–95; 8 (1938): pp. 79–107.

97. Taché, *Vingt années*, p. III.

98. Ibid., pp. 110–11.

99. Walter Nigg, *The Heretics*, edited and translated by Richard and Clara Winston (New York: A. Knopf, 1962), pp. 9–12.

100. "Rapport de Mgr Grouard," *Missions* 40 (1902): pp. 267–68.

101. Huel, "Jean L'Heureux Canadien errant et prétendu missionnaire auprès des Pieds-Noirs," pp. 209–13.

102. Olive Dickason, *Canada's First Nations: A History of Founding Peoples From Earliest Times* (Toronto: McClelland and Stewart, 1992), p. 328.

103. "École pensionnat du Fort Frances, Ontario," *Missions* 55 (1921): p. 308.

104. PAA, OMI, Dunbow 21, Grandin to Rév. et bien cher père Guy, 23 juillet 1921.

105. PAA, Duck Lake 58, Grandin to Mon cher père Delmas, 7 mars 1922.

106. PAA, OMI, Adm., Brocket IRS, Correspondance 1922–24, Levern to Loft, 18 Jan. 1922.

107. Ibid., Scott to Grandin, 2 Feb. 1922.

108. Sluman, *John Tootoosis*, p. 163.

109. Ibid., p. 191.

110. Ibid., pp. 195–201.

111. Carter, *Lost Harvests*, p. ix, p. 13.

112. Ibid., pp. 13–14.

113. Grant, *Moon of Wintertime*, ch. 9.

11   THE CANONICAL VISIT OF SUPERIOR GENERAL T. LABOURÉ

1. "Rapport du Vicariat de Saint-Boniface," *Missions* 36 (1898): p. 262.

2. AD, L 1D51 M27C 1, *Codex historicus*, Mission de Pelly; ibid., HEB 3Z97 J94C 3, A. Philippot, o.m.i., Decorby manuscript, Decorby to Sévigny, 23 juin 1888.

3. PAA, OMI, Cochin 1.

4. PAA, OMI, Calgary Sainte-Marie 1, *Codex historicus*, mission Notre-Dame de la Paix, 4–5 jan. 1884, avril 1884, 22 mai 1884, pp. 3–8.

5. AD, L 2221 A33R 3, Leduc to l'Hermite, 31 déc. 1887.

6. AD, L 531 M27R 11, Rapport annuel 1922–23, Mission indienne Notre-Dame de l'Espérance.

7. AD, L 535 M27l 188, Poulet to Beys, 30 juillet 1924; "La mission-école de l'Espérance, Lestock," *Missions* 62 (1928): p. 53.

8. AD, L 535 M27L 196, Kalmès to Mon Rév. Père, 10 jan. 1925.

9. AD, L 1027 M27L 95, Carrière to Rév. et Cher Père Provincial [Beys], 24 avril 1924.

10. AD, L 1052 M27K 172, Tétreault to Lavigne, 27 sept. 1942.

11. PAA, OMI, Adm., Questionnaire pour une visite canonique, Labouré to NN ss les Vicaires des Missions et aux RR PP Provinciaux, 21 nov. 1934.

12. PAA, OMI, Adm., Correspondance avec l'Administration Générale 1935, Langlois to Desnoyers, 12 mars 1935.

13. Ibid., Desnoyers to Langlois, 13 avril 1935; 28 nov. 1935.

14. *Acte général de visite des missions indiennes*, pp. 31–35.

15. Ibid., pp. 27–28.

16. Raymond Huel, "The Irish-French Conflict in Catholic Episcopal Nominations: The Western Sees and the Struggle for Domination Within the Church," Canadian Catholic Historical Association, *Study Sessions* 42 (1975): pp. 50–70.

17. AD, L 31 M27R 6, Les Oblats du Manitoba et leurs responsabilités envers les missions, p. 35.

18. *Acte général de visite des missions indiennes*, p. 35; AD, HR 8004 C37R 0.1, Procès verbal, comité de direction, Commission oblate des oeuvres indiennes et esquimaudes [COOIE], 24 nov. 1937.

19. *Acte général de visite des missions indiennes*, p. 31.

20. AD, HPK 2033 N82R 3–72, Questionnaire pour les Supérieurs de Maisons et Districts, les Directeurs de Résidences et les Principaux d'Écoles, 1935.

21. *Acte général de visite des missions indiennes*, p. 29.

22. Ibid., p. 39.

23. Ibid., pp. 60–62.

24. Ibid., pp. 60–64.

25. Ibid., pp. 64–67.

26. Ibid., pp. 67–68.

27. Ibid., pp. 46–49.

28. Ibid., p. 49.

29. Ibid., p. 93.

30. Ibid., pp. 51–52, 88.

31. Ibid., pp. 52–53.

32. Ibid., pp. 55–56.

33. Ibid., p. 54.

34. Ibid., pp. 89–90, 93.

35. Ibid., pp. 86–88.

36. Ibid., pp. 68–69.

37. Idid., pp. 74–76.

38. Ibid., pp. 78–79.

39. Ibid., pp. 79–80.

40. Ibid., p. 83.

41. AD, L 221 M27R 6, Pacelli to Labouré, 6 Augusti 1935, reproduced in *Missions* 69 (1936): pp. 708–9.

42. AD, HPK 2033 N82R 3, Questionnaire pour les Supérieurs de Maisons et Districts, les Directeurs de Résidences et les Principaux d'Écoles, 1935, No 3.

43. *Acte général de visite des missions indiennes*, pp. 98–101.

44. Grant, *Moon of Wintertime*, chs. 9–11.

45. AD, HR 8001 C73R 7, J.E.Y. Levaque, o.m.i., Aug. 1972.

12   THE OBLATE APOSTOLATE: ONE HUNDRED YEARS LATER

1. *Acte général de visite des missions indiennes*, pp. 70–71.

2. AD, HR 8001 C73R 2, Notes tirées des minutes de la Commission des Affaires indiennes, 17 jan. 1936.

3. PAA, OMI, Adm., Correspondance avec J.O. Plourde, Plourde to Langlois, 15 oct. 1936.

4. AD, HR 8001 C73R 2, Notes tirées des minutes de la Commission des Affaires indiennes, 25 nov. 1937.

5. AD, HR 8004 C73R 0.1, Procès verbaux, comité directeur COOIE, 17 jan. 1936, p. 1, 24 nov. 1937, p. 23.

6. Ibid., 12 oct. 1939.

7. Ibid., 24 nov. 1936, p. 11.

8. Ibid., 23 nov. 1936, p. 6; 24 nov. 1937, p. 17.

9. Ibid., 25 nov. 1937, pp. 36–38.

10. Ibid., 13 oct. 1939, pp. 52–53.

11. Ibid., 22 mai 1940, p. 58.

12. Ibid., 12 oct. 1939, pp. 46–47.

13. PAA, OMI, Duck Lake 4, Plourde to Mon rév. père, 27 nov. 1941. An examination of Anglican sources suggests that the proposed reduction of grants would cause "very great difficulty" and that this financial consideration motivated the joint meeting with Crerar. Anglican Church of Canada Archives, MSCC, Executive Committee Minutes GS75–103 Series 1–4, 22 Sept. 1941. The Board of Home Missions of the United Church had suggested that the government be asked to provide a bonus to cover the operating costs of residential schools, ibid., MSSC, Indian and Eskimo Residential School Commission Minutes, GS 75–103, Series 2–15, 21 Oct. 1941. On the government's proposal to close two Anglican residential schools and replace them with day schools, however, the MSCC stated

that "any alteration in the status of the Society's Schools must be contingent upon similar action being taken in connexion with Schools administered by other Church societies, and in due proportion to the number of those Schools," ibid., 9 Dec. 1941. That the various denominations were able to come together in such a meeting is amazing given traditional Protestant-Catholic jealousies and animosities. In 1940, Anglicans attempted to persuade the minister of National Defence to reduce the number of Catholic chaplains in the Canadian armed forces. The following year, Baptist Churches described their efforts to convert Catholics to Protestantism as a positive contribution to the Canadian war effort. At a conference of United Church Indian Workers held in Norway House, Manitoba, in 1942, the Rev. E. Young stated that the progress of Catholic missions was a loss to the United Church and concluded that "we must fight it [the Catholic Church], not merely to save our investment and effort, but also to save the Indians from a system which more and more reveals itself as a pagan and perverted thing." United Church of Canada Archives, Board of Home Missions, General Files, 83.050C, Box 25, File 376, Report of Conference of Indian Workers, p. 10.

14. United Church of Canada Archives, Board of Home Missions, General File: Re Indian Co-operation Committee, 83.050C, Box 25, File 376, Memorandum for the Honourable T.A. Crerar, 10 Jan. 1942.

15. PAA, OMI, Duck Lake 4, Plourde to Mon rév. père, 27 nov. 1941.

16. Ibid., Plourde to Latour, 31 oct. 1942.

17. Ibid.

18. Ibid., Plourde to Hoey, 9 Aug. 1941.

19. Ibid., Hoey to Plourde, 22 Aug. 1941.

20. *Acte de la visite générale de la province du Manitoba par le T.R.P. Rousseau, O.M.I. Mai-Octobre 1941*, p. 71.

21. Nowakowski, "Indian Residential Schools," pp. 70–75.

22. PAA, OMI, Duck Lake 64, Plourde to Latour, 31 juillet 1942.

23. PAA, OMI, Hobbema 143, Plourde to Hoey, 3 May 1945.

24. Ibid.

25. PAA, OMI, Adm., Correspondance avec le gouvernement 1945–56, Routhier to Crerar, 4 April 1945.

26. Ibid., Crerar to Routhier, 10 April 1945.

27. *Acte général de visite des missions indiennes*, pp. 59–60.

28. AD, L231 M27R 116, Séjour des enfants indiens au scolasticat de Lebret entre le 13 nov. 1932 et 23 mars 1936.

29. Ibid.

30. AD, L 281 M27C 4, *Codex historicus*, École industrielle des Saints-Anges; "Province du Manitoba," *Missions* 73 (1939): p. 132.

31. *Semaines d'études missionnaires du Canada, Ottawa, 1934* (Ottawa: Le Secrétariat des Semaines, Université d'Ottawa, n.d.), p. 15.

32. Ibid., p. 12.

33. Ibid., "La missionologie et les Semaines missionologiques," p. 43–44.

34. "Province du Canada," *Missions* 70 (1936): p. 171.

35. Lajeunesse, *Directives missionnaires*, 629 pages.

36. Ibid., pp. vi–viii.

37. Joseph-Étienne Champagne, *Manuel d'action missionnaire*, pp. 15–18.

38. AD, HF 224 C44R 5, J.-É. Champagne, o.m.i., Projet d'institut scientifique missionnaire, 1 mai 1948.

39. "Vicariat du Keewatin," *Missions* 73 (1939): p. 138.

40. "Goldfields «Aux mines d'or du Lac Athabasca»" *Missions* 70 (1936): pp. 66–67.

41. "Vicariat du Mackenzie," *Missions* 73 (1939): p. 405.

42. "Vicariat du Keewatin, Rapport annuel, 30 juin 1935–30 juin 1936," *Missions* 71 (1937): pp. 37–38.

43. Ibid., p. 39, "Vicariat du Keewatin," p. 387.

44. AD, HPK 2033 N82R 1, Jean-Baptiste Ducharme, OMI, Report on the Indians and Half-Breed Question, 10 August 1939, La Loche, Saskatchewan.

45. Ibid.

46. Murray Dobbin, *The One-And-A-Half Men: The Story of Jim Brady and Malcolm Norris Metis Patriots of the 20th Century* (Vancouver: New Star Books, 1981), ch. 4, "L'Association des Métis d'Alberta et des Territoires du Nord Ouest," pp. 54–65.

47. Ibid., p. 64.

48. "Vicariat de Grouard, "*Missions* 69 (1935): p. 445.

49. PAA, OMI, DP, I. Gauthier 1934–39, Gauthier to Blair, 24 July 1937, AD, L2681 A33R 1, Roméo Levert, Fishing Lake, p. 2.

50. AD, L 2681 A33R 1, Levert, Fishing Lake, p. 2.

51. Ibid.

52. PAA, OMI, Paroisses noninventoriées, Fishing Lake Correspondance 1939–50, Gauthier to Buck, 5 April 1940.

53. AD, L2681 A33R 1, Levert, Fishing Lake.

54. PAA, OMI, Paroisses noninventoriées, Fishing Lake Correspondance 1939–50, McNally to Levert, 22 Dec. 1942.

55. Ibid., Routhier to The Métis, Missionaries and People, 4 Jan. 1943.

56. Ibid., Gauthier to Maynard, 7 jan. 1943.

57. PAA, OMI, DP, I. Gauthier 1940–52, Rapport sur la situation des Métis, 1943.

58. PAA, OMI, DP, I. Gauthier 1934–39, Gauthier to Mon rév. père [Routhier], 22 fév. 1939.

59. AD, L 301 M275 16, Lessard to Joyal, Religious Vacation School, 23 Aug. 1935.

60. AD, L 301 M275 15, P. Dumouchel, G. Michaud, Catéchisme aux enfants métis, [1936].

61. AD, L 301 M27S 3, Welsh to Lamontagne, 27 oct. 1936.

62. AD, L 301 M27S 4, Lamontagne to Welsh, 29 nov. 1936.

63. AD, L 282 M27T 4, Welsh to Lamontagne, 2 nov. 1936.

64. AD, L 282 M27T 9, Memorandum of Agreement, 10 June 1940.

65. AD, L 282 M27T 17, Memorandum of Supplementary Agreement, 25 April 1941; ibid., Lamontagne to Dawson, 22 May 1941.

66. AD, L 282 M27T 24, Duplain to Parker, 2 Feb. 1943.

67. AD, L 282 M27T 23, Memorandum of Agreement, 1 Jan. 1943.

68. AD, L 282 M27T 30, Magnan to Lavigne, 17 fév. 1943.

69. AD, L 282 M27T 38, Jalbert to Lavigne, 19 déc. 1944.

70. AD, L 102 M27C 3, Procès verbal, Conseil provincial, Manitoba, 20–21 fév. 1945, p. 251.

71. AD, L 282 M27T 47, White to Franke, 15 Oct. 1945.

72. AD, L 282 M27T 48, Franke to White, 12 Oct. 1945.

73. AD, L 282 M27T 49, Silman to Dear Sir, 21 Oct. 1946, ibid., 50, Lavigne to Silman, 9 Nov. 1946.

74. *Acte général de la visite de la province d'Alberta-Saskatchewan, Avril-Octobre 1941* (Montréal: 1201 rue de la Visitation, 1942), p. 13.

75. Ibid., p. 16.

76. Ibid., p. 23.

77. Ibid., p. 18.

78. Ibid., p. 4.

79. Ibid., pp. 4–5.

80. Ibid., pp. 5–6.

81. Ibid., pp. 8–10. Catholic Action involved activities by lay groups under the authority and supervison of the local bishop. Within this context, Catholic Action "denotes a highly structured organization that serves as an arm of the hierarchy in lay life," see: "Catholic Action," *New Catholic Encyclopedia*, vol. 3, pp. 262–63.

82. Ibid., pp. 12–16.

83. Ibid., pp. 16–17. The club is only identified by its acronymn HIPC [possibly Hobbema Indian Progress Club?].

84. Ibid., pp. 18–19.

85. AD, L 2031 A33R 2, Victor Le Calvez, o.m.i., Quelques notes.

86. Ibid.

87. *Acte de la visite générale de la province du Manitoba, Mai-Octobre 1941*, p. 70.

88. Ibid., p. 77; AD, L 3 M27C 16, p. 5.

89. *Acte de la visite générale de la province du Manitoba, Mai-Octobre 1941*, pp. 73, 79–80.

90. AD, L 1052 M27K 148, Perreault to bien cher père [Lamontagne], 21 nov. 1936.

91. AD, L 1052 M27K 175, Tétrault to Lavigne, 8 oct. 1942.

92. PAA, OMI, Hobbema 141, Rhéaume to Plourde, 6 sept. 1939; ibid., Adm., St. Paul IRS, Blue Quills, Correspondence 1937–42, Balter to Routhier, 9 oct. 1939.

93. PAA, OMI, DP, C. Chataigner: Divers Documents, Réflexions sur l'avenir de nos oeuvres oblates."

94. PAA, OMI, DP, J. Angin: Divers, Mémoire sur l'évangélisation des Indiens, [1943].

95. PAA, OMI, DP, C. Chataigner: Divers Documents, évangélisation des Indiens et Métis.

96. PAA, OMI, Adm., Vicariat Apostolic Keewatin, Correspondance 1938–40, Rossignol to Mgr [Lajeunesse], 25 nov. 1938.

97. "Province du Manitoba," *Missions* 73 (1939): p. 307; "Vicariat de Grouard," ibid., pp. 415–16.

98. AD, LC 3 M14R 11, A. Autilly, Références sur les missions du Mackenzie, 1934; ibid., LC 3 M14R 4, Suzor to S.E. Mon. le Ministre des Affaires Étrangères, 10 juillet 1934.

99. "Vicariat du Keewatin," *Missions* 67 (1933): p. 224.

100. "L'avion au service du missionnaire," *Missions* 70 (1936): p. 177.

101. AD, LC 6003 K26R 8, "Au Pays du Keewatin," 22 juin au 31 juillet 1937," p. 1.

102. "Vicariat du Mackenzie," *Missions* 71 (1937): p. 385.

103. AD, HEB 1646 E24C 3, Ducharme to Chers parents et amis, 27 juin 1940. For an account of Oblate air travel in the Arctic consult William Leising, OMI, "Air Transportation in the Arctic," in *Western Oblate Studies 2 / Études Oblates de l'Ouest 2*, ed. by R. Huel (Lewiston: Edwin Mellen Press, 1992): pp. 31–36 and the same author's *Arctic Wings*.

104. In a political context George Potter argues that the United States' mission

to preach the gospel of democracy to the world failed because American freedom was based on abundance. When the concept of democracy is exported "to countries which see no means of attaining abundance, the message does not convey the message which it is meant to convey." There was a similar flaw in the preaching of the Christian message. David M. Potter, *People of Plenty: Economic Abundance and the American Character* (Chicago: University of Chicago Press, 1954), p. 127.

105. Dickason, *Canada's First Nations*, ch. 22, "Shift in Attitudes."

13 EPILOGUE: REDEFINING CHURCH AND SPIRITUALITY

1. Gresko, "Everyday Life at Qu'Appelle Industrial School," p. 94.
2. Titley, "Dunbow Indian Industrial School: An Oblate Experiment in Education," pp. 95–113.
3. Grant, *Moon of Wintertime*, p. 263.
4. Gaston Carrière, o.m.i., "Contribution des Oblats de Marie Immaculée de langue française aux études de linguistique et d'éthnologie du Nord canadien," *Culture* 12 (1951): pp. 213–26.
5. AD, LC 2109 G87R 2, Congrès missionnaire, Fahler, Alberta, 1966, p. 6.
6. Cf., Guertin to Rainville, 1 juillet 1877, *Missions* 16 (1878): pp. 193–97 on the Cariboo country of British Columbia; and Deltour to Martinet, 1 déc. 1879, *Missions* 18 (1880): pp. 213–23 on the Kaffirs of Basutoland; "Missions du Célan: Esquisse sur les Véders," *Missions* 10 (1872): pp. 36–47; "Rapport du Vicariat du Texas," *Missions* 11 (1873): pp. 420–29 on Mexicans north and south of the Rio Grande.
7. Vincent J. Donovan, CSSp., *Christianity Rediscovered* (Maryknoll, NY: Orbis Books, 1991).
8. "Le clergé indigène à Jaffna-Colombo," *Missions* 61 (1927): pp. 149–50.
9. Ibid., pp. 155–57.
10. "Ordination sacerdotale du premier Indien des tribus du traité, le R.P. Marvin Fox, o.m.i.," *Missions* 90 (1963): p. 98.
11. PAA, OMI, PP, V. Végréville, Reilly to Rev and Dear Sir [Végréville], 15 May 1890.
12. Ronnald P. Zimmer, OMI, "Early Oblate Attempts for Indian and Métis Priests in Canada," *Études Oblates* 32 (1973): pp. 277–83.
13. "Le R.P. Patrice Beaudry O.M.I., (1873–1947)," *Missions* 76 (1949): p. 92.
14. "Rapport du Rme Vicaire de l'Athabaska [sic]," *Missions* 61 (1927): p. 415. In 1939 the Vicariate of Grouard supported nine young boys at the juniorate in Edmonton, ibid., 72 (1939): p. 418.

15. AD, HF 225 C44R 2, Notes sur les vocations indigènes dans les missions du Nord-Ouest, p. 2.

16. Ibid., p. 5, 9.

17. AD, HEB 5675 G34C 23, Forbes to Very Rev. and Dear Father Provincial, 3 April 1942.

18. F. O'Grady, OMI, 16 April 1984, "Réactions au texte d'Achiel Peelman / Reaction to Achiel Peelman's Paper to the CCCB, September 1983," *Kerygma* 18 (1984): p. 120.

19. AD, HEB 5675 G34C 23, Forbes to Very Rev. and Dear Father Provincial, 3 April 1942.

20. C. Champagne, *Les débuts de la mission*, p. 241.

21. Zimmer, "Early Oblate Attempts," p. 287.

22. "Le clergé indigène à Jaffna-Colombo," *Missions* 61 (1927): p. 139.

23. Jacques Johnson, OMI, "Kisemanito Centre Training Native Men for the Priesthood," *Kerygma* 15 (1981): p. 111.

24. Ibid., p. 113. See also John Webster Grant, "Indian Missions as European Enclaves," *Sciences Religieuses / Studies in Religion* 8 (1978): p. 275.

25. Johnson, "Kisemanito," p. 113.

26. Ibid., p. 112.

27. Dianne Persson, "The Changing Experience of Indian Residential Schools: Blue Quills, 1931–1970," in *Indian Education in Canada*, vol. 1, *The Legacy*, ed. by Jean Barman et al (Vancouver: University of British Columbia Press, 1986), pp. 150–51.

28. Dickason, *Canada's First Nations*, pp. 336–37.

29. "La Semaine d'études des principaux d'écoles indiennnes," *Missions* 84 (1957): p. 83.

30. Yvon Levaque, OMI, "The Oblates and Indian Residential Schools," in *Western Oblate Studies 1 / Études Oblates de l'Ouest 1*, ed. by R. Huel (Edmonton: Western Canadian Publishers and Institut de recherche de la Faculté Saint-Jean, 1990), p. 188.

31. Persson, "The Changing Experience," p. 151.

32. Guy Voisin, o.m.i., "La coordination de l'activité missionnaire des oblats à travers le Canada: Le Conseil oblat des oeuvres indiennes et esquimaudes," *Kerygma* 2 (1968): p. 79.

33. AD, HR 8001 C73R 8, "Indianescom Past and Present," J.E.Y. Levaque, 7 Dec. 1973, pp. 2–3.

34. AD, HR 8001 C73R 10.

35. Dickason, *Canada's First Nations*, pp. 328–31.

36. Achiel Peelman, OMI, "The Mission of the Church After Vatican II and the Native Peoples of Canada," *Kerygma* 18 (1984): p. 2.

37. Achiel Peelman, o.m.i., "L'Émergence de l'Église aborigène au Canada: Un fait socio-culturel dans la société canadienne," *Kerygma* 16 (1982): p. 24.

38. Achiel Peelman, OMI, "The Amerindian Church: Dream or Reality?" Canadian Catholic Conference of Bishops, *Insight: A Journal for Adult Religious Education* (1987): p. 35; AD, HR 8001 C73R 1, "Indianescom Past and Present," J.E.Y. Levaque, 7 Dec. 1973.

39. Peelman, "The Amerindian Church," cited on p. 35.

40. Peelman, "L'Émergence de l'Église aborigène," pp. 26–27. The emergence of the "Third Church" also coincided with the coming of age of the Third World in international affairs. Peelman also argued that if the Oriental Church dominated for the first thousand years and the Western Church for the second thousand then the third millenia belongs to the faithful of the Third World. Consult A. Peelman, "The Mission of the Church," p. 3.

41. Peelman, "L'Émergence de l'Église aborigène," p. 27.

42. Ibid., p. 28.

43. Peelman, "The Mission of the Church," pp. 4–5.

44. Ibid., pp. 2–3.

45. "Réactions au texte d'Achiel Peelman / Reactions to Achiel Peelman's paper," *Kerygma* 18 (1984): pp. 106–24.

46. Ibid.

47. Ibid., p. 155.

48. Ibid., p. 161.

49. René Jaouen, OMI, "Conditions for Authentic Inculturation: Some Observations of a Missionary in Cameroun," *Kerygma* 19 (1985): p. 4, p. 6.

50. Ibid., pp. 9–11, italics in original. Once this encounter has taken place, the missionary must verify that the resulting church is an authentic expression of the faith. Directions and guidelines for inculturation and verification are to be found in Francis E. George, OMI, "The Process of Inculturation: Steps, Rules, Problems," *Kerygma* 22 (1988): pp. 93–113.

51. Johnson, "Kisemanito Centre," pp. 114–15.

52. Ibid., p. 115.

53. "Missions of the Canadian North: Statement by the Bishops of the Eight Dioceses of the Canadian North at the Plenary Assembly of the Canadian Conference of Catholic Bishops in 1985," *Kerygma* 21 (1987): pp. 128–29.

54. Peelman, "The Amerindian Church," p. 34.

55. For an insightful analysis consult Miller, "Native Residential Schools in Historical Context."

56. Robert Carney's study of residential schools at Ft. Chipewyan and Ft. Resolution demonstrates that "only a minority of school-age Métis

and Indian children" attended these institutions (p. 125). Examining school registers, Carney concludes that "the average time in school was about four years for boys and about five for girls" (p. 127). Only three per cent of children enrolled at Ft. Resolution (Saint Joseph's) reached grade six and the figures for Ft. Chipewyan (Holy Angels) are similar (p. 127). Robert Carney, "Residential Schooling at Fort Chipewyan and Fort Resolution 1874–1974"; in *Western Oblate Studies 2 / Études Oblates de l'Ouest 2*, ed. by R. Huel (Lewiston: Edwin Mellen Press, 1992): pp. 115–38; Brian Titley, in "Dunbow Indian Industrial School: An Oblate Experiment in Education,"demonstrates that Dunbow opened its doors in 1884 with eight students and admitted 156 between 1884 and 1892 and discharged 79. Of this number, 49 "had not stayed long enough to be affected by the experience" (p. 101). The highest enrolment, 120 students, occurred in 1895 (p. 101), followed by a gradual decline: 1897, 117; 1899, 90; 1901, 75 (p. 103); 1915, 47; 1917, 39 (p. 109). Jacqueline Gresko states that only 25 to 30 per cent of eligible Indian pupils attended Qu'Appelle between 1884 and the 1900s and that the majority attained only a grade four level, "Everyday Life at Qu'Appelle Industrial School," p. 81.

57. Sluman, *John Tootoosis*, pp. 95–97.
58. Eleanor Brass, *I Walk in Two Worlds* (Calgary: Glenbow-Alberta Institute, 1987), p. 14.
59. Sluman, *John Tootoosis*, p. 103.
60. Ibid.
61. "An Apology to the First Nations of Canada by the Oblate Conference of Canada," in *Western Oblate Studies 2 / Études Oblates de l'Ouest 2*, ed. by R. Huel (Lewiston: Edwin Mellen Press, 1992): p. 262.

△ △

BIBLIOGRAPHY

The majority of documents consulted in the preparation of this book were housed in Oblate archives. The central archives of the Oblate order in Canada are the *Archives Deschâtelets* located in Ottawa and they contain documents pertaining to all Oblate jurisdictions, including the archives of the Oblate Province of Manitoba. The *Archives oblates de Montréal* are administrative archives but, nevertheless, contain valuable information on the early Oblate missions in the Canadian North West. Material from the former Alberta-Saskatchewan Province is currently housed in the Provincial Archives of Alberta in Edmonton. Other relevant manuscript collections consulted in the National Archives of Canada include the records of the Department of Indian Affairs, the Hudson's Bay Company and the John A. Macdonald papers. The Hayter Reed papers were consulted to a lesser extent as were the Archives of the Anglican Church of Canada and the United Church of Canada. Time did not permit an examination of the voluminous archives of the female religious communities associated with the Oblates. Researchers interested in a more detailed analysis of some of the themes identified in the Preface and other parts of this study should be prepared to consult those sources that were not central to this specific study on the Oblates.

An excellent overview of the encounter between Christian missionaries and Native populations is to be found in John Webster Grant's *Moon of*

Wintertime. The Native perspective is lacking in most studies but Olive Dickason's well documented *Canada's First Nations: A History of Founding Peoples from the Earliest Times* will initiate the reader. The Oblates themselves were prolific in their production of memoirs and reminiscences but these have not been consulted extensively for reasons indicated in the Preface. An obvious exception is Alexandre-Antonin Taché's *Vingt années de missions dans le Nord-Ouest de l'Amérique* that was more contemporary and compiled as a report.

No serious study of the Oblates can be undertaken without consulting *Missions de la Congrégation des Missionnaires Oblats de Marie Immaculée*. This quarterly publication has appeared since 1862 and contains valuable information on the missions of the North West as well as reports from missionaries in the field. Specialized articles on the Oblates, their apostolate and spirituality, are to be found in *Vie Oblate Life*, formally *Études Oblates*. The new missiology evident since the sessions of Vatican II are reflected in the pages of *Kerygma* initiated in 1966 as a medium of communication between Oblate missionaries.

OBLATE REPORTS AND PUBLICATIONS

Acte de la visite générale de la province du Manitoba par le T.R.P. Rousseau, O.M.I. *Mai-Octobre 1941.*

Acte de visite du R.P. Soullier, premier assistant général pour le vicariat de Saint-Albert. Octobre 1883. St-Albert: Typographie privée O.M.I., [1885].

Acte de visite du vicariat d'Athabasca 1912, R.P. W.J. Murphy, o.m.i., Visiteur. Bordeaux: Imprimerie Victor Cambette, 1913.

Acte général de la visite de la province d'Alberta-Saskatchewan, avril-octobre 1941. Montréal: 1201 rue de la Visitation, 1942.

Acte général de visite des missions indiennes du Nord-Ouest canadien par le T.R.P. Théodore Labouré O.M.I., Supérieur Général, Juin 1935–Février 1936. Rome: Maison Générale, 1936.

Acte général de visite du vicariat apostolique d'Athabasca-Mackenzie par le R.P. Antoine, o.m.i., Assistant Général, Mai-Sept. 1895. Paris: Typographie privée O.M.I., 1895.

Acte générale des visites canoniques faites dans le vicariat de Saint-Albert. Paris: Typographie privée O.M.I., 1885.

Audruger, Alexandre, o.m.i. *Directoire pour les missions à l'usage des Missionnaires Oblats de Marie Immaculée.* Tours: A. Mame et Fils, 1881.

Champagne, Joseph-Étienne, o.m.i. *Manuel d'action missionnaire*. Ottawa: Éditions de l'Université d'Ottawa, 1947.

Constitutiones Et Regulæ Congregationis Missionariorum Oblatorum Sanctissimæ Et Immaculatæ Virginis Mariae. Parisiis: E Typis priv. O.M.I., 1887.

de Mazenod, Bx. *Lettres aux correspondants d'Amérique, 1841–1850*. Écrits Oblats I. Rome: Postulation générale O.M.I., 1977.

———. *Lettres aux correspondants d'Amérique, 1851–1860*. Écrits Oblats II. Rome: Postulation générale O.M.I., 1977.

———. *Lettres à la Sacrée Congrégation et à l'Oeuvre de la Propagation de la Foi, 1832–1861*. Écrits Oblats V. Rome: Postulation générale O.M.I., 1981.

Instruction de notre Vénéré Fondateur relative aux missions étrangères. Rome: Maison générale, 1936.

Lajeunesse, Martin, o.m.i. *Directives missionnaires*. le Pas: Évêché, 1942.

BOOKS

Allaire, Gratien, Gilles Cadrin and Paul Dubè. *Après Dix Ans . . . Bilan et Prospective*. Les actes du onzième colloque du Centre d'études franco-canadiennes de l'Ouest. Edmonton: Institut de recherche de la Faculté Saint-Jean, 1992.

Axtell, James. *The Invasion Within: The Contest of Cultures in Colonial North America*. New York: Oxford University Press, 1985.

Anderson, James T.M. *The Education of the New Canadian: A Treatise on Canada's Greatest Educational Problem*. Toronto: J.M. Dent & Sons, 1918.

Barman, Jean, Yvonne Hèbert and Don McCaskill, eds. *Indian Education in Canada*. Vol. 1, *The Legacy*. Vancouver: University of British Columbia Press, 1986.

Berkhofer, R.F., Jr. *Salvation and the Savage: An Analysis of Protestant Missions and American Indian Responses, 1787–1862*. Lexington: University of Kentucky Press, 1965.

Brass, Eleanor. *I Walk in Two Worlds*. Calgary: Glenbow-Alberta Institute, 1987.

Breton, Paul-Émile, OMI. *The Big Chief of the Prairies: The Life of Father Lacombe*. [Edmonton?]: Palm Publishers, [1955].

———. *Blacksmith of God*. Edmonton: Éditions de l'Ermitage, 1960.

———. *Le grand chef des prairies: Le père Albert Lacombe, o.m.i., 1827–1916*. Edmonton: Éditions de l'Ermitage, 1954.

———. *Vital Grandin: La merveilleuse aventure de l'évêque des Prairies et du Grand Nord*. Bibliothèque Ecclesia 58. Paris: Librairie Arthème Fayard, 1960.

Bourassa, Henri. *La langue gardienne de la foi.* Montréal: Bibliothèque de l'Action française, n.d.

Breynat, Gabriel, OMI. *Bishop of the Winds: Fifty Years in the Arctic Region.* New York: P.J. Kennedy, [ca. 1955].

———. *Cinquante ans aux pays des neiges.* 3 vols. Montréal: Fides, 1945–48.

———. *Évêque volant: Cinquante ans au Grand Nord.* Paris: Amiot-Dumont, 1953.

Carrière, Gaston, o.m.i. *L'Apôtre des Prairies: Joseph Hugonnard, o.m.i., 1848–1917.* Montréal: Rayonnement, 1967.

———. *Dictionnaire biographique des Oblates de Marie Immaculée au Canada.* 3 vols. Éditions de l'Université d'Ottawa, 1976–79.

———. *Histoire documentaire de la Congrégation des Missionnaires Oblats de Marie-Immaculée dans l'Est du Canada.* Vol. 3. Ottawa: Les Éditions de l'Université d'Ottawa, 1961.

———. *Le père du Keewatin: Mgr Ovide Charlebois, o.m.i., 1862–1933.* Montréal: Rayonnement, 1962.

Carter, Sarah. *Lost Harvests: Prairie Indian Reserve Farmers and Government Policy.* Montreal and Kingston: McGill-Queen's University Press, 1990.

Champagne, Claude, o.m.i. *Les débuts de la mission dans le Nord-Ouest canadien: Mission et Église chez Mgr Vital Grandin, o.m.i., 1829–1902.* Ottawa: Éditions de l'Université d'Ottawa, 1983.

Champagne, Joseph-Étienne, o.m.i. *Les missions catholiques dans l'Ouest canadien (1818–1875).* Ottawa: Éditions des *Études Oblates,* 1949.

Cronin, Kay. *Cross in the Wilderness.* Toronto: Mission Press, 1976.

Crunican, Paul. *Priests and Politicians: Manitoba Schools and the Election of 1896.* Toronto: University of Toronto Press, 1974.

Delalande, Lucien, o.m.i. *Sous le soleil de minuit.* Montréal: Rayonnement, 1958.

D[e]. L[a]. S[eine]. [Morice, Adrien-Gabriel, OMI]. *Fifty Years in Western Canada: Being the Abridged Memoirs of A.G. Morice, O.M.I.* Toronto: Ryerson Press, 1930.

de Trémaudan, Auguste-Henri. *Histoire de la nation Métisse dans l'Ouest canadien.* Montréal: Éditions Albert Lévesque, 1936.

———. *Hold High Your Heads (History of the Métis Nation in Western Canada).* Trans. by E. Maguet. Winnipeg: Pemmican Publications, 1982.

Dickason, Olive. *Canada's First Nations: A History of Founding Peoples From the Earliest Times.* Toronto: McClelland and Stewart, 1992.

Dobbin, Murray. *The One-And-A-Half Men: The Story of Jim Brady and Malcolm Norris, Metis Patriots of the 20th Century.* Vancouver: New Star Books, 1981.

Dolphin, Frank. *Indian Bishop of the West: The Story of Vital Justin Grandin, 1829–1902*. Ottawa: Novalis, 1986.

Dom Benoit, c.r.i.c. [Augustin, Joseph-Paul]. *Vie de Mgr Taché, Archevêque de St-Boniface*. Vol. 1 and 2. Montréal: Librairie Beauchemin, 1904.

Donovan, Vincent J., CSSp. *Christianity Rediscovered*. Maryknoll, NY: Orbis Books, 1991.

Duchaussois, Pierre, OMI. *Hidden Apostles: Our Lay Brother Missionaries*. Buffalo, NY: Missionary Oblates of Mary Immaculate, 1937.

———. *Mid Snow and Ice: The Apostles of the North-West*. London: Burns, Oates and Washbourne, 1923.

Frémont, Donatien. *Monseigneur Provencher et son temps*. Winnipeg: Éditions de La Liberté, 1935.

Fernand-Michel [Fortuné, François]. *Dix-huit ans chez les sauvages: voyages et missions dans l'Extrême Nord de l'Amérique britannique*. Paris: Régis Ruffert et Cie, 1870.

Flanagan, Thomas. *Louis "David" Riel: Prophet of the New World*. Toronto: University of Toronto Press, 1979.

———. *Riel and the Rebellion: 1885 Reconsidered*. Saskatoon: Western Producer Prairie Books, 1983.

Gagnon, François-Marc. *La conversion par l'image: Un aspect de la mission des Jésuites auprès des Indiens du Canada au XVII Siècle*. Montréal: Éditions Bellarmin, 1975.

Gilbert, Maurice, o.m.i., and Normand Martel, o.m.i. *Dictionnaire biographique des Oblates de Marie Immaculée au Canada*. Tome 4. Montréal: Maison provinciale, 1989.

Grant, John Webster, *Moon of Wintertime: Missionaries and the Indians of Canada in Encounter Since 1534*. Toronto: University of Toronto Press, 1984.

Greenshields, Malcolm, and Thomas Robinson, eds. *Orthodoxy and Heresy in Religious Movements: Discipline and Dissent*. Centre for the Study of North American Religion Series, no. 2. Lewiston: Edwin Mellen Press, 1992.

Grouard, Émile, o.m.i. *Souvenirs de mes soixante ans d'apostolat dans l'Athabasca-Mackenzie*. Winnipeg: La Liberté, 1922; Lyon: Oeuvre Apostolique de Marie Immaculée, [1922].

Gualtieri, Antonio. *Christianity and Native Traditions: Indigenization and Syncretism Among the Inuit and Dene of the Western Arctic*. Vol. 2, *The Church and the World*. Notre Dame, Indiana: Cross Road Books, 1984.

Hanley, Philip M. *History of the Catholic Ladder*. Ed. by Edward J. Kowrach. Fairfield, WA: Ye Galleon Press, 1994.

Harrod, Howard L. *Mission Among the Blackfeet*. The Civilization of the

American Indian Series, vol. 122. Norman, OK: University of Oklahoma Press, [1971].

Huel, Raymond, ed. *Western Oblate Studies 1 / Études Oblates de l'Ouest 1.* Edmonton: Western Canadian Publishers and Institut de recherche de la Faculté Saint-Jean, 1990.

———, ed. *Western Oblate Studies 2 / Études Oblates de l'Ouest 2,* Centre for the Study of North American Religion Series, no. 1. Lewiston: Edwin Mellen Press, 1992.

———, ed. *Western Oblate Studies 3 / Études Oblates de l'Ouest 3.* Edmonton: Western Canadian Publishers, 1994.

Jonquet, Émile, o.m.i. *Mgr Grandin, o.m.i., Premier évêque de Saint-Albert.* Montréal: 20 rue Saint-Vincent, 1903.

Kennedy, Dan (Ochankugahe). *Recollections of an Assiniboine Chief.* Toronto: McClelland and Stewart, 1972.

Lacombe, Albert, o.m.i. *Le catéchisme en images pour l'instruction des sauvages.* Montréal: Imprimerie de l'Asile de la Providence, 1874.

Le Chevalier, Jules, o.m.i. *Saint-Michel de Duck Lake: Épreuves et progrès d'une école indienne durant un demi-siècle, 1894–1944.* Edmonton: Imprimerie de *La Survivance,* 1944.

Leising, William, OMI. *Arctic Wings.* Garden City, NY: Echo Books (Doubleday), 1965.

Levasseur, Donat, o.m.i. *Les Constitutions et Règles des Missionnaires Oblats de Marie Immaculée à la lumière de Vatican II.* Bibliothèque Oblate XV. Ottawa: Éditions des Études Oblates, 1967.

———. *Histoire des Missionnaires Oblats de Marie Immaculée: Essaie de Synthèse.* Vol. 1, 1815–1898. Montréal: Maison Provinciale O.M.I., 1983.

———. *Les Oblats de Marie Immaculée dans l'Ouest et le Nord du Canada, 1845–1967.* Edmonton: University of Alberta Press, 1994.

McCarthy, Martha. *From the Great River to the Ends of the Earth: Oblate Missions to the Dene, 1847–1921.* Edmonton: University of Alberta Press, 1995.

———. *To Evangelize the Nations: Roman Catholic Missions in Manitoba, 1818–1870.* Papers in Manitoba History, Report No. 2. Winnipeg: Manitoba Culture, Heritage and Recreation Historic Resources, 1990.

Macleod, Rod C., ed. *Swords and Ploughshares: War and Agriculture in Western Canada.* Edmonton: University of Alberta Press, 1993.

Meyer, Patricia, ed. *Honoré-Timothée Lempfrit, O.M.I.: His Oregon Trail Journal and Letters from the Pacific Northwest, 1848–1853.* Fairfield, Washington: Ye Galleon Press, 1985.

Morice, Adrien-Gabriel, o.m.i. *Souvenirs d'un missionnaire en Colombie britannique.* Winnipeg: Chez l'auteur, 1933.

———. *La race métisse: Étude critique en marge d'un livre récent.* Winnipeg: Chez l'auteur, 1938.

Mulhall, David. *Will to Power: The Missionary Career of Father Morice.* Vancouver: University of British Columbia Press, 1986.

Muise, David A. *Approaches to Native History in Canada.* Ottawa: National Museums of Man, Mercury Series, History Division paper no. 25, 1977.

Nigg, Walter. *The Heretics.* Ed. and trans. by Richard and Clara Winston. New York: A. Knopf, 1962.

Nock, David A. *A Victorian Missionary and Canadian Indian Policy: Cultural Synthesis vs. Cultural Replacement.* Editions SR/9. Waterloo: Wilfrid Laurier University Press, 1988.

Nute, Grace L., ed. *Documents Relating to the Northwest Mission, 1815–1827.* St. Paul: Minnesota Historical Society, 1942.

Owens, Brian and Claude Roberto, eds. *The Diaries of Bishop Vital Grandin, 1875–1877.* Vol. 1. Trans. Alan D. Ridge. Edmonton: The Historical Society of Alberta, Amisk Waskahegan Chapter, 1989.

Pannekoek, Frits. *A Snug Little Flock: The Social Origins of the Riel Resistance, 1869–70.* Winnipeg: Watson and Dwyer Publishing, 1991.

Payment, Diane. *Batoche (1870–1910).* Saint-Boniface: Les Éditions du Blé, 1983.

Potter, George. *People of Plenty: Economic Abundance and the American Character.* Chicago: University of Chicago Press, 1954.

Rasporich, Anthony W. *Western Canada Past and Present.* Calgary: McClelland and Stewart West, 1975.

Sluman, Norma. *John Tootoosis as told by Jean Goodwill and Norma Sluman.* Winnipeg: Pemmican Publications, 1984.

La Société Historique de Saint-Boniface. *Histoire de Saint-Boniface.* Tome 1, *A l'ombre des cathédrales: Des origines de la colonie jusqu'en 1870.* Saint-Boniface: Les Éditions du Blé, 1991.

Sprague, Douglas N. *Canada and the Métis, 1869–1885.* Waterloo: Wilfrid Laurier Press, 1988.

Stanley, George F.G. *Louis Riel.* Toronto: Ryerson Press, 1963.

Une Soeur de la Providence. *Le Père Lacombe «L'Homme au bon coeur» d'après ses mémoires et souvenirs.* Montréal: au *Devoir*, 1916.

Taché, Alexandre-Antonin, o.m.i. *Esquisse sur le Nord-Ouest de l'Amérique.* 2e éd. Montréal: Beauchemin et Fils, 1901.

———. *Vingt années de missions dans le Nord-Ouest de l'Amérique.* Montréal: Eusèbe Senécal, 1866.

Titley, Brian. *A Narrow Vision: Duncan Campbell Scott and the Administration of Indian Affairs in Canada.* Vancouver: UBC Press, 1986.

Trigger, Bruce. *Natives and Newcomers: Canada's "Heroic Age" Reconsidered.* Montreal: McGill-Queen's University Press, 1986.

Venini Byrne, M.B. *From the Buffalo to the Cross: A History of the Diocese of Calgary.* Calgary: Calgary Archives and Historical Publishers, ca. 1973.

Whitehead, Margaret. *The Caribou Mission: A History of the Oblates.* Victoria: Sono Nis Press, 1981.

———, ed. *They Call Me Father: The Memoirs of Father Nicolas Cocolla.* Vancouver: University of British Columbia Press, 1988.

Zaslow, Morris. *The Opening of the Canadian North, 1870–1914.* The Canadian Centenary Series, vol. 16. Toronto: McClelland and Stewart, 1971.

ARTICLES AND PRESENTATIONS

"An Apology to the First Nations of Canada by the Oblate Conference of Canada." In *Western Oblate Studies 2/ Études Oblates de l'Ouest 2*, ed. by R. Huel (Lewiston: Edwin Mellen Press, 1992): 259–62.

Axtell, James. "Some Thoughts on the Ethnohistory of Mission." *Ethnohistory* 29 (1982): 35–41.

Beaumont, J.-C., J. Gadille, and Xavier de Montclos. "L'Exportation des modèles de christianisme français à l'époque contemporaine. Pour une nouvelle problématique de l'histoire missionnaire." *Revue d'Histoire de l'Église de France* 63 (1977): 5–23.

Benoit, Barbara. "The Mission at Île-à-la-Crosse." *The Beaver* (Winter 1980): 40–50.

Brass, Eleanor. "The File Hills Ex-Pupil Colony." *Saskatchewan History* 6 (1953): 66–69.

Breton, Paul-Émile, o.m.i. "Le Fondateur des Oblats d'après les écrits de Mgr Grandin." *Études Oblates* 18 (1959): 331–62.

Carrière, Gaston, o.m.i. "Contribution des missionnaires à la sauvegarde de la culture indienne." *Études Oblates* 31 (1972): 165–204.

———. "Contribution des Oblats de Marie Immaculée de langue française aux études de linguistique et d'éthnologie du Nord canadien." *Culture* 12 (1951): 213–26.

———. "Fondation et développement des missions catholiques dans la Terre de Rupert et les Territoires du Nord-Ouest." *Revue de l'Université d'Ottawa* 41 (1971): 253–81, 397–427.

———. "L'Honorable Compagnie de la Baie-d'Hudson et les mission dans l'Ouest canadien." Société Canadienne d'Histoire de l'Église Catholique, *Sessions d'Études* 32 (1965): 63–80.

———. "L'Honorable Compagnie de la Baie d'Hudson et les missions dans l'Ouest canadien." *Revue de l'Université d'Ottawa* 36 (1966): 15–39, 232–57.

———. "Letter from Bishop Alexandre Taché to his Mother Concerning his Life with the Chipewyan Nation [4 Jan. 1851]." *Prairie Forum* 3 (1978): 131–56.

———. "Méthodes et réalisations missionnaires des Oblats dans l'Est du Canada (1841–1861)." *Études Oblates* 16 (1957): 37–65.

———. "Une mission de paix: le père André et les Sioux, 1863–1865." *Études Oblates* 27 (1968): 189–224, 299–340.

———. "Mgr Ignace Bourget et les Oblats." *Revue de l'Université d'Ottawa* 30 (1960): 400–420.

———. "Le père Albert Lacombe, o.m.i., et le Pacifique canadien." *Revue de l'Université d'Ottawa* 37 (1967): 287–321, 510–39, 611–38; 38 (1968): 97–131, 316–50.

———. "La réponse des Oblats de l'Ouest canadien à la perception de la «mission» chez Mgr de Mazenod." *Vie Oblate Life* 42 (1983): F193–213.

Carter, Sarah. "Demonstrating Success: The File Hills Farm Colony." *Prairie Forum* 16 (1991): 157–83.

Champagne, Claude, o.m.i. "La formation des Oblats, missionnaires dans le Nord-Ouest canadien." Société Canadienne d'histoire de l'Église Catholique, *Sessions d'Études* 56 (1989): 21–33.

Champagne, Emery, p.b. "Le missionnaire, ses qualités sa préparation." *Semaines d'études missionnaires* (Ottawa: Le Secrétariat, Université d'Ottawa, 1934): 171–90.

Champagne, Joseph-Étienne, o.m.i. "Aux origines de la mission de la rivière Rouge (1818–1845)." *Études Oblates* 4 (1945): 37–59.

———. "Les méthodes missionnaires dans l'Ouest canadien, 1845–75." *Études Oblates* 5 (1946): 143–60.

Choquette, Robert. "Les rapports entre catholiques et protestants dans le Nord-Ouest du Canada avant 1840." In *Western Oblate Studies 1 / Études Oblates de l'Ouest 1*, ed. by R. Huel (Edmonton: Western Canadian Publishers and Institut de recherche de la Faculté Saint-Jean, 1990): 129–40.

Crunican, Paul. "Father Lacombe's Strange Mission: The Lacombe-Langevin Correspondence on the Manitoba School Question." Canadian Catholic Historical Association, *Report* 26 (1959): 57–72.

"Feu le R.P. Joachim Allard, o.m.i." *Les Cloches de Saint-Boniface* 16 (1917): 21, 52–56.

Foster, John E. "*Le missionnaire* and *le chef Métis*." In *Western Oblate Studies 1 / Études Oblates de l'Ouest 1*, ed. by R. Huel (Edmonton: Western Canadian Publishers and Institut de recherche de la Faculté Saint-Jean, 1990): 117–27.

Francis, E. George, OMI. "The Process of Inculturation: Steps, Rules, Problems." *Kerygma* 22 (1988): 93–113.

Grant, John Webster. "Indian Missions as European Enclaves." *Sciences Religieuses / Studies in Religion* 8 (1978): 263–75.

Gresko, Jaqueline. "Creating Little Dominions Within the Dominion: Early Catholic Schools in Saskatchewan and British Columbia." In *Indian Education in Canada*, vol. 1, *The Legacy*, ed. by Jean Barman et al, 88–109. Vancouver: University of British Columbia Press, 1986.

———. "White 'Rites' and Indian 'Rites': Indian Education and Native Responses in the West, 1870–1919." In *Western Canada Past and Present*, ed. by A. Rasporich, 163–82. Calgary: McClelland and Stewart West, 1975.

Hanley, Philip M. "Father Lacombe's Ladder." *Études Oblates* 32 (1973): 82–99.

Huel, Raymond. "The Chipewyan Prophets, Louis Riel, and the Oblates of Mary Immaculate: Who Were The True Heralds of the Word in the Canadian North West?" In *Orthodoxy and Heresy in Religious Movements: Discipline and Dissent*, ed. by M. Greenshields and T. Robinson, 93–119. Lewiston: Edwin Mellen Press, 1992.

———. "The Irish-French Conflict in Catholic Episcopal Nominations: The Western Sees and the Struggle for Domination Within the Church." Canadian Catholic Historical Association, *Study Sessions* 42 (1975): 50–70.

———. "The French Language Press in Western Canada: *Le Patriote de l'Ouest, 1910–41.*" *Revue de l'Université d'Ottawa* 46 (1976): 476–99.

———. "Jean L'Heureux canadien errant et prétendu missionnaire auprès des Pieds-noirs." In *Après Dix Ans . . . Bilan et Prospective*, ed. by G. Allaire et al, 207–22. Edmonton: Institut de recherche de la Faculté Saint-Jean, 1992.

———. "Louis Schmidt Patriarch of St. Louis." *Saskatchewan History* 40 (1987): 1–21.

———. "La mission Notre-Dame des Victoires du lac la Biche et l'approvisionnement des missions du nord: le conflit entre Mgr V. Grandin et Mgr H. Faraud." In *Western Oblate Studies 1 / Études Oblates de l'Ouest 1*, ed. by R. Huel (Edmonton: Western Canadian Publishers and Institut de recherche de la Faculté Saint-Jean, 1990): 17–36.

"Indian and Eskimo Commission Observes Silver Jubilee." *Agence romaine des Oblats de Marie Immaculée*, Nov. 1961.

Jaenen, Cornelius. "Missionary Approaches to Native Peoples." In *Approaches to Native History*, ed. by D.A. Muise. Ottawa: National Museums of Man, Mercury Series, History Division Paper No. 25, 1977, 5–15.

Jaouen, René, OMI. "Conditions for Authentic Inculturation: Some Observations of a Missionary in Cameroun." *Kerygma* 19 (1985): 3–15.

Johnson, Jacques, OMI. "Kisemanito Centre Training Native Men for the Priesthood." *Kerygma* 15 (1981): 111–22.

Lamirande, Émilien, o.m.i. "L'Annonce de la parole de Dieu selon Mgr de Mazenod. Le ministère évangélique de la Congrégation." *Études Oblates* 18 (1959): 105–26.

———. "Le père Honoré-Timothée Lempfrit: son ministère auprès des autochtones de l'île de Vancouver (1849–1852)." In *Western Oblate Studies 1 / Études Oblates de l'Ouest 1*, ed. by R. Huel (Edmonton: Western Canadian Publishers and Institut de recherche de la Faculté Saint-Jean, 1990): 53–70.

Leising, William, OMI. "Air Transportation in the Arctic." In *Western Oblate Studies 2 / Études Oblates de l'Ouest 2*, ed. by R. Huel (Lewiston: Edwin Mellen Press, 1992): 33–36.

Leonard, David. "Anglican and Oblate: The Quest for Souls in the Peace River Country 1867–1900." In *Western Oblate Studies 3 / Études Oblates de l'Ouest 3*, ed. by R. Huel (Edmonton: Western Canadian Publishers, 1994): 119–38.

Levaque, Yvon, OMI. "The Oblates and Indian Residential Schools." In *Western Oblate Studies 1 / Études Oblates de l'Ouest 1*, ed. by R. Huel (Edmonton: Western Canadian Publishers and Institut de recherche de la Faculté Saint-Jean, 1990): 181–91.

Lewis, Maurice. "The Anglican Church and its Mission School Dispute." *Alberta Historical Review* 14 (1966): 7–13.

MacKinnon, Joan. "Oblate House Chapels in the Vicariate of Athabasca-Mackenzie." *Western Oblate Studies 2 / Études Oblates de l'Ouest 2*, ed. by R. Huel (Lewiston: Edwin Mellen Press, 1992): 219–30.

McCarthy, Martha. "The Founding of Providence Mission." In *Western Oblate Studies 1 / Études Oblates de l'Ouest 1*, ed. by R. Huel (Edmonton: Western Canadian Publishers and Institut de recherche de la Faculté Saint-Jean, 1990): 37–49.

McGovern, Margaret, SP. "Perspective on the Oblates: The Experience of the Sisters of Providence." In *Western Oblate Studies 3 / Études Oblates de l'Ouest 3*, ed. by R. Huel (Edmonton: Western Canadian Publishers, 1994): 91–108.

McNally, Vincent. "A Lost Opportunity? A Study of Relations Between the Native People and the Diocese of Victoria." In *Western Oblate Studies 2 / Études Oblates de l'Ouest 2*, ed. by R. Huel (Lewiston: Edwin Mellen Press, 1992): 159–78.

Miller, James R. "The Irony of Residential Schooling." *Canadian Journal of Native Education* 14 (1987): 3–14.

"Missions of the Canadian North: Statement by the Bishops of the Eight

Dioceses of the Canadian North at the Plenary Assembly of the Canadian Conference of Catholic Bishops in 1985." *Kerygma* 21 (1987): 127–31.

Morton, W.L. "The Battle at the Grand Coteau, July 13 and 14, 1851." *Papers Read Before the Historical and Scientific Society of Manitoba*, Series III, 16 (1961): 37–49.

Peelman, Achiel, o.m.i. "L'Émergence de l'Église aborigène au Canada: Un fait socio-culturel dans la société canadienne." *Kerygma* 16 (1982): 17–33.

———. "The Amerindian Church: Dream or Reality?" Canadian Catholic Conference of Bishops, *Insight: A Journal for Adult Religious Education* (1987): 34–40.

———. "The Mission of the Church After Vatican II and the Native Peoples of Canada." *Kerygma* 18 (1984): 1–9.

Persson, Dianne. "The Changing Experience of Indian Residential Schools: Blue Quills, 1931–1970." In *Indian Education in Canada*, vol. 1, *The Legacy*, ed. by Jean Barman et al, 150–67. Vancouver: University of British Columbia Press, 1986.

Philippot, Aristide, o.m.i., "Mgr H.-J. Faraud, o.m.i., 1823–1890." *L'Ami du foyer* (Sept. 1959): 10.

Pielorz, Josef, o.m.i. "L'affirmation: «Les Oblats sont les spécialistes des missions difficiles» est-elle de Pie XI?" *Vie Oblate Life* 51 (1992): 99–101.

Pouliot, Léon, s.j. "Mgr Ignace Bourget et la mission de la Rivière Rouge." Société Canadienne d'Histoire de l'Église Catholique, *Sessions d'Études* 37 (1970): 17–30.

Quenneville, Jean-Guy. "Le R.P. Alexis André, o.m.i., et quelques autres plénipotentiaires auprès des Sioux." In *Western Oblate Studies 2 / Études Oblates de l'Ouest 2*, ed. by R. Huel (Lewiston: Edwin Mellen Press, 1992): 51–70.

Quéré, Martin, o.m.i. "Monseigneur de Mazenod et le missionnaire oblat." *Études Oblates* 20 (1961): 237–70.

"Réactions au texte d'Achiel Peelman / Reaction to Achiel Peelman's Paper to the CCCB, September 1983." *Kerygma* 18 (1984): 106–24.

Roberto, Claude. "Relations entre les Oblats et les autres communautés religieuses dans le fonds oblat de l'Alberta-Saskatchewan." In *Western Oblate Studies 3 / Études Oblates de l'Ouest 3*, ed. by R. Huel (Edmonton: Western Canadian Press, 1994): 65–73.

Roy, D. "Monseigneur Provencher et son clergé séculier." Société Canadienne d'Histoire de l'Église Catholique, *Sessions d'Études* 37 (1970): 1–16.

Titley, Brian. "Dunbow Indian Industrial School: An Oblate Experiment in Education." In *Western Oblate Studies 2 / Études Oblates de l'Ouest 2*, ed. by

R. Huel (Edmonton: Western Canadian Publishers and Institut de recherche
de la Faculté Saint-Jean, 1990): 95–114.

———. "Hayter Reed and Indian Administration in the West." In *Swords and
Ploughshares: War and Agriculture in Western Canada*, ed. by R.C. Macleod,
109–47. Edmonton: University of Alberta Press, 1993.

Turquetil, Arsène, o.m.i. "Le mariage chez les Esquimaux en regard des facultés de
dispense accordées aux missionnaires." *Revue de l'Université d'Ottawa* 5 (1935).

Tourigny, Irénée, o.m.i. "Le père Joseph Hugonard, o.m.i. Son oeuvre apostolique." Société Canadienne d'Histoire de l'Église Catholique, *Sessions
d'Études* 15 (1948): 23–38.

"Vicar Apostolic." *New Catholic Encyclopedia*. Vol. 14: 638–39.

Vanast, Walter. "Compassion, Cost and Competition: Factors in the Evolution
of Oblate Medical Services in the Canadian North." In *Western Oblates
Studies 2 / Études Oblates de l'Ouest 2*, ed. by R. Huel (Lewiston: Edwin
Mellen Press, 1992): 179–98.

Venini, Bernice. "Father Constantine Scollen, Founder of the Calgary Mission."
Canadian Catholic Historical Association, *Study Sessions* 9 (1942): 75–86.

Voisin, Guy, o.m.i. "La coordination de l'activité missionnaire des oblats à travers le Canada: Le Conseil oblat des oeuvres indiennes et esquimaudes."
Kerygma 2 (1968): 76–81.

Woestman, W.H., OMI. "Juridical History of the Oblate Brothers." *Vie Oblate
Life* 44 (1985): 219–62.

Zimmer, Ronnald P., OMI. "Early Oblate Attempts for Indian and Métis
Priests in Canada."*Études Oblates* 32 (1973): 277–83.

THESES

Boswell, Marion Joan. "Civilizing the Indian: Government Administration of
Indians." Ph.D. thesis, University of Ottawa, 1977.

Dionne, Gabriel, o.m.i. "Histoire des méthodes missionnaires utilisées par les
Oblats de Marie Immaculée dans l'évangélisation des Indiens du «versant
pacifique», au dix-neuvième siècle." M.A. thesis, University of Ottawa, 1947.

Gainer, Brenda. "The Catholic Missionaries as Agents of Social Change." M.A.
thesis, Carleton University, 1978,

Huel, Raymond. "L'Association Catholique Franco-Canadienne de la
Saskatchewan: A Response to Cultural Assimilation, 1912–1934." M.A. thesis,
University of Regina, 1969.

Hanley, P.M. "The Catholic Ladder, and Missionary Activity in the Pacific
Northwest." M.A. thesis, University of Ottawa, 1965.

Kennedy, Jacqueline, "Qu'Appelle Industrial School: White Rites for the Indians of the Old Northwest." M.A. thesis, Canadian Studies, Carleton University, 1970.

McCarthy, Martha. "The Missions of the Oblates of Mary Immaculate to the Athapascans, 1846–1870: Theory, Structure and Method." Ph.D. thesis, University of Manitoba, 1981.

Moodie, D.W. "The St. Albert Settlement: A Study in Historical Geography." M.A. thesis, University of Alberta, 1965.

Nowakowski, R. "Indian Residential Schools in Saskatchewan Conducted by the Oblate Fathers." M.A. thesis, University of Ottawa (Institute of Missiology), 1962.

UNPUBLISHED MANUSCRIPTS

Carrière, Gaston, o.m.i. "Le martyr du devoir Mgr Ovide Charlebois, o.m.i." Vol. 1, "Le missionnaire."

Miller, Jim R. "Indian-White Relations in Canada. The Case of Residential Schooling." Paper presented at the Association for Canadian Studies in Australia and New Zealand, Griffith University, Nathan, Qld., May 14–16, 1986.

Miller, Jim R. "Native Residential Schools in Historical Context." Paper presented to the annual meeting of the Canadian Catholic Historical Association, Calgary, June 14, 1994.

△ △ △ △ △ △ △ △ △ △ △ △ △ △ △ △ △ △ △ △

INDEX

N.B. The terms Oblate, Métis, Indian, Catholic and Christian have not been indexed because of the frequency of their appearance.

233, 241, 248, 265, 276, 278, 281, 283–85, 289

Canadian Conference of Catholic Bishops, 282–83, 285

Canadian government, 9, 36, 39, 105, 110, 112, 117, 120, 123–24, 126, 130, 132, 138, 144, 147–48, 160–61, 164, 172, 175, 177–81, 185–90, 197, 202–4, 206, 209–14, 216, 241, 243–44, 246, 254, 280

Canadian Pacific Railway, 209, 225, 255

Canadian Publishers Ltd., 242

Canoe Lake (Saskatchewan), 78

Canon Law, 6, 91

Cardston (Alberta), 166

Carrière, Gaston, OMI, xxiii–xxiv

Carrier Indians, 277

Carter, Sarah, 221

Catholic Action, 259, 263, 267

Catholic Church Extension Society, 251, 264

Catholic Columbian, 275

Catholic Ladder, 94–96

Catholic News, 72

Champagne, Claude, OMI, xxiv, 4

Champagne, Joseph-Étienne, OMI, xxiv, 249–50

Chapellière, Gérasime, OMI, 80–81

Chapleau, Adolphe, 181

Charlebois, Ovide, OMI, xxiii, 101, 150, 172, 203, 213, 247, 249, 265

Charlebois, Sister, 112

Chataigner, Clément, OMI, 263

Chicago (Illinois), 142

Chilcotin Indians, 277

China, 72

Chipewyan Indians, xviii, 17, 21–22, 30–32, 38, 42, 82, 100–101, 160, 203, 207, 219, 234, 260

Christianity and Native Traditions, xxvi

Christie, W.S., 102

Churchill basin, 49, 58

Church Missionary Society, xxvii, 14, 182

Church of England, 125

Cinquante ans au pays des neiges, xxiii

Citeaux (France), 119–20, 124

Claresholm (Alberta), 134

Claude, Charles, OMI, 130

Cluny (Alberta), 52, 132, 166–67, 189, 275

Clut, Isidore, OMI, 28, 31–32, 40, 49, 63, 85, 91, 202–3

Coastal Indians, xviii

Collège Mathieu, 196

Columbian Exposition, 142

Comité Historique de l'Union Nationale Métisse, 217–18

Commissioner of Indian Affairs, 112

Commission Oblate des Oeuvres Indiennes et Esquimaudes (COOIE), 242–44, 280

Congregation of Notre-Dame, 94

Constitutions et Règles, 5

Conversion de Saint-Paul Mission (Brocket, Alberta), 52, 169

Cooperative Commonwealth Federation, 255

Council of the Northwest Territories, 181

Cowesses Indian Residential School (Marieval, Saskatchewan), 163

Cranbrook (British Columbia), 167, 277

Cree Indians, 28, 30–33, 51, 53–54, 78, 80, 92, 96–97, 101, 103, 105, 113, 130, 135, 140–41, 150, 160, 206, 233, 260

Wabossimong (Manitoba), 17–19

War of 1812, 13

Washington (District of Columbia), 124, 186

Waterhen Lake (Saskatchewan), 80

Wesleyans, 15

Western Canadian Publishers, xii

Western Oblate History Project, xii

White Horse Plains (Manitoba), 13

White, Thomas, 186–87

Will to Power, xxvi

Winnipeg (Manitoba), xi, 11, 229, 242, 244, 265

Winnipeg River, 17, 52

Winterburn (Alberta), 92

Woodland Cree Indians, xviii

Wood Mountain (Saskatchewan), 54

York Factory, 79

Yukon, xii, 188

THE MISSIONARY OBLATES OF
MARY IMMACULATE IN THE CANADIAN NORTHWEST

Raymond J.A. Huel, General Series Editor

Published by The University of Alberta Press
   and
Western Canadian Publishers

*Les Oblats des Marie Immaculée dans L'Ouest
et le Nord du Canada, 1845–1967*
Donat Levasseur, o.m.i. (1995)

*From the Great River to the Ends of the Earth:
Oblate Missions to the Dene, 1847–1921*
Martha McCarthy (1995)

*Proclaiming the Gospel to the Indians and the Métis:
The Missionary Oblates of Mary Immaculate
In Western Canada, 1845–1945*
Raymond J.A. Huel (1996)